D0959820

IRAN RISING

Iran Rising

The Survival and Future of the Islamic Republic

Amin Saikal

PRINCETON UNIVERSITY PRESS
PRINCETON AND OXFORD

Published by Princeton University Press
41 William Street, Princeton, New Jersey 08540
6 Oxford Street, Woodstock, Oxfordshire OX20 1TR

press.princeton.edu

LCCN 2018936897
ISBN 9780691175478

British Library Cataloging-in-Publication Data is available

Editorial: Eric Crahan and Pamela Weidman
Production Editorial: Debbie Tegarden
Jacket design: by Spencer Fuller at Faceout Studio
Jacket photograph: Milad Tower in Tehran, during sunset. Courtesy of BornaMire / Getty Images
Production: Jacquie Poirier
Publicity: James Schneider
Copyeditor: Gail K. Schmitt

This book has been composed in Adobe Text Pro and Gotham

Printed on acid-free paper. ∞

Printed in the United States of America

10 9 8 7 6 5 4 3 2 1

CONTENTS

PREFACE

The Islamic Republic of Iran has been in the eye of a political storm for forty years. Few states in the modern world have experienced as many domestic and foreign policy challenges, and have circumvented so many of them, as the Islamic Republic. These challenges have emanated primarily from two variables. One is the Islamic Republic's revolutionary rhetoric and theocratic, but politically pluralist, system of governance, its fear of outside hostile actions, and the need to protect itself through various national and regional security-building machinations. The other is the way in which the regional and world actors, most importantly the United States, have treated the Islamic Republic as an oddity and have sought to protect their interests based on a view of the Islamic Republic as a destabilizing and metastasizing force in an oil-rich and strategically important part of the world. The two variables have mutually reinforced one another, resulting in the devastating Iran-Iraq War (1980–88), a stringent regime of international sanctions against Iran, driven largely by the United States, and semiglobal isolation of the country for virtually all of its life over the last four decades.

The pressures to which the Iranian Islamic regime has been subjected could not initially have augured well for its long-term survival. Yet, it has managed to deal with these in an increasingly pragmatic rather than ideological fashion in order to neutralize or get around them, while persisting with its base of religious legitimacy. It has pursued the *jihadi-ijtihadi*, or combative/reformist, approach of its founder, Ayatollah Ruhollah Khomeini, in the conduct of Iran's domestic and foreign policy, transforming the country into an influential actor or, according to a particular set of criteria, an important "middle power" in the region. It has succeeded in building such domestic structures, processes, and resources capability and a foreign policy posture that have enabled it to ensure order at home and deter aggression from outside.

This endurance and capability have not been free of costs for its people and its international standing. Given Iran's abundant natural resources and human capital, many seasoned critics have argued that the theocratic nature of the Islamic Republic's political order has held back its subjects from achieving their full potential and from ensuring the development of their country as a progressive and prosperous state. They contend that the Islamic system has proved to be as autocratic and corrupt in many of its operational aspects as that of the Shah's dictatorial rule. As such, the Republic has indeed a long way to go before a majority of its people could enjoy a standard of living that would enable them to remain solidly behind their Islamic government out of devotion rather than coercive obligation. Undoubtedly, the Islamic Republic has had a very turbulent journey so far, and there is no evidence to suggest that its path of change and development is likely to be less rocky in the foreseeable future.

What makes the Islamic Republic tick? What direction is it likely to take in its evolution, especially in light of the changing dynamics of the regional and international strategic environment? In the years ahead, it is bound to face a range of hostilities and opportunities. Its ability to deflect hostilities and leverage opportunities will depend on whether it continues on its seesawing *jihadi-ijtihadi* path of evolution, or whether one approach will dominate more than the other.

I have been researching and writing on Iran for most of the forty years of my academic life. My first major work on the country was *The Rise and Fall of the Shah,* published by Princeton University Press (PUP) in 1980, with an abridged paperback edition published in 2009. The motivation for the current volume came to me after delivering a lecture at Princeton University in 2015. Eric Crahan of PUP encouraged me to develop the ideas in my lecture into a substantial volume to mark the fortieth anniversary of the Iranian Revolution of 1978–79, which toppled the Shah's rule and replaced it with Khomeini's Islamic government. This book takes up the tale of the development of Iran in both regional and international contexts from where *The Rise and Fall of the Shah*'s discussion ended.

The book is not designed to advance a major theoretical discourse or examine certain theories of state building or international relations with a focus on Iranian developments. Its primary objective is to provide a comprehensive discussion and analysis of the evolution of the Islamic Republic of Iran over the last four decades. However, various relevant theoretical tools and concepts are deployed to unpack the complexities of the Republic's domestic and foreign policy situation against the backdrop of complicated but changing national and international settings. The book's approach is multidisciplinary, involving usage of those disciplines that are conducive to an in-depth understanding of the vicissitudes and endurance of the Islamic Republic. The main theme running through the volume is that of the *jihadi-ijtihadi* within the framework of which the story of the Islamic Republic is best explained and analyzed.

In writing this volume as a product of years of accumulative knowledge and contemplation, I owe a depth of gratitude to many individuals and institutions. In Iran—the country that I have visited and where I have carried out research numerous times—I am very thankful to a number of policymakers, academics, and friends who have continuously enriched me with their knowledge, analyses, and gracious hospitality. I cannot mention all of them, for most are still in active service and would not want to be named. Even so, it is appropriate to express my sincere thanks to the current foreign minister, Javad Zarif, for enlightening me about the Islamic Republic's foreign policy issues, as well as the Institute of Political and International Studies (IPIS) and Islamic Culture and Relations Organization, whose scholars and foreign service personnel have been more than willing to discuss with me the affairs of their country freely and frankly.

I am equally grateful to many specialists and current and former policymakers in the United States, including most importantly the former US undersecretary of state Thomas Pickering, and a number of friends at Princeton University, including the director of

LISD Wolfgang Danspeckgruber, whose knowledge of the region and depth of understanding of US policy behavior toward it have been invaluable to me.

Meanwhile, had it not been for the valuable support of three young and brilliant research and editorial assistants, I would have struggled to complete the manuscript for this book on time. I owe a world of gratitude to Andrew Feng for being a very meticulous and energetic researcher; to William Jenkins, for his valuable knowledge of Iran and the Persian language and for reading a draft of the manuscript; and to Stephanie Wright, for her enormous editing skills and insightful comments.

I am also very thankful to Professor James Piscatori, an extremely valuable colleague in the field, from whose expertise I have enormously benefited over the years. This also applies to a number of colleagues at the Centre for Arab and Islamic Studies (the Middle East and Central Asia)—CAIS—at the Australian National University (ANU), where I have been based as an academic for more than three decades, for their support and illuminating discussions. They include Dr. Zahra Taheri, whose rich insights about the various aspects of Iranian culture and society have consistently elevated my understanding of Iran. My sincere thanks also to Professor Catherine Waldby, director of the Research School of Arts and Social Sciences, ANU, for her delightful leadership and generous support throughout this project. It is also a great pleasure to acknowledge the administrative help and backing of my executive assistant, Ms. Rachel Larobina, and our research and publication officer, Dr. Anita Mack.

I am grateful to the ANU, which has provided me with a first-class working environment and generously helped me to engage in research and writing for this and other books. ANU's chancellor and former Australian foreign affairs minister, the Hon. Professor Gareth Evans, has been a source of inspiration and support for CAIS and my academic endeavors. I am indeed thankful to him for this and to the ANU's chancellor, Professor Brian Schmidt, for his dynamic leadership of the university and support for academics like me.

Above all, I cannot praise enough Mary-Louise Hickey, my partner, the love of my life, and a very accomplished editor. She has been the rock behind this work and my other publications and has never failed to be my loveable companion, confidant, and supporter, with an enormous capacity to endure all my idiosyncrasies and temperamental moments. I dedicate this book to her and to my three beautiful, charming, witty, and highly accomplished daughters, Rahima, Samra, and Amina. They are all my golden treasures.

Amin Saikal
Canberra, August 2018

A NOTE ON TERMS AND TRANSLITERATION

"Islamic Republic," "Republic," and "Iran" are used interchangeably in the volume, as are also the terms "traditionalists," "conservatives," and "hard-liners" to refer to *jihadis*, and "reformist" and "moderates" to identify *ijtihadis*. For Persian names and terms, the normal Persian transliteration is used.

ABBREVIATIONS

AAC	Assembly of Assertive Clerics
AI	Anjuman-e Islami
AID	Anjuman-e Islami-e Daneshjuyan
AIOC	Anglo-Iranian Oil Company
APOC	Anglo-Persian Oil Company
AQAP	Al-Qaeda in the Arabian Peninsula
BBC	British Broadcasting Corporation
CIA	Central Intelligence Agency
CNPC	China National Petroleum Corporation
E3	France, Germany, and the United Kingdom
EU	European Union
FDI	foreign direct investment
GCC	Gulf Cooperation Council
GDP	gross domestic product
IAEA	International Atomic Energy Agency
ICRO	Islamic Cultural and Relations Organization
IKRC	Imam Khomeini Relief Committee
IRC	Islamic Revolutionary Court
IRGC	Islamic Revolutionary Guard Corps
IRIB	Islamic Republic of Iran Broadcasting
IRP	Islamic Republican Party
IS	Islamic State

JCPOA Joint Comprehensive Plan of Action
JMIBNA Jebheh-ye Mujtahed-e Islami Bara-ye Nejat-e Afghanistan
JPA Joint Plan of Action
JRM Jame'eh-ye Ruhaniyyat-e Mobarez
mbpd million barrels per day
MENA Middle East and North Africa
MOIS Ministry of Intelligence and Security
NATO North Atlantic Treaty Organization
NGO nongovernmental organization
NPT Nuclear Non-Proliferation Treaty
OECD Organisation for Economic Co-operation and Development
OPEC Organization of Petroleum Exporting Countries
P5+1 China, France, Russia, the United Kingdom, the United States, and Germany
SAVAK Sazman-e Ettela'at Va Amniyat-e Keshvar
SNSC Supreme National Security Council
SOE state-owned enterprise
SWIFT Society for Worldwide Interbank Financial Telecommunication
UAE United Arab Emirates
UN United Nations
WMD weapons of mass destruction

IRAN RISING

1

Introduction

In late December 2017, a series of public protests broke out in the Islamic Republic of Iran, starting in the country's second-largest city of Mashhad and spreading soon to many other towns and cities, including Tehran. The protestors' initial demand was for better economic conditions of living and employment, especially among the youth, but it rapidly came to include slogans against the government, criticizing the country's ruling clerics, including the Supreme Leader Ayatollah Ali Khamenei, and calling for an end to the theocratic rule and costly involvement in regional conflicts, most specifically Syria and Lebanon. US president Donald Trump and several of his senior aides, especially his ambassador to the United Nations, Nikki Haley, as well as his strongest regional ally, Prime Minister Benjamin Netanyahu of Israel, suddenly found their moment to voice strong support for the protestors against the Islamic regime, with a warning that the US and the world were watching it. Haley convened a meeting of the UN Security Council to condemn the regime. However, neither Trump's efforts nor the Security Council's meeting produced any results, as other permanent members of the council, like most of the rest of the world, adhered to the principle of noninterference in the internal affairs of a state. In his response, the Iranian ambassador to the UN, Gholamali Khoshroo, condemned the Washington interference as a "preposterous example" of US bullying tactics and accused it of having "lost every shred of moral, political and legal authority and credibility in the eyes of the whole world."[1]

Washington's interventionist approach indeed enabled Tehran to label the protests as foreign-led and to castigate the American and Israeli leaders as the enemies of the Iranian people. Rhetoric aside, the conservative opponents of the moderate president, Hassan Rouhani, had a hand in the protests and exploited the protesters' grievances. The Islamic regime soon quelled the unrest at the cost of dozens killed and hundreds arrested. The whole episode, whose importance was exaggerated by the US and its regional allies, demonstrated Washington's misjudgment of the strengths and weaknesses of the Islamic regime. This was not the first time that the regime had to deal with domestic disturbances, foreign intervention, and a poor understanding of its nature. The regime has proved to be more resilient and at the same time vulnerable. It has oscillated between its religious legitimacy and pragmatic policies.

The central concern of this book is to explore and analyze this oscillation over the last four decades and the reasons for it. In so doing, it focuses on the evolution of the Islamic Republic of Iran in its domestic and foreign policy settings in changing regional and international contexts. It also offers an analysis of the salient issues and developments that enabled the founder of the Republic, Ayatollah Ruhollah Khomeini, to implement his unique vision of a Shia theocratic order. While this order continues to be governed by his legacy, it has sufficiently reinvented itself to endure and survive numerous interlinking internal and external challenges.

The Context over Time

The Islamic Republic of Iran has experienced trials and tribulations ever since its inception, following the momentous Iranian Revolution of 1978–79. The revolution was remarkable in many ways. It was a mass uprising of unprecedented scale and social breadth in modern history, even as it predated social media. It began with the aim of reforming the rule of pro-West Mohammad Reza Shah Pahlavi in order to transform Iran into a constitutional monarchy. However, it ultimately delivered a new Islamic type of government under the leadership of the Shia cleric Ayatollah Khomeini, who emerged as the most high-profile political opponent of the Shah. At one level, the revolution inaugurated a dramatic departure from the past by replacing a secular monarchy with an Islamic government. At another level, however, it merely perpetuated a political culture of authoritarianism that had underpinned Iranian politics for most of the country's 2,500-year-long history. In short, one form of autocracy—the Shah's secular monarchy—was merely substituted with another—Khomeini's modern revolutionary Islamic theocracy. The transition altered Iran's domestic and foreign policies in dramatic ways. It resulted in the severance of ties with the United States, Iran's major sponsor under the Shah, which Khomeini demonized as a "hegemonic" and "evil" world power. The Iranian Revolution ushered in a new Islamic government that, from its inception, has challenged the prevailing norms of the regional and, indeed, the global order.

The Islamic system of governance that the revolution ultimately established was deeply informed by Khomeini's particular, politicized interpretation of Twelver Shia Islam, the dominant sect in Iran but the minority vis-à-vis the Sunni sect that predominates in most other states in the Muslim world. Khomeini promoted his interpretation of Islam as the most authentic and applicable under contemporary national and international conditions. He regarded it as the most conducive instrument for creating an Islamic government that could give full expression to the supreme will of God, and to the necessarily subordinate will of the people, in the contemporary world. Khomeini also believed that his interpretation of Islam alone could create a polity capable of serving humanity to the highest standard—which for him could only mean an Islamic standard. For him, there were only two possible ideological positions: Islamic and un-Islamic, with nothing in between or beyond. He pronounced that his Shia theological paradigm, which some of his followers subsequently promoted as *Islam-e naabi-e Mohammad* (the quintessential Islam of Prophet Mohammad), stood above all other interpretations of the faith, but he nonetheless called for pan-Islamic solidarity, including from Sunni coreligionists.

Khomeini desired to create an Islamic polity that would be durable in a changing modern world. To achieve this, he adopted a two-dimensional approach to Islamic government: *jihadi* ("combative") and *ijtihadi* ("reformist"). The former was to focus on the Islamization of politics and everyday life, and the latter to apply a novel interpretation of Islam based on independent human reasoning, to the degree necessary to forge a strong, modern Islamic Iran. He drew on an ideological interplay between the two dimensions in the context of a broader rhetorical framework that centered on the struggle between *mosta'zafin* (the "have nots," or the "oppressed and downtrodden") and *mostakbarin* (the "haves," or "arrogant oppressors"). Although Khomeini never endorsed Marxist thought, his dichotomization of the social strata rhymed with the Marxist division of social classes in capitalist countries: between the ruling bourgeoisie and oppressed proletariat. To legitimize the construction of his new Islamic Republic, he emphasized the empowerment of the *mosta'zafin* over the *mostakbarin* by an *ijtihadi* interpretation that combined divine and earthly themes from Islamic theology and jurisprudence. As Supreme Leader of the Islamic Republic from 1979 until his death on June 3, 1989, Khomeini oversaw the establishment of an Islamic political paradigm that has guided the management of Iran under his successor Ayatollah Khamenei and the successive elected Islamic governments and that continues to shape Iranian politics to this day.[2]

Khomeini's transformation of Iran along these lines challenged and even threatened the US geopolitical dominance that had prevailed in the oil-rich and strategically significant Middle East under the so-called Pax Americana. Prior to the revolution, Iran itself had acted as a critical pillar for this US policy under the Shah. The advent of the Islamic Republic not only alarmed the United States, which lost a critical ally in the region, but also caused deep ideological, political, and security concerns for many neighboring Arab states, which feared the Republic would embolden Shia and other minorities to rise up across the region. While Khomeini initially played down his Shia sectarian allegiance in favor of a pan-Islamist stance, his radical political Islamism was deeply rooted in Twelver thought and revolutionary rhetoric, with a call for the export of the Iranian Revolution in support of the oppressed peoples of the world. The revolution also jolted the Soviet Union to an awareness of political Islam.

Never before had a political leader as theologically driven, defiant, and popular as Khomeini burst onto the world scene to lock horns with a superpower like the United States while loudly denouncing another, the USSR. Khomeini shunned the United States in particular, but he had no time for its "Godless" communist global rival either, condemning the December 1979 Soviet invasion and decade-long occupation of Afghanistan as "socialist imperialism." Iran was no longer a compliant actor for an international superpower but rather a resistant and independently transformative force. Khomeini's defiance injected a new catalyst for global political realignment that alarmed regional ruling elites and the United States.[3] The rise of the Ayatollah was to shake the post–Second World War Pax Americana at its foundations in the Middle East—with a dramatic and lasting impact on regional geopolitical dynamics.

The US not only was suspicious of the forces that had toppled its Pahlavi ally but also saw Khomeini's political Islamism and Islamic system of governance as repugnantly fundamentalist; a view that intensified during the "hostage crisis." On November 4, 1979, a group of Khomeini's militant student supporters invaded the American embassy in Tehran and took dozens of diplomats and employees hostage. Their demands were the extradition of the Shah from the US, where he had been admitted for medical treatment, to face trial in Iran for crimes against the people. After thirty-seven months, unable to rescue or negotiate the release of the hostages, Washington cut off all relations with Iran, imposed unprecedented sanctions on the country, and condemned the new order in Iran, which was becoming increasingly repressive as Khomeini moved to consolidate his power at the cost of thousands of lives.

Iran's erstwhile ally also decided on a policy of backing whoever opposed the new Islamic regime, including Israel, which was alarmed by Khomeini's call for the destruction of the "Zionist state" and which set out to undermine his Islamic order in whatever way available. Iraq, Egypt, and the Arab monarchies, all of which shared American and Israeli concerns, adopted the same approach to Iran. The Islamic Republic thus found itself immediately isolated. The US sought to shore up Pax Americana not only by strengthening its strategic partnership with Israel but also by increasing arms sales and military assistance to anti-Iranian Arab states, especially in the Gulf. Iran's main regional Sunni rival today, the Kingdom of Saudi Arabia, was selected as Washington's main regional counter to the newly militant Iran.

In its determination to marginalize Iran, the US even proved willing to aid its erstwhile foe, the Iraqi dictator Saddam Hussein. With the Shah no longer an obstacle to his quest for regional supremacy and the country engulfed in postrevolutionary turmoil, the Iraqi leader saw his opportunity to invade. The Gulf Arab states, plus Egypt and Jordan, backed Iraq financially and logistically on a large scale. In Syria, the ruling Arab socialist Ba'ath party under Hafez al-Assad supported Iran as much out of strategic interest as out of their schismatic dislike for their cousin Ba'athists in Iraq. Iraq's attack on Iran in mid-1980 ignited a bloody and costly war that lasted eight years and inflicted terrible devastation on both sides, resulting in massive loss of human life and widespread damage of infrastructure that has had a lasting impact on both countries' people.

During the war, however, the US ceased to look on Saddam Hussein as a repressive dictator hostile to the West and came to regard him as a useful pawn or even potential ally against Khomeini's Iran. The US assisted him in the war against the Islamic Republic primarily because it perceived its own interest in letting Iraq and Iran wear each other down in a cycle of mutual destruction, thus dramatically weakening two of the region's strongest states. Israel played its part in this plan by channeling some arms to Iran, although indirectly, in such a way as to make sure that the two antagonists were locked in indefinite hostilities and that no united

Arab or Islamic front could be formed against the Jewish state—a policy that informs Israeli behavior to date.[4] Unsurprisingly, the war ended in stalemate. The Islamic Republic had staved off its first existential threat, largely because of Khomeini's ability to mobilize the Iranian population against Iraqi forces by invoking a combination of Iranians' fierce sense of Shiism and nationalism in defense of the new Islamic Republic and the old motherland, Iran.

During the war, the resistance to Iraqi and Arab aggression and the stance against the United States and its allies provided Khomeini and his devotees with a powerful platform from which to wage *jihad* concurrently against two sets of enemies: external and internal. While fighting the Iraqi forces and fending off their regional and international supporters, Khomeini used the cover of war to engage in forceful processes of power centralization. The war was instrumental in promoting his leadership and the Islamic Republic as the resolute and fearless defender of true revolutionary Islam from internal and external threats. During the same period in which Khomeini's supporters and ordinary Iranians stemmed the tide of the Iraqi aggression, they also virtually wiped out or neutralized all those who either actually opposed or were suspected of opposing Khomeini's Islamic direction for Iran.[5] Those complicit in the violence and arrests included a number of ranking clerics who had either actively or tacitly supported the revolution and Khomeini's leadership.

No regional or distant Muslim country embraced Khomeini's system of Islamic governance as it stood, despite his efforts at "export of revolution," which became the Islamic Republic's policy for a time. However, his political Islamism appealed to some minorities in the region, predominantly to marginalized Shia communities. The most successful case in this respect was in Lebanon, where Iranian Hezbollahis (followers of the Party of God) assisted the formation of the Lebanese Hezbollah (Party of God), which over time has grown to be a formidable Iranian protégé force in Lebanese political and military life.

Khomeini used a mixture of religious imagery, rhetorical power, political violence, and moral persuasion to implement a unique new

Islamic order based on a two-tiered system of divine and popular sovereignty. He developed an *ijtihadi* concept of the "sovereignty of God"—*velayat-e faqih* (the guardianship, or governance, of the Islamic jurist). Through this concept, he argued that Islam empowers a *faqih* (strictly a jurist, but in Khomeini's reading also a deputy to the last hidden Shia imam and related to Prophet Mohammad) to have custodianship over the people,[6] whose sovereignty was represented by an elected president and Majles (the National Assembly). Khomeini's political theology legitimated and furnished what could be considered a form of religious polyarchy, as defined by Robert Dahl.[7] It gave rise to a theocratic but politically pluralistic Islamic government, where the "sovereignty of God," vested in the *faqih*, would nevertheless prevail over the will of the people on contentious governance issues.

Khomeini—the first *faqih*—was not oblivious to the need for his Islamic system to be robust and resilient. Indeed, he saw internal and external adaptability as necessary to safeguard the continuity of the Islamic government in the context of a changing modern world, and it was here that the *ijtihadi* dimension of his thinking and actions mattered most. Despite his emphasis on and reputation for ideological purity, he proved to be remarkably pragmatic when the survival of his regime was at stake. The system he established allowed the participation of diverse groups of his followers, so long as they operated within the Islamic framework that he had laid down. The Supreme Leader's umbrella dictate underpinned the emergence, by the end of the 1980s, of three main theo-political factional clusters: *jihadi* (revolutionary conservatives and traditionalists, popularly referred to as "hard-liners," characterized by a confrontational streak), *ijtihadi* (reformists, progressives, and internationalists), and *amalgaran* (pragmatists).[8] Hereafter, the terms "traditional," "conservative," and "hard-line" will be used interchangeably to refer to the *jihadi* side of the spectrum, while "reformist" and "internationalist" will be used to refer to the *ijtihadi* side.

The same adaptability applied to Khomeini's stance on the conduct of the Islamic Republic's foreign relations. For example, to compensate for sanctions and hostilities with the United States, he was content to allow the cultivation of good relations with the Soviet Union, China, and India and, ultimately, to swallow his pride and accept a ceasefire with his mortal enemy, Saddam Hussein, despite his long-standing vow to fight to the end.[9]

By the time of his death, Khomeini had left behind not only a politically pluralist theocratic order but also a seesawing *jihadi-ijtihadi* approach to its governance. This approach has been very diligently pursued by his successor Ayatollah Khamenei. Having risen, somewhat unexpectedly, to the heights of the Supreme Leadership, Khamenei has successfully used and consolidated his religious and constitutional powers as well as various vetting and power-enforcement bodies, particularly the state's coercive instruments, in order to subordinate the executive and legislative branches of the Islamic government to his authority and to preserve his power to act as the final arbiter of all significant domestic and foreign policy issues. In this, he has performed both conservatively and pragmatically within Khomeini's framework, depending on the nature of the issues and their implications for regime survival.

In many cases, Khamenei has insisted on ideological adherence, but there have also been occasions when he has accommodated pragmatic and reformist policies. He has done so especially when he and his conservative entourage have judged such flexibility as necessary. As such, they have allowed reform and renewal measures in both domestic and foreign policies, as long as those measures do not open the way for radical changes to the Islamic system that could undermine the basis of their power. Whenever confronted with complex or significant policy innovations, Khamenei has made sure to qualify his endorsement of them with precautionary statements to ensure their reversal if required.

Within this paradigm, Khamenei has thus far interacted with four elected presidents, all of whom have ultimately bowed to his authority over policy differences with him. The president who has had the most success in gaining Khamenei's backing has been the moderate, Hassan Rouhani (2013–present). Rouhani was elected in a landslide with the combined support of the reformist and pragmatist factions in 2013 and again in 2017. He has campaigned on a platform of political moderation, economic reform, and flexibility in foreign policy to resolve the long dispute over Iran's nuclear program with the West and widen Iran's foreign relations. In this instance, the president's quest for reforms has aligned with the position of the Supreme Leader (who has been aided by an array of advisors within the Beit-e Rahbari, or House of the Leader). By 2013, Khamenei appeared to have reached the conclusion that there was probably no other viable option but a diplomatic resolution of Iran's nuclear dispute in order to bring an end to international sanctions. Since Rouhani's election, both the president and the Supreme Leader also apparently agreed in viewing the broadening of Iran's interactions with the West as a necessity for improving an increasingly moribund economy, which had fueled serious political and social unrest, as demonstrated by the 2009 Green Movement and again by the December 2017–January 2018 protests.[10]

Khamenei, however, styled his endorsement of Rouhani's approach to the nuclear issue—controversial among conservatives who oppose any negotiations with Iran's archenemy, the United States—as *narmesh-e qahramaneh* (heroic flexibility). He also accompanied his endorsement with a clear warning that the US cannot be trusted and emphasized that any agreement must be in compliance with Iran's sovereignty and Islamic system.[11] Nevertheless, the Supreme Leader gave his consent, and the Joint Comprehensive Plan of Action (JCPOA, or simply, the "nuclear agreement") between Iran and the five permanent members of the UN Security Council and Germany (P5+1) was concluded on July 14, 2015, enforceable from January 2016. Under this agreement, Iran downgraded its nuclear program for demonstrably civilian use only for the next fifteen years in return for the lifting of sanctions. Yet the agreement still faced obstacles; not all the sanctions were lifted and hard-liners in both the United States and Iran remained highly skeptical of the agreement, not to mention the objections it raised among Israel and the Saudi-led Arab states.

While the Democrat US president Barack Obama was able to override his domestic critics to clinch the nuclear deal, his highly divisive, temperamental, populist Republican successor, Trump, who took office on January 20, 2017, strongly sided from the start with the critics. President Trump painted the nuclear agreement as "the worst deal ever" and promised to "scrap" it. The Trump administration accused Iran of "provocative" and "destabilizing activities" in the region[12] and lambasted the Islamic Republic as the biggest supporter of terrorism, comparing it to North Korea as a "rogue" state, and putting it "on notice."[13] The Europeans responded to Trump's threats by insisting on the nuclear agreement's multilateral nature. The European Union foreign policy chief Frederica Mogherini stated, in a press conference in July 2017 alongside the Russian foreign minister Sergei Lavrov, that "the nuclear deal doesn't belong to one country, it belongs to the international community."[14] Until March 2018, the Trump administration retained the deal and verified Iran's adherence to it, but with a focus on canceling America's participation and containing the Islamic Republic in whatever way necessary.

Trump's secretary of defense, General James Mattis, stood fast in favor of a military confrontation with the Islamic Republic in order to remove what he asserts is a menace to American interests, especially in Iraq and Syria, and a threat to its Arab and Israeli allies in the region. Mattis's vehement opposition to Iran goes back to his time as commander of the United States Central Command (2010–13) and commander of the United States Joint Forces Command (2007–10), when he played a key role in managing US operations in Iraq and Afghanistan. His direct experience of Iranian operations in Iraq and Syria led him to regard the Islamic Republic as the biggest danger to the region and to view the Islamic Republic not as a state but rather as "a revolutionary cause devoted to mayhem."[15] In light of these views, he grew frustrated by the Obama administration's unwillingness to adopt his recommendations against negotiating the nuclear deal, which he, like Trump, considered disastrous, although at the end he favored the retention of the nuclear agreement as important to US security interests[16] Trump—backed by Mattis; the president's former special advisor, Steven Bannon, who sees the Iranian regime as part of what he calls the "cancer" of radical Islam[17]; and the current national security advisor, John Bolton, who has advocated a hawkish stance against Iran over a long period of time[18]—continues to view Iran as America's real enemy and main culprit for regional instability and insecurity. Trump finally withdrew the US from the JCPOA in May 2018, vowing to reimpose sanctions with such severity as to destroy the Iranian economy.

Tehran had already stated that in the event of a US withdrawal from the agreement or any US aggressive action against Iran, it would respond in kind. There is a "snapback" clause in the deal that applies if either side violates the agreement. It had vowed that in the case of America's violation, Iran will return its nuclear program to its pre-JCPOA state of development and not only restore all its centrifuges but also upgrade them. With Trump in the White House, Mattis in charge of America's military power, and the Iranian Supreme Leader remaining defiant in the face of increasing American pressure, the risk of a US-Iranian military confrontation is at a critical level.

Whatever progress had been achieved in improving US-Iranian relations under Obama and Rouhani has been reversed under Trump's presidency, placing the US and Iran once again on a collision course.[19] This situation has pleased the forces of the Right in the United States and Israel and emboldened Saudi Arabia to pressure its partners in the Gulf Cooperation Council (GCC; Bahrain, Kuwait, Oman, Qatar, and the United Arab Emirates) to treat Iran as more of a threat than the Jewish state, although Kuwait, Oman, and Qatar (which has been subjected to a blockade by Riyadh, Abu Dhabi, Cairo, and Manama since June 2017 partly because of its good relations with Iran) have not wholeheartedly embraced this view. The powerful Saudi crown prince and defense minister, Mohammad bin Salman, has categorically ruled out any rapprochement with Iran, accusing Tehran of plotting a Shia takeover of the holy sites in Saudi Arabia. He has threatened to take the battle to Iran.[20] Regional hostility to Iran has helped to forge an unprecedented degree of cooperation not only between Saudi Arabia, its Arab allies, and the US under Trump but also between Saudi Arabia and Israel, although the latter has taken place largely behind the scenes.[21]

Tehran has not been an innocent party in its international isolation by any means—for two important reasons. The first is its involvement in Iraq, Syria, Lebanon, and Yemen and its growing influence in the region, and the second is the sense of ideological, sectarian, and civilizational superiority with which the Islamic regime has approached the neighboring Arab states. This state of affairs has deeply worried the GCC and some other Arab countries, including Egypt under the authoritarian rule of President Abdel Fattah al-Sisi, with whom the Trump leadership has forged a close alliance against what it has described as "the crisis of Islamic extremism and the Islamists and Islamic terror of all kinds" in the Middle East.[22]

Conversely, Washington's stance toward Iran has prompted the latter to strengthen ties with Russia and China as counterweights against the United States and its regional allies. Despite its historical trepidation about Russia, Tehran and Moscow have entered into an enhanced strategic cooperation not only in war-torn allied Syria but also in Afghanistan. Here the two countries have common cause in denying the US the opportunity to determine that country's conflict and shape its status according to its interests. This cooperation does not rest on any firm ideological or even geopolitical foundations, because Russia's regional interests do not necessarily converge with those of Iran. It nonetheless serves the pragmatic interests of both sides for the time being.[23]

Iran, through its actual and perceived actions, has acquired a reputation as a threatening, powerful regional actor, especially among its Arab neighbors and the US. Anoushiravan Ehteshami, for example, writes that Iran's foreign policy "reinforce[s] the impression and image of a powerful Iran acting in its national interest on the international stage." He further notes that "Iran's apparent prowess has invited counterbalancing rather than 'bandwagoning,' leading to relative international isolation."[24]

Positioning Revolutionary Iran

Despite all of the difficulties and hostility that the Islamic Republic has faced, many pundits contend that it has succeeded in rising to the position of a "middle power," although what this specifically means is often debated.[25] Louis Bélanger and Gordon Mace write that "middle stateness . . . is not characterized by a clearly determined position in the international hierarchy of power but by vague locational parameters—somewhere between the major powers and the small states—and role conceptions."[26] This vagueness has underpinned the inclination of some policymakers and analysts to label the Islamic Republic as a "rogue" state. It has also underpinned the extraordinary anxiety around its foreign policy intentions.[27] Given the popular perception of Iran as a destabilizing regional actor, a thorough and dispassionate analysis of Iran's actual power capabilities in its historical and current political context is both relevant and necessary.

Of all the approaches defining and measuring the status of a state as a middle power, including the functional and behavioral perspectives,[28] the hierarchical view offers the most useful theoretical reference with which to quantify Iran's national power. This view defines middle powers as states that occupy the middle range in a ranking of states established by a quantitative measure of national power. Many popular conceptions of what constitutes a "middle power" come from Martin Wight's classic definition:

> A middle power is a power with such military strength, resources and strategic position that in peacetime the great powers bid for its support, and in wartime, while it has no hope of winning a war against a great power, it can hope to inflict costs on a great power out of proportion to what the great power can hope to gain by attacking it.[29]

This definition invokes the unavoidable centrality of materiel factors in defining how we perceive and critically assess notions of greatness, size, and power.[30]

A hierarchical approach to the conceptualization of national power underpins this book's analytical and empirical investigation of Iran's material capabilities. The reason is that such an approach offers the most conceptually coherent and intuitive understanding of a "middle power" while remaining relatively free from the normative and ideological assumptions that would necessarily impede a judicious appraisal of so controversial a case as Iran. From the realist premise that state power constitutes the most important criteria in organizing international relations—a premise that is shared and acted upon by the policy and political elite of all states across the world—it follows that any analysis of the relations between states must take account of the power differences between them.

Within the hierarchical approach, there are many different views on how to measure national power. Gregory Treverton and Seth Jones suggest that state power is typically conceptualized in three ways: (1) resources and capabilities, (2) the conversion of resources into power through domestic processes, and (3) outcomes.[31] In this approach, the difficulty in measuring outcomes makes it impractical as a way of quantifying power, particularly when it comes to military power. On the other hand, a purely resources-based approach would face similar empirical limitations. Because power is not necessarily fungible, it might not be possible to compare different aspects of national power.[32] Indeed, one of the weaknesses of the hierarchical approach is that there is no universal or standard method of measuring or quantifying power, because any effort involves implicit assumptions about the nature of power itself. Another major criticism of the hierarchical approach is that it is imprecise, lacking a unified methodology. As a result, different metrics used for measuring power produce different results.[33]

One solution is to combine all three measures of state power—in particular focusing on measurements of resources and processes of conversion, given the inherent difficulty in measuring outcomes—into an assessment of a state's capabilities. In this way, it is possible to develop a measure of a state's power through its potential ability to use its resources effectively to achieve its goals. Jonathan Ping notes that capabilities are a more fruitful method of quantifying power, concluding that "statistics [capability measurements] are a useful form of defining middle power if it is accepted that states are not required to use their capacity to influence others unless they see fit to do so."[34]

Measuring a state's capabilities involves looking at three different but interrelated areas. The first is the traditional arena of "hard" (military) power, which Hans Morgenthau defined as a combination of geography, natural resources, industrial strength, military capacity, population, "national character" and morale, and the quality of government and diplomacy.[35] Meanwhile, Kenneth Waltz proposed that hard power should "be defined in terms of the distribution of capabilities," including "size of population and territory, resource endowment, economic capability, military strength, political stability and competence."[36]

The second is Joseph Nye's concept of "soft" (nonmilitary) power, which has gained greater currency in the post–Cold War era. Nye defined soft power as

> the ability of a country to structure a situation so that other countries develop preferences or define their interests in ways consistent with its own through cultural or ideological attraction, institutions, and transnational corporations.[37]

Soft power is qualitatively different from hard power because it is "co-optive" rather than "coercive." However, the most common instruments of soft power—such as culture, language, and ideology—are inherently difficult to quantify. Jonathan McClory and Olivia Harvey, looking at the Soft Power 30 index—an aggregation of multiple "subjective" and "objective" quantitative measures of soft power—found that the increasing "diffusion of power" away from hegemony toward multipolarity (and nongovernmental organizations, NGOs), alongside the evolution of digital communications and media, are increasing the importance of soft power.[38]

The third area of analysis is the normative shift toward a neoliberal paradigm that has changed the role of the economy in society as well as academic understandings of that role and that has triggered an increasing profusion of non-state actors in the international system. While the economy, as traditionally defined, is still important—if only because of its role in fueling and funding material and military capabilities central to a state's power—scholars' understanding of economic power has developed to encompass subtler soft-power dimensions. Strong economic growth, for instance, can have a normative effect on a state's soft power that is positive, whereby the state becomes a model of emulation that ostensibly attests to the superiority of particular political systems. At the same time, economic power can also be used to "buy" the goodwill and support of target audiences through foreign investment and philanthropic efforts, notably through the dispensation of foreign aid at the simplest level.[39] The proliferation of affordable everyday technology to "consumers"—the basis of the global neoliberal economy—has also contributed to the diffusion of power to non-state actors and interconnected individuals and movements. These phenomena extend the battlefield for states in international relations from the economic influence of state economic agencies down to the consumer of everyday goods.

Organizational Plan

Unpacking the complexities of the evolution of the Islamic Republic raises a number of questions. What is the nature and structure of the Islamic Republic's theocratic order? Why has its existence aroused so much regional and international opposition, especially from a world power like the United States? What has enabled the Islamic Republic to ride out this fierce opposition, and what has given rise to its unorthodox domestic and foreign policy behavior, which has, at least in part, fed outsiders' fear of the Republic? How far has it progressed in its resources capabilities, and to what extent has this progress allowed it to maintain domestic order, an adequate popular base of support, and its status as a key player in the region and possibly beyond? In what ways has it pursued its interests against those of its neighbors and world powers, while proffering itself as an amicable and stabilizing force within the international system? Will it be able to deflect the Trump administration's hostile attitude, as it had done vis-à-vis previous American leaderships?

The book's approach to addressing these questions is mainly analytical and empirical rather than theoretically elaborative. In other words, it seeks to elucidate and analyze those issues that have prominently underpinned the foundation, development, continuity, and vulnerability of the Islamic Republic of Iran in both its domestic and foreign policy exposition within the changing regional and international circumstances. It posits that the Islamic Republic has a unique and multidimensional, and at times tragic, theo-political story that needs to be narrated and heard if one is to gain realistic and valid insights into how it has functioned and managed to move forward in the face of all its many adversities.

This approach does not mean that various conceptual and theoretical tools are not deployed to examine the case of the Islamic Republic. Nor does it imply that the various issues covered in this book have not been tackled elsewhere. On the contrary, the Iranian Revolution and its resulting Islamic system have been the subject of many scholarly and popular publications, albeit of varying depth, breadth, and quality. What primarily distinguishes this book from others is the detailed analysis that it offers of the *interplay* between the domestic politics and foreign relations of Iran, and the manner in which this interplay has interacted with the vicissitudes of the regional and international situation to ensure the survival of the Islamic regime. In other words, although the regime's behavior has more often than not taken shape in reaction to outside provocations, it has at the same time played a key role in generating these provocations and responding creatively to them. In providing a holistic picture of change and continuity in the development of the Islamic Republic, this book also provides the most up-to-date study of the Islamic Republic over the span of the last forty years.

The book is divided into eight chapters, including a conclusion. Chapter 2 sets the scene by explaining the concept of revolution and analyzing the internal and external conditions that helped to unleash the Iranian Revolution and paved the way for Khomeini's rise to power. The nature, structure, and processes by which Khomeini established his Islamic order and managed to overcome domestic opposition and outside hostilities are outlined in chapter 3. Chapter 4 critically discusses the evolution of Khomeini's system under his successor, Khamenei, who has managed to accumulate as much power, if not more, than his predecessor in domestic and foreign policy matters. The issue of the Islamic Republic's resources capability in terms of its economic and hard and soft power is examined in detail in chapter 5 as an essential base for evaluating Iran's capacity to act as a key regional player. Chapters 6 and 7 provide a critical analysis of the Islamic Republic's relations with its neighbors and world powers, respectively. The concluding chapter examines some of the preeminent challenges facing the Islamic Republic and poses the question of whether the Iranian Islamic system can survive outside Khomeini's *jihadi-ijtihadi* tradition or whether at some point that tradition will run its course, raising the potential for Iran to take a different direction. As part of this, it gives particular consideration to the effect that the hard-line policy attitude of the Trump presidency may have on US-Iranian relations and the destiny of the Islamic Republic itself.

2

Revolution and Transition

The Iranian Revolution of 1978–79 constituted one of the most significant events of the twentieth century. The revolution transformed Iranian politics and society in ways that confounded the expectations of those who had instigated it and toppled a major pillar of the regional and global order, shaking it at its foundations. While some seasoned analysts and observers of the country pointed to the clouds that had been gathering over Iran, none confidently predicted the scale of the coming storm. Not even the US Central Intelligence Agency (CIA), which had nurtured a deep and pervasive presence in Iran for a quarter of a century, foresaw the revolution or the dramatic changes that it would entail. On the eve of the revolution, it was confident that the Pahlavi regime, whose close alliance was central to US geopolitical and strategic interests, was so unquestionably secure that no force—whether from inside or outside—could possibly upend it.

Since the beginning of the Cold War, Iran's oil riches and strategic location on the border of the Soviet Union had made the country a centerpiece in the US policy of containing the rival superpower and maintaining dominance in the Persian Gulf and its environs. Yet, within a year, the cornerstone of America's Cold War strategy in the Middle East collapsed, as the Iranian Revolution gave rise not only to an Islamic government hostile to the US but also to serious regional power imbalances and conflicts that eroded its status as an unassailable world power in the region.

Revolution

The term "revolution" is broadly applied to describe a range of events, developments, and processes that have caused radical transformative changes at a national or transnational level in modern human history. In its most reductive political definitions, revolution is described as a singular, monolithic, and dramatic event resulting in the transformation of formal political structures. Richard Davis, for example, states that revolution is "the overthrow of an existing regime."[1] Apart from this political sense, the term is also used to denote a variety of phenomena—from "industrial revolution" to "feminist revolution" to "digital revolution"—that change human life in unprecedented ways.

There is a more specific application of the term in studies of politics that guides our discussion here; that is, the movement that overthrows one political regime and replaces it with a new system that changes the political, social, cultural, economic, and legal institutions and operations, as well as the external orientation, of a state and society.[2] This conception of revolution aligns with what Theda Skocpol calls "social revolution," which combines a political revolution in the state structure with "rapid, basic transformations of a society's state and class structures."[3] Whereas social revolutions involve long-term transformations across multiple spheres of life, the initial explosion of "political" revolutions tends to fizzle out once the overthrow of the old regime is achieved. Revolutions, in the sense we intend, are not only intense and rapid political events but also ongoing processes of, and movements for, social transformation that are driven by their instigators and social dynamics long after political change has been achieved.

The scope and content of revolutionary change are shaped by the composition and internal power dynamics of the movement that drives it. The revolutionary movement may arise from the bottom up or be instigated from the top. In other words, it may swell from a popular base, involving a cross section of social elements pursuing fundamental or wide-ranging change, or be implemented by a leadership or elite whose messages strike a chord with a receptive public because of favorable political and social conditions. In either case, revolution is usually built on the promise of specific ideological and concrete goals or nationalist agendas (or both) that encapsulate the desires of a discontented or restless public for a new system of governance and better living conditions. Yet, in history, few revolutions of this nature have succeeded in toppling the existing political system, and fewer still have delivered comprehensively on the ideals and values propounded by their original spokespersons. Revolutionary movements are invariably made up of coalitions of political and social forces with diverse platforms. Most, however, end up being dominated by a single group that succeeds in assuming leadership and shaping the revolution's direction to its preferences—often by authoritarian means. As such, political revolutions have often devoured their makers, taking shapes contrary to what the latter had originally envisioned.

The Russian and Chinese Revolutions fit this description in many ways. The October Revolution of 1917—which some historians dismiss as a Bolshevik coup d'état—resulted in the overthrow of the Provisional Government that had replaced tsarist imperial rule following the revolution of February in the same year.[4] It led to the establishment of a new political order: a union of "soviets" (peasants' and workers' collective), as envisaged by the Bolshevik Party leader and theorist Vladimir Illyich Ulyanov (known as Lenin). The Bolsheviks' success could not have been achieved without the popular support that it had gained by promising human freedoms, like those enshrined in the party's slogan: "peace, land, and bread."[5] Yet, in spite of Lenin's own dictum that the revolution would deliver all power to the proletariat, the Bolsheviks moved rapidly and successfully to secure their party's dominance by marginalizing their rivals, centralizing the Soviets, and subordinating them to the absolute authority of the Bolshevik Party.[6] This centralization laid the foundations for Joseph Stalin's dictatorship in pursuit of building what he claimed to be a Marxist–Leninist socialist and later a communist Soviet state. Stalin's successors continued a variation (albeit a less bloody one) of his authoritarianism. Even after the collapse of Soviet communism and the disintegration of the Soviet Union in December 1991, Russia's political culture has not been able to entirely divest itself from the Soviet legacy of authoritarianism. The dramatic success that the revolutionary movement achieved in overthrowing the old regime set in train revolutionary political and social changes. But whereas multiple factions and social forces had combined to achieve the first revolution, the second was fundamentally dominated by a single group.

The same can be said for the Chinese Revolution, which culminated in 1949 in the declaration of a communist order under the leadership of the Great Helmsman, Mao Zedong. Undoubtedly, the Chinese Communist Party had a broader social base than its Bolshevik counterpart, as its strategy focused on grassroots support and mobilization among the peasantry rather than on the organization of the urban industrial classes.[7] Nevertheless, the Chinese Revolution ultimately took the same path as the Russian, by betraying the promises that had inspired its original creators. In its political aspects, the communist order has succeeded only in enduring at the cost of Mao's successors relinquishing the socialist organization of the economic and social spheres in favor of a state-guided capitalist mode of development. This is just one example of the many "obvious discrepancies between [Marxist] theory and practice" that became evident in the post-revolutionary period.[8] Indeed, Deng Xiaoping justified his shift in economic policy exactly on the grounds of preserving revolutionary gains, arguing that "if we again fail to implement reform, our modernization program and socialist cause will be doomed"[9]—something that has guided his successors to date. The jury is out on how this will work in the long run.

Like the Russian and Chinese Revolutions, the Iranian Revolution overthrew one system of government and established a new one, changing the polity's domestic and foreign policy settings in fundamental ways. It swept the pro-Western autocratic monarchy of Mohammad Reza Shah Pahlavi out of power and opened the arena for what emerged as a radical Shia Islamic order under the leadership of the Shah's main political and religious opponent, Ayatollah Ruhollah Khomeini. It began as a diverse movement uniting the disaffected masses with an array of political groups but ended in the triumph of one victorious faction.

The trajectory of the revolutionary movement in Iran paralleled various developments in Russia and China: with a significant exception. Whereas in Russia and China, the dominant faction deployed varying versions of Marx's secular philosophy to advance revolutionary change, in Iran it was a Shia version of political Islamism that provided legitimation for shaping the revolution and the post-Shah transformations.

How Khomeini's Islamist faction succeeded in co-opting the Iranian revolutionary movement, and with what consequences, will be addressed in more detail later in this chapter. However, for any political revolution to succeed, four key interrelated variables are essential: the internal and external conditions, leadership, ideology, and organization. It is within the framework of these variables that the political success of the Iranian Revolution can be best explained.

Internal and External Conditions

The domestic situation conspired with regional and international circumstances to precipitate the outbreak of the Iranian Revolution. Since the two dimensions were interwoven in the Iranian political fabric, they cannot be analyzed in isolation from one another. No factor was more effective in generating favorable conditions for a revolution than the interplay between the Shah's autocratic regime, its alliance with the United States, and Iran's turbulent historical experiences at the epicenter of global power rivalries. The manner in which the Shah assumed and then reassumed his throne, his increasingly repressive rule, and his growing dependency on the United States to keep his throne paved the road to the end of the Pahlavi dynasty.

TURBULENT HISTORICAL EXPERIENCES

Mohammad Reza Shah was made Shah of Iran not once, but twice—on both occasions, by foreign powers. He first ascended the Peacock Throne in 1941, following the forced abdication of his father, Reza Shah Pahlavi, in the wake of the joint Anglo-Soviet invasion of Iran, which sought to open a direct route for the supply of wartime materiel from the United States to the Soviet Union during the Second World War. Reza Khan founded the Pahlavi dynasty—the briefest in Iranian history—when he assumed power through a coup d'état in 1921 and ascended the Peacock Throne as Reza Shah in 1925. An autocrat and modernizing nationalist, Reza Shah used his acute awareness of Iran's strengths and vulnerabilities to effect, sometimes violently, social and political change that continued through his son's rule. Iran (called Persia in the Western world until 1935) had been the seat of many great empires, both prior to and following its conversion to Islam in the late seventh century. From these empires, Iran inherited a civilizational and cultural richness, a fierce sense of Persian nationalism, and an identity rooted in Shia Islam, to which Iran's Safavid rulers forcefully converted their subjects from the start of the sixteenth century.[10] While these factors smoothed the path for Reza Shah's modernization programs, the country's strategic position on the Persian Gulf and on the Russian border, as well as the discovery of its oil riches, made it increasingly vulnerable to outside interference and serious domestic volatility.

Iran's emergence to a position of global geostrategic importance began in the middle of the nineteenth century, when the country became a centerpiece of Anglo-Russian rivalry. At the time, imperial Britain and Russia were locking horns across Central Asia in the Great Game,[11] which the two empires played against one another for regional domination from Tibet to Istanbul.[12] The rivalry of the two imperialist powers, which continued (albeit in a different form and with less intensity) after tsarist Russia's transformation into Soviet Russia in 1917, had several negative consequences for Iran. Two of these, however, would prove especially decisive for later events.

The first was a formal division of Iran into spheres of influence between the two powers by the Anglo-Russian Convention of 1907, signed at St. Petersburg. Britain largely dictated the terms, as the tsarist regime had been weakened by military defeat in the Russo-Japanese War of 1904–5 and an abortive revolution in 1905. Under the terms of the agreement, northern Iran was apportioned to Russia and the southeastern Iranian provinces to Britain, with the central strip and southwestern region remaining under the control of the government in Tehran. The whole development voided Iran's sovereignty in practice, seriously undermined the authority of the autocratic Qajar dynasty, and thwarted the Iranians' capacity to build strong domestic structures of enduring stability and security.[13]

The second was the discovery of oil in Iran at the beginning of the twentieth century. A British-born Australian, William D'Arcy, had purchased from the Shah a concession granting him exclusive rights to prospect for oil, gas, and minerals in an area amounting to three-quarters of Iran. The British, eager to secure an independent source of oil (in particular for their modernizing naval fleets) and to acquire prospecting rights on Russia's doorstep, soon purchased D'Arcy's concession. In 1909, the Anglo-Persian Oil Company (APOC; renamed the Anglo-Iranian Oil Company, or AIOC, in 1935) was established to develop, exploit, and control Iranian oil resources, largely for the benefit of British interests. Apart from adding another bone of contention between Great Britain and Russia, the oil concession set the pattern for a client-patron relationship between the rulers of Iran and world powers. This, as well as the convention, heightened Iranians' distrust of outside powers, a factor that has grown to be an important element of their political culture alongside a traditional sense of fierce independence and national pride.

These internal and external developments drove the coalescence of a nationalist and reformist movement in the first decade of the twentieth century. The movement was spearheaded by an unlikely alliance between members of the intelligentsia, the *bazaaris* (petit bourgeois, composed of mainly small traders and merchants who traditionally formed the backbone of the Iranian economy), and the Shia clerical establishment. These groups were united in the aim of transforming Iran into a constitutional monarchy and ending the Anglo-Russian rivalry in and over Iran. The movement had some success: a new constitution came into effect in 1906, marking Asia's first constitutional revolution; a parliamentary system was enacted; and the clerical establishment secured a constitutional role in overseeing and approving the passage of all national laws to ensure they stayed on the path of Shia Islam.[14] These successes, however, were rapidly eroded by a dysfunctional parliament, continual interference from Britain and Russia, and the ascent of a new Qajar Shah who reasserted autocratic rule with indispensable support from Russia.[15] In the face of these challenges, the alliance that had formed the Constitutional Movement broke up. Iran faced political fragmentation and economic and social stagnation, with the decaying Qajar monarchy struggling to hold on to power in the face of bankruptcy, a corrupt and inefficient administration, popular unrest, and a weak army.[16] Its deteriorating relationship with the British, who by the late 1910s were extracting far more exorbitant profits from the Iranian oil industry than the Iranians, did not help the situation.

The combination of domestic fragility and vulnerability to external forces opened the way for the commander of the Russian-trained Cossack Brigade, Brigadier General Reza Khan, to march from the north to take power in Tehran in 1921. Four years later, Iran's Majles elected to depose the Qajar dynasty and declared Reza Khan the new Shah. Reza Shah had risen through the military ranks from a very humble background. After losing his father (from the Iranian province of Mazandaran) while still an infant, he was raised by an uncle and his Muslim Georgian mother. His mother's family had migrated to Iran following the Russo-Persian War (1804–13), during which Iran had lost the territory of today's Georgia to Russia. Reza Khan's military training endowed him with not only a regimented attitude but also a single-mindedness about the problems—both internal and external—that had beset his country and the region.

By the time Reza Khan assumed power, the First World War had restructured the regional political landscape. The British and French colonial powers had carved up the Arab Middle East between themselves along the lines of the 1916 Sykes-Picot Agreement, which preempted the defeat and disintegration of the Ottoman Empire, along with its two Axis allies, Germany and Austria-Hungary. In 1923, the secular reformist Mustafa Kemal Ataturk had founded the new republic of Turkey. Reza Shah was deeply impressed by Ataturk's modernization program, as was King Amanullah Khan, who had taken the reins of power around the same time in Afghanistan.[17] After dissolving parliament, suspending the constitution, banning political activities, and engaging in politics of suppression, the Shah instituted a top-down process of modernization, with emphasis on infrastructure building and the expansion of social services, most importantly in education and health.[18] His crowning achievement was the construction of a railroad that linked Iran from the Persian Gulf to the Caspian Sea.

At this time of relative calm in the Anglo-Russian rivalry, Reza Shah was able to neutralize, with British assistance, Soviet encroachments in northern Iran in the late 1920s, while also managing to prevent British incursions into the territories that were consolidating into the Soviet Union.[19] Doing so, he realized, was essential in order to buffer Iran's own integrity against the Russians and the British. Like several of his predecessors, Reza Shah was keen to forge close ties with the more distant United States, a nascent power with a reputation untarnished by a history of imperialist expansion in the region.[20] However, despite American Christian missionaries visiting Iran in the second half of the nineteenth century, the signing of the US-Iran Treaty of Friendship and Commerce as far back as 1856, and the establishment of political relations between the two sides from 1883, full diplomatic ties at the ambassadorial level between the two states did not materialize until 1944. Up to this point, the US treated Iran largely as part of the British sphere of influence and did not reciprocate Tehran's diplomatic overtures.

To compensate for this, Reza Shah not only entered the defensive regional Saadabad Treaty with Turkey, Iraq, and Afghanistan in 1937 but also forged close relations with Nazi Germany at around the same time. In fact, by the turn of the 1940s, Germany had become Iran's largest trading partner, with some six hundred German personnel involved in different fields of activity in Iran, where "German prestige stood high."[21] Under a rising tide of nationalism, he also renegotiated the first oil concession with the British in 1932, which did not increase Iran's control over its oil industry, but gave it a better cut of the profits.

Reza Shah's repressive politics at home and his ties with Nazi Germany set the stage for his undoing. In 1941, he rejected a US-backed Anglo-Soviet request to use Iranian territory for the transfer of wartime supply to the USSR. Although Reza Shah had declared Iran's neutrality in the war, the British and Soviets responded to his refusal by invading and occupying Iran along the lines of their previous spheres of influence to guarantee oil flows to the Allies and war materiel supply routes to the USSR. The occupying powers left Reza Shah little choice; he agreed to abdicate, but in return for the continuation of the Pahlavi dynasty under his oldest son, Crown Prince Mohammad Reza, who became Shah on September 16, 1941. His father sailed out to Johannesburg, South Africa, as a frustrated nationalist and modernizer, only to die in July 1944 in exile. Thirty-eight years later, his son would share his father's fate.

Reza Shah's departure ushered in another turbulent phase in Iran's historical evolution. At the time of his ascent to the throne, Mohammad Reza Shah was young and inexperienced. Aged only twenty-two, he had not expected to be thrust into such a position of responsibility so soon or so suddenly. After completing his primary education in Switzerland, he returned to Iran in 1935, where he graduated from a military school in Tehran three years later. As such, he was largely out of depth in the art of governance and led a largely boisterous life that left him with little understanding of the complexity of Iran's political and social dynamics and their connection with regional and global affairs. In any case, as his father's autocratic structures rapidly loosened, the emergence of a more assertive parliament, combined with interference from the occupying powers, meant that the Shah had little real power.[22]

To maintain his position, Mohammad Reza Shah found himself with no choice but to engage in the politics of compromise and consensus-building between two antagonistic forces. On the one hand, he was confronted with a new wave of nationalism, which sought to achieve what the Constitutional Movement had failed to accomplish. This movement was headed by a veteran reformist politician of noble origin, Dr. Mohammad Mosaddegh, who had opposed Reza Shah's accession to the throne on the grounds that it would perpetuate dictatorial rule, and who had subsequently been imprisoned for his political activities in 1939. On the other hand, the new monarch was pressured by the occupying powers to comply with their competing political, strategic, and ideological agendas. The conflicting pressures from the domestic and the international front strongly conditioned the policy behavior of the Shah and his advisors, including even the highly experienced Prime Minister Mohammad Ali Foroughi, and a succession of another ten, short-term prime ministers over the next decade.[23]

Cajoled by the United States, which by now had abandoned its relatively noninterventionist policy in favor of an active involvement in the Middle East, Britain, the USSR, and Iran signed what became known as the Tripartite Treaty of Alliance in January 1942. The treaty acknowledged the presence of foreign troops in Iran, with a firm declaration that the signatories would respect the independence, sovereignty, and territorial integrity of Iran and that Allied troops would withdraw from Iran within six months of the termination of the war.[24] However, the treaty commitments did nothing to prevent the occupying powers from being closely watchful of each other's activities in Iran. To prevent this, the Soviets rapidly closed off the five northern provinces of Iran and set up Azeri and Kurdish socialist governments there. Meanwhile, the British sought to do everything possible to strengthen their hold on the oil-rich southern regions of Iran. Both powers forced the Iranian government to expel the Germans and competed against one another for its favor.[25] This competition, in effect, served as a precursor to the strategic rivalry of the Cold War, which would continue to drag Iran into the main fray of regional and global geopolitics.

While the Soviets relied on the Iranian communist party Tudeh (Masses) and disaffected Iranian ethnic Kurdish and Azeri minorities as their main political weapons, the British patronized various southern tribes and such parties as Erade-ye Melli (National Will) and Edalat (Justice) to achieve their objectives. They did so, as Sir Winston Churchill put it, to make "the Persians keep each other quiet while we get on with the war."[26] Meanwhile, the American oil companies found an opportunity to demand access to Iran's oil resources, which the Soviets countered with a request of their own. Iran thus became the site of a three-way contest between the three supposedly allied powers. When the Second World War ended in 1945, the British honored their treaty commitment by withdrawing their forces, but the Soviets were reluctant to do so, particularly because Stalin considered northern Iran as critical to the security of the southern flanks of the USSR, where the key oilfields were located.[27] He argued that given that the British had already used Iran to invade Bolshevik Russia in the 1920s, withdrawing the troops would allow anyone with a box of matches to ignite the oil fields of the Soviet republic of Azerbaijan.[28] However, under threat of US and British retribution, and realizing that it had more at stake in Eastern Europe, Moscow found it expedient to announce the withdrawal of its troops in late March 1946. It did so only after signing an agreement with the Iranian government that Tehran would respect the autonomous status of the Soviet-installed Kurdish and Azeri republics. Yet, once the Soviets had gone, the Iranian government, supported by Britain and the US, sent its army to those republics and regained full control over them—a move that naturally soured relations with Moscow.[29]

Meanwhile, the Iranian people had good reason to be distrustful of the British and concerned about the role of the United States in their country. These concerns fed into a growing call for an end to outside interference in Iran and to the authoritarian rule that had historically defined Iranian political culture. By 1949, Mosaddegh had succeeded in coalescing a rainbow alliance of different ideological, political, and social groups—secular, communist, socialist, liberal democratic, and devoutly religious—within the Jebhe-ye

Melli (National Front), which, according to the British ambassador Sir Francis Shepherd, "were playing a chord which awoke strong echoes among many classes of Persians."[30] As the National Front gained a parliamentary majority and the Majles voted in Mosaddegh as prime minister, the Shah had little choice but to appoint Mossadegh to the position on April 30, 1951.[31] The Shah, who did not like Mosaddegh and who was also conscious of the fact that the absolute power of Iran's monarchs had been the historical basis of their survival, had by now forged close links with the military as commander in chief and with the British and Americans.

MOSADDEGH'S REFORMS AND THE DISMANTLING OF THE BRITISH REGIONAL ORDER

As prime minister, Mosaddegh began work on a substantive, largely secular, reform agenda that focused on three major interrelated goals: regaining full control over Iran's national resources (most importantly oil) and curtailing major power rivalry and interference in the country; instituting long overdue socioeconomic reforms for the benefit of the Iranian people; and transforming Iran into a constitutional monarchy, thereby limiting the traditional powers of the Shah in favor of a publicly mandated system of governance.[32] Mosaddegh considered his reforms to be not only politically and socially right but also morally so.[33] He believed that he had an ethical responsibility to empower Iran to be a truly sovereign, independent, and prosperous state. Mosaddegh was not a middle-of-the-road leader—he had been a political activist for most of his adult life, with a burning desire for radical change. He was also a shrewd political actor, although unorthodox in his habits and dealings.[34] He had a broad nationalist and social base of support. Among his supporters were prominent and influential clerics such as Ayatollah Abol-Ghassan Kashani, who was known for his advocacy of a Shia Islamic government, opposition to oppression and foreign interference, and support of oil nationalization.[35]

Mosaddegh saw the British monopoly of the Iranian oil industry as a main reason for foreign rivalry in Iran. He had authored the

1944 parliamentary bill demanding that there be no oil concession to any power, after American oil companies had demanded a share and the Russians had made a similar request. Unsurprisingly, then, his first major act on May 1, 1951, was to declare the nationalization of the AIOC. In return, he promised to financially compensate the British and invited their personnel to continue their operations in the industry. He set up the National Iranian Oil Company to replace the AIOC as the body to run the oil industry. Washington was initially supportive of Mosaddegh's nationalization, viewing it as within Iran's national right to self-determination. The US State Department's response stated that "no Government can deny itself the sovereign rights to nationalize an industry within its territory."[36] Yet, at the same time, American oil companies were pressuring Iran to cut them in on the Iranian oil industry, as part of an emerging ambition to build a US-led order in the region. London, on the other hand, rejected the nationalization, fearing it would set a precedent for other British assets to be nationalized in the region. These fears proved well founded: in Egypt in 1956, President Gamal Abdul Nasser took control of the main highway of British commerce, the Suez Canal.

Mosaddegh's nationalization was a decisive and globally significant first episode in the waning of British supremacy in the Middle East. The British responded, as they had in the early 1930s during renegotiation of the oil concession, with gunboat diplomacy, imposing an economic blockade.[37] British Petroleum reached a secret agreement with six other major Western oil companies to boycott Iranian oil, thereby undermining Iran's main source of revenue, preventing Mosaddegh from implementing his promised social and economic reforms and causing widespread economic hardship for the Iranian people.[38] Meanwhile, Mosaddegh's efforts to limit the Shah's powers caused the relationship between the two to sour to a point that threatened the country's very political stability. The Shah decided to leave Iran for a temporary stay in Switzerland in August 1953, which could have easily turned into permanent exile.

Yet despite Tehran's success in presenting its case before the UN Security Council, London was able to persuade Washington to intervene, convincing them that the country was under threat of a takeover by the pro-Soviet Tudeh communists, which would turn Iran into a Soviet ally. In Operation Ajax, a covert operation typical of the Cold War, the CIA, encouraged and backed by Britain's MI6, staged a coup d'état on August 19, 1953. Fronting the coup were the Iranian security and conservative social forces.[39] The result was the overthrow of Mosaddegh's government and the return of a reluctant Shah to his throne just one week into his Swiss exile.[40]

Mosaddegh was put under house arrest until his death in 1967. He was allowed to live as a precaution against him becoming a martyr, a high risk in a nation where martyrdom and heroism have long been symbolically intertwined. The Shah was now ruling Iran on sufferance and never more conscious of owing his seat on the Peacock Throne to foreign powers—this time, to the United States.

THE SHAH'S RULE AND THE US-ESTABLISHED REGIONAL ORDER

The nationalization episode marked a turning point for both Iran and the United States. The CIA's intervention was widely resented inside Iran. No Persian ruler had ever succeeded to the throne as a result of direct foreign intervention of this nature. Mosaddegh himself referred to this in his trial, declaring that "numerous sins have been attributed to me, but I know that I have committed no more than one, and that is that I have not yielded to the whims of foreigners."[41] Foreign backing both underpinned and undermined the legitimacy of the Iranian monarch and the institution of the Shah. Meanwhile, in the rest of the region, the Arab nationalist forces (converging under the leadership of Nasser) were calling for the unity of all Arabs against colonialism, imperialism, and Zionism and viewed the CIA's reinstallment of the Shah on his throne with serious apprehension. The Soviet Union condemned the US intervention in Iran as an act of imperialism.[42]

On the domestic front, the Shah imposed a military dictatorship and made extensive use of the secret police, Sazman-e Ettela'at va Amniyat-e Keshvar (the Organization of Information and Security, known as SAVAK), which was hurriedly set up for him by the CIA and the Federal Bureau of Investigation in cooperation with the Israeli intelligence agency, Mossad.[43] On the foreign policy front, the Shah's regime drew ever closer to the United States, depending heavily on it for political, financial, economic, and military support. It rapidly signed various bilateral agreements in all these areas with the United States to shore up its position.[44] Iran became the largest recipient of American aid outside North Atlantic Treaty Organization (NATO) countries, reflecting its key status in US Middle Eastern policy. This relationship entailed a dramatic change that transformed Iran from a neutral state to a US ally against Soviet communism. These developments laid the groundwork for Iran's long-term dependence on, and vulnerability to, the United States.[45]

The Shah's regime essentially became a bridgehead for the United States to penetrate a frontline oil-rich state, while preventing the USSR from gaining access to the equally oil-rich Persian Gulf. Of particular importance was Iran's control of the northern tip of the Strait of Hormuz, through which the bulk of the Gulf oil was and still is exported. The US-Iranian alliance also complemented the de facto alliance that the United States had begun to forge with another of Iran's oil-rich Arab neighbors to the south of the Persian Gulf: the Sunni Islamic Kingdom of Saudi Arabia.[46] US-Saudi ties first emerged out of an exchange in which the US agreed to provide security to the ruling Ibn Saud family, who, in return, guaranteed an uninterrupted supply of oil to America and its allies. The US-Iranian and US-Saudi relationships, in effect, formed the two important foundational pillars of Pax Americana in the Persian Gulf.[47] The subsequent forging of a US-Israeli strategic partnership in the late 1950s, and the British withdrawal from the Gulf (as part of a wider retreat from east of Suez at the turn of the 1970s), provided wider but hazier scope for such an order.

The Shah pursued two contradictory goals in his reign. First, following the precedent of Iranian shahs for more than two millennia, he sought to make himself central to the operation of Iranian politics. Second, he engaged, like his father, in a pro-capitalist secular mode of national development that complemented his special relationship with the US. The first, to be successful, required political centralization. The second demanded political decentralization and liberalization of the economy. While the Shah was initially able to stave off the threat to his rule, it was clear to him and Washington that the manner in which he had regained his throne had created a serious problem of political legitimacy. He formally ended martial law in 1959 and subsequently under pressure from the administration of President John F. Kennedy set out to secure a wider base of popular legitimacy.[48] In 1961, he embraced wide-ranging land reform, which was initiated by Prime Minister Ali Amini, a close friend of the Kennedys who was forcefully recommended to the Shah by Washington.[49] However, by 1962, the Shah prompted Amini to resign and took over the land-reform process himself while also initiating a number of other social and economic reforms, such as the establishment of a rural literacy corps and the introduction of female suffrage.[50] He called these reforms the White Revolution, or "the revolution of the Shah and the people," not only because they were carried out without bloodshed or overt class warfare but also to distinguish them from a communist "red revolution" similar to the 1917 Russian Revolution.[51]

Meanwhile, he sought to maximize Iran's benefit from its oil resources. He had criticized Mosaddegh's approach to the oil nationalization as "negative nationalism" that "led straight to the sort of political and economic chaos which foreign agents found ideal for their purposes."[52] In 1960, he joined three other oil-producing states—the conservative Saudi Arabia and "revolutionary" Iraq and Venezuela—in forming the Organization of Petroleum Exporting Countries (OPEC) as a "cartel of producers" vis-à-vis the powerful Western international oil companies and their supporting governments. He called his approach "positive nationalism," which he defined as

> a policy of maximum political and economic independence consistent with the interests of one's country, which necessitates making any deals that are in the [national] interest, regardless of the wishes or policies of others.[53]

This move put him at odds with Washington. The US Secretary of State, John Foster Dulles, had in 1953 declared American oil companies an "instrument" of US foreign policy that required government protection.[54] However, by now the Shah had become sufficiently confident in his relationship with Washington that he began to pursue some nationalizing reforms and Iranian interests more assertively.

Whatever steps he took, he still could not expunge the indignity of owing his throne to the CIA. Nor could he bridge the contradiction in his goals or transform his relationship with the US from a client-patron relationship into one of interdependence. Consequently, he was unable to legitimize his rule in the eyes of most of the Iranians and the countries of the region. He continued to govern on the basis of the politics of suppression, co-optation, patronage, and divide-and-rule. SAVAK was developed into and projected as such a pervasive force that a majority of the Iranian people came to believe that most of their compatriots were either members or informants of the organization. Frances Fitzgerald, a well-known American journalist, wrote:

> SAVAK has agents in the lobby of every hotel, in every government department and in every university classroom. . . . Educated Iranians cannot trust anyone beyond a close circle of friends, and for them the effect is the same as if everyone else belonged. SAVAK intensifies this fear by giving no account of its activities. People disappear in Iran, and their disappearances go unrecorded.[55]

Fear of SAVAK reached the point where "people could not trust people."[56]

By the late 1960s, four major sources of opposition to the Shah were beginning to coalesce. The first was drawn from political groups and organizations that opposed the Shah on ideological grounds. They included not only the remnants of the center-left National Front but also such Marxist-Leninist groups as the Tudeh and Fedayin-e Khalq (People's Sacrificers), as well as the radical semi-Islamist Mojahedin-e Khalq (People's Strugglers), which preached a mixture of Marxist and Islamic messages. These varied leftist groupings formed into the Organization of Communist Unity, which was a key mobilizing front for Iranian revolutionary fervor and a major contributor to the revolutionary "ground game."[57]

The second group was drawn from the professional and intellectual strata of Iranian society. It included public servants, lawyers, journalists, academics, and university students, most of whom could no longer accept servitude. In general, they had no consolidated political agenda beyond seeking a democratic reformation of the political system.

The third were the *bazaaris,* and to a lesser extent the landowners aligned with them who had been negatively affected by the White Revolution. These groups had traditionally constituted a coherent middle-class stratum with close ties to the Shia religious establishment. Although some benefited from the Shah's policies, most were targeted by his anti-*bazaari* drive, which sought to "[break] down their economic power and . . . [reduce] their socio-culturally conservative influence throughout society."[58] Many were also concerned about the transfer of economic power away from the *bazaari*s to a class of large merchants known as oil bourgeoisie, a process that was happening under the Shah's modernization drive. They were neither content with the increased taxes and regulations nor satisfied with the growing cost of living and operating businesses.

The fourth was the Shia religious establishment. The Pahlavi dynasty, composed of the Shah and his late father, embraced Shia Islam as the state religion and used the clerical establishment for political purposes on occasion but would not allow it to undermine the dynasty's authority in the operation of state and society. The Shah, even more so than his father, aggressively promoted secular politics, partly to prevent any religious center of power from challenging his position.[59] His constant attempts to erode the power base of the Shia establishment caused widespread disquiet among the clerics. Many of their leading figures, especially in the historical city of Qom—a traditional Shia seat of learning and political power that had counterbalanced the temporal authority of the Shah since the early sixteenth century—did not approve of the Shah's regime or his pro-Western secular modernization drive.[60]

While public grievances gathered pace at different levels of society, two related factors predominantly coalesced to trigger widespread active popular opposition to the Shah's rule by the late 1970s. The first was the dramatic increase in Iran's oil revenue, which led him to entertain ambitious plans of transforming Iran into the world's fifth-largest economic and military power by the mid-1980s and therefore remold the country into what he called *Tamadun-e Bozorg* (great civilization, or welfare state). Iran's oil revenue increased from $1.36 billion in 1970 to the post-OPEC "revolution" of $18.5 billion in 1974 and $20 billion in 1975.[61]

The second factor concerned Washington's unqualified complicity in the Shah's quest for grandeur. Under the Nixon Doctrine, the Shah's regime was entrusted with the responsibility not only to look after Iran's interests but also to champion those of the US in the region. In a 1972 visit to Tehran, President Richard Nixon, who was keen to recycle the dramatic increases in OPEC members' oil revenues back into the US economy, gave the Shah carte blanche to purchase any conventional weapon system he desired (nuclear weapons were excluded) and boost substantially Iran's trade ties with the United States.[62] The Shah used the increase in the oil wealth to purchase a horde of technologically impressive American weaponry, notably F-14 fighters for his air force. In a 1975 agreement, military trade between the two sides, which had totaled about $10 billion from 1973 to 1976, was augmented by another $15 billion during the same period.[63] Commercial trade also was to expand, growing from $10 billion in 1974–76 to $40 billion during the period 1976–80, making the US Iran's largest trading partner.[64]

Washington's broader objective was to make Iran one of the three pillars, alongside Saudi Arabia and Israel, that would provide an enduring support upon which the structure of American geopolitical dominance in the Gulf (and possibly the wider Middle East) could rest secure. This policy approach appeared to pay little or no attention to the possibility of regime change in Iran or to how

Saudi-Iranian and Saudi-Israeli differences might undermine efforts to engage in regional cooperation.

While expecting Iran's oil revenue to continue to grow for the foreseeable future, the Shah's journey of socioeconomic change and military modernization soon proved to be poorly conceived and badly implemented. It turned out to be unresponsive to Iran's needs and deaf to internal political pressures, while the sheer scale and speed of the reforms were beyond the country's capacity to handle. The Shah's ambitions exceeded the country's infrastructural, technical, and trained labor force capacity, resulting in bottlenecks, congestion, malfunctions, and malpractices. It created situations where "food imports rotted" in inadequate storage facilities or on ships that "had to wait weeks at Iranian ports" to unload their goods. The education system was unable to absorb the high numbers of students, producing high joblessness in a country forced to import foreign workers.[65] While over 70 percent of Iranians could not read and write, an equal number suffered from curable diseases and poor sanitary conditions, and unemployment hovered around 30 percent, especially among the Iranian youth.[66] Out of the $69 billion budget for the Fifth Development Plan (1973–78), the Shah spent more than two-thirds on economic modernization and military build-up.[67]

This approach produced serious social and economic dislocation and imbalances that caused great confusion and uncertainty among Iranians, particularly in the face of rising inequality, as the country's newfound wealth was not shared in an equitable manner. Those who could not be the beneficiaries of the Shah's policies (and these constituted a majority of Iranians from both urban and rural backgrounds) could not identify with any of his goals. The Shah cannot have been unaware of the mounting opposition, as the Mojahedin-e Khalq, Fedayin-e Khalq, and Fadayan-e Islam (Devotees of Islam) had already engaged in violent actions, killing some of the Shah's trusted advisors and American personnel. The Mojahedin, for example, had by 1975 bombed Reza Shah's mausoleum, killed a US advisor to the Shah, and assassinated the chief of the Tehran police force.[68]

However, the Shah dismissed these forces as Islamic, Marxist, and terrorist (and therefore not representative of broader social currents) and remained confident of his security apparatus's ability to wipe them out. Even so, on the political front, he found it expedient to allow a parliament to function, but he set up a three-faction political party called Rastakhiz (Resurgence) from early 1975 and called on Iranians of different ideological convictions to join either its right, left, or central wing. Evidently, Iranians did not view the party as anything more than a ploy. Its membership and popular base remained minute, composed primarily of those who benefited from the Shah's policies and thought that joining the party would give them power and a better life. When the Shah was asked why he would not allow free and fair parliamentary elections, his response was that there would be more candidates than voters.

Meanwhile, the Shah's policies caused alarm in the region. Although the Soviets appeared to have come to terms with Iran's transformation into a firm US ally and were reluctantly content to settle for good working relations with Tehran in return for its refraining from open hostility, they could not but view the Shah's military build-up with trepidation. Moscow was horrified at the prospect of the Shah serving as the regional policeman.[69] Nor could it remain indifferent to the Shah's opposition to what he called "foreign-backed subversive forces" in the region that were aligned with the Soviet Union, such as the Popular Front for the Liberation of Oman, which was backed by pro-Soviet regimes in Syria, Iraq, and the People's Democratic Republic of Yemen.[70] Beyond this, Moscow had reason to be mindful of Tehran's close intelligence and economic cooperation with Israel and its possible impact on the regional balance and the Palestinian-Arab cause, which Moscow, from the mid-1950s, had made the centerpiece of its Cold War competition with the US in the wider Middle East.

By the same token, both radical and conservative Arab states, which were experiencing a surge of pan-Arab nationalism during this period, found the Shah's vision of an all-powerful Iran disturbing. While the radicals had long been critical of the Shah's regime, their ranks were now swelled by the conservatives, led by Saudi Arabia. The Saudis countered the development by not only engaging in a process of military modernization of their own but also using their position as the largest producer within OPEC to keep oil prices steady, thus starving the Shah of the increased oil revenue on which he had staked his modernization pipedreams. By 1975, this caused a serious shortfall in Tehran's income, forcing the Shah to raise a $500 million loan from Europe in order to meet the costs of his planned projects. By 1977, the budget deficit had increased to $4.5 billion.[71] Meanwhile, he had to dampen the expectations that he had initially elevated among the Iranian people. Doing so could only raise the ire of many, who now questioned the Shah's whole approach to Iran's transformation.

The change of the American administration in 1977 from the Republican Nixon to the Democrat President Jimmy Carter did not help the situation. President Carter had made human rights a foreign policy priority, and although his prime target was the Soviet Union, this also put pressure on the Shah to engage in a degree of limited liberalization. Despite declaring off-limits any criticism of the monarchy, the constitution, and the armed forces, once the Shah had opened the gates for political expression, he was unable to turn back the tide. Despite the regime's strict control of the media and other means of communication, many Iranians took advantage of the small window of opportunity not only to criticize the working of the government but also to refer negatively to the prevalence of authoritarian rule and the lack of democratic rights and freedoms, which basically amounted to criticism of the regime.

In spite of growing signs of the build-up of opposition, Washington continued to stand behind the Shah's regime and its policies unequivocally. In November 1977, when hosting a dinner for the Shah at the White House, President Carter declared: "We look upon Iran as a very stabilizing force in the world at large."[72] In December 1977, during a visit to Tehran, President Carter praised the Shah's strong stewardship and Iran's close relations with the United States. He described Iran as "an island of stability in one of the more troubled areas of the world" and attributed this stability to the Shah's "great leadership" and, as he put it, "to the respect and admiration and love which your people give to you."[73] However, as events soon proved, Carter's comments had completely missed the realities of Iranian popular politics.

Iranian students studying in the US had already begun a wave of protests abroad, which were picked up by Tehran University students and snowballed into a nationwide uprising and popular revolution in the first half of 1978. The participants came to include a wide range of social groups, forming a mass-based, popular movement. Its participants came from diverse ideological, political, and social backgrounds and included secular liberals and democrats, socialists and communists, and *bazaaris*, who were progressively joined by industrial workers, most importantly those in the oil industry. While it was initially spearheaded by political, professional, and intellectual elements, these forces had no organizational network or shared platform beyond a common opposition to the Shah's regime and two aspirations: the reformation of the regime and a withdrawal of US support for it. Some were keen to see democratic changes, whereas others pronounced demands that ranged from socialist changes to better standards of living. Few openly demanded, far less expected, a Shia religious metamorphosis of the country.

The Shah originally appeared confident (as did his American and British allies) that he had sufficient coercive resources and a base of popular support to impose stringent security measures, accompanied by some political concessions, to contain and quell the uprising. However, the more he clamped down on the protestors—at the cost of hundreds of lives—the less he was able to persuade them to give ground, despite his promises of some reforms to liberalize the polity for wider public participation. It was in this context that the Shia *ulema* (learned critics) were able to step in and seize control of the revolutionary strands, which leads us to the second variable for the success of the revolution.

Leadership

Up to this point, the Shia establishment lurked largely in the background, encouraging protestors actively, but from the sidelines. Once it became clear that the opposition movement had solidified, it sensed an acute opportunity to assume a frontline position and, more important, fill the leadership vacuum. The figure who emerged from the ranks of its leading clerics to spearhead the protests was Ayatollah Khomeini (1902–89). Khomeini had been a stern and relentless critic of the Shah's regime for most of his adult life. Born in Khomeyn, Markazi Province, Iran, he was brought up by his mother and an uncle following the assassination of his father, Seyyed Mostafa Hindi, when Khomeini was five months old. He was a trained scholar of Islamic theology, as well as of Islamic and Western philosophies, and a great admirer of Aristotelian thought. After studying under various prominent Shia theologians, he taught in Iran at Qom and in Iraq at Najaf, one of the holiest Shia sites because it is the burial place of Ali ibn Abi Talib (the fourth Caliph of Islam and son-in-law and cousin of Prophet Mohammad, whom the Shias took as their first imam, or leader, and successor to the Prophet leadership). Until the early 1960s, he remained dutifully in the shadow of his mentor, Ayatollah Mohammad Hussein Borojerdi. However, after the latter's death in March 1962, he became an active political opponent of the Shah's regime, although he had supported a limited monarchy in the 1940s.

It was at about this time that Khomeini's peers, led by Grand Ayatollah Mohammad Kazem Shariatmadari, elevated him to the rank of *Ayatollah* (Sign of Allah) and *marja-e taqlid* (source of emulation)—the highest positions in the Shia hierarchy—providing him a religious rank that could ensure his security against the Shah's regime.[74] While stepping up his criticism of the monarchy and its special relationship with the US, in a series of sermons Khomeini castigated the Shah for violating the Constitution of 1906 and deviating from the path of Islam. When the Shah granted diplomatic immunity to American military personnel who had committed crimes in Iran, he condemned it as a "capitulation." He derided the Shah's White Revolution as mere theater.[75] To silence him, SAVAK first detained him in 1964 for less than a year and then forced him into exile, which took him via Turkey to Najaf in Iraq. Iraq's leftist-nationalist Ba'athist regime granted Khomeini protection as leverage in Baghdad's political, ideological, and territorial disputes with Tehran. The exile distanced him from his country but did not prevent him from reaching his supporters through his sermons, which were smuggled into Iran on cassettes and played during Friday prayers in mosques.

When it became clear that the uprisings were heading toward a full-blown revolution, Khomeini took center stage. The Shah's regime had decimated the overtly organized political opposition and even driven some underground to take up arms. But it had not been able to uproot the Shia establishment, despite its crusade against the opposition. The establishment and its clerical network had remained fairly cohesive and active, largely because SAVAK's ability to penetrate the network of mosques and seminaries was constrained by the Shah's own need to project himself as a devout Shia Muslim to a pious public.[76]

Although the leader of the National Front, Karim Sanjabi, had thus far acted intermittently as the main spokesperson for the revolution, Khomeini rapidly overshadowed him and all others in both stature and influence. Within the Shia clerical hierarchy, Khomeini was not the most senior Ayatollah. He was junior to a number of his peers at the time, of whom three were most prominent. The first was Grand Ayatollah Mahmoud Taleghani (1911–79)—an Islamic reformer and promoter of democracy, who was widely respected within the Shia establishment and masses. He supported the revolution but did not survive to have much impact on what transpired after it. The second was Grand Ayatollah Shariatmadari (1905–86), who was a strong supporter of the traditional Shia dictum that the clerics had a duty to oversee and guide the working of the government but not to run it. The third was Grand Ayatollah Ali Montazeri (1922–2009), who played a leading role in the revolution as a prominent Islamic scholar and theologian, democracy advocate, and human rights activist.

None of these figures, nor several other Grand Ayatollahs—all *marja*—could match Khomeini's image as a bold, resolute, resilient, visionary, and politically savvy theologian, far less rival his qualities as a unifying revolutionary leader. Khomeini articulated his religious political views and objectives in a language far more radical and accessible than any of his peers. He often couched his messages in simple terms, laced with historical Shia symbols and events and imbued in the Iranian political discourse and public consciousness over centuries. Khomeini's hearkening to the core Shia theme of justice tapped into the emotions, sensitivities, and vulnerabilities of a wide cross section of Iranians who had accumulated grievances against the Shah's regime. In one speech, he declared:

> I don't know where this White Revolution is that they are making so much fuss about. God knows that I am aware of . . . the remote villages and provincial towns, not to mention our own backward city of Qum. I am aware of the hunger of our people and the disordered state of our agrarian economy. Why not try to do something for this country, for this population, instead of piling up debts and enslaving yourselves?[77]

He went on to link these poor socioeconomic conditions to foreign interference, stating that "[the US and the Shah] have reduced the Iranian people to a level lower than that of an American dog."[78] Through his vivid, striking, and unambiguous language, Khomeini distinguished himself from the leaders of all other revolutionary groups, whose ideological and jargon-laden messages flew over the heads of ordinary Iranians.

By the end of 1978, Khomeini was clearly a national religious and political hero in the eyes of many Iranians. Millions viewed him as the leader who would be capable of standing up not only to the Shah but also to the US. He exuded a mystical charisma, power, and authority, projecting a messianic, invincible, and decisive image. It, together with a firm, fatherly demeanor, found wide appeal among Iranians, especially among the poor and those who were from rural areas or had recently migrated to the cities. His courageous stance made him a source of admiration for many Iranians, to whom he exemplified the combined virtues of Shia Islam, Iranian nationalism, and Persian historical traditions. No other leader inspired such popular adulation and following.

Most of the Iranian public knew enough about Khomeini's longstanding opposition to the Shah's regime to respect him but not to make a critical assessment of him or his ideas and intentions. In this respect, he was indeed an enigma. Some even came later to believe that he was the Hidden Imam Mohammad ibn Hassan al-Mahdi (864–941), who according to the belief of Twelver Shias went into major occultation at the age of four but would return, together with Jesus Christ, to bring peace and justice to the world, save it from decadence, and prepare it for the Day of Judgment.[79] Khomeini initially appeared to be quite content to allow such an elevation to run its course, happily acquiring the title imam. However, there was nothing mysterious about the circumstances that led him to formulate his Shia revolutionary theology.

Ideology

Khomeini was unique among Iranian revolutionary leaders in his ability to formulate a coherent and popular ideology to serve as a viable alternative to the Shah's secular, ethnonationalist monarchy. He had already outlined his broad vision for a post-monarchy Iran some years before the revolution. While some of his peers and devotees, especially in Qom, were familiar with his theological writings, neither the general Iranian public nor the global community, the West in particular, had much awareness of them. This may well have been due to the fact that no one, not even the most seasoned scholars of Iran, imagined a day when Khomeini's political thoughts might become a reality.

Since the early 1960s, Khomeini had said and written much about what might constitute an Islamic order within a Shia, or "partisan" or "heterodox" (as against a Sunni, or "orthodox") discourse. However, it was not until the early 1970s that he solidified his position on the issue in a series of lectures that he delivered in Iraq. Forming the conceptual core of these lectures was Khomeini's doctrine of *velayat-e faqih* (the guardianship of Islamic jurist). The lectures were subsequently published in a single-volume, English translation under the title of *Islamic Government*. They expounded Khomeini's view of an Islamic system of governance presided over by a *velayat-e faqih* (guardian jurist, or supreme religious and political leader), which some have likened to the Platonic concept of the philosopher king.[80]

Khomeini, indeed, was not the first ayatollah with political ambitions to pioneer the idea of an Islamic government. Several ayatollahs before him had advocated such a position since the turn of the twentieth century. As mentioned earlier, one of his most prominent and influential predecessors was Ayatollah Kashani (1882–1962), who served as Chairman of the Majles during Mosaddegh's premiership. Known for his advocacy of Islamic government, he initially made common cause with the political secularist Mosaddegh over oil nationalization. However, when Mosaddegh refused to give Kashani's supporters a meaningful share of executive power, he turned against the prime minister, which helped precipitate his downfall.[81] However, Khomeini's detailed and innovative exposition of the doctrine of Islamic government was unique. His writings, statements, and sermons attest to an unwavering conviction in the superiority of Islam as a system for governing all aspects of human life and in the unique authenticity of his own theological interpretation.[82]

As a Shia *faqih* (jurist), Khomeini relied on four sources to substantiate the theoretical system of Islamic government that he would develop. The first and most authoritative, as for all Muslim theologians, was the Qur'an (the book of God's revelations to Prophet Muhammad). The second was the Sunna, which in Twelver Shiism includes not only the traditions, sayings, and deeds of the Prophet but also those of his *ahl al-bayt* (household). Two particularly influential sources in Twelver Shia jurisprudence are the teachings of the sixth Shia imam Ja'far ibn Muhammad al-Sadeq (702–65) and Sheikh Abu Ja'far Mohammad ibn Ya'qub al-Kulayni's (864–941) *hadith* collection, *Kitab Al-Kafi* (the Sufficient Book). Third, Khomeini relied on the concept of the *ijma* (consensus) of the time of the Prophet and Shia imams, including Ali ibn Abu Talib, the Prophet's son-in-law. The fourth source was *aql* (intellect or reasoning)—a term with a variety of technical meanings in Islamic theology and philosophy. All Sunni and Shia schools of jurisprudence recognize *aql* as a source of law. However, it is used more extensively and creatively by Shia jurists, and by those of the Twelver (Ja'fari) sect in particular, because the Sunni schools restricted and, by the fifteenth century, abolished the creative interpretation and application of Islam (*ijtihad*) based on individual reasoning (*aql*).

The Twelver Shias uphold Ali ibn Abu Talib as the Prophet's legitimate successor and consider him the first imam and Amir al-Mu'minin (Commander of the Faithful). They base this on a *hadith* attesting that Muhammad designated Ali as his first and only successor, so that leadership of Islam would remain within his house. Sunni Islam rejects the authority of this hadith, recognizing Ali instead as the last of the four Khulafa-e Rashideen (Rightly Guided Caliphs), after Abu Bakr, Omar, and Othman.

The Sunni-Shia schism, which originated from the succession crisis after Prophet Mohammad's death in 632, continues to haunt the Muslim world. Ali's own reign (656–61) was marked by civil unrest and a struggle for the *Khilafat* (caliphate, the Islamic system of rule and governance as defined in Sunni Islam until its abolition by Ataturk in 1924). Ali's reign was successfully challenged by Mu'awiyah, the governor of Syria and son of Abu Sufyan, an Arab from a noble Meccan house. Mu'awiyah proclaimed himself caliph, inaugurating the Umayyad dynasty, which lasted for nearly a century. Meanwhile, Ali was attacked by a Kharijite (a member of a group that appeared in the first century of Islam in opposition to the *Khilafat*) and died in Kufa. He was buried in Najaf in January 661, although it is also claimed that his body was carried to today's Afghanistan and buried there in the northern city of Mazar-i-Sharif.

Succeeding Ali in opposition to Mu'awiyah were his two sons, Hasan and Hussein, who the Twelver Shias regard as their second and third imams. However, under pressure from Mu'awiyah, Hasan abdicated in less than a year. His brother Hussein, however, refused to pledge allegiance to Mu'awiyah's son and successor, Yazid. In the ensuing battle of Karbala, Yazid's army slaughtered Hussein and all of his followers on October 10, 680. Only Hussein's wife, Zaynab, her daughters, and youngest son were spared. For Shias, this episode is a powerful symbol of righteous resistance and heroic sacrifice. The martyrdom of Hussein and his companions is marked as *Ashura* (tenth), a day of mourning marked annually by Muslims, but mainly by the Shias, as a day of sorrow, passion, and emulation. Khomeini drew heavily on this central event as an effective means to legitimize his resistance to the Shah, whom he compared to the tyrant Yazid, and to mobilize the public in support of his leadership and Islamic political doctrine.[83] He held the application of his version of Islam not only as obligatory in Iran but also as one to be emulated across the rest of the Muslim world.

In his lectures on Islamic government, Khomeini drew on these sources to argue that the task of governing the Muslim community should be entrusted to a single *faqih*, who, as the representative of the Prophet and the Twelve Imams, could rule over other jurists but not dismiss them, as "there is no hierarchy ranking one *faqih* higher than another or endowing one with more authority than another."[84] He insisted that the rule of the jurist does not usurp the infallible authority of the Prophet or the Imams, for to rule "means governing the people, running the state and applying the laws of the *shari'a*." For Khomeini, then, the Islamic government held an essentially administrative function; it was "a means for implementing the laws and for establishing the just Islamic system." Governing is therefore not an end in and of itself but is "only a means . . . for attaining noble aims."[85]

Elaborating on the suitability of *faqih*, Khomeini wrote that "in addition to general qualifications like intelligence and administrative ability, there are two other essential qualifications: knowledge of the law [*shari'a*] and justice."[86] He stressed that the *faqih* who possessed these two qualities would be qualified to preside over the Islamic government and would "possess the same authority as the Most Noble Messenger . . . in the administration of society, and it will be the duty of all people to obey him."[87] Viewing *shari'a* as the only basis of a legitimate legal system, he argued that "since Islamic government is a government of law, those acquainted with the law, or more precisely, with religion—i.e., the *fuqaha* [jurists; plural of *faqih*]—must supervise its functioning."[88] He therefore asserted that the jurists, as "scholars [who] are the heirs of the prophets," possess judicial and executive authority above even "kings and their appointed judges."[89] Thus, "the *faqih* has authority over the ruler."[90] The *fuqaha,* however, "should be foremost in knowledge of the laws and ordinances of Islam and just in their implementation."[91] Khomeini also discussed the necessity of an efficient and effective bureaucracy in the Islamic government, which could be staffed by ordinary Muslims who were not *alim* (learned scholars of Islam) or well versed in Islam.

Khomeini's religious-political doctrine, along with his bitter life experiences, including the years of exile and the mysterious death of his son, Mostafa, in October 1977, for which he blamed SAVAK, also shaped his worldview. In a subsequent elaboration, he dichotomized the world between the realm of *mostakbarin* (the oppressors, or the "haves") and *mosta'zafin* (the downtrodden, or the "have nots") and called for the empowerment of the latter under the leadership of a *faqih*, supported and guided by the clerical establishment. He attributed this dichotomy to the work of the Americans. In *Islamic Government*, he wrote:

> Through the political agents they have placed in power over the people, the imperialists have also imposed on us an unjust economic order, and thereby divided our people into two groups: oppressors and oppressed. Hundreds of millions of Muslims are hungry and deprived of all form of health care and education, while minorities comprised of the wealthy and powerful live a life of indulgence, licentiousness, and corruption.[92]

His classification paralleled the division of the world by classical Sunni jurists—especially Nu'man ibn Thabit ibn Zuta ibn Marzuban, also known as Abu Hanifah (699–767), the founder of the Hanafi Sunni school of *fiqh* (jurisprudence)—between *dar al-Islam* (the domain of Islam) and *dar al-Harb* (the domain of war), or the domains of Muslim and non-Muslim rule. It also resembled the Marxist and Leninist division of the industrialized world into two adversarial classes: the proletariat (the industrial workers, or suppressed) and the bourgeoisie (the wealthy owners of the means of production, or oppressors), including in its prophecy of an inevitable revolutionary struggle between the two and of the victory of the former over the latter. There is no evidence that Khomeini directly imitated Karl Marx's views, but he had nonetheless studied

Western philosophical thought and would have been familiar with Marxist ideas.

Khomeini's *velayat-e faqih* resembles the Sunni concept of *khilafat* in its concern with the question of who is authorized to rule and govern instead of the Prophet of Islam. However, in the case of Twelver Shias, this ruler also acts on behalf of the imams, especially the last one, Mohammad Hasan al-Mahdi. A more critical difference between the two is that, according to Khomeini's doctrine, the imam needs to be a jurist of a very high standing, who is extremely knowledgeable of Islam in all its divine aspects and earthly manifestations. By contrast, Sunni Islam does not postulate the same degree of qualifications for *khalifa*: he needs to be a respected practicing Muslim, but not necessarily a theologian, exercising power in temporal affairs and with a more defined separation from religious scholars than in Shia Islam.[93]

Until the start of the revolution, Khomeini's ideological vision was raw and undeveloped. He was operating mainly in the realm of theory, with little expectation that one day he would have the opportunity to enact any part of it. Yet, as the revolution intensified and Khomeini was catapulted into the leadership, the picture changed for both him and his supporters. He now had to develop, refine, and adjust his ideological views in ways that could make them practical. He must thereby wear the mantle of a theological politician. Before discussing how Khomeini sought to achieve this, it is important to look at the fourth variable that contributed to his success and that of the revolution.

Organization

Rarely has a revolutionary movement succeeded in history without a solid yet flexible organizational network for public mobilization in its support. In the case of Iran, the Shia Islamist faction that formed Khomeini's bedrock held the organizational advantage in the revolutionary movement. This factor is critical in explaining their ability to rally the support of the public and solidify the revolutionary movement under their leadership.

The Ruhaniyyat (the clerical stratum) provided the backbone for Shia political organizing. Within its broad ranks were three networks: Jame'eh-ye Ruhaniyyat-e Mobarez (the Society of Combative Clergy, JRM), Anjuman-e Islami-e Daneshjuyan (Islamic Students Associations, AID), and Anjuman-e Islami (Islamic Society, AI). Each proved critical in the revolutionary movement. Despite having initially divergent approaches to its application in Iran, there was a great deal of cooperation between the three networks. In the wake of the revolution, they found it expedient to defer to JRM's dominant position in support of Khomeini and his political Shia Islamic preferences.

The Ruhaniyyat had its base in the seminaries of Qom and in its organic links with mosques and various other religious institutions around the country. Qom had historically been the most significant center of Twelver Shia learning and scholarship. It is the burial place of the venerated sister of the eighth Shia imam Ali ibn Musa al-Reza (789–816), Fatema Ma'sume, although Twelver Shia doctrine was forged primarily in Isfahan following Safavid dynastic rule (1501–1722, 1729–36). As such, the Ruhaniyyat had been at the forefront of Shia clerical political activism for a long time. Mohammad Reza Shah's attempts to weaken and control the Qom clerical establishment could not erode its religious and cultural bonds or lessen its popularity among a majority of the Iranian public.[94] While Qom continued in its traditional function as a source of religious authority and political ferment, its clerics, alongside their local followers, were on call to serve as the foot soldiers of the religious establishment if the right conditions arose.

The group that emerged from the Ruhaniyyat as its dominant representative, and which played the most pivotal role in support of Khomeini's leadership rise, was the JRM. The JRM was secretly established in Tehran in early 1977 with the specific aim of overthrowing the Shah's regime in favor of an Islamic order, modeled on Khomeini's concept of *velayat-e faqih*. Initially, the JRM operated as a close-knit, behind-the-scenes mobilizing unit. However, once the anti-Shah public uprising gained momentum, its members became more vocal in their efforts to drive the revolution in an

Islamic direction. They were intensely active in organizing marches, delivering sermons and lectures in mosques, and providing religious slogans to demonstrations.

Its founding members, many of whom formed the JRM's Central Committee and included several of Khomeini's former students, rose to occupy significant positions of authority and power in the postrevolution organs of government. Although these organs and their prominent figures will be profiled in chapters 3 and 4, it is important to identify briefly some of them here. Three of its members, Ayatollah Mohammad Beheshti, Abdolkarim Musavi Ardebili, and Mohammad Yazdi, came to serve as head of the judiciary, while two others, Akbar Hashemi Rafsanjani and Ali Akbar Nateq Nuri, rose to be Speakers of the Majles, each for two terms. Rafsanjani also served as president, chairman of the Assembly of Experts, and head of the Expediency Council—a position that he held from 1989 until his death on January 8, 2017. Three other members, Ayatollahs Mahdavi Kani, Yazdi, and Emami Kashani, became members of the Council of Guardians. Finally, another very active founding member was the current Supreme Leader, Ayatollah Ali Khamenei, as well as Grand Ayatollah Montazeri, whom Khomeini initially designated as his successor.

AID, which emerged as somewhat distinct from the JRM, had multiplied and become active prior to the outbreak of the revolution, especially in educational institutions: Tehran University, Ferdowsi University of Mashhad, and many more. Inspiring these societies was Ali Shariati (1933–77), one of Iran's leading and legendary Islamist intellectuals of the twentieth century. With a bachelor's degree from the University of Mashhad and a PhD in sociology from the Sorbonne, Shariati used a blend of Western and Islamic philosophies to advocate a revolutionary modern Shia Islam, calling it red Shiism, Alavi Shiism (named after Ali), or authentic Shiism, relating back to the Shia's first imam, Ali. In this, he promoted a *jihadi* (assertive) approach to bringing about structural changes in society. This philosophy is evident in one of his most popular sayings, "Every palace should be turned into Karbala, every one month into Moharram, and every day into Ashura."[95] As a dynamic orator and passionate writer, he was a motivational figure to many university students and a younger generation of clerics, whom he encouraged to abandon their past passivity in favor of assertive actions to transform Iran into a vibrant modern Shia state. Shariati paid a high price for his revolutionary Islamist stand because the state authorities imprisoned him twice. He was released from his second, eighteen-month-long incarceration in 1975, after which he moved to Britain, where he was reported to have died of a heart attack, although some have alleged that he was killed by SAVAK.[96] The legacy that he left behind was an enormous boon to the Ruhaniyyat, especially the JRM.

AI represented a form of social organization that had a longstanding tradition in Iran since the early 1940s. While from the early 1970s overlapping with AID, AI sprang from within multiple religious, cultural, educational, and occasionally political groupings, especially in Tehran and other major urban centers, as well as among Iranian students abroad. In fact, it was a demonstration by such students against the Shah, during his visit to the US in November 1977, that sparked the beginning of the revolution. For a long time, AI promoted largely nonpolitical causes, such as presenting Islam as a religion compatible with modernity and science. It was only after the outbreak of the revolution that it began to promote Islam as a "revolutionary socio-political system."[97] Theologically, these societies were influenced by Ayatollah Mahmud Taleqani, a prominent *marja*, who had founded the organization of Kanun-e Islami (Islamic Centre) in 1941, with Mehdi Bazargan as its intellectual patron. The latter was a prominent French-educated academic in engineering and an Islamic scholar who had served as a deputy minister under Mosaddegh, and cofounded Nehzat-e Azedi-e Iran (the Liberation Movement of Iran) in 1961 along the lines of the National Front's platform advancing a nontheocratic Islamic reformation of Iran. Bazargan supported the revolution and served as a close advisor to Khomeini during his time in Paris, who subsequently appointed Bazargan as the first prime minister of Islamic Iran in April 1979, only for him to resign a year later in protest against the theocratic trajectory of the new Islamic order and against the

Iranian student militants' takeover of the American embassy on November 4, 1979—an issue that will be detailed in chapter 3.

There was also a fourth column that surfaced in close cooperation with the Ruhaniyyat: Hezbollahi (Partisans of God) cells, which by 1977 had begun to coalesce around militant clerics and *ulama*, but more or less on an ad hoc basis. These cells, whose generic name Hezbollah (Party of God) is derived from a Qur'anic verse declaring the victory of the Party of God, rapidly rallied behind whatever local religious leaders were sympathetic to their goals. This type of organization had some historical precedents in Iran; cells with loose networks had also become operational during the Constitutional Movement in the first decade of the twentieth century. JRM was quick to penetrate Hezbollahi circles and make use of their cadres as the revolution progressed. However, the groups gained prominence in the immediate aftermath of the revolution when, under JRM's auspices, a coherent network known as Hezbollah was developed as an assassination squad to eliminate the "enemies" of the revolution.

Although it is not clear who precisely led and guided Hezbollah, some suspect that Khomeini's trusted and strategically minded ally, Beheshti, may have directed it under the Supreme Leader's direct instructions.[98] Beheshti, who founded and activated the Islamic Republican Party as the core party organization of the new Islamic order, was later killed in a bomb blast on June 28, 1981. While Hezbollah was formally disbanded within a year of the revolution, it has nonetheless remained operational at informal levels and in different ways to the present day.

Triumph

Internal and external conditions, decisive leadership, ideological disposition, and organizational networks proved central to enabling Khomeini and his followers to seize leadership of the revolution by the middle of 1978. However, along the way there were also a few watershed events that played their role in the process. The most important ones included the appearance of an article by the Shah's information minister Daryoush Homayoun in the government's mouthpiece, *Ettela'at* newspaper, under the title of "Black and Red Imperialism" on January 7, 1978. The article accused Khomeini of "homosexuality and misdeeds," an accusation that its author later confessed to have been written on orders from the Shah.[99] This incident outraged and infuriated Khomeini and his Ruhaniyyat supporters and marked a turning point in their opposition to the Shah's regime. Another decisive event occurred on May 10, when the security forces invaded the house of the popular Grand Ayatollah Shariatmadari in Qom and killed one of his followers. The incident led the Ayatollah to trade his past quiet and peaceful demeanor for support of the opposition forces.

No single incident was more responsible for turning the tide dramatically in favor of the revolutionaries, and propelling Khomeini and his zealots to the forefront of the revolution, than the Shah's decision to impose martial law on September 7, 1978, and the slaughter of three to four hundred protestors the following day by the Iranian army. The massacre caused unprecedented public anger, grief, and resentment toward the Shah. It drove even those societal segments that had hitherto remained on the sidelines to take up the cause of the protestors. By the time oil industry workers went on strike in late October, the Shah's administration was paralyzed, the Iranian economy was in free fall, and foreign investments and investors had begun to flee, along with capital and wealthy loyal supporters of the Shah, from Iran. The only elements that remained obedient were the high echelons of the armed and security forces, but the same could not be said about the loyalty of the lower-level officers and conscripts. With the unrest showing no signs of abating, on November 6, 1978, the Shah dissolved the civilian government and appointed General Gholam Reza Azhari as prime minister. When Azhari's military government also failed to restore order, the image of the Shah as a strong and fearless leader collapsed, along with the perception of SAVAK as an omnipotent and unflinching power. The dam had burst, and the people no longer viewed the Shah and his forces as invincible.

Against this backdrop, Khomeini's denunciation of the Shah and his government as illegitimate, unconstitutional, and in violation of the Shia Islamic tenants reached its zenith. As a man of faith first and a politician second, Khomeini was no longer willing to settle for anything less than the removal of the Shah's regime—something that struck a chord with the public. On December 10–11, some seventeen million Iranians came out in Tehran and other cities in peaceful protest calling for the dismissal of the Shah's regime and the return of Khomeini. No number of concessions by the Shah—from his August 1978 commitment to hold free parliamentary elections to his November declaration that he had heard the voices of the people and approved of their revolution—could stem the tide of an ever more resolute revolutionary movement.

In a desperate bid, the Shah finally decided to appoint a longtime National Front opposition figure, Shapour Bakhtiar, as prime minister on December 29, 1978, in the hope that this would placate the opposition. However, within two weeks, his position had become untenable. The Bakhtiar government could not last very long in the face of mass defections, especially among public servants and junior- to middle-ranking military officers and conscripts. Khomeini's rejection of Bakhtiar and the subsequent formation of a revolutionary council on January 12, 1979, heralded the doom of the Bakhtiar government, and with it, the Shah's fate.

Meanwhile, Khomeini and his close aides also appeared to be very conscious of America's long-standing involvement in Iran and the bonds that the Shah had forged with Washington over the past twenty-five years. He had been highly critical of the United States for supporting the Shah's regime and for acting as a hegemonic power in the Middle East. He believed that neither the Shah's dictatorial rule nor the "Zionist state" of Israel's aggressive usurpation of Palestinian lands (most importantly East Jerusalem, one of the holiest Islamic sites) would have been possible in the absence of US support. Washington, in his eyes, was therefore complicit in the Shah's crimes against the Iranian people. In a December 1978 interview, he stated: "The measures taken so far to repress the movement of our people have all been the results of American intervention."[100] He was also very apprehensive of America's role in backing many Arab regimes, especially Saudi Arabia, and equally damning of Saddam Hussein's repression of Iraq's Shia majority.

In the final phase of the revolution, Khomeini feared that the United States would launch a military intervention or instigate a coup d'état (as they had done in 1953) to save the Shah's regime or install a military government in its place. There was a considerable amount of chatter about a military takeover in both Tehran and Washington. Khomeini's leadership reportedly found it expedient to open a backdoor channel of communication with Washington in order to stall such a development.[101] In Paris, Khomeini was closely advised by Ebrahim Yazdi and Ayatollah Beheshti. Yazdi was an Iranian-American physician who acted as a "go-between" for the Americans and Khomeini's camp and who subsequently served as deputy prime minister and foreign affairs minister during the interim government of Bazargan (February–November 1979). Beheshti was a highly educated cleric; he was also an astute and pragmatic political operator and organizer, with years of experience as the imam of a mosque in Hamburg, Germany. At the advent of Khomeini's rule, he was appointed chief justice of Iran and played a key role in Khomeini's Islamic government in different capacities until his assassination.

Khomeini's concerns about a coup were alleviated to some extent after he received word that America's ambassador to Iran, William Sullivan, had warned Washington in a November 9 cable that the Shah was doomed and that the US should get the Iranian leader and his top generals out of the country. Although at first, Sullivan's warning caught President Carter by surprise, by the start of January the president and his national security advisors had fallen in line with the ambassador's conclusions. On January 7, 1979, one advisor to Zbigniew Brzezinski concluded: "The best deal that can result, in my view, is a military coup against Bakhtiar and then a deal struck between the military and Khomeini that finally pushes the Shah out of power."[102] Earlier on January 3, 1979, President Carter dispatched the Air Force general Robert E. Huyser to Tehran, not to meet the Shah, but to advise his generals to sit tight and "not jump into a coup."[103] Washington's objective by now was to see if the Iranian military and Khomeini's leadership could reach an agreement that would allow for a relatively smooth transfer of power. This move constituted the clearest indication that the US was willing to trade off the Shah in exchange for Khomeini, which some have speculated to have been part of an American strategy to put a ring of anti-communist religious forces around the Soviet Union.

This plan, in some ways, tallied with Khomeini's view of the US as a useful counterweight to the neighboring Soviet Union. He was almost as distrustful of the USSR as he was of the US, in part because of its "Godless" communist ideology, and in part because of the history of Russian interventions in Iran. Many Iranians also remained suspicious of the Russians and had not forgotten the Russo-Persian War of the early nineteenth century, the negative impact of Anglo-Russian rivalry on Iran, the tsarist support of the Qajar monarchy against Iran's Constitutional Revolution in the early twentieth century, or the Soviet occupation of and reluctant withdrawal from northern Iran after the Second World War.

Although the current Iranian Supreme Leader, Ayatollah Khamenei, has publicly denied that Khomeini maintained contacts with Washington at any time, according to recently declassified US documents Khomeini was cognizant of America's role in countering Soviet influence in Iran as far back as 1963.[104] Evidently, fifteen years later he still found the US useful for such a role. On this basis, Yazdi conveyed a message from Khomeini to Washington in early January 1979 in which he assured the Carter administration that in the wake of the Shah's fall, it need not be concerned about the preservation of US strategic interests in Iran.[105] In other words, a Khomeini-led government would not seek to diminish America's position as a security buffer against the USSR.

However, US maneuverings to forge some kind of coalition between the Shah's generals and Khomeini's clerical allies, as well as the latter's assurances to preserve America's Cold War interests, ultimately amounted to nothing. Once Khomeini was convinced that the US was ready to abandon the Shah, he was no longer prepared to engage in any compromise. Instead, he hardened his long-held conviction that the US was essentially an evil and destructive power and resolved to settle for nothing less than the end of the Shah's rule and the removal of any vestiges of American influence in Iran and, if possible, in the region.

On January 17, 1979, accompanied by his wife Farah Diba and their three children, the Shah found it necessary to depart Iran for another "temporary stay" abroad—which, in this case, turned into a permanent exile until his death from cancer in Cairo on July 17, 1980, at the age of sixty-two. While the Shah's fall bore close resemblance to his father's, Reza Shah had not endured as much humiliation as his son, who was at the end abandoned even by Washington. The United States had only agreed to allow the Shah to enter the US for treatment under intense lobbying by the Shah's old friend, former American secretary of state Henry Kissinger. However, Washington soon denied the Shah anything longer than a short stay when Khomeini's leadership threatened to retaliate against the US if it did not consent to return the Shah to Iran in order to stand trial. The British government of Prime Minister Margaret Thatcher also denied him asylum.[106] With the Bakhtiar government crumbling, Khomeini returned to Iran on February 1, 1979, where he received a tumultuous welcome from some five million people in Tehran who had gathered to witness the inauguration of a new era in the history of Iranian politics and society.

While the Iranian Revolution predated social media, it was unquestionably a broad-based and bottom-up revolution, riding on the back of grassroots mass participation and the people's willingness to make sacrifices for fundamental change. The nature of the Shah's autocracy, combined with the deep-rooted spirit of uncompromising nationalism and the peculiarities of Iranian Shia political culture, proved instrumental in generating the necessary conditions and the process for such a change. While non-Iranian media outlets became more vocal in reporting the Iranian events as they progressed, within Iran one outlet that played a very prominent role in the revolutionary movement, especially in its final stages, was the British Broadcasting Corporation (BBC). The BBC frequently broadcast the time and place of demonstrations, keeping the millions of Iranians who tuned in to its Persian service abreast of key developments as they unfolded. These factors aside, the revolution could not have materialized and changed the course of Iran's development without Khomeini's leadership and America's handling of the Iranian crisis.

Whatever one's opinion of Khomeini, it is difficult to deny that he was one of the most astute theo-political leaders in modern history. His conduct in the course of the Iranian Revolution and eventual triumph against the Shah set him apart from many revolutionary leaders before him. Some may compare him to Lenin, as both men rose from exile to change their countries. However, the circumstances under which Lenin operated and eventually succeeded in giving a new direction to his country were very different from those that drove Khomeini in redirecting his nation. During his years of exile for nearly one and a half decades from 1901, Lenin still managed to secretly visit Russia several times before finally reentering the country in April 1917, with considerable German support, to lead the Bolshevik's seizure of power in October. Yet Khomeini spent a similar continuous length of time in exile without return or respite. He was banished to Iraq from 1964 until, under pressure from the Shah, the Iraqi dictator Saddam Hussein expelled him in early October 1978, only to be given political asylum by France. Paris, where he arrived on October 8, proved to be a turning point for him; there, he came under the limelight of the international media, enabling him to communicate with and guide his supporters more easily. Khomeini did not seize power; he was elevated to it by the Iranian public. Lenin forced his country down the path of secularist dictatorship, whereas Khomeini steered his country down the lane of an indigenous form of theocracy, if only playing his hand at a late stage. Lenin successfully battled a pluralist transitional government that had already ended tsarist rule, whereas Khomeini clawed his country back from the grasp of a model dictator and his superpower backer and remolded it as an anti-hegemonic, theo-political actor, challenging both the regional and international orders.

3

Khomeini's Theo-Political Order

Khomeini's triumphant return from Paris marked the beginning of a new era full of hope and expectations but was also beset with confusion, uncertainty, and conflicts, which characterized the first few years of the revolution. These features of the early revolutionary years were exacerbated by a long and devastating war with Iraq from 1980 to 1988. After the fall of the Shah, all those who had come together to make the revolution a reality now wanted their divergent and often conflicting wishes to be fulfilled. They had relinquished leadership of the revolution to Khomeini and his devotees in the expectation that they would still be able to participate in building a new Iran and that their political and ideological ideals would be accommodated. However, as it soon became evident, they had underestimated the determination of Khomeini and his Ruhaniyyat supporters to settle only for an Islamic order under Khomeini's leadership. Riding on a wave of popular support, Khomeini was able to move resolutely to implement his Islamic political vision. What commenced primarily as a popular movement for the reformation of Iran into a constitutional monarchy now empowered Khomeini and his devotees to take the helm not only to transform Iran but also to launch a project for politicizing the Muslim world.

Until a couple of months before his return to Iran, Khomeini was careful to maintain conciliatory appearances toward all the participatory groups and strata in the revolution. While rejecting the Shah's allegation that Khomeini and his supporters were in league with communists to perpetuate "red and black colonialism,"[1] Khomeini had promised that even the communists would have a free voice in an Islamic Iran. In an interview on May 6, 1978, with *Le Monde*'s special envoy, Lucien George, he had declared:

> In the society we intend to establish, the Marxists will be free to express their opinions, for we are convinced that Islam has all the answers our people need. . . . We have never denied them the freedom or infringed upon it. Everyone is free to express his opinions, but not to conspire.

When asked in the same interview whether he intended to head the government personally in the event of the success of the revolution, his reply was: "Personally? No. Neither my age, nor my position, nor my own inclinations make me suitable for such a task," stipulating that "if proper circumstances arise, we will choose qualified persons from among those who are well acquainted with Islamic ideas and concepts of government."[2]

However, once Khomeini was assured of the success of the revolution, he incrementally changed his tone on the role that he envisaged for the clerics in the post-Shah political system and about the way his Islamic vision would be implemented. In another interview with *Le Monde* on October 17, 1978, when asked what he meant by an "Islamic Government," he replied: "We do not intend to take over the government. But the religious leaders direct the people in order to define the goals and the demands of Islam. Because the majority of the Iranian people are Muslim, an Islamic government also means that it is a government supported by the majority." He further asserted that the Islamic government would be established in stages:

> In the first stage, our objective is to make the country independent, and to eliminate foreign control, as well as those internal

> factions which are paid by foreign interests. Today, our country is enslaved in every respect of its life: political, economic, cultural and military. We must therefore expel the exploiters and colonizers whoever they may be. . . . We will have to devote all the rich resources of our country to bettering the lot of our people, who are today oppressed workers, living in sickness and poverty. The second will see the complete purging of ministries, the administration, and of public associations; the weeding out of traitors, the corrupt, and those who are only out for their own profit. All responsibilities must be put in the hands of competent, honest and patriotic people. Other stages will follow gradually. But above all, if the Islamic government is to achieve its goals, it is essential that the Pahlavi dynasty be removed. No reform is possible while this dynasty and its servants remain.[3]

Largely along these lines, Khomeini set out to establish his Islamic order. Yet, neither he nor the people in his inner circle had ever expected the Shah's rule to crumble so quickly and so spectacularly. They had little preparation, let alone a developed strategy, for how to deal with the situation. They were forced to improvise their way through the transformation of Iran in both a reactive and proactive fashion and to keep a keen eye on constantly shifting political dynamics.

Khomeini's inner sanctum at this stage included a number of notable clerical and nonclerical figures, some of whom had accompanied him from Paris to Tehran and others who were already on the ground in Iran. In the clerical category, four emerged as most influential. One of their highly deft religious and political players was Ayatollah Dr. Mohammad Beheshti, whose alleged connection to the Hezbollahis cells was mentioned in the chapter 2. He rapidly proved to be a very shrewd political strategist, tactician, and organizer, who soon came to be known by his critics as Ayatollah Rasputin. He had served as the director of the Islamic Centre at Hamburg, an old Shia mosque, from 1965 to 1970. As Khomeini's close confidant and first in line as his heir, Beheshti played a key role in the initial stages of the construction of the Islamic order, but his career was cut short when he was killed in a bomb blast allegedly organized by Mujahideen-e Khalq, in June 1981. Hashemi Rafsanjani, Ali Khamenei, and Mohammad Reza Mahdavi Kani were the other three who gained prominence after Beheshti's assassination in implementing Khomeini's vision. The first two had nurtured a close camaraderie between themselves from the late 1950s. Rafsanjani, who had maintained contact with anti-Shah groups and with Khomeini personally in the years before the revolution and who had acquired the latter's trust, initially emerged to head the Majles and was later elected as president for two terms (1989–97). Khamenei rose to be president from 1981 to 1989 and succeeded Khomeini as Supreme Leader after his death in July 1989. Kani was a hard-line cleric who served in the Islamic government from the beginning in various important positions, notably as head of the Assembly of Experts, and remained an influential player on the Iranian political scene until his death in October 2014.[4]

Among the most notable nonclerical advisors to Khomeini was the French-educated son of an ayatollah, Seyyed Abul Hassan Bani-Sadr. In Paris he had been a close companion to Khomeini, who favored him as a knowledgeable Islamist economist. A second important figure was the French-educated, mild-mannered, and liberal-minded Mehdi Bazargan, who had remained in Iran, where he had a popular base. He served as the Islamic Republic's first prime minister for nearly a year in 1979. Also accompanying Khomeini in Paris was a former National Front student activist in the United States, Sadegh Ghotbzadeh. He had ingratiated himself with Khomeini and had joined his circle of close advisors in exile. Another figure, who also acted as a close aide to Khomeini in Paris and accompanied him upon his return to Tehran, was the Iranian-American physician, Ebrahim Yazdi. As mentioned in chapter 2, Yazdi was reportedly the main go-between for Khomeini's communications with Washington in the last month of the revolution.

It is difficult to quantify the influence of these figures on Khomeini, but without their support and dedication, in different degrees, ways, and stages, Khomeini would not have been able to carry out his mission effectively. They played valuable roles in enabling Khomeini to move rapidly from what he had expounded as conciliatory and inclusionary politics to a faith-focused politics of power and governance-building, and to act as the ultimate determinant in setting the pace and direction of Iran's transformation. Khomeini recognized that building a viable Shia Islamic state required more than being an idealized theocracy focused on religious rather than temporal government. He wanted to build an Iran that was not only Islamic but also modern, strong, influential, and capable of enduring any domestic and foreign challenges.

To achieve this goal, he adopted a two-dimensional approach: *jihadi* and *ijtihadi*. Although each term has a complex history in Islamic thought, *jihadi* may be taken here to signify a combative, revolutionary, and inward-looking approach to the implementation of Islam. *Ijtihadi*, as summarized in chapter 2, denotes a creative interpretation of Islam according to changing times and conditions, based on independent human reasoning (*aql*). While many have identified Khomeini with the first approach, he was in fact renowned among Shia clerics for his *ijtihadi* and pragmatist tendencies. Many of the ideas he advanced, such as *velayat-e faqih*, and policy actions in response to changing national and international situations, were both innovative and unorthodox.[5] Some Iranian *ulama* even denounced some of his rulings as *bida'a* (illegitimate innovation).[6] Let us now examine his transformative actions within these two, interrelated *jihadi* and *ijtihadi* approaches.

The *Jihadi* Dimension

The first few years after the Shah's overthrow were dominated by a *jihadi* approach that has never entirely vanished from Iranian politics. Through this approach, Khomeini aimed to assertively implement his vision of an Islamic order and consolidate his own power and that of his followers. This early *jihadi* phase saw a Khomeini who was uncompromising, exclusionary, and self-righteous, driven by a steely determination to overcome anyone or anything that stood in his way. Khomeini was a man of conviction, and had full faith that his vision of an Islamic order was the correct one. For him, there were only two choices: either something fell within his interpretation of Islam and was therefore "Islamic," or it contradicted it and was un-Islamic altogether. This standpoint led him to denounce critics of the *velayat-e faqih* as being "enemies of the Prophet" or fronts for "American Islam."[7]

Khomeini's actions in power showed that he was not prepared to accommodate any interpretations of Islam that did not accord with his own. In this, his stance was comparable to that of the Bolshevik leader Vladimir Ilyich Lenin, whose self-belief as the true interpreter of Marxism knew no limits.[8] Khomeini was deeply familiar with Iran's historically authoritarian political culture and quickly showed himself willing to make use of the tools of his predecessors. He spared no effort in crushing all those who might jeopardize the religious, national, and international mission that he envisaged for himself and for Iran. To implement his Islamic political vision in Iran and to project it as revolutionary throughout the Muslim world, Khomeini focused his resolution on three main *jihadi* objectives: the dismantling of the state apparatus he had inherited from the Shah; the total Islamization of Iranian state and society; and the elimination of all political opposition to the Islamic Republic.

The violent retribution that Khomeini had foreshadowed in his October interview with *Le Monde* came swiftly on the tails of the revolution. Hundreds who were closely associated with or worked for the Shah's regime were swiftly dismissed from their positions, imprisoned, or executed. Those executed, often without trial or in summary trials, included Amir Abbas Hoveyda, the Shah's longest-serving prime minister (1965–77), and scores of his former ministers, high-ranking public servants, and military and intelligence personnel. The person responsible for most of the summary executions was the infamous "hanging judge," Ayatollah Sadegh Khalkhali (1926–2003), a member of the Society of Combative Clerics and whom Khomeini had appointed head of the Islamic Revolutionary Court (IRC).[9] A 1982 Amnesty International report claimed that some thirty-eight hundred actual or suspected opponents had been eliminated since the revolution—most within the first few months.[10]

Meanwhile, the IRC passed hundreds of death sentences against Iranians who had fled the country, and Khomeini showed no mercy toward the now cancer-ridden exiled Shah, demanding that he return to Iran to face judgment for his crimes against the Iranian people. By the mid-1980s, virtually all vestiges of the Shah's governance structures were uprooted or unrecognizably reformed, and his men dismissed from all senior administrative, management, security, and military positions, which were then filled with the largely inexperienced Ruhaniyyat and their adherents.

Having effectively dismantled the Shah's political apparatus, Khomeini set about establishing the structures and mechanisms that would bring about his *velayat-e faqih* system of governance. For Khomeini, this demanded a wholesale Islamization of state and society—if necessary, by use of violence. Khomeini commenced the processes for building the new Islamic order with a national referendum on March 30–31, 1979, in which the people were simply asked a yes-or-no question on whether they wanted an Islamic Republic. While the public had not widely been appraised of what this meant or what it might entail, the results of the referendum—which was approved by an overwhelming 97 percent of voters—provided Khomeini with a clear mandate to claim the revolution as Islamic and Iran as an Islamic Republic. Emboldened by this outcome, he set out vigorously to put in place the structures and institutions he judged necessary for his Islamic government and to promote a foreign policy posture consistent with his ideal of an Islamic Republic.

Khomeini oversaw the construction of a legal-political framework within which to legitimize and define the perimeters of his Islamic order. An Islamic constitution (*Qanun-e Asasi*, meaning literally "fundamental law"), establishing *shari'a* as the ultimate foundation of state and society, was rapidly formulated and adopted by another referendum in October 1979.[11] The constitution, which was largely authored by Khomeini's clerical devotees, provided for a political order in which the divinely ordained position of *vali-e faqih* (supreme religious and political leader) would provide overarching and determining guidance, while a government beneath it would embody the will of the people within an Islamic paradigm.

The result was a two-tiered system of governance based on Khomeini's understanding of the relationship between divine and popular sovereignty. It was designed both to reflect the "sovereignty of God," echoed through the indirectly elected and appointed Supreme Leader (*vali-e faqih*), and to represent the will or "sovereignty of people" through participation and contestation in the political system. For the latter tier, which would ensure that Islamic governance also rested on a pillar of popular legitimacy, the constitution prescribed an elected presidential system of government composed of executive, legislative, and judicial branches. Thus, the sovereignty of the people was to materialize through a government composed of an elected president, a unicameral national assembly (Majlis), and an appointed judiciary. The legislative reforms retained much of the old civil code-based constitution that dated back to the Constitutional Revolution, especially in more everyday aspects of governance. Yet Khomeini's two-tiered Islamic political system was innovative in combining transcendental theocratic aspects (which extended Iran's long autocratic tradition) with institutions that seemed almost liberal, especially when compared to those that existed under the Shah.

The resulting system was highly complex: monolithic on the one hand, but malleable on the other. The position of Supreme Leader—which Khomeini assumed in spite of earlier professions to the contrary—was endowed by the constitution with extraordinary powers of jurisdiction over the entire system. He possessed the ultimate authority to determine all important matters of state and society. He was empowered to approve the government beneath him and to appoint the heads of the judiciary and the armed and security forces. At the same time, stringent checks and balances were put in place to ensure that the whole system functioned and endured within Khomeini's Islamic framework and that no individual or force could succeed in assuming power to act outside of it. An organic relationship between the system's two tiers was assumed, based on the intricate and shifting interrelationships between the Supreme Leader and the government, the three intermediary bodies, the three branches of the government, and the Islamic Republican Party (IRP) and law enforcement and security agencies. As the Islamic order took shape, this complexity left it prone to fragmentation, conflict, and manipulation by the various forces within it. The presidential system and National Assembly were to be counterbalanced by three powerful bodies that mediated the two divine and popular tiers of the system. One was the unelected twelve-member Shora-ye Negahban-e Qanun-e Asasi (Council of Guardians), made up of experts in Islamic law, of whom six were nominated by the Supreme Leader and six by the head of the judiciary (who was himself appointed by the Supreme Leader). The council was entrusted with the power to vet presidential and parliamentary candidates, hold referenda, veto legislation passed in the Majles, and declare the results of elections. The second was the eighty-six-member Majles-e Khobregan-e Rahbari (Assembly of Experts), whose members were to be elected every eight years, subject to the vetting of their candidacies by the Council of Guardians. This body was tasked with appointing the Supreme Leader, ensuring his adherence to the precepts of Shia Islam, and terminating his appointment if necessary. The third was the Majma'e Tashkhis-e Maslahat-e Nezam (Expediency Council), created later than the first two, an administrative assembly appointed by the Supreme Leader with the power to adjudicate legislative disputes between the National Assembly and the Council of Guardians and advise the Supreme Leader.

To buttress and secure the system, three more significant organizations were hastily created in 1979. One was the Hezb-e Jomhuri-ye Islami (the IRP), instigated and led by Ayatollah Beheshti. This was an umbrella organization set up in order to incorporate a number of political Islamic groups that had sprung into existence before and during the revolution into a single organization under the leadership of the Society of Combative Clerics. These groups, which were ideologically analogous to the latter, included the Jame'eh-ye Modarresin Hozeh-ye Elmiyeh (Society of Instructors of the Seminaries), the Hayat-e Mo'talefeh Islami (Board of the Islamic Coalition), and the Jame'eh-ye Islami-ye Mohandesin (Islamic Society of Engineers), with the last two representing the *bazaaris* and technocrats.

Crystallizing in tandem with the IRP were two other forces—the Sazmane Basiji-e Mostaza'afin (Organisation for Mobilisation of the Oppressed, or simply Basij) and the Sepah-e Pasdaran-e Enqelab-e Islami (Islamic Revolutionary Guard Corps, IRGC, or simply Sepah). The Basij was established as a voluntary paramilitary force, made up of young Iranians who were recruited from the age of ten, to act as the eyes and ears of the new Islamic regime. Recruits were indoctrinated in the precepts of Khomeini's theology of Islamic government, trained to maintain internal security, and operated in branches all over Iran under the guidance or control of the regime's clerics. The Sepah, however, was entrusted with a constitutional responsibility to act as the guardian of the Islamic system and was granted extensive powers to do so. The Basij works in tandem—both organizationally and doctrinally—with the Sepah, which has grown to be the most powerful and pervasive security actor in the country.[12] These organizations were in addition to the *artesh* (military), which was rapidly reconstituted and restructured under a new command and tasked not only with defending Iran's borders but also with maintaining domestic order when needed. The leaders of all these forces, who became paramount in Iranian politics in the context of the Iran-Iraq War (1980–88), were appointed by the Supreme Leader and owed their loyalty to him. The interrelations of Iran's political and military institutions are discussed in detail in chapter 5.

To boost and consolidate the clerical hold on the economy and to manage the wealth expropriated from the Shah and his alleged associates and sympathizers, the Islamic Republic developed a system of *bonyads* (Islamic foundations) and, in the process, aligned the latter with the new regime's ideology.[13] While some *bonyad*s had existed prior to the revolution, mainly in the form of *waqfs* (religious endowments), the scope and significance of their operations grew dramatically after 1979 with the founding of a number of private and public *bonyads*. Although the *bonyads* were ostensibly nonprofit organizations established to provide social and public services, many also engaged in commercial and financial activities such as banking, trade, and manufacturing, with some developing into massive conglomerates. The Bonyad-e Mostaza'fan va Janbazan (Foundation of the Oppressed and Disabled), for example, is involved in multiple economic areas, notably tourism, real estate, petrochemicals, and transportation.[14] Legally exempt from taxation and some government regulations, and politically safe from others, the *bonyads* have been the key economic instrument by which the clerics assumed control of various national resources, which they have subsequently operated in conjunction with rich merchants for a variety of purposes, including charitable and humanitarian ones. The *bonyads* remain a cornerstone of clerical and conservative power in Iran, accounting for an estimated 30 percent of the country's gross domestic product (GDP).[15] They also underpin Iran's "soft power" as flexible actors outside the Iranian state by funding various humanitarian, educational, and cultural projects in different Muslim countries, especially in Iran's neighborhood.[16]

The Shah's internal security force, SAVAK, was immediately disbanded, and many of its personnel dismissed and executed. In its stead, various *komiteh-ha-ye enghelabi* (revolutionary committees) sprang up in neighborhoods, as mosques, police stations, and youth clubs became the headquarters of the ideological enforcement agency of the new clerical authorities. Khomeini's close aide Ayatollah Kani took over the general supervision and coordination of these committees. The latter were soon supplemented by various other intelligence and counterintelligence organizations, ranging from the Daftar-e Ettla'at Nokhostvaziri (Prime Minister's Intelligence Office), established in 1980, to the IRGC, the army, and police force. In 1983, most of the intelligence units merged to form the super Vezarat-e Etella'at va Aminiyat-e Keshvar (Ministry of Intelligence and Security), which continues to operate as the Vezarat-e Ettela'at-e Jomhuri-ye Eslami-ye Iran (Ministry of Intelligence of the Islamic Republic of Iran).

Along with the dismantling or remodeling of existing structures and the establishment of a revolutionary Islamic economy and society, Khomeini sought the creation of a compliant and unified Islamic movement under his leadership. This move involved expunging any opponent who carried the potential to challenge

Khomeini's particular Islamic order. They included not only secular and semi-secular political figures but also some of Khomeini's peers and followers, who either doubted the efficacy of Khomeini's approach or disagreed with his vision of political Islam.

Among the nonclerical liberal-minded figures, one of the early casualties was Bazargan (1907–95). As noted earlier, Bazargan had a long history of prodemocracy activism and opposition to the Shah's rule. However, he was not in favor among some of the ambitious clerics around Khomeini.[17] His prime ministerial tenure lasted nine months (February 11–November 6, 1979), during which time he developed major political differences with Khomeini, especially over the American hostage crisis—an episode that will be discussed subsequently.

The other significant nonclerical figure who fell out of favor with Khomeini early on was Bani-Sadr, who had opposed the Shah's regime and had been incarcerated for a period before leaving for Paris in 1963. He met Khomeini in Iraq in 1972 and had maintained contact with him. Khomeini affectionately referred to him as a son, which in Muslim and Iranian tradition designates a relation of exceptional trust. After serving as a close advisor to Khomeini in Paris, he returned with him to Tehran and was appointed foreign minister in the Bazargan interim government. As Khomeini's favorite, Bani-Sadr was elected as the first president of the Islamic Republic in February 1980, only to be dismissed by his former patron sixteen months later, prompting him to flee into self-exile in Paris.[18]

Beheshti is said to have had a strong hand in the ousting of Bani-Sadr, who fell under suspicion due to his close relations with the leader of the militant Mujahideen-e Khalq, Massoud Rajavi (1948–2015). Wanting to see a politically pluralistic Iran, Rajavi had violently opposed the Shah's rule, which led him to be imprisoned by SAVAK. He was also put forward as a candidate in the 1980 presidential election, but Khomeini struck out his candidacy. When Bani-Sadr left Iran secretly, Rajavi escaped with him, declaring his support for the popularly elected president of Iran. In 1982, after Rajavi's first wife, Ashraf Rabiei, was killed, he married Bani-Sadr's daughter, Firouzeh, although they divorced a few years later. In

1986, Rajavi moved his Mujahideen group to Iraq, where Saddam Hussein had granted it safe haven, content to provide a base for foreign fighters to attack the Khomeini regime. Tehran denounced the Mujahideen as a "terrorist organization," as did the European Union until 2009 and the United States from 1997 to 2012. The 2003 US-led invasion of Iraq and the overthrow of Saddam Hussein's dictatorship severely limited the group's operational ability. When an Iraqi Shia majority assumed the levers of power in Iraq, the Iranian and Iraqi governments coordinated to hit the Mujahideen hard, rendering it virtually defunct. Rajavi went into "hiding," with unconfirmed reports of his death emerging in 2016.[19]

Yazdi and Ghotbzadeh who, like Bani-Sadr, had been locked in serious political rivalry, also fell victim to the purges. Yazdi was initially appointed deputy prime minister and minister of foreign affairs in Bazargan's interim government, but, like Bazargan, he could not accept Khomeini's position on the hostage situation and was relieved of his post. Ghotbzadeh was appointed to succeed Yazdi as foreign minister on November 30, 1979, but his tenure lasted only nine months. He was executed on September 15, 1982, on charges of conspiracy to kill the Supreme Leader and overthrow his Islamic government.

Among the Ruhaniyyat, the ranks of those who grew uncomfortable with Khomeini's implementation of the Islamic order and harbored misgivings about his version of political Islam included several grand ayatollahs and ayatollahs, the most important of whom were Mohammad Kazem Shariatmadari and Hussein Ali Montazeri. Both were in fact senior to Khomeini and had supported the revolution. Montazeri played a proactive role as a founding member of Ruhaniyyat-e Mobarez. Shariatmadari had saved Khomeini from execution at the hands of the Shah in 1963 and commanded a strong popular following among Iran's Azeri minority, who comprised some 15–20 percent of the country's population. He favored a gentler and more humane application of Islam than Khomeini had pursued, and supported respect for human rights. He could neither approve of Khomeini's empowerment of the clerics to run the government nor support the occupation of the US embassy in Tehran. Khomeini viewed Shariatmadari's disagreements and popularity among the Azeris as a liability. In 1982, Shariatmadari was accused of plotting against Khomeini and the new Islamic state and was sentenced to house arrest until his death in 1986.

Similarly, Montazeri, whom Khomeini had anointed as his successor in 1985 after Beheshti's death, fell out of favor for criticizing Khomeini's harsh approach. He was ultimately marginalized and spent years under house arrest, with Khomeini revoking his succession entitlement to the leadership in early 1989. A collection of tapes released by Montazeri's son, Ahmad, in August 2016, revealed that Montazeri had grown highly critical of Khomeini as a result of the mass executions and atrocities committed under his leadership. In the tapes, which provoked much controversy in Iran, Montazeri laments in particular the execution of hundreds of Mujahideen-e Khalq political prisoners in 1988. While stating emphatically his opposition to the Mujahideen and their doctrine, he intimates that the executions took place with Khomeini's approval and expresses his fear that the crimes perpetrated under the Islamic system could tarnish the reputation and legacy of Khomeini, the Islamic Republic, and the dignity of Islam in history.[20] He stated: "We were opposing the Shah for executing the political activists, but let's now compare the number of the executions during his time and the ones done in the Islamic Republic."[21] Montazeri persisted in his staunch criticism of the Islamic regime, especially following the disputed results of the June 2009 presidential elections, which is discussed in chapter 4. The man whom the Islamic government disparaged as the "rioters' cleric" died of natural causes in December 2009. For revolutionaries of a more humanist and pluralist bent, however, his legacy has always loomed large.[22]

The forces that had played so great a part in making the revolution a reality thus found themselves at ideological and political variance with Khomeini's Islamic system to varying degrees. This was true also for leftist political groups—such as the Mujahideen-e Khalq, Fadayan-e Khalq, Tudeh, and Jebheh-ye Melli—who were now castigated as the enemies of the revolution and of Islam. Tudeh had initially pursued a policy of cooperation with Khomeini's *jihadis*, in the misplaced belief that the *jihadis'* political incompetence would open the way for them to shape the postrevolution order. The *jihadis* accepted the alliance out of convenience, because it freed them to deal with other groups, which were given two choices: either accept Khomeini's terms or resort to violent resistance. Many opted for the latter, resulting in a period of open conflict and bloodshed between leftist revolutionaries (the Mujahideen-e Khalq and Fadayan-e Khalq in particular) and Khomeini's *jihadi* supporters. The situation became so bloody, unstable, and unpredictable that some analysts predicted the Islamic regime would soon self-destruct. The belief that the Islamic Republic had little capacity for longevity seemed increasingly plausible in light of several of its senior figures being killed, most importantly Ayatollah Beheshti and Prime Minister Ali Rajai in 1981. At this time they decided to take on the Tudeh, whose members were now subjected to the same degree of purges and elimination as the other leftist groups. Khomeini's *jihadi* fighters ultimately triumphed, but at a terrible cost. It is estimated that some ten to twenty thousand Iranians were eliminated on charges of being opponents of the regime during the first three years of the Islamic Republic.[23] The Iranian Revolution thus repeated the fate of many other revolutions in history, with many of those who had ensured its triumph, now sidelined, destroyed, and condemned as traitors to their religion and country.

Khomeini's *jihadi* supporters were thus availed of all the means necessary to pursue their mandate as the moral guardians of the Islamic order. They acted vigorously to enforce the wide range of Islamic rulings that were passed to Islamize Iranian society, from dress codes, almsgiving, education, sound and movement, and theatrical and artistic performances, to the treatment of minorities and the conduct of relations with the outside world, as elaborated in Khomeini's book, *A Clarification of Questions* (*Resaleh Towzih Al-Masael*).[24] In education, the emphasis on Iran's pre-Islamic history, which had predominated under the Shah, was replaced with a focus on its Islamic past, especially the period following its conversion to Shia Islam, but above all the modern history of Islamic resistance to Pahlavi dynastic rule. However, this dimension of

Khomeini's *jihadi* approach was applied in a way that made it prone to the same abuses for which the Shah's rule had been condemned: the personalization of politics and the institutionalization of patronage, nepotism, malpractice, poor governance, and corruption. This paradox is discussed in greater depth in chapters 4 and 5.

Among the chief beneficiaries of the new order were members of the IRP, the zealous, newly united, and highly conservative political vanguard of the new regime. Initially the IRP was a powerful organization with close ties to the IRGC, the Basij, and the *artesh*, forming their parliamentary political wing. Together, they constituted the driving forces behind the regime's consolidation of power and wartime efforts against Iraq. However, since the dissolution of the IRP in 1987, a number of other political groupings have become active on the political scene. The IRGC, the Basij, and the *artesh*, however, have continued to grow and function largely as the repository of the *jihadi* aspect of Khomeini's approach, with the IRGC retaining a commanding position and commensurate privileges in the life of the nation.[25]

On the foreign front, Khomeini made a policy out of a popular revolutionary chant, "neither East nor West, but Islamic." He called for the export of the Iranian Revolution to the Sunni Islamic regions, the liberation of all oppressed people, and opposition to the extortionist imperialist powers, in particular the United States. He derided Israel—an ally of Iran during the Shah's reign—and denounced the pro-Western Arab regimes as America's instruments for enforcing its geopolitical dominance in the Middle East. He also excoriated Saddam Hussein, who had expelled him from Iraq at the Shah's behest, as an irredeemable oppressor and urged the Iraqi Shia majority to rise up against his illegitimate rule. As such, he challenged the existing Pax Americana and the major-power–dominated international order. He labeled the US as the Great Satan, and Israel as a colonialist-imperialist and Zionist occupier that needed to be removed in order to liberate Jerusalem and to restore the Palestinians to their rightful homeland. He declared an annual Jerusalem, or Quds, Day of public rage against Israel and all other imperialist aggressors:

> Quds Day is an international day, it is not a day devoted to Quds alone. It is the day for the weak and oppressed to confront the arrogant powers, the day for those nations suffering under the pressure of Zionist oppression and oppression by other powers to confront the superpowers.[26]

Khomeini viewed the other superpower, the Soviet Union, with great trepidation. While past Russo-Persian wars and Soviet interventions in Iran gave Khomeini plenty of reasons to be distrustful of Moscow, he was equally perturbed by the pro-Soviet coup in Kabul in late April 1978. Twenty months after the small pro-Soviet cluster, the People's Democratic Party of Afghanistan, seized power in Afghanistan, the Soviets invaded. This action reinforced his concerns about the Soviet Union as a powerful, expansionist, and "Godless" neighbor against which Iran must always be on its guard.

In response to the Soviet occupation of Afghanistan, Khomeini decided to back an alliance of several Islamic resistance groups, particularly from Afghanistan's Shia minority who reside in the western part of the country that borders Iran. This alliance's role in the overall Afghan Islamic resistance was nowhere near as significant as the Sunni groups, which represented some 80 percent of the Afghan population and which were supported by the US and its allies. It nonetheless underscored Khomeini's concerns about Russia's ideological and irredentist tendencies.[27]

Khomeini expressed his views on Soviet communism in a historic letter to the last Soviet leader, Mikhail Gorbachev, written in early January 1989, in which he opined: "It is clear to everyone that Communism should henceforth be sought in world museums of political history," adding that "materialism cannot save humanity from the crisis of disbelief in spirituality, which is the basic affliction of human societies in the West and the East."[28] He invited Gorbachev to turn to Islam, with an offer that "the Islamic Republic of Iran as the greatest and most powerful base of the Islamic world can easily fill the vacuum of religious faith in Russia." He nonetheless added: "In any case, our country honors good neighborhood and bilateral relations as in the past. Peace be upon those who follow the guidance."[29]

In Iran, Khomeini's anti-US stance emboldened public outbursts of anti-Americanism. This position instigated a series of events that contributed substantially to the entrenchment of hostile relations between Iran and the United States. In protest against Washington's decision to admit the Shah into the US for medical treatment rather than deport him to Iran for trial, a number of Khomeini's militant student supporters invaded the US embassy on November 4, 1979. Declaring the embassy a "den of spies," they took fifty-two American personnel hostages and demanded the Shah be released in exchange for their release.[30] The incident generated the infamous "hostage crisis" that lasted for 444 days, with the Iranian side refusing to free the hostages. As the crisis dragged on, Washington severed all diplomatic relations with Iran and imposed economic and military sanctions on the country. Acrimonious exchanges ensued; President Jimmy Carter labeled Khomeini as "nutty," and the latter likened Carter to "Yazid," the Umayyad ruler responsible for the murder of Imam Hussein and his companions.[31]

The whole episode crystalized an American perception of Khomeini's brand of political Islam as unflaggingly fundamentalist and therefore a source of serious danger to the United States and its allies. Washington rapidly came to the opinion that Khomeini and his followers were anti-modern fanatics beyond the reach of reason and that their Islamic order was incompatible with the international system. Donette Murray, a reputed foreign policy scholar, reflects that "much of what emanated from Tehran was taken at face value. More often than not the clerical regime was viewed as difficult, venomous, uncompromising and bitter."[32] Although the born-again President Carter was a man of faith like Khomeini, from the beginning of the hostage crisis this did nothing to stop the Iranian leader from seeking to humiliate his American counterpart. By the same token, nothing deterred Carter from demonizing Khomeini in equal measure.[33] On April 24, 1980, the Carter administration launched a desperate military operation to rescue the American hostages. But the operation failed in an Iranian desert far from Tehran, partly due to poor weather conditions, which caused mechanical problems in several of the helicopters that were crucial for the mission, and partly because the planning was ill-conceived and inadequate for the rescue mission. President Carter was forced to abort the mission; eight US servicemen lost their lives.[34]

The incident empowered Khomeini with more ammunition to discharge against the American power, whose humiliating military debacle he could now contrast to the resilience of Iran's Islamic faith, ideas, and politics. He now also reinforced his long-standing claim that the US was indeed an "evil," "hegemonic" power, determined to engage in military action against his Islamic government and the Iranian people instead of returning the Shah for trial in exchange for the freedom of the American hostages. He also used the attack to bolster the Islamic Republic's international image as a champion of Muslim countries. In a speech condemning the operation, he stated: "Carter must know that an attack on Iran is an attack to all Islamic countries. The Muslims around the world are not indifferent in this matter. . . . It has left so deep an effect in America."[35] Thus, Khomeini used the hostage crisis to establish a tradition of anti-American defiance that proved useful not only for domestic power consolidation but also for foreign policy distinction in the conduct of Iran's regional and wider relations.

He rarely failed to act with similar opportunism in response to international controversies as they emerged. In February 1989, he issued a nonbinding Islamic legal opinion (*fatwa*) pronouncing the Indian-born British author Salman Rushdie guilty of blasphemy in his book *The Satanic Verses*. His ruling of blasphemy, which carries the death penalty in Islam, caused an anti-Rushdie rage in Iran and sparked protests in several other parts of the Muslim world, South Asia in particular. It inspired death threats against Rushdie, resulting in a deterioration of Iran's relations with Britain, where the author held citizenship, and elicited condemnation from the US and many of Britain's other Western allies. However, it ultimately came to naught, for two reasons. First, Khomeini's *fatwa* was mostly overlooked in many of the Sunni-dominated Arab countries, because they did not want to be seen as endorsing Khomeini as a mainstream Islamic cleric.[36] Second, many within the Supreme Leader's ruling circles feared the *fatwa* would embroil Iran in another international controversy similar to the hostage crisis. Eventually, the post-Khomeini Islamic government came to gently dissociate itself from acting on the execution of the *fatwa* by pointing out that Khomeini had not specifically directed the Islamic Republic to undertake the task.[37] Yet to many in Iran and the outside world, the whole episode was a powerful demonstration of Khomeini's *jihadi* stance against the West in general and the US in particular.

Khomeini's condemnation of regional Arab states and his call to their populations to emulate the Iranian example to overthrow their regimes caused mounting political and security anxieties for most Arab rulers. As many Shia minorities became encouraged and restless in the region, most Sunni Arab regimes adopted both costly and stern measures to deflect Khomeini's inspirational and consequential impact. In Saudi Arabia, for example, the government increased investment, as well as surveillance, in the predominately Shia Hasa province, where most of the 10–15 percent of the kingdom's Shia minority lives, to improve living standards and prevent civil unrest. In Bahrain and Kuwait, the government cracked down on Iranian-influenced Shia opposition.[38] Ultimately, Khomeini's quest to incite popular uprisings and revolutions, bore little success except in Lebanon. There, the deprived Shia community was motivated to bolster mainstream and moderate Shia groups, such as the Amal party, and, more directly, to give birth to the Lebanese Hezbollah. The organization, which was established with assistance from Iranian Hezbollahis (many of whom had spent time training in Lebanon in the lead-up to the revolution), grew over time to be a formidable Iranian-backed political and military group in Lebanese politics and in opposition to Israel and the United States.

The Iraqi dictator, Saddam Hussein, who had long harbored ambitions of claiming regional Arab leadership, sensed in the Islamic Revolution a unique opportunity. He decided to act while Iran was in the midst of postrevolution turmoil, proclaiming Iraq as the bulwark of "the Arab nation" against the universalist Islamism of

Khomeini's regime. Iraqi forces attacked Iran on September 22, 1980, commencing the longest, bloodiest, and costliest war in the history of the modern Middle East. Saddam Hussein's aim was to overthrow Khomeini's regime in favor of a more receptive one and to replace the fallen Shah as the regional superpower. In this, the Iraqi leader was supported by other major Arab players—Saudi Arabia, Kuwait, Jordan, and Egypt in particular. The US also now found it expedient to court Saddam as a counter to Khomeini's regime, despite Washington's past criticism of the Iraqi dictator for his repressive rule and massive human rights violations, close ties with the Soviet Union, and maverick behavior in the region.

Yet Khomeini skillfully managed to turn these developments to his political advantage in pursuit of consolidating his Islamic order. He used a combination of Iranians' traditional nationalist stance and their allegiance to Shiism to harness public support and mobilize against Iraqi aggression, while allowing his hard-line Islamist supporters to assume most levers of power under his leadership. The public's preoccupation with the war and its human and material consequences availed Khomeini of a significant diversion that enabled him to push through forceful theocratic measures that would have faced stiff social resistance but for the exigencies of foreign invasion. Thus, he and his close entourage proceeded with the enactment of the new Islamic Constitution, which was ushered in under the marginalization or elimination of hundreds of opposition elements on the grounds of treason or subversion.[39]

The war effort against Iraq and the adversarial attitude toward the United States and its regional allies proved to be very costly for Iran. They severely affected the export of Iranian oil and the country's income from it, which dropped substantially, from $21.2 billion in 1983 to $13.7 billion in 1984 and $6.3 billion in 1986.[40] This decline had a savage impact on Iran's economic and social development. Income inequality increased and urban poverty more than doubled between 1983 and 1988, while exports fell from 20 percent of GDP in 1978 to 4 percent in 1987, as the war came to consume 60–70 percent of the Iranian national budget.[41] However, the Islamic Republic's organs justified these costs and the sacrifices and suffering of the Iranian people on the grounds of defending Islam and the Iranian nation.

While many factors accounted for the prolongation and devastation of the war, three were especially important: the Islamic regime's dismantling of the Shah's military and security forces and the transfer of the Iranian high command from regular military leaders to clergy in mid-1982[42]; the regime's fear of an American invasion; and Arab support of Saddam Hussein's war efforts. The conservative littoral Gulf Arab monarchies, led by Saudi Arabia, had formed the intergovernmental organization Gulf Cooperation Council (GCC) in May 1981. Although the GCC was created primarily as a trade organization, it emerged in reaction to a perceived political threat from the Iranian Islamic regime. The GCC states also sought to deepen and widen their strategic ties with the United States as the mainstay of their external security. Saudi Arabia took the lead as the largest and most resourceful GCC member, engaging in an accelerated military build-up and modernization.

The only Arab countries that did not back Saddam Hussein's adventure were Syria and Libya. Iran and Syria, under the dictatorship of the Shia-affiliated Alawite minority led by Hafez al-Assad, forged a strategic partnership, underwritten by the Syrian Ba'ath party's dislike of their Iraqi ideological cousins. The Libyan ruler, Colonel Muammar al-Qaddafi, who sought to distinguish himself from the rest of the Arab world as an anti-Western actor, also found it expedient to maintain a "revolutionary" relationship with the Islamic regime.

The war with Iraq and the confrontation with the United States as part of a wider, anti-hegemonic stance enabled Khomeini and his devotees not only to project themselves as champions of the oppressed but also to divert the Iranian public's attention from their quickly worsening domestic situation. Thus, Khomeini earned for himself and his new Islamic Republic an internal and international reputation of uncompromising resistance to hegemonic international norms, whether capitalist, communist, or Zionist. From Khomeini's perspective, this stance was merely the application of a *jihadi* struggle against oppression of many shades.

The *Ijtihadi* Dimension

Khomeini's goal was not just to construct an Islamic state; he wanted to build an Islamic republic that was sufficiently resilient to continue to function and thrive within a very complex national, regional, and international setting. While uncompromising in his core religious and political ideals, Khomeini was politically and socially savvy enough to see that if the Islamic Republic was to endure, it must act within the bounds of pragmatism and realism on both domestic and foreign policy fronts. When circumstances required the innovative application of Islam to modern requirements and evolving social contexts, Khomeini thus deployed an *ijtihadi* approach.

The *ijtihadi* dimension of Khomeini's approach to state building had always been present beneath his primarily *jihadi* thinking. Contrary to many critics' characterizations of Khomeini as an ideologically determinist and monolithic thinker, the ayatollah had a long history of practicing *ijtihad* that dated back to the start of his anti-Shah activities in the early 1960s, when he began to call for Iran's reformation along Shia Islamic lines.[43] His opposition to the Shah's rule and his proclamation that the Shia establishment should take over the government constituted major *ijtihadi* actions. By the time of the Revolution, he had already earned the rank of *mujtahid-e a'lam*—a title that qualified him to act as a leading creative interpreter, reformist, and activist of Shia Islam. Khomeini now used *ijtihad*, in combination with *taqiyya* (a judicial term that in the Twelver Shia tradition designates the permissibility of lying when necessary for a greater good, such as the defense of faith and religious and fraternal unity), to construct an Islamic government capable of adjusting to the needs of the changing times.

Khomeini was conscious of the diverse nature of his supporters and Iranian society, as well as international complexities. As a result, the Islamic system of governance that he established contained a degree of internal elasticity and external flexibility, with some necessary mechanisms and safety valves, to address this diversity and to adjust to changing domestic and foreign circumstances within the broad parameters of his Islamic framework. It was endowed with a capacity for reinvention and renewal. To illustrate this, it is important to look at Khomeini's *ijtihadi* actions in three main areas.

The first relates to his management of the popular tier of the system of governance, which was to provide for public participation and contestation in politics within the limits permitted by the divine tier. After 1983–84, by which time the consolidation of the Islamic order against its ideological and political opponents had been largely accomplished, Khomeini seemed to be increasingly mindful of the danger of ideological differences among his supporters, particularly within the Ruhaniyyat. He was also conscious of the fact that many of his followers had undergone a major metamorphosis in their thinking since the initial triumph of the revolution. Having established his Islamic order beyond serious contention, he now found it expedient to allow a degree of pluralism in Iranian political life. By the late 1980s, it had come to provide for the rise of three informal factional clusters within the ruling clerical stratum: the *jihadi*s, or revolutionary traditionalist conservatives; the *ijtihadis*, or reformist or internationalists; and *amalgaran*, or centralist pragmatists.[44]

The first to form was the *jihadi* cluster, which had coalesced around such figures as Khamenei and Kani. By the mid-1980s, this faction had succeeded in taking over and instrumentalizing state power in the Islamic order. As discussed above, a key factor in the *jihadis*' early political predominance was its militancy; the faction played an active role in the war with Iraq, echoed Khomeini's vehement opposition to the United States and Israel, and aided his attempts to export the revolution to the region. It generally argued for the strengthening of the Islamic order and promoted the consolidation of the revolution's gains as necessary for preserving traditional forms of social life, promoting Iranian self-sufficiency and minimizing dependence on the outside world to the greatest degree possible, and maintaining the ideological and cultural purity of the Islamic Republic. In foreign policy, the *jihadis* favored the continued treatment of the United States and its regional allies as major threats to Iran, in part because this position was an effective means of mobilizing the public in support of their own faction.[45]

However, a second *ijtihadi* cluster began to take shape in 1988 with the establishment of the Majma-e Ruhaniyun-e Mobarez (Assembly of Assertive Clerics, or AAC). The AAC formed under the leadership of a distinguished Shia cleric, Mehdi Karroubi, with the strong support of his equally prominent peer, Mohammad Khatami. Both Karroubi and Khatami had actively supported Khomeini in the revolution but had grown more moderate and reformist in their ideological dispositions through the tumult of the postrevolution period. Karroubi was a former student of Khomeini and Montazeri and a trained theologian and lawyer who was recognized as a *mujtahid*. After the revolution, he headed the Komiteh Emdad-e Imam Khomeini (Imam Khomeini Relief Committee, IKRC) and the Martyr's Foundation—a major *bonyad*—before entering parliament and serving two terms as Speaker (1989–92 and 2000–2004). He founded the Hezb-e E'temad-e Meli (National Trust Party) in 2005 and ran for the presidency in that year and in 2009, only to be defeated in a disputed outcome and ultimately placed under house arrest. Khatami, on the other hand, was a high-ranking Islamic scholar who had served as a member of parliament and minister of Culture and Islamic Guidance from 1982 to 1992, prior to becoming Iran's first reformist president (1997–2005) in two landslide election victories (see chapter 4).

The AAC was united in its support for a pluralistic, democratic, Islamic political system. Some of its leading figures, most prominently Khatami, discreetly favored the promotion of Islamic civil society, the relaxation of political and social controls, economic openness, a cultural renaissance, and wider interactions with the outside world, including the United States. They were inspired by the Iranian Islamic political theorists Ali Shariati and Abdul Karim Saroush, who blended Islam with Enlightenment ideas to imagine a modern Islamic society that was also democratic.[46] Meanwhile, some of the cluster's leaders, whose realism nonetheless took precedent over their idealism, emphasized the importance of maintaining a balance of power in domestic politics.[47]

The third cluster—*amalgaran*—on the other hand, crystallized around Ali Akbar Hashemi Rafsanjani, who had studied theology with Khomeini in Qom and who, following the revolution, played a key role in shaping and maintaining Khomeini's Islamic order. Those who formed this entity, which tends to fall politically between the first and the second clusters, were organized into two parties, reflecting its diverging positions on social and cultural issues—the Hezb-e Kargozaran Sazandegi (Executives of Construction Party), who supported the reformists' approach to culture, and the Hezbe E'tedal va Tose'eh (Justice and Development Party), who leaned toward the conservatives on the same issues. The camp as a whole was motivated by the intellectual work of a number of academic economists, with a belief in economic modernization from above, favoring technical and economic relations with the West but with little evident interest in the democratization of politics.[48]

Khomeini appeared quite comfortable with a degree of political pluralism, as long as the clusters remained loyal, operated within his Islamic paradigm, and refrained from public displays of interfactional frictions. However, when the IRP descended into factionalist disorder, he pragmatically reversed his earlier position on whether a political organization should have a monopoly of power in an Islamic society. In 1987, he reverted to the traditional theological position, declaring that the existence of any kind of political party in an Islamic entity was inappropriate, formally abolishing the IRP, and declaring Iran a nonpartisan Islamic Republic. However, he did not call for an end to political factionalism, nor was he able to put an end to it. Hence, modern Iran under the Islamic Republic has maintained a fluid set of factional clusters rather than a rigid party alignment in its formal politics.

The second sphere in which Khomeini displayed *ijtihadi* pragmatism was in social and cultural changes. This is not to say that a *jihadi* dimension was absent from these realms. On the contrary, Khomeini presided over a comprehensive Islamization of the Iranian polity, which sought to make all social and cultural practices conform in both substance and style with what he regarded as "Islamic" standards. Implementation involved a considerable degree of moral compulsion. In Iranian schools, Islamic studies and Arabic as the language of the Qur'an were given primacy at all levels of education, and daily prayers were established as the norm. While advocating virtue and austerity as the foundation of a rewarding Muslim life, he empowered his *jihadi* supporters to act as the guardians and enforcers of the new moral order. Khomeini's loyalists in the security and police forces were given wide constitutional and legal sanctions to punish the perpetrators of the Islamic Republic's rapidly expanding list of "vices."

Among the most visible and socially symbolic changes was the imposition of a dress requirement on women, who were legally required to wear the *hijab* (head scarf) despite Khomeini's prerevolutionary promises that women under an Islamic Republic would have some freedom of dress, particularly as concerned the *hijab* (an example of his *taqiyya* dissimulation for the purposes of gaining power). Whereas the new dress laws required women to veil and completely cover their bodies except for their face and hands, men were pressured to sport beards and wear collarless shirts to appear appropriately Islamic and to distinguish themselves from the Western suits and clean-shaven styles favored during the Shah's era. In the literary and political sphere, individual rights, civil liberties, and freedom of expression were subordinated to ideological dictates. State censorship and self-censorship became the order of the day. In this respect, Khomeini's theocratic practices simply replaced those of the Shah's autocratic secular rule, perpetuating Iran's historically authoritarian political culture.

Khomeini, however, was realistic enough to recognize that his Islamic impositions would fail if they proved too uncompromising or solely regressive. Moreover, he appeared to be conscious of the role that Iranian women could play in the reconstruction of the new Islamic order. Women and girls, who outnumbered their male counterparts by a considerable margin, largely due to the loss of an estimated three to five hundred thousand men in the war, were given the same educational opportunities under the Islamic Republic as their male counterparts and were employed in both public and private sectors. The Islamic tradition (*hadith*) praising the role of education and acquisition of knowledge for both men and women was given particular emphasis in state propaganda. In postrevolution

Iran, women were granted greater freedom of movement and personal autonomy than in some of the neighboring Gulf Arab states: they were allowed to drive, participate in political, commercial, and civil activities as well as the security sector without a legal male chaperone. The Islamic order also provided for health and sanitary care, accompanied by the opening of women's clinics. One of Khomeini's most significant *ijtihadi* innovations laid the ideological groundwork for the progressive family planning and birth control policies that were put in place from the 1990s. This is not to downplay the segregationist and participatory restrictions to which women and girls were subjected, which include a prohibition against women attending sporting events.[49] It is merely to point out that in implementing his vision, Khomeini was as much of a constructionist as he was a combatant.

The third *ijtihadi* sphere was foreign policy. While declaring an unabashedly pro-Islamic foreign policy, Khomeini was not impervious to the need to engage in *ijtihadi* actions when necessary to preserve the interests of his Islamic regime. On a number of occasions, he found it expedient to depart from his declared foreign policy approach and goals. For example, to compensate for his bitter opposition to the US and its regional allies as well as Iraq, Khomeini was willing to let his Islamic government look more to the "East." Despite his rejection of communism, the Islamic Republic sought to maintain good working relations with the USSR and China as trading partners and arms suppliers. He followed a similar line with another Asian rising power, India.

As early as January 1979, Khomeini sent a warm note congratulating President Gorbachev on the occasion of the anniversary of the Bolshevik Revolution. A year later, he supplemented it with the only personal letter that he ever wrote to a foreign head of state, as detailed earlier. While Moscow was initially ambivalent toward the new regime, relations between the two countries experienced an upswing with the rise of Khomeini's anti-American rhetoric. The two sides signed a number of deals, such as the February 15, 1982, Protocol on Economic and Technical Cooperation.[50] Indeed, in the first three years after the revolution, two-way trade between Iran and the Soviet Union reached a new record of over $1 billion, with the total volume of trade more than tripling, from 1 million tons in 1978 to 3.4 million tons in 1984.[51] While the relationship between the two countries fluctuated with the regional situation (such as the Soviet invasion of Afghanistan in 1979), the Soviet Union remained a valuable strategic partner for Iran, providing weapons and arms exports through Soviet-aligned states such as Syria. By 1989, the relationship had stabilized, as indicated by Soviet foreign minister Eduard Shevardnadze's visit to Tehran to meet Khomeini.[52]

Like Russia, China also became a partner capable of providing strategic benefits to Iran. Its early transactions with Iran consisted primarily of arms sales, which began in 1981 and accounted for 41 percent of all arms trade to Iran between 1980 and 1988.[53] In addition to small arms, China provided Iran with important technologies, particularly in the field of ballistic missiles, such as the HY-2 anti-ship missile (known as the Silkworm), which was delivered in 1986.[54] Relations with China developed further after 1984, when the governments on both sides were beginning to adopt more pragmatic foreign policy positions. In 1985, China initiated civilian nuclear cooperation with Iran.[55] Rafsanjani visited Beijing in his capacity as Speaker of the Majles in 1985, with the aim of expanding Iran's foreign relations; Khamenei, did the same as president in 1989. From the Chinese side, Wan Li, the chairman of the National People's Congress, visited Iran in 1988.[56] Trade between the two countries also expanded dramatically over a decade, tripling from $627 million in the early 1980s to $1.7 billion by 1990.[57]

Iran's relations with India primarily focused on economic and diplomatic issues. Economically, Iran was interested in India's potential as a trading partner through which it could circumvent US sanctions; diplomatically, it was attracted to India as a country with a soft, nonaligned international stance. In 1980, the Iranian commerce minister Reza Sadr visited India to investigate India's potential as a secure source of importing spare parts and raw materials.[58] The goal of expanding economic ties was again pursued in 1983, when the Indian prime minister Narasimha Rao and a delegation of businesspeople and politicians visited Iran and signed an agreement to create the India-Iran Joint Commission.[59] More recently, in 2016 the two countries signed a memorandum of understanding for further cooperation in the fields of industry, research, and commerce.[60]

Khomeini died of natural causes on June 3, 1989, just short of his eighty-eighth birthday. His passing caused widespread grief among Iranians, with hundreds of thousands attending his funeral. The crowd that gathered to mourn his departure was the largest since the funeral of Egypt's Arab nationalist president Gamal Abdul Nasser (1918–70), which was attended by two million people. Khomeini was buried in a strategic location between Tehran and Qom—the two places that had intertwined his political and religious life—a place that now lies on the main thoroughfare between Tehran's Imam Khomeini International Airport and the city itself. His tomb, permanently ensconced by a large scaffolding complex, has become a site of pilgrimage for his supporters within and beyond Iran.

While Khomeini remains an object of admiration for many, since his death he has also become the target of both overt and guarded criticism within the country. Some of his initial supporters have taken issue with Khomeini for having instituted an excessively repressive theocratic system. These critics view the regime's legalization and sanctioning of violence and human rights violations, and its use of foreign confrontations to shore up the power of the clerical rulers, as contrary to the humane precepts of Islam. One of his highest-ranking critics in this respect was Ayatollah Montazeri, who remained relentless in his criticism of Khomeini and the system that he established until his death, despite being placed under house arrest. Montazeri continued to command a sizable following within the Ruhaniyyat even after his passing. His views are shared by other prominent living clerics, including Karroubi and Khatami, although to varying degrees.

Outside the Ruhaniyyat, Khomeini has many critics, who have gone as far as to claim that his theocratic rule was a disaster that held Iran back from achieving the greatness that it deserves among the world's nations. They contend that his system of governance has been repressive and regressive, with little room for individual rights, freedoms, initiatives, and creativity, but with wide scope for patronage building, corruption, nepotism, and administrative dysfunction at many levels. Changing perceptions of Khomeini have also been reflected in the decreasing number of visitors to his mausoleum. One cleric lamented the mausoleum's dwindling crowds—a sign, in his opinion, that "the Iranian people do not sufficiently appreciate their leader and his revolution." Khomeini's legacy may reflect Iranians' growing disillusionment with stagnating economic conditions. As one Iranian man recently reflected, "No one remembers the revolution or Imam Khomeini anymore. He was a good man on a righteous path, but the revolution died with him. There is no help for disenfranchised people anymore."[61]

Whatever his critics' views and the nature of the order that he established, the Shia majority in Iran, and even some circles outside of Iran, continue to recognize Khomeini as a steely champion of the Islamic faith and as a wildly successful revolutionary who fundamentally transformed his country, challenging the regional and international order in defiance of the major powers, especially the United States. He left behind a legacy of *jihadi* and *ijtihadi* revolutionary politics in Iran that sent shock waves through the Muslim and non-Muslim world. Through the first approach, he had forged a tightly structured Islamic order, and through the second, he had provided room for adjustments and reinvention within changing circumstances. It is within this paradigm that the post-Khomeini Islamic government has evolved and endured to the present day. The life of the Islamic Republic after Khomeini's death would prove to be no less tumultuous or controversial than during the ten years of his rule.

4

The Islamic Order under Khamenei

FROM RAFSANJANI TO ROUHANI

The Supreme Leader's passing meant the collapse of the epicenter of gravity of the Islamic system, which had been designed to revolve around Khomeini alone. This event inevitably opened up the system to potential changes, confronting his successor, Ayatollah Ali Hossein Khamenei, and his supporters with the difficult task of preserving and strengthening the Islamic order without compromising the framework that Khomeini had established. Naturally, questions were raised inside and outside of Iran about what would become of the Islamic Republic now that it had lost its founder. However, Khomeini's *jihadi-ijtihadi* approach had endowed the Islamic system with enough flexibility to allow his successors to make policy adjustments when and where required without eroding the foundations on which the system rested. This resilience and dynamism propelled the journey of the Islamic Republic under its new Supreme Leader, Khamenei, who (despite lacking the necessary religious qualifications at the time of assuming the leadership) has succeeded in exercising as much, if not more, power and authority than his predecessor. Four elected presidents have so far served beneath Khamenei. Each has sought to swing the political pendulum in different directions and at strategic moments, but ultimately all of them have deferred to the authority of the Supreme Leader as the overarching power holder and element of continuity in Iranian politics.

Khamenei at the Helm

Khamenei had been a key loyalist of Khomeini prior to and during the revolution and remained so as president from October 13, 1981, until August 3, 1989. In this capacity, he had also played an important role, along with Prime Minister Mir-Hossein Mousavi (1981–89), in the war with Iraq. Born in Mashhad in July 1939 from Azeri heritage, Khamenei hails from a Seyyed family, a title reserved for direct descendants of Prophet Mohammad. Khamenei commenced his Islamist political activities in the early 1960s following a modest seminary education, a sojourn in Najaf, and a period in Qom, where he studied under Khomeini and another prominent Shia scholar, Seyyed Hossein Borujerdi. This marked the beginning of his association with Khomeini, which led to the beginning of his anti-Shah activities, for which he served a jail sentence in 1963. In the Shia clerical ranking, he never progressed to ayatollah, let alone *marja*, the rank required by the Iranian Islamic Constitution for the positions of *faqih* and Supreme Leader of the Islamic Republic.

At the time of his nomination to succeed Khomeini, Khamenei held only the middling rank in the Shia hierarchy of *hojjat-ol-eslam* (Authority on Islam). Few of his peers ever seriously expected him to reach the position of *faqih* by religious qualification. When Khomeini consented to his nomination for Supreme Leader on the recommendation of the then Speaker of Majles, Akbar Hashemi Rafsanjani, Khamenei did not consider himself qualified for the position. Instead, he joined with a number of other members of the Assembly of Experts in promoting the idea of a collective leadership to replace Khomeini. It was only after he won the largest number of votes in the assembly that the title of ayatollah was bestowed upon him, leading to his recognition as a *marja* and rendering him eligible for the position.

Initially, Khamenei found his position quite tenuous, given the disdain of several *marjas* and senior ayatollahs, who could not accept his authority on the basis of a rank attained by political intercession rather than traditional Islamic study and proven excellence in jurisprudence. However, Khamenei's shrewdness as a tactician and skill as a political operator soon confounded his critics and rendered their objections moot. Despite his rank, Khamenei had been a passionate revolutionary cleric and student of Islamic studies, gaining fluency in Arabic in addition to his native Azeri and Persian tongues. He had translated several discourses from Arabic to Persian, including the works of the prominent Egyptian Sunni Islamist theorist and activist, Sayyed Qutb (1906–66). He had developed a particular admiration for the latter, whose writings have influenced a generation of radical Islamists, most importantly those in the Muslim Brotherhood.

Upon assuming the Supreme Leadership on June 4, 1989, Khamenei found it imperative to address three issues. One was to consolidate his leadership by building a power base of his own. Another was to manage the relations between the two tiers of the Islamic government, including the different factions that had emerged within the ruling clerical stratum, in order to ensure that the government remained subordinate to his leadership. The third was to fill the ranks of the clerical and state administrative and security structures under him with favorable elements of the upcoming post-revolution generation, without entirely stifling the elected governmental bodies in the second tier. Let us look at each of these issues separately.

Leadership Consolidation

Hailing from the *jihadi* camp as an ardent student of theology, Khamenei had loyally served Khomeini in entrenching and defending his *velayat-e faqih* system.[1] He saw his mission as pursuing Khomeini's line and regarded any deviation from it as a gross betrayal and detrimental to the Islamic system. He shared Khomeini's belief in the superiority of Shia Islam over its Sunni counterpart, as well as his dedication to the goal of a unified Shia Islamic government.[2] In foreign policy, Khamenei also resembled his predecessor, viewing the United States as a hegemonic oppressor and scorning Israel as an imperialist outpost of the superpower and an illegitimate occupier of the Palestinian homeland. Similarly, he detested Saddam Hussein's Iraqi regime and castigated the latter's Arab allies for supporting the Iraqi dictator's aggression against Iran and for acting as proponents of American imperialism in the region. He cast Iraq's reliance on foreign governments and Arab cooperation with the US as a stain on their honor, stating:

> Foreigners' defense of regional governments brings shame and disgrace to these governments. . . . If these governments had relied on their nations they would have defended their national prestige, honor and dignity through resistance and devotion. Those governments defending themselves with the help of foreigners have humiliated their nations. The stain of such humiliation will not be effaced for years.[3]

Although well versed in the complexities of Iran's internal and external settings, Khamenei had very limited world experience. He had been outside Iran only three times, spending a year in Najaf during his studies and undertaking two short visits to Libya and China during his presidency. Drawing on the legitimacy and structures established under Khomeini, he set out to leverage his theological authority and constitutional powers as the Supreme Leader, head of state, and commander in chief of the armed forces to make himself as pivotal to the operation of the Islamic system as possible.

Two days after Khomeini's death, he moved swiftly to establish his authority by dispatching his representatives to various provinces with notes of goodwill. By the same token, he disseminated messages to solicit the obedience of the mosques and other religious organizations as well as official outlets across the country. He also very actively engaged like-minded thinkers, both clerics and nonclerics, in order to surround himself with loyal and influential agents to advise him on domestic and foreign affairs and liaise between him and the governmental, semigovernmental, and religious organizations, as well as the public at large. In particular, he sought out ranking clerics in the Ruhaniyyat and Hezbollahis, the ideological heirs of the now-defunct Islamic Republican Party. Finally, Khamenei moved rapidly to appoint his loyalists to important strategic positions, not only within his personal administration but also in the top ranks of the three branches of the armed forces, the Basij, Sepah, the security agencies, the judiciary, state information services, religious organizations, and the *bonyads*.[4] Khamenei's close ties to Sepah, forged during his tenure as deputy defense minister in Mehdi Bazargan's provisional government and during his subsequent presidency, came in handy in this process of power consolidation. In his strategic use of political appointments and diligent cultivation of his personal connections, Khamenei made up for what he lacked in Khomeini's natural charisma, popular support, and legendary revolutionary legacy.

Over time, Khamenei succeeded in building networks of dedicated supporters within and outside of the Council of Guardians, Assembly of Experts, and Council of Expediency, as well as government structures at all levels. His residential compound, Beit-e Rahbari (House of Leadership), has developed into a center of theological and political power and bureaucratic gravity. Functioning almost as an informal government operating above the formal one,[5] it is reminiscent of the Royal Court, the Shah's parallel government that controlled policy decision-making to a greater degree than the formal government. Today, Khamenei wields as much, if not more, power and authority as his predecessor or, for that matter, the Shah.

Dealing with the Two-Tiered System and Factionalism

Chapter 3 related how Khomeini's *jihadi* posture enabled the conservative/traditionalist cluster, or "hard-liners," to secure most levers of power, while at the same time his *ijtihadi* dimension generated space for pragmatic and reformist clusters to emerge by the end of the 1980s. At the time of Khomeini's death, however, there was still considerable fluidity between these clusters, and the policy and personality differences had not become so pronounced as to define relations and political contestation between them. So long as the Islamic Revolution was still under ostensible threat from inside and out, the three political factions cooperated respectfully and functionally to ensure the success of the new order, to which all of their fortunes were tied.

By the time of Khamenei's ascendancy, the relationship between the two tiers of the Islamic system of governance had been firmly established, and factionalism among the ruling clerics had taken on a definitive shape. Given his intimate involvement in the establishment of the Islamic system, Khamenei was well informed of its very complex components and their interrelations. This knowledge left him well equipped to follow Khomeini's *jihadi-ijtihadi* approach to managing the system to his advantage. While relying on the dominance of his own *jihadi* cluster, he followed Khomeini's style of power balancing through largely indirect and informal means, falling back on his religious authority whenever necessary or appropriate. In this way he was able to build up his power over the elected executive and legislature (the presidency and Majles) and to deflect any factional challenge.[6] To illustrate this, it is important to take a closer look at the tenure of each of the four presidents who have served under Khamenei.

RAFSANJANI'S PRAGMATISM

Rafsanjani, the man largely responsible for Khamenei's succession, was elected president for two terms (1989–97), the maximum permitted by the constitution. He had been a close friend of Khamenei's since the late 1950s, and the two had worked in close alliance to ensure the success of the revolution. As explained earlier, like Khamenei, Rafsanjani had studied under Khomeini in Qom and gained the latter's trust and confidence to become one of the few figures in the leader's inner circle who could speak openly to him and prompt him to act on his advice and recommendations. Rafsanjani had earned a reputation as a charismatic, capable, articulate, and eloquent political cleric. However, in contrast to Khamenei's modest background, Rafsanjani, born in 1934 in the province of Kerman, came from a wealthy family of pistachio growers and had a knack for trade and business. A practical, business-minded cleric, Rafsanjani did not entirely share Khamenei's religious orthodoxy and political conservatism. On the contrary, he had become known as a pragmatist who was prone to political fluctuations when he judged it necessary to maintain the support of different factional clusters for his pragmatic outlook.

At the beginning of his first term, Rafsanjani appeared to enjoy more popularity among the ruling stratum and public than Khamenei. This favor made him both a source of support and a potential threat to Khamenei, requiring the Supreme Leader to remain watchful of his ambitions and influence. Khamenei initially remained well disposed toward Rafsanjani, who was equally keen to work with him to steer the post-Khomeini Islamic Republic toward a blend of conservative Islamic and pragmatic politics. Khamenei and his conservative supporters were quite content to let Rafsanjani engage in some reforms, especially in the economic arena. Khomeini's reluctant acceptance of a cease-fire with Iraq, effective from July 20, 1988 (largely at Rafsanjani's urging), thus ending the active conflict, provided an opening to pursue the constructionist dimension of Khomeini's vision, which had been severely impeded by the war.

Rafsanjani commenced his first term of office with a promise of domestic and foreign policy openness in order to relieve the Iranian people of the abominable conditions imposed on them by war austerity, US economic sanctions, and the *jihadi* centralization of power. He launched a number of policy initiatives in pursuit of economic liberalization and a market economy, involving the establishment of free economic zones (discussed in chapter 5). He also initiated a number of foreign policy gestures to ease the Islamic Republic's international isolation and bring its Islamic government to a level of cordiality within the world order. However, he was not interested in political reform and maintained a firm commitment to the *velayat-e faqih* system. Having been a key architect in the building of the boat, he had never intended to rock it or to upset the *jihadi* cluster in any way. Throughout his presidency, his focus remained on economic reforms and foreign policy openings.

As part of a charm offensive to improve relations with Iran's Arab neighbors, he visited Saudi Arabia on a goodwill mission and sought to alleviate the Arab governments' concerns over the threat of the export of the Iranian Revolution. He also made a concerted effort to widen trade with Russia, India, and China and to make common cause with them on certain international issues. While unable to revoke Khomeini's *fatwa* (religious ruling) that called for the killing of Salman Rushdie, he downplayed the role of the Iranian state in encouraging the execution of the ruling.[7] Beyond this, he used Iran's influence to secure the release of some of the Western hostages detained by Iran's Hezbollah allies in Lebanon. In so doing, he expected an improvement in Iran's relations with the West, and possibly a thaw in US-Iranian relations. However, ultimately, the United States did not trust him. Washington's hostile policy attitude was motivated partly by its mistrust of the Islamic Republic, as shaped by the experience of the hostage crisis, Tehran's human rights violations, and alleged support of international terrorism. Yet it was also driven partly by geopolitical objectives, including America's commitment to Israel, close ties with oil-rich conservative Gulf Arab states, and a sense of "loss" of Iran as a vital strategic foothold in the Middle East.

Meanwhile, Rafsanjani's pragmatic agenda rattled the conservative forces, which grew concerned about its implications for their advocacy of ideological purity and their hold on power and privileges. They gradually but surely set in motion a low-level campaign of resistance to his policies of economic liberalization and foreign policy openings by using their dominance inside and outside the state power structures, with growing effect. It eventually became clear that the president could expect little or no support from his conservative counterparts. Referring to Rafsanjani's liberal economic policies, one hard-liner publication wrote that "preserving revolutionary values and principles is vital and should not be sacrificed for the sake of freedom and development" and that "political and economic openness in Iran will cause the collapse of the revolution."[8] Concurrently, the conservative Islamist quarterly *Mashreq* declared that "democracy is nothing but the dictatorship of capital, consumerism and selfishness. Democracy is reactionary; it is a return to *jāheliyya* [the pre-Islamic age of ignorance], paganism, and disbelief."[9] Khamenei did not take a public stance against Rafsanjani, but given his personal conservative convictions and base of support among the traditionalist cluster, his silence can only have implied his consent with the hard-line forces' activities to check the president's pragmatic moves.

By Rafsanjani's second term in office, the rift between the president and his supporters, on the one hand, and Khamenei's conservative associates and operators, on the other, was highly visible. Any earlier semblance of political unity that the two sides had displayed was now evaporating. While this did not entail an outbreak of open hostility between the Supreme Leader and the president, the two were increasingly unable to see eye to eye on policy issues. The tables had turned: Khamenei was now in a position to obstruct and disrupt the political moves of his old friend and ally indirectly through his supporters in the conservative faction. At the same time, Rafsanjani was coming under growing pressure from the emerging third column—the *ijtihadis*. As a result, he found himself treading an increasingly fine line between the *jihadi* and *ijtihadi* clusters. Toward the end of his presidency, he was placed in an even tighter political corner. He consequently made the difficult choice of seeking to ingratiate himself with the *ijtihadi* faction,[10] which distanced him even further from the conservative cluster.

Under the prevailing circumstances, the most that Rafsanjani could achieve was to keep the Islamic Republic afloat and slightly improve its regional and international standing. A majority of Iranians experienced no tangible positive change in their living conditions under his presidency. Indeed, one study found that average household expenditures and the standard of living in urban areas actually decreased from 1993 to 1996 as a result of rising accommodation prices, high inflation, and unemployment.[11] As his pragmatic efforts reached a deadlock, Khamenei and his supporters, in effect, had successfully managed to deflect the challenge from the pragmatists. Along with this, patronage, corruption, administrative dysfunction, moral lapses, and poor governance continued on an upward trajectory. There were a number of high-profile corruption cases in which close associates and allies of Rafsanjani were exposed as enriching themselves from the privatization process, earning them the moniker of *aghazadeh* (offspring of men of means and influence). *Bonyads* in particular became an emblem of corruption among the elite. The Bonyad e-Mostazafan va Janbazan (Foundation for the Oppressed), the largest organization encompassing multiple businesses, was subject to a parliamentary investigation in 1995–96 that concluded that it had engaged in "influence peddling."[12] Two of Rafsanjani's sons were also involved in cases, charged with benefiting from their father's position of power and influence: one of them had been put in charge of a multibillion-dollar development of the Tehran metro system, and another had been given a prominent position in the Oil Ministry.[13]

Following his presidential term, however, Rafsanjani remained an important figure in the pragmatist cluster of Iranian politics, at first as the head and subsequently as deputy head of the Expediency Council, while developing increasingly strong leanings toward the reformist camp. Despite his daughter and son being prosecuted and jailed periodically on charges of undermining the sanctity of the Islamic government and fraud, respectively, he continued to act with a degree of influence. As a result, Khamenei could not but recognize the need to remain on good terms with the former president. When Rafsanjani passed away from a heart attack on January 8, 2017, Khamenei and all other leading clerical figures attended his funeral amid a wave of popular mourning. While Rafsanjani had been frustrated in many of his ambitions as a pragmatist, his attempted changes emboldened the reformist forces, which ascended to prominence under Mohammad Khatami's leadership and later under that of Hassan Rouhani, although the latter was a pragmatist of Rafsanjani's ilk. Rafsanjani's changes posed an even stronger challenge to the conservative cluster.

KHATAMI'S REFORMISM

Khatami assumed office in an electoral landslide on August 2, 1997, amid mounting public disenchantment with the traditionalists' hard-line policies, economic mismanagement, and corruption and Rafsanjani's pragmatic reform efforts, which had failed to deliver the promised changes. Many citizens were now looking for a fresh approach capable of improving their living conditions and opening up the country to the outside world. Khatami, known for his advocacy of a humane and participatory Islamic order and an internationalist rather than combative *jihadi* approach to the conduct of the Islamic Republic's foreign relations, seemed to have the answer.

Born in the Iranian province of Yazd to a renowned ayatollah, Khatami completed his higher education at the Universities of Isfahan and Tehran, receiving degrees in Western philosophy and educational sciences, respectively, before going on to Qom, where he received his doctorate in Islamic sciences. He had served as the chair of the Islamic Centre in Hamburg, Ayatollah Mohammad Beheshti's old stomping ground, between 1978 and 1980. His post-revolution public service included two periods serving as a member of the Majles (1980–82, 1989–92) and one as minister of Culture and Islamic Guidance (1982–86). From the start a strong supporter of Khomeini and his *velayat-e faqih* system, Khatami over time came to favor a more *ijtihadi* approach to the institution and operation of the Islamic order. In this, he had much in common with a number of liberal-minded senior ayatollahs, such as Mahmoud Taleqani, Mohammad Kazem Shariatmadari, and Hussein Ali Montazeri. He was also actively involved in the founding of the reformist organization and clerical political party the Assembly of Assertive Clerics, in 1988, as noted in chapter 3.

Khatami campaigned for the presidency on a platform of reform and liberalization, based on a firm conviction that the time had come to redirect Iran's political culture from a *jihadi* to an *ijtihadi* course. His candidacy survived the vetting of the Council of Guardians, the body in charge of endorsing or disqualifying presidential candidates, which has over the years allowed fewer and fewer aspirants to enter the race. While Khatami's reformist views may have given rise to some misgivings among the Supreme Leader and his conservative supporters, his credentials as a religious scholar and member of the Ruhaniyyat proved to them that he was sufficiently trustworthy to take on the presidency. More important, Khatami seemed a promising candidate to fill the need that they now perceived to soften aspects of the Islamic government to contend with growing public demand for change and openness. The conservatives were thus willing to allow Khatami to proceed with certain reforms, provided they remained in a position to set the limits.

Working within the constitution and Khomeini's Islamic system, Khatami called for domestic political reforms that would promote "Islamic civil society" and the rule of law as a precondition for, and in tandem with, the pursuit of "Islamic democracy." He strongly maintained that Islam was compatible with democracy, arguing that many of its values harmonized with those enshrined in Western democracies and in the Universal Declaration of Human Rights. An exception was capital punishment, which Islam endorses and which the Islamic Republic permits and practices. In a television interview in 2001, Khatami presented Islamic democracy as one of democracy's multiple forms, stating:

> The existing democracies do not necessarily follow one formula or aspect. It is possible that a democracy may lead to a liberal system. It is possible that democracy may lead to a socialist system. Or it may be a democracy with the inclusion of religious norms in the government. We have accepted the third option.[14]

He also emphasized the importance of full adherence to the constitution and the right of citizens to criticize high-ranking authorities (including, according to some interpretations, the Supreme Leader) and advocated dialogue among the Iranian people and between followers of different faiths inside and outside Iran.[15] In a speech delivered at the Islamic Summit Conference in 1997, he argued:

> Citizens of the Islamic civil society enjoy the right to determine their own destiny, supervise the administration of affairs and hold the government accountable. The government in such a society is the servant of the people and not their master, and in every eventuality is accountable to the people whom God has entitled to determine their own destiny. Our civil society is not a society where only Muslims are entitled to rights and are considered citizens. Rather, all individuals are entitled to rights, within the framework of the law.[16]

Furthermore, he oversaw the reorganization of the Ministry of Intelligence in the wake of the 1998 "chain murders" and the jailing of many political prisoners without due process.[17] Khatami's actions demonstrated an acute awareness that the longevity of the Islamic regime and Iran's sociocultural progress and economic prosperity depended on the loosening of political and social control. The Islamic Republic's survival needed wider public participation, freedom of thought and expression, and greater room for individual initiative and creativity, as well as constructive engagement within an increasingly interdependent world.

In the sphere of foreign policy, he went further than Rafsanjani, calling for what he termed the "dialogue of civilizations" as a counter to Samuel Huntington's concept of the "clash of civilizations."[18] He wished for friendly relations with all countries, even the United States, which, he stressed, could start on the basis of people-to-people dialogue and exchanges. In his presentation at a United Nations Educational, Scientific and Cultural Organization (UNESCO) conference in 2000, he stated:

> In order to provide natural unity and harmony in form and content for global culture and to prevent anarchy and chaos, all the parties concerned should engage in a dialogue in which they can exchange knowledge, experience and understanding in diverse areas of culture and civilization.[19]

Like his predecessor, Khatami also made a special effort to assuage the fears of Iran's Arab neighbors, notably in his 1999 visit to

Riyadh in order to promote his dialogue of civilizations.[20] His efforts paid off: Western European embassies were reopened in Tehran, goodwill was generated in Iran's regional relations, and Iran's trade and economic ties with the main European powers and regional actors were boosted.[21]

Khatami was conscious that Iran's nuclear program had become a defining issue in the country's relations with the West and was eager to negotiate a settlement. The program, as mentioned earlier, had started under the Shah, with German expertise and construction as well as America's blessing.[22] Although the program was put on hold by the Islamic regime during the eight years of war with Iraq, it was restarted from the 1990s with Russian expertise and institutional collaboration. The US and its main European allies, as well as Israel, had rejected the Islamic Republic's claim that the program was for peaceful purposes only, insisting that Tehran's intent was to develop nuclear weapons. They were therefore resolved that the program be stopped at all costs and that Iran be made to fulfill its obligations as a signatory to the Nuclear Non-Proliferation Treaty (NPT). Although Iran had been negotiating for some time with the UN's nuclear watchdog, the International Atomic Energy Agency (IAEA), and with three European powers—the UK, France, and Germany—these negotiations had not produced any tangible outcome.

In order to demonstrate that Iran had no secret military nuclear objectives, the Khatami leadership engaged in a number of policy actions to assist the process of negotiations and to entice Washington to meet them halfway. It instituted a temporary suspension of Iran's uranium enrichment and signed in December 2003 the Additional Protocol to Iran's existing NPT safeguard agreement with the IAEA, which allowed the latter wider inspection and verification rights. A November 2007 US intelligence agency report titled "Iran: Nuclear Intentions and Capabilities" stated: "We judge with high confidence that in fall 2003, Tehran halted its nuclear weapons program . . . [and] we do not know whether it currently intends to develop nuclear weapons"[23]—something that the former US Secretary of Defense, Robert Gates, subsequently described as a "grievous blow" to US policy toward Iran at the time.[24] From 1989 to 2005, Iran's top nuclear negotiator was Rouhani—a moderate whose 2013 and 2016 elections to the presidency and subsequent policies and position on this issue are discussed below.

Yet, despite all his reformist efforts, Khatami received little more than lip service from the United States and its major European allies in response to his overtures, which continued to view him and his reformist supporters as powerless and incapable of prevailing over the conservative factions. Meanwhile, the European powers maintained a cautious policy of "constructive engagement" toward the Islamic regime, largely to preserve their lucrative trade arrangements with the country. The European Union (EU) was at that time Iran's largest trading partner, with the total volume of trade reaching €25.4 billion (27.8 percent of total trade) in 2006. Indeed, trade actually increased from 2002 (when it was revealed that Iran was constructing two previously undeclared nuclear facilities at Natanz and Arak), as the EU sought to use economic incentives and cooperation to reach a nuclear agreement. The US sanctions imposed on Iran, which barred American citizens and businesses from exporting to or investing in the country, left Europe the main trade beneficiary.[25] The administration of the Democratic president Bill Clinton (1993–2001) made no more than superficial gestures in response to Khatami's reforms. It lifted sanctions on the import of a few insignificant items, such as pistachios and caviar, and called for a road map to move forward but without taking concrete steps to build mutual confidence.

The US continued to accuse Tehran of having a secret military nuclear program and supporting international terrorism. Under heavy lobbying from the American Israel Public Affairs Committee, the Clinton administration committed itself to a policy of "dual containment" of Iran and Iraq, after the latter's August 1990 invasion of Kuwait and the US-led military intervention six months later. The policy was intended to make the two mortal regional enemies check and weaken one another, enabling America to contain both of them. However, the policy proved to be unworkable, since both countries were able to circumvent it.[26] It was heavily criticized by several senior American political figures, including Zbigniew Brzezinski and Brent Scowcroft, former national security advisors to former presidents Jimmy Carter and George H. W. Bush, respectively.[27]Although the policy was quietly killed, much to Tehran's delight and Washington's embarrassment, US-Iranian animosity showed no signs of abating.

America's hostility toward the Iranian government intensified with the presidency of Republican George W. Bush (2001–9). In the wake of al-Qaeda's September 11, 2001 (9/11), terrorist attacks on the United States, masterminded from Afghanistan under the medievalist Islamic rule of the Taliban, President Bush, in his January 2002 State of the Union speech, condemned Iran, along with Syria and North Korea, as part of an "axis of evil" and therefore liable to punishment by the United States.[28] Bush did so despite the fact that the Khatami leadership had not only loudly denounced the attacks but also fully cooperated with the United States at the December 2001 Bonn Conference on Afghanistan, which endorsed the formation of the internationally backed government of Hamid Karzai and the interventionist role of the United Nations and the United States in the country.[29] The head of the Iranian delegation was the current foreign minister, Mohammad Javad Zarif, who had not only cooperated with his American counterpart, James Dobbins, on the Afghanistan issue but also signaled to the latter Iran's strong desire to open a way to settle the two countries' differences. Dobbins communicated the Iranian desire to Washington, but it fell on deaf ears. The US National Security Advisor, Condoleezza Rice, did not even respond to the memo.[30] As the US leadership turned a blind eye to Iran's repeated overtures, its media ignored Iranians' outpouring of compassion in response to the 9/11 attacks. The public response in Iran was unparalleled in the Muslim world but unheeded elsewhere: vast crowds turned out in Tehran's streets for candlelit vigils and sixty thousand attendees at a Tehran soccer event two days later observed a minute of silence.[31]

By the end of his first term, Khatami and his reformist supporters remained extremely popular. Not only did Khatami win the 2001 presidential election in another landslide, but his reformist cohorts also succeeded in gaining a majority in the Majles election of the same year. However, this good fortune did not endure for much longer. Khatami's reformist policies alarmed the Supreme Leader and his supporters, who viewed them as radical enough to risk posing a serious threat to their hold on power. That apprehension, combined with the lack of any substantive responses from the US and its main European allies to Iranian overtures for peace and cooperation, played right into the hands of Khatami's factional opponents, emboldening and empowering them to increase their efforts to frustrate and undermine his reforms.

As in the case of Rafsanjani, there was no public brawl between Khatami and Khamenei, who tended toward political timidity. But this could not hide Khamenei's displeasure with some of the president's ideals and policy measures, especially those that made the Supreme Leader vulnerable to public criticism on the cultural and social policy front. As Khamenei's conservative supporters pursued a campaign of publicly criticizing Khatami and fueling public agitation and protests as a means to discredit and stifle his reforms, the Supreme Leader sat tight, refusing to give his full backing to Khatami. This refusal to rein in the conservatives from lambasting Khatami and frustrating the implementation of his reforms spoke volumes and has become an effective tactic of Khamenei in achieving his political goals as final arbiter of the system. The conservative clusters had invested heavily in the existing system and therefore remained opposed to any changes that could undermine their position and privileged status. Meanwhile, many of those voters, especially the youth, who had put their trust in Khatami as an Islamist reformist and had voted for him to the presidency on two occasions, became disillusioned, because he proved unable to fulfill their expectations. In June 2003, thousands of students, disappointed with the lack of reforms and the human rights violations committed under Khatami's government, marched against the government to protest and call for Khatami's resignation.[32] They found themselves caught between the conservatives and reformists, with the question: which side should they turn to next?

This situation, however, did not mean that Khatami's reformist efforts had no impact on the Iranian political and social landscape. On the contrary, they had great influence in bringing to the public an awareness of a softer, gentler, humane, and liberalist version of Shia political Islamism that Iranians could pursue under their existing Islamic Republican system, by working toward civil society, democracy, and peaceful coexistence with followers of other sects and with the governments of other nations. He demonstrated that if Muslims adhere to the Qur'anic ordinance that there is no compulsion in religion and understand their faith as one that advocates peace, harmony, and virtuous existence, they could apply Islam to bring about positive transformation of their societies in today's world. This legacy left the door open for the *ijtihadi* cluster to make a comeback when circumstances turned in their favor.

For the time being, though, the traditionalist forces succeeded once again in preserving their control and in projecting themselves as a more stable and reliable alternative to their pragmatist and reformist counterparts. Backed by the Islamic Revolutionary Guard Corps as the "praetorian guard," as well as by other powerful bodies within and outside of the governmental structures, the traditionalists regained the majority in the Majles in the February–May 2004 elections. The presidential election of the following year brought to power a man from their ranks: Mahmoud Ahmadinejad. This was a development that shifted Iranian Islamic politics to the right once again—at first to the relief of the Supreme Leader and his supporters, and later to their dismay.

AHMADINEJAD'S CONSERVATISM

In the 2005 presidential election, Rafsanjani still decided to run, this time with the support of die-hard reformists. However, among the several other candidates that the Council of the Guardians had endorsed to contest the ballot was also the conservative mayor of Tehran, Ahmadinejad, who defeated the heavyweight Rafsanajni and assumed Iran's presidency on August 3, 2005, winning 62 percent of votes cast.[33] His success was due largely to his anti-reform agenda along factional and class lines. In other words, he invoked the issues that appealed to both the conservative camp and to the category of citizens whom Khomeini had called *mosta'zafin* (the "have-nots" or the downtrodden). The year before, the conservatives had also won a large majority in the parliamentary elections following the disqualification of more than two thousand reformist candidates—a major victory for the *jihadi* cluster and a serious setback for pragmatists and reformists.[34]

Ahmadinejad was relatively unknown in Iranian politics until his rise to the presidency.[35] Born in Semnan province in 1956, he came from an unsophisticated, nonclerical but pious family and from a poor, rural socioeconomic background. Although a staunch follower of Khomeini, he did not play a leading role in the Iranian Revolution. He had been a member of the radical student group responsible for the takeover of the American embassy but reportedly did not take part in the action.[36] During his time working in the intelligence and security apparatus of the Sepah in the 1980s, he gained close identification with the *jihadi* cluster and developed links with the security establishment. He was educated as an engineer, receiving his doctorate in 1997, and served as a teacher for a while before assuming administrative/political positions in various Iranian provinces, culminating in his appointment as governor of Ardabil province in 1993. He resumed his teaching career in 1997 after Khatami removed him from the position of governorship.

Despite his humble origins and unimpressive revolutionary credentials, Ahmadinejad had emerged as the main leader of a coalition of conservative groups called the E'telaf-e Abadgaran-e Iran-e Islami (Alliance of Builders of Islamic Iran), which opposed Khatami's domestic reforms and foreign policy, believing these would compromise Khomeini's Islamic vision and make Iran vulnerable to Western (especially American and Israeli) influence. The alliance formed Ahmadinejad's political power base and was instrumental in his appointment by the city council of Tehran as mayor in 2003. From this platform, he was able to gain wider visibility. He had all along viewed himself as a champion of the *mosta'zafin*, as expressed in his famous promise to "put the oil money on everyone's dinner table."[37] His brand of conservatism was very much influenced by Ayatollah Mohammad Mesbah Yazdi, a powerful hard-line cleric and member of the Assembly of Experts who strongly opposed any form of democratic rule and reformism.

During his first term, Ahmadinejad worked in tandem with Khamenei to consolidate the *jihadis*' hold on power. Sharing the Supreme Leader's worldview, he deferred to him on most important state issues. Claiming that the United States and its allies, especially Israel, were determined to destroy the Islamic regime, he focused predominantly on three priorities: ingratiating himself with the *mosta'zafin*, especially in the rural areas which he visited more frequently than any of his predecessors, breaking bread with families and providing financial assistance to them to build his reputation as a concerned pious Shia and devoted disciple of Khomeini; expanding Iran's military power and nuclear program; and maintaining and strengthening Iran's support for its regional allies, including Syria, Lebanon's Hezbollah, and some powerful Shia factions in Iraq.[38] All this suited the conservatives' agenda and conformed to Khamenei's stance.

The *jihadi* faction's growing dominance in all governmental branches, at least by the time of Ahmadinejad's second term, prompted an effective merger between the reformist and pragmatic factions. Both sides found Ahmadinejad's populist, ad hoc approach to Iran's social and economic development alarming and viewed his policies as regressive and detrimental to the country. Those policies involved wealth redistribution through salary and subsidy increases, as well as pet projects and cash handouts, especially in the rural areas. This approach, along with state patronage of selected groups and institutions that formed the bulwark of the conservatives' power, generated little sustainable development, administrative efficiency, or clean and effective governance. In terms of monetary policy, Ahmadinejad directly intervened in the banking sector and forced state-owned commercial banks to provide low-interest loans to "preferred geographic areas and economic activities." These loans caused banks to suffer large losses, increased both inflation and government debt, and left a legacy that is still evident in Iran's widespread nonperforming-loans banking crisis.[39] A number of ministers and business heads were fired or resigned under his administration.

According to the foreign policy analyst Suzanne Maloney, these "resignations over Ahmadinejad's fiscal policies were representative of a broader cycle of bureaucratic instability and unprecedented turnover at the highest levels of government." Maloney notes that none of the officials who had entered the government when he was first elected in 2005 "remained by the end of his second term."[40] The dissatisfaction was expressed by Ahmadinejad's finance minister Davoud Danesh-Jafari, who, upon his resignation, accused the administration of having "no positive attitude towards previous experiences or experienced people" and "no plan for the future."[41] Ahmadinejad went through four different deputy governors for foreign exchange matters, with some officials only lasting a year (or less) in office. He often replaced technocrats and ministers with members of the Basij and the Sepah, thus expanding their reach and influence across the economy and in the political sphere.

Unlike Khatami and Rafsanjani, Ahmadinejad adopted an assertive and confrontational policy attitude toward the West and established camaraderie with heads of state who displayed a similar distaste for the United States and its allies (Israel in particular), such as the late Venezuelan president Hugo Chavez and Zimbabwean leader Robert Mugabe.[42] His foreign policy was defined by a stance of uncompromising isolation that shunned foreign investment in favor of national self-sufficiency. He reiterated Khomeini's reproofs against the United States as an evil power and Israel as an aggressive "Zionist state," questioning the legitimacy of Israel's existence and, famously, branding the Holocaust a Zionist ploy.[43] He appointed a hard-line conservative, Saeed Jalili, as his deputy foreign minister and chief nuclear negotiator and adopted a defiant stance on Iran's nuclear program.[44]

These policies further isolated Iran and brought about three rounds of UN sanctions and increasingly crippling American and European financial and economic sanctions in relation to Iran's nuclear program, especially from mid-2012. Those measures, in conjunction with growing corruption, fraud, and inefficiency in governmental operations, as well as a chronically underdeveloped taxation system, caused the Iranian economy to slide into stagnation. This occurred despite the fact that the government had finally decided to act on subsidy reform, instituting a phase-out program for food and fuel subsidies, the first stage of which was rolled out in December 2010. Public disquiet and popular opposition caused the government to delay the program's subsequent phases.

Rouhani, Ahmadinejad's successor, subsequently claimed that "Iran's oil and gas export incomes during Ahmadinejad's two-term presidency reached some $800 billion, and his administration had spent some $640 billion of that on importing goods until March 2013."[45] Rouhani further criticized Ahmadinejad for abusing around $100 billion of the country's annual revenue.[46] As public discontent with the Islamic government soared during Ahmadinejad's first term, the reformist and pragmatist factional leaders decided to stridently oppose him in the June 2009 presidential election. Mir Hossein Mousavi, who had served as prime minister for five years during the war with Iraq, and Mehdi Karroubi, as mentioned earlier, a prominent cleric, former Speaker of the Majles, and previous contender for the presidency, put themselves forward with the public support of Khatami (who had initially intended to run himself) and Rafsanjani. The two were vetted and approved by the Council of Guardians to run against Ahmadinejad, which could not have been done without the endorsement of Khamenei, who now enjoyed majority support in the Council. It has been a matter of debate as to why the Council ratified Mousavi and Karroubi, given their well-known reformist tendencies. The most probable explanation is that while Khamenei still wanted Ahmadinejad to serve a second term, he was also fully aware of the public discontent with the president's policies and wished to sate the public's thirst for change by indicating that the Islamic system was still politically pluralist and that the voters could have a relatively diverse choice of candidates.

The election results, however, proved to be highly controversial. The pragmatist and reformist coalition argued that they had won the election, based on exit polls and the high level of voter turnout at their rallies. Yet shortly after the vote count, but before the customary declaration of the results by the Council of Guardians, Khamenei broke his normal political silence on election results to declare Ahmadinejad as the victor and "a blessing from God."[47] This statement provoked a showdown between the conservative camp and the pragmatist-reformist coalition, whose leaders, including Khatami, Mousavi, Karroubi, and Rafsanjani, now turned publicly against the government. They condemned Ahmadinejad's election as "fraudulent" and alleged that his victory was a result of vote rigging. By extension, they were also challenging the authority of the Supreme Leader, who had thrown his support so publicly behind Ahmadinejad.[48]

The supporters of the coalition, the bulk of which were young people of the postrevolution generation, poured onto the streets in peaceful protests, inaugurating what became known as the Green Movement. Protests of this size had not been seen since the revolution thirty years before. Many who took part or followed the movement believed that it heralded a second revolution, this time against the conservative clerics' monopoly of power, if not the Islamic system as a whole.[49] In haste and with a sense of panic, under the command of the Supreme Leader, the government resolved to crush the uprisings in order to prevent a repeat of the revolutionary mobilizations that had led to the downfall of the Shah's regime.

The bloody crackdown, involving the Sepah and Basij, resulted in the killing of dozens of people and the arrests of hundreds more, most of them coalition supporters. Government censorship prevented the Iranian official print and electronic networks from broadcasting the events, but the Iranian reformist publications, foreign news networks (especially the BBC), and social media revealed the extent of the protests and the ensuing bloodshed. During the 1978–79 revolution, the BBC and other foreign media outlets had played a vital role in reporting events in Iran to the wider world and enabling Iranians to circumvent the official state media. This time, their role was supplemented by social media, which served as a critical means of informing and connecting opposition groups and documenting the violence of the repression, as protestors shared raw images and videos of bleeding and dying protestors on Facebook and other platforms. Khamenei branded the protestors as conspirators working at the behest of foreign enemies of the Islamic Republic to subvert it from within.[50]

Mousavi and Karroubi were subsequently put under house arrest, where they remain to date, although under less severe conditions since 2013. Some one hundred opposition figures were also thrown into jail. Many were from the Central Council of the AAC, such as Khatami's former vice-president Mohammad-Ali Abtahi and Karroubi. Others were members of the reformist Jebhe-ye Mosharekat Iran-e Islami (Islamic Iran Participation Front), including the former deputy foreign minister Mohsen Aminzadeh (one of the party's founding members) and Mohammad Reza Khatami, an erstwhile party leader and brother of the former president. Abtahi was released within a year after making a public confession of guilt, which many claimed was made under duress. Aminzadeh was kept in prison until his transfer to a hospital for treatment in 2012.[51] In the eyes of many in Iran and the international community, Khamenei's handling of the situation revealed him to be no less of an oppressor than the Shah. While at least one commentator in the US labeled Khamenei "the new Shah,"[52] in Iran, Mousavi declared that the crackdown showed that "the roots of despotism" still remained even after the Revolution.[53] The splits between the *jihadis* and *ijtihadis*, and between the "sovereignty of God" and the "sovereignty of the people," were now so deep and so public that they seriously threatened the legitimacy of the regime.

By and large, Iranian politics during Ahmadinejad's two terms witnessed "a progressive shift of the Iranian Revolution from popular republicanism to absolute theocratic sovereignty."[54] Yet the 2009 election also highlighted a second schism within the conservative faction itself. Several powerful elements, most notably the faction of the Supreme Leader and the Majles Speaker Ali Larijani, moved to limit Ahmadinejad's autonomy and reinforce their hold on state power.[55] Aware of these machinations, the president made some overtures to the *ijtihadi* and pragmatist clusters. Between 2009 and 2012, several clear signs of dissent within the conservative cluster surfaced, with a split emerging between the ultraconservatives, who emphasized the Islamic character of the polity and rallied behind Khamenei, and supporters of Ahmadinejad's Iranian-Islamic nationalist rhetoric.[56] By 2012, the rift between the Supreme Leader and the president had widened to such an extent that there was a complete breakdown of communication between the two, as neither trusted the other.

This distrust was reflected in Khamenei's growing tendency to intervene in Ahmadinejad's political decisions. For instance, when Ahmadinejad dismissed the minister of intelligence, Heydar Moslehi, in April 2011, the Supreme Leader reinstated him.[57] At one point, the president disappeared without any explanation for two weeks. It was rumored he was in Tehran securing a "dirt file" on Khamenei's son Mojtaba, who had initially backed Ahmadinejad in the 2009 election but had since grown disillusioned with him. A hard-line cleric with a reportedly vast fortune (most of it allegedly gained from illicit activities),[58] Mojtaba is said to harbor ambitions to succeed his father. Whatever the truth of these claims, Ahmadinejad could never seriously contest the Supreme Leader's control of the very organs of state power that he had helped to grow and strengthen during the period of his presidency, regardless of his efforts to cultivate a network of supporters within the system as Khamenei had done.[59] The Sepah and the Basij, the *bonyads*, and the *artesh*, all of whose leaders owe their appointment to the Supreme Leader and are therefore loyal to him, continue to exercise greater influence in the political, economic, and social life of Iran than its popularly elected president. Among these forces, the Sepah in particular assumed a more powerful and pervasive role in the Iranian polity during Ahmadinejad's presidency than ever before.[60]

Given Ahmadinejad's possession of government secrets, including information about the allegedly illegal activities of Khamenei's son, and the network of supporters that he had built within the conservative forces inside and outside the government during his presidency, Khamenei tactfully opted to keep him inside the tent after the completion of his term as president. In August 2013, the Supreme

Leader appointed him a member of the Expediency Council, a position that he holds to the present day. However, this show of appearances could not hide the growing rift between the two and Khamenei's increased displeasure with the former president. When Ahmadinejad indicated in September 2016 an interest in running again for presidency in the June 2017 election, the Supreme Leader resolutely barred him from doing so.[61] Ahmadinejad registered to run in the election anyway, but was, unsurprisingly, disqualified by the Council of Guardians.[62]

At the close of Ahmadinejad's second term, Iran was in a dire situation. It suffered from severe stagflation, an almost depleted national treasury, crippling sanctions, growing discord between its two tiers of government, and more power in the hands of coercive organs of the state. The country was now also deeply embroiled in costly operations in the Syrian conflict, providing increasing financial, economic, and military assistance to Iran's only strategic ally in the Arab world, the regime of Bashar al-Assad, against its many internal opponents. It also had to bear the cost of maintaining Iran's proxy Hezbollah force in Lebanon, while facing the threat of military action from Israel and the United States over its nuclear program. The scene was once again set for the Iranian political pendulum to swing back toward the *ijtihadi* pole.

ROUHANI'S ANTI-EXTREMISM

Ahmadinejad's presidency generated the need for a degree of political reinvention to make the Islamic system more palatable domestically and internationally. The tenth presidential election, which was held on June 14, 2013, provided the opportunity. The Supreme Leader and his supporters might have preferred the election of a conservative, but they were also conscious of the fact that the Iranian electorate harbored widespread disillusionment with conservative rule. They were also wary of the fact that the Islamic Republic had become entangled in more foreign policy complications than it could afford. As a result, they found it expedient to allow the election results to reflect the will of the people, considering this the most effective way to dampen public discontent and ease Western pressure on Iran. From the ten original presidential candidates that the Council of Guardians approved, including one conservative and one reformist who dropped out prior to the election, the reformist- and pragmatist-backed moderate cleric, Rouhani, emerged triumphant. Rouhani's success was primarily due to his moderate reformist stance. He had campaigned on the promise of combating extremism, improving the living conditions—economic, social, and also to an extent political—of all Iranians, and developing a foreign policy that would support his domestic reformist agenda.

Rouhani assumed office on August 3, 2013, as a highly seasoned, experienced, and deft *ijtihadi*-inclined clerical and political figure. A widely respected academic, diplomat, political activist, and British-educated lawyer with a doctoral degree, he had a long and intimate association with the Islamic system, and operated within the *jihadi-ijtihadi* framework of the Ruhaniyyat Islamism laid down by Khomeini, from the early days of the Islamic Republic. He had risen through the ranks of the Islamic state apparatus, serving in a range of positions in the Assembly of Experts, the Expediency Council, and the Supreme National Security Council, of which he was also secretary from 1989 to 2005. Further, he had been an elected member of the Majles, serving as deputy speaker twice. He also possessed diplomatic experience, having served as an economic and trade negotiator and as Iran's chief nuclear negotiator under Khatami. He headed the Center for Strategic Research—Iran's premier think tank for influential policymakers—from 1992 until the beginning of his presidency and authored several monographs with a focus on Iran's foreign relations and its place in world politics.[63] More important, he had maintained effective organizational ties with the Supreme Leader and good working relationships with all other factions in Iranian politics. As such, Khamenei viewed him as a loyal insider and competent interlocutor, capable of strengthening the regime by reconnecting it to its original popular base and improving its international standing. Rouhani was therefore a figure whom all factions in the Islamic system could respect, although to varying degrees, and who could be trusted by the Supreme Leader.

Rouhani was now well placed to address a set of problems that required political tact, ingenuity, and creativity if he were to fulfill his election campaign promises. After eight years of Ahmadinejad's hard-line policies, the Islamic Republic of Iran was in a dire predicament on many fronts. This was partly due to its international isolation over its nuclear program, which had emerged as the critical issue in Iran's relations with the West, particularly the US. After assembling a reform-minded cabinet, which included Zarif, a US-educated and highly experienced diplomat, whom he appointed as foreign minister with the endorsement of the Supreme Leader and the conservative Majles, Rouhani identified four priorities for his government: to improve social and economic living conditions for the Iranian people; to engage the West, and the United States in particular, in pursuit of a settlement of the nuclear dispute that would safeguard Iran's right to uranium enrichment for peaceful purposes; to uphold the rights of ethnic and religious minorities and initiate a "civil rights charter"; and to relax political and social controls and secure the release of political prisoners.[64]

As a matter of urgency, he found it imperative to pursue two intertwined goals simultaneously: political and socioeconomic reforms and the lifting of Western sanctions. To do this, he needed to chart a new direction for Iran to achieve foreign policy breakthroughs, especially with the United States, which in turn would earn him points on the domestic front. The task that he set for his government was difficult and laborious but not insurmountable.

To stabilize the economy, and the Iranian currency rial in particular, whose value had significantly fallen, Rouhani needed to engage in structural reforms involving tighter fiscal and monetary measures. They included reining in the money supply, which had ballooned, fueling high inflation under Ahmadinejad, as well as devising a more effective tax system and overhauling the oil industry, for which Iran was in dire need of technological and financial investment. To attract this investment and to diversify the economy and Iran's trade links, he also needed to streamline bureaucratic processes and reduce red tape, as well as address inefficiency, patronage, and corruption in the governmental system and the public service.[65] At the same time, he needed to end food and fuel subsidies and reduce public spending while expanding the private sector.

In addition, it was imperative for Rouhani to curtail the activities and influence of forces such as the Sepah, the Basij, and the *bonyads*, which have a vested interest in the preservation of the existing factional power balance. At the same time, he also had to be adept at tackling or warding off the conservative factions within the Majles, around the Supreme Leader, and throughout the governmental system in ways that could enable him to implement his reforms. Moreover, he needed to expand political and civil liberties and improve the rights of the restless minorities, which had overwhelmingly voted for him in the elections and formed a major base for his presidential ascendancy. Above all, he was required to reach an accommodation with the United States and its European allies over Iran's nuclear program in order to end sanctions, which would help him with his domestic reforms and open the way for a possible US-Iranian rapprochement. Without it, he was unlikely to be able to attract the capital and technological resources necessary to implement his domestic reforms.

Rouhani therefore deemed it highly appropriate to give priority to the foreign policy objectives so crucial for the implementation of his domestic agenda. He launched a concerted diplomatic effort and a so-called charm offensive to secure a resolution of the nuclear issue and to reassure Iran's Arab neighbors of his commitment to a peaceful nuclear program and cordial relations. Interestingly, the Supreme Leader was now willing to support Rouhani on his endeavors, both at home and abroad—a privilege that Rafsanjani and Khatami were not accorded (the latter more so than the former). This was for two main reasons. First, Khamenei's long experience, after twenty-two years at the helm, had left him confident in his capacity to handle any adverse or unforeseen situation that Rouhani's initiatives might create. Second, Khamenei could not think of a better way out of the predicament in which Iran was placed than Rouhani's intertwined domestic and foreign policy approach. He had previously echoed Khomeini's assertion that Iran would never produce nuclear weapons because they were "un-Islamic." Now, he not only reemphasized this position in support of Rouhani's efforts but also personally defended the president against his conservative critics whenever he deemed appropriate.[66] However, his support came with a clear caveat. Iran would not forgo its right to develop its nuclear program for nonmilitary purposes, and would not capitulate to the West over its national and security interests. For the first time, the Supreme Leader and the Iranian president had voiced a common position on the nuclear issue.

The Supreme Leader's backing proved crucial in determining what Rouhani has achieved in his domestic and foreign policy goals. On the nuclear issue, it enabled the president to pursue negotiations, the end result of which was the July 14, 2015, Joint Comprehensive Plan of Action with the five permanent members of the UN Security Council plus Germany. The agreement, which materialized after two years of negotiations, committed Iran to reducing its nuclear program to a level that would satisfy the international powers' concerns over Iran's military capabilities without compromising the country's pursuit of nuclear energy for peaceful purposes. In return, the Western powers, most importantly their main leader, the United States, agreed to lift sanctions, which they began to do in January 2016, as discussed in detail in chapter 7.

Meanwhile, Rouhani moved urgently to unfold a number of reforms aimed at fostering economic and sociopolitical cohesion in the country. While a detailed analysis of his economic reforms must wait until chapter 5, at this stage it is important to mention one of his signature moves, which carried strong national political undertones—the creation of a Charter of Citizens' Rights, which he had promised to undertake as one of his first actions in office. While the charter was by no means groundbreakingly liberal, it nonetheless provided a basis for reassuring national minorities—Arabs, Azeris, Bahais, Baluchis, Kurds, and Turks—and may therefore provide a cornerstone for developing a robust and pluralistic civil society within Khomeini's Islamic framework. Article 15 of the charter states:

> Citizens have equal right to participate in determining their political, economic, social and cultural destiny, and may exercise this right in free and fair elections or referendums.[67]

In addition, Article 13 adds: "No authority shall, in the name of security, violate or threaten legitimate rights and freedoms of citizens and their human dignity and integrity."

Rouhani's Charter of Citizens' Rights was officially launched on December 19, 2016, and drew mixed responses.[68] While conservative hard-liners criticized the document for being a distraction from the real (i.e., economic) issues, reformists and pragmatists broadly welcomed it. Some, however, criticized Rouhani for speaking of abstract rights while failing to curb actual abuses, particularly those committed by agencies controlled by the Supreme Leader, such as the Ministry of Intelligence.[69] Furthermore, some rights groups have derided the charter as "toothless," pointing out that much of its provisions can be overridden by existing laws. Article 26, for example, guarantees that "every citizen has a right to freedom of speech and expression," but adds that "this right shall be exercised within the limits prescribed by law."[70] Although the document is not yet legally binding and Rouhani has not succeeded in fulfilling his other promised political reform to secure the release of political prisoners, including of Mousavi and Karroubi from their ongoing detention under house arrest, it may nonetheless provide a basis for political and social change over time.

The political presence of the reformist and pragmatist camps has never been more commanding than in Rouhani's era. They have forged a strong organizational base of support in the Hezb-e E'tedāl va Towse'e (Moderation and Development Party). Founded in 1999, this party today has a stronger presence in the executive, legislature, and Assembly of Experts than ever before, although it is not yet able to outweigh the conservative cluster's dominance in the system.

On May 20, 2017, Rouhani was reelected, defeating the main conservative candidate, Ebrahim Raisi, a cleric closely identified with the Supreme Leader and touted as his possible successor. Rouhani's second victory was as decisive as his first, dispensing with the need for a run-off election. During his inauguration ceremony on August 3, 2017, in which he received once again the Supreme Leader's blessing, Rouhani reiterated his resolve to persist with his reform agenda, including enhancing Iran's cooperation with other states. He also expressed a willingness to launch the "mother of all negotiations," while chastising the new US Trump administration for its hostile attitude toward Iran and for seeking to undermine the nuclear agreement of July 2015.[71]

The Post-Revolutionary Generation

The third issue facing Khamenei was how to deal with the growing postrevolution generation. Iran is the most populous state in the Gulf. Its population has doubled since 1978, to just over eighty million people, more than half of whom are aged under thirty. This new generation of Iranians has either little or no recollection of Khomeini or the Iranian Revolution or, for that matter, Iran's transformation from a secular, autocratic monarchy into an Islamic Republic. This is not to claim that the public is not constantly reminded of Khomeini. His writings, tape and video orations, and publications about him remain compulsory content in seminaries, schools, colleges, and universities. He also still looms large over the nation with his commanding photos, either alone or together with those of the current Supreme Leader, on display in public squares, shops, factories, institutions, and homes throughout Iran. Iran's official media outlets, educational curricula, and religious institutions extol him not only as the founder of the Islamic Republic but also as a Shia religious leader whose sacrifices and achievements for Iran demand the reverence and adulation of all its citizens.

However, it is clear that he has increasingly become an abstract and removed historical figure to Iranians who were either very young during the revolution or born after the events. Among these Iranians today, especially in urban areas, Khomeini's Islamic political legacy is widely perceived as stifling, suffocating, regressive, and anti-modern. This critique, expressed more often in private than in public settings (for obvious reasons), sees Khomeini's Islamic order as a key impediment to Iran's cultural, economic, and national potential as a nation rich in resources and manpower.[72] It argues that had it not been for his establishment of such a highly personalized Islamic framework, Iran could have been a far more powerful and respectable regional and international actor than it has managed to become since 1979. Most of Khomeini's critics are young but generally well informed and connected with other young people across the country and the world. They harbor a strong desire for political, social, and artistic freedom, economic prosperity, and a life free of theocratic restrictions and clerical domination.[73] This is reflected in Iran's vibrant underground (and increasingly public) youth movements, which have demonstrated considerable ingenuity in circumventing official censorship in music, creative art, and writing.[74] Despite its determination to keep a lid on dissent, the ruling clerical stratum has not been all that successful. For reasons of expediency or under pressure from the public, it has instead found itself with little choice but to loosen social and cultural control to some extent over time. Grassroots opposition and artistic resistance among the youth have been and will continue to be an important factor in moderating the theocratic dimension of the Islamic Republic.

The scale of youth participation in the Green Movement has not been lost on Khamenei and the conservative cluster, given the changes in the demographic composition of Iranian society since the consolidation of the Islamic system in the 1980s. Khamenei's strategy of allowing pragmatist and reformist clusters to contest and win elections has been the chief way in which he has attempted to cater to the demands of the postrevolution generation. He and his ruling apparatus have shown themselves conscious of the need to include this generation in the politics and running of the country in order to supplement but not surpass the workings of the regime's cadres, who act as its guardians. Indeed, some of the youths of the postrevolution generation have already been incorporated into these cadres, attracted in part by the perks and privileges of membership in organizations such as the Basij. In addition, if one looks at the series of cabinets since Rafsanjani, the trend toward the appointment of progressively younger and well-educated people at different state levels is clearly visible. Similarly, although the morality police still seek to enforce Islamic codes of dress and social behavior, its activities have become increasingly sporadic. Compared to the early phase of the revolution, Iranians today are left alone in their attire and public comportment, so long as this does not pose a serious threat to the Islamic regime. This has involved growing social and cultural nonconformity.

The Islamic Republic has even become beset by a culture of drugs, rock and roll, temporary marriage, and prostitution. Temporary marriages (*sigheh*), for example, have become a concept almost promulgated by officials "as a possible solution to the problems of Iran's youth" that is legal and in accordance with the religious establishment's rulings as a Shia religious practice.[75] In recent years, these marriages have begun to be arranged online.[76] Meanwhile, many scholars have written about the role of pop, rock, and electronic music as expressions of cosmopolitan cultural identification as well as forms of political resistance among Iran's youth.[77] As the number of rock bands and concerts has increased under Rouhani, state censorship of foreign media has been somewhat relaxed. Whereas foreign television networks such as the BBC and CNN (Cable News Network) were blocked until 2015, a year later the BBC was available to interview guests in a hotel like the Parsian Esteghlal International Hotel in Tehran. Some of these measures merely authorize what Iranians had been doing illegally for years. For instance, many Iranian households learned how to get around the government's ban on satellite dishes, allowing them to access foreign broadcasts and telecasts. While attempting to control foreign social media platforms such as Facebook, Twitter, and Instagram, the authorities have learned that it is better not to punish those who access them. Indeed, many political figures use them, despite their official bans.

All of this means that the pluralist dimension of the theocratic system has been used by the Supreme Leader and conservative echelons whenever needed to ensure the longevity of the system within a reinventive and flexible wheel. As such, the Supreme Leader has pursued a policy of give-and-take in a *jihadi-ijtihadi* fashion to control the Islamic system, manage factional in-fighting, deflect threats to the existing order arising from within or outside, and co-opt and accommodate the postrevolution generation as far as possible. This strategy has worked so far and may continue to remain the case in the conduct of the Islamic Republic's politics for the foreseeable future. At the same time, the forces of reform have gained momentum, requiring the leadership to be increasingly cognizant of them in a changing national and international environment.

5

Resource Capabilities

The ability of a state to influence its internal and external settings in pursuit of its national interests depends not only on the nature of its political system and policy orientation but also on its ability to harness the necessary resources to convert this into action and into policy outcomes. In other words, the extent of a state's capability to mobilize the required "input" to achieve a desired "output" or outcome can serve as a good indication of that state's strengths and weaknesses. In a hierarchical approach, as explained in the chapter 1, economic, military, and "soft-power" resource capabilities underpin a state's success and failure not only in maintaining a viable domestic order but also in exerting influence beyond its borders. However, such capabilities are not always easy to quantify, and this is especially true in relation to a country like the Islamic Republic of Iran, for which precise and accurate data is not readily available. Most of the existing data carries a good margin of error, underestimation, or exaggeration, depending on the source. The best that can be done in these circumstances is to corroborate the available sources as much as possible in order to demonstrate the extent of the Islamic Republic's resource capabilities as a basis for its ability to project power. This chapter examines the Islamic Republic's economic, "hard-power," and "soft-power" resource capabilities, in order to evaluate their significance in underpinning the Islamic Republic's regional and international relations in chapters 6 and 7.

The Economy

Since the revolution, the Islamic Republic has followed a state-led, oil-dependent, or rentier, model of economic development, as had been pursued by the Shah's regime before it. It has achieved what can be described as an upper-middle-income economy.[1] By 2016, it had a GDP of $412.2 billion and a population of just over eighty million, making it the second-largest economy with the second-largest population in the Middle East and North Africa (MENA) region.[2] However, the Republic's growth has been volatile. From 1999 to 2006, Iran's GDP grew by an average of 5.8 percent per annum, while in 2012, it shrank by 6.6 percent.[3] An estimated 40 percent of the population remains below the unofficial poverty line (defined as an annual income of $900 for a family of five), although absolute poverty is almost nonexistent.[4] Iran's economy is characterized by fluctuating periods of growth and sharp decline, due to structural imbalances, international sanctions, institutionalized factional competition spilling into economic spheres, and political involvement in economic activities. Unemployment and inflation have been two perennial problems. Inflation reached as high as 40 percent in 2013, as US-led sanctions targeted Iran's oil exports and President Mahmoud Ahmadinejad pursued profligate fiscal policies, although it has been reined in to 9.5 percent under President Hassan Rouhani.[5] Unemployment, on the other hand, has remained above 10 percent since 1979. Estimates from government data put it at 14 percent for 2016, and 32 percent among youth aged fifteen to twenty-four, although the real figures may well be higher.[6]

The Islamic Republic's uneven economic development reflects the severe strains imposed on the country since 1979. Iran's successive presidential administrations have sought to address these strains in different ways and with varying degrees of success. The most salient of these deserve a closer analysis to reveal the strength and weakness of the economy as a basis for evaluating Iran's capabilities as a player in the region and beyond.

WAR ECONOMY

The first is the war economy, which Iran endured for eight years of conflict with Iraq (1980–88). The economy and all national policy priorities were geared to support the country's war efforts. During this period, restrictive policies—most notably price controls, import limitations, and subsidies—were introduced to ensure a functioning economy that provided reliable if diminished livelihood for Iranians. The government adopted a policy of import substitution industrialization and a multiple exchange system to free up foreign currency to purchase military equipment and resources. The war focus meant that investment in other areas of the economy declined. Gross domestic investment fell by an average of 6.6 percent per year. As the war dragged on, materiel and parts shortages reduced productivity, with some industries only working at 30 percent capacity.

The decline in oil prices in the 1980s also undermined economic growth, increasing deficits (which reached 44 percent of government spending and 9 percent of GDP by 1988) and leading to an inescapable reduction in government expenditure.[7] Overall, GDP fell by 1.8 percent a year in this period, with income per person declining by 55 percent compared to the 1977–78 level. Downward pressure on per capita incomes was exacerbated by high population growth, pushed by Ayatollah Khomeini's pro-natalist policies.[8] The war caused an estimated $592 billion in economic damage to Iran.[9] In addition, Iran lost more than half a million of its young in the fighting, with a lasting impact on the country's trained manpower and national development. When the conflict ended, the task of postwar recovery confronted successive presidents as Iran's most urgent priority.

POPULISM AND REFORM

The pragmatist president Hashemi Rafsanjani sought to tackle this issue by instituting the first Five Year Development Plan (1989–94). The plan focused on investing in government spending.[10] These conditions were exacerbated by an abortive attempt to unify the multiple exchange rates, which led to a rapid depreciation of the rial and forced the reintroduction of a dual, and then multiple, system of foreign trade and reserve limits.

Between 1993 and 1994, oil prices fell further, leading to a 30 percent decline in oil revenue. That, together with increases in domestic consumer demand (reflected in imports), exceeded export revenues and led to negative terms of trade, balance of payment problems, and increased debt, which reached 11.4 percent of GDP by 1997.[11] Rafsanjani's second Five Year Development Plan (1994–99) did little to improve the declining situation. Not only was the president frustrated in his pragmatic efforts toward reform, because they were resisted by elements of the conservative camp, but he, his family, and several high-ranking government figures were also embroiled in public scandals for corruption and nepotism, as was detailed in chapter 4.

In light of Rafsanjani's experience, his successor, the reformist president Mohammad Khatami, opted for a gradual, incremental approach to economic reform. As mentioned in chapter 4, he favored political and social reform, believing it would pave the way for economic reform. The third Five Year Development Plan (2000–2005) continued the process of measured liberalization: eliminating import and export restrictions in favor of a more rationalized tariff system, reforming the tax system, and defining a legal framework for foreign direct investment (FDI). An important policy was the establishment of the Oil Stabilization Fund, a sovereign wealth fund fed by profits from oil exports to insulate the Iranian economy from oil-price volatility. The plan also reformed the banking sector (lifting the ban on private banks) and, most importantly, unified the multiple exchange rates into a single, floating exchange rate.[12] Although the economy was often considered a weakness of Khatami's presidency, he introduced a number of reforms that structurally improved its balance, which between 1999 and 2006 grew by an average of 5.8 percent a year.[13] By 2005, Iran's per capita GDP had returned to its prerevolutionary peak of 1976.[14] However, Khatami was unable to overcome institutional and conservative opposition to subsidy reform, although energy subsidies accounted for 17.5 percent of GDP in 2006, while food subsidies consumed 7.5 percent of GDP in the same year.[15]

By the beginning of Ahmadinejad's presidency, all members of the political stratum had acknowledged that subsidy reform was a ticking time bomb. Ahmadinejad had campaigned on a populist platform of redistribution, promising to portion out the oil wealth to all ordinary Iranians, as he championed the cause of *mosta'zafin*. While his initial plan to cut subsidies to 90 percent of market prices was rejected by the Majles, a compromise reform was passed that cut $20 billion in energy subsidies, replacing them with payments to low-income groups. Ahmadinejad reversed the emerging economic liberalization policies enacted by his predecessors, adopting an interventionist and populist approach. He shut down the Development Plan Authority and subordinated the economy to military and security interests and overt political objectives. These actions increased rentierism and corruption while enabling the military and other deep-state actors, such as the IRGC, to expand involvement in the economy. By 2013, the IRGC controlled an estimated 21 percent of the Tehran Stock Exchange's listed value.[16]

Ahmadinejad's aggressive rhetoric toward Israel and the West, along with his management of the nuclear issue, resulted in the imposition of UN sanctions against Iran in 2010, with additional, intensified US-led Western measures in 2012. As a result, oil exports plummeted from 2.3 million barrels per day (mbpd) in 2011 to 1.2 mbpd in 2012 and less than 1 mbpd in 2013,[17] costing the Iranian government an estimated $133 million a day in revenues. The rial tumbled to half its value and inflation spiraled to an official rate of 31.5 percent. This in turn increased the cost of basic goods—the price of vegetables increased by 81 percent and chicken by 74 percent by October 2012.[18] High inflation produced goods shortages reminiscent of the 1980s, epitomized in the so-called chicken crisis, in which a nationwide shortage of chicken due to falling supplies of feedstock produced civil unrest.[19] Ahmadinejad maintained a dual rate system with a preferable fixed exchange rate for the rial, which was highly overvalued in order to keep imports and consumer goods cheaply available to the government and its favored companies or individuals. This approach, ironically, increased the country's dependence on global markets as the artificially supported exchange rate undermined the efficiency and competitiveness of domestic production and manufacturing, while the dual rates had disastrous economic effects on imports including for essentials such as pharmaceuticals and foodstuffs.

In terms of monetary policy, the state reversed previous reforms reducing government regulation of the banking sector and took control of the Central Bank. It maintained low interest rates, which were extended to make borrowing easier for lower-income groups. However, the special rates offered by some banks discouraged savings and investment and intensified already-high inflation. They created a proliferation of nonperforming loans that had to be written off, adding to government debt, and constituted an underlying threat to Iran's economy that continues to this day. The entire lending market was distorted: interest rates skyrocketed for liquidity-starved banks seeking to attract capital but dropped for other institutions. By 2013, the rial was worth only 50 percent of its 2010 value. This occurred despite the fact that oil and gas exports, which make up 80 percent of the country's total export earnings and 60 to 70 percent of the Iranian government's revenues, actually rose between 2008 and 2011 on the back of increased international demand and Middle East volatility, generating revenues of $75–$95 billion a year.

Under Ahmadinejad, GDP growth fell from 6.9 percent in 2005 to 3.7 percent and −6.6 percent in 2011 and 2012. Unemployment among women and young people (the under-twenty-fives, the generation of the post–Iraq War baby boom) increased, while the overall labor force declined from 41 percent of the working-age population in 2005 to 37.3 percent in 2012, demonstrating the government's inability to keep job creation in line with demographic trends. By the end of Ahmadinejad's presidency in 2013, Iran's official year-on-year inflation rate was estimated to be 40 percent and its unemployment rate 12.9 percent (14.9 percent in urban areas), although the real rates for both were probably closer to 30–40 percent and increasing as Western sanctions accelerated.[20] Youth unemployment rates became particularly acute, possibly doubling the official figure of 25 percent.[21]

Ahmadinejad spent too much time and resources on pet projects, notably the Maskan-e Mehr housing project, which promised to construct 600,000 low-income homes across Iran. However, his use of cheap credit to fund the project in the midst of a credit crisis "had a devastating impact on the economy."[22] His use of the Central Bank to provide easy money to low-income families and to fund his populist initiatives, especially in rural areas, "was emblematic of his approach to economic policy: populist, redistributive initiatives [that] turn[ed] into a herd of white elephants."[23]

President Rouhani inherited a weak and unstable economy with negative growth and high debt, inflation, and unemployment. In addition to existing structural weaknesses in the economy, his administration had to contend with rapidly falling oil prices and a substantially diminished national GDP.[24] He had little choice but to begin by acting upon his campaign promises to repair the economic issues resulting from Ahmadinejad's policies. During his first term, Rouhani's economic policy primarily focused on stabilizing macroeconomic indicators and encouraging growth through a more disciplined fiscal policy, structural reform, and anti-corruption initiatives. He spent the first two years of his presidency improving fiscal discipline and staving off a recession. A major task was to reduce inflation. To this end, he adopted a pro-austerity approach, as reflected in the 2015 budget, which outlined reductions in government spending (particularly on subsidies), an increase in taxes, and continued privatization.[25] At the same time, he reviewed and rescinded many of the populist policies enacted under Ahmadinejad, including the Maskan-e Mehr housing project,[26] as well as the substitution of cash payments for subsidies. In the case of subsidy reform, the government launched a campaign to encourage wealthier Iranians to voluntarily withdraw from the program while also introducing residency and income requirements that excluded Iranians living overseas from receiving benefits.[27]

In addition, Rouhani sought to promote domestic production and diversification while also improving the business environment. In this, he tried to enact broader structural reforms designed to promote long-term growth and to prepare Iran for its reintegration into international markets. In particular, he focused on attracting foreign investment and technology transfer as key to stimulating economic conditions and on improving the efficiency and productivity of domestic industries. This has not been, coincidentally, consonant with the Supreme Leader's conservative rhetoric of a "resistance economy," which insists on economic self-sufficiency.[28] As a result, in 2015, tax revenues outstripped oil exports as a revenue source.[29] In the same year, Iran achieved a positive balance of trade from non-oil exports, with a trade surplus of $916 million.[30] Rouhani has used these outcomes to claim that his administration "is the least oil dependent ever."[31] Critics, however, note that the surplus was a result of economic contraction, with imports and exports shrinking by 25 percent and 18 percent, respectively, compared to the previous year.[32] Furthermore, falling imports were tied to weaker economic conditions because they indicated lower demand from local manufacturers.

Finally, Rouhani's economic policies focused, at least rhetorically, on fighting corruption. According to Transparency International's Corruption Perceptions Index, the Islamic Republic ranked 29th out of 100 countries surveyed in 2016.[33] A 2016 report by the World Justice Project ranked Iran 86th in the world, up thirteen places from the previous year and ahead of Turkey (99th) and Lebanon (89th), but below the United Arab Emirates (UAE) (33rd), Jordan (42nd), and Tunisia (58th).[34] Corruption in Iran stems from several major sources—international sanctions, which encourage black market and illicit activity; state control and involvement in the economy, particularly among conservative elites and the IRGC; oil rentierism and property speculation; and a lack of transparency and accountability mechanisms. While there have been several high-profile corruption prosecutions since 2013—notably the execution in May 2014 of Mahafarid Amir Khosravi, a billionaire businessman convicted for his part in a 2011 $2.6 billion embezzlement scandal[35]—Rouhani's anti-corruption drives have faced significant resistance from the conservative factions and the IRGC, whose major economic interests have been threatened by these reforms. The parliamentary elections in February 2016, however, gave Rouhani a Majles with a solid reformist bloc that could be more receptive to passing his economic reforms, although this was not assured, given the stalwart opposition from conservative opponents.[36]

In late 2015, Rouhani shifted toward a more Keynesian approach, introducing a $2.5 billion stimulus package to be invested in infrastructure and development projects in a bid to boost growth.[37] Although the announcement of the package was timed with a view to upcoming parliamentary elections in February 2016, it nonetheless reflected concerns about sluggish growth rates affected by low oil prices, delayed foreign investment, and weaker-than-expected growth in the global economy. In another sign of this shift toward spending, the budget proposal for 2017 envisioned an increase in government expenditure, totaling $328 billion, with much of the increase projected to come from a rise in oil revenues from production and price jumps, as well as from improving growth and production due to the removal of sanctions.[38] However, Iran requires a price of about $110–$130 per barrel to balance its budget, which is not likely to eventuate in the foreseeable future. Meanwhile, Rouhani has sought to limit the power of the IRGC and *bonyads*, especially in the economy, and to rescind their tax-exempt status, although with not much success so far, given the pervasive influence of these organizations and their close links with the conservative forces in the country.

POOR ECONOMIC MANAGEMENT

Three features of the Islamic Republic political structures are key to explaining the poor management of the Iranian economy. One is the bifurcation of the political system into two tiers, which has given birth to a multitude of competing and sometimes conflicting institutions. The system of parallel institutions has amplified factional infighting, competition over resources, and waste from duplication. It has also created an environment characterized by a lack of transparency and accountability. These developments are exacerbated by the state's large, unwieldy, and inefficient bureaucracy, equally a feature and legacy of the Shah's state-led modernization program. Rigid labor regulations, such as the 1990 Labour Law, which heavily penalizes employers for laying off workers,[39] have posed a further barrier to raising economic efficiency or productivity.

Another is the ethos of state-led development—with its focus on full employment and social welfare, rather than efficiency—which means that state-owned enterprises (SOEs) tend to maintain inefficient arrangements of overemployment. This, combined with the preferential treatment that SOEs receive, removes incentives to increase efficiency, productivity, and competitiveness. As a result, SOEs are often unprofitable, usually running large budget deficits that need to be subsidized by the government. The problem is compounded because the government and its affiliated organs, including, most importantly the IRGC and *bonyads*, remain the main economic actors, ultimately controlling up to 70 percent of the economy.[40] Thus, both the state bureaucracy and SOEs impose a significant burden on the government's budget and sap much of the country's potential economic vitality. Privatization has failed to change the nature of the state's involvement and control over the economy because it has largely advantaged political insiders, resulting in the transfer of state enterprises to parastatal organizations and individuals linked to the ruling elite, who are, after all, the only actors with the capital available to buy privatized enterprises. In this regard, privatization has simply reinforced existing distorted economic conditions and strengthened oligarchical interests.

A third feature is the size and dominance of the public sector, which has produced a restricted environment for foreign investment. Parvin Alizadeh calls this the "structural trap," in which "political and economic obstacles avert the reallocation of capital from low productivity firms to high productivity ones."[41] A bloated bureaucracy and expansive statist intervention thus produce over-regulation. Iran's private sector is correspondingly weak, due to the nationalization of most major industries following the revolution, as well as to discriminatory policies favoring large businesses owned by political elites.

In 2017, the World Bank ranked Iran 124th out of 189 countries in ease of doing business. It takes ninety-seven days to start a business and twenty-five days to process construction permits in Iran.[42] Such obstacles pose a significant problem if Iran wants to attract the foreign investment that it desperately needs. During the next decade, Iran will need an estimated $1 trillion to invest in its aging infrastructure, including in the oil industry on which its economy so heavily depends. Much of this needs to come from foreign investment, given the low levels of available domestic capital, the weakness of its non-oil sectors, and the residual impact of sanctions.[43]

POLITICAL RENTIERISM

Iran's economy is characterized by the close link between political actors and economic interests that amounts to political rentierism, which results in the subordination of economic policy to political realities. Despite the Supreme Leader's commanding position, the Iranian system still has "multiple centers of power" that involve "a ponderous process of checks and balances among different organizations." Because of this, "there is a default drift toward 'behind-the-scenes' bargaining and informal network[s]."[44] As a result, the economy has become a field of competition between different political actors struggling to maximize their share of the country's rents. The ruling strata often use their political influence, particularly through *bonyads* and the IRGC, to gain favorable contracts, subsidized imports, and cheap loans, as well as to undermine competitors through measures such as imposing regulations or increasing taxes. Like many IRGC and military-linked companies, *bonyads* are exempt from taxation and enjoy subsidized imports and preferential treatment in the allocation of contracts. The Imam Reza Foundation, for example, is worth an estimated $15 billion and is involved in car manufacturing, agriculture, and real estate.[45] Similarly, the Foundation of the Oppressed and Disabled, one of the largest *bonyads*, is a conglomerate involved in multiple economic areas, notably tourism, real estate, petrochemicals, and transportation.[46]

Here, the powerful conservative and cleric-linked elites have deployed liberalizing measures, notably privatization, to capture large parts of the economy. For example, the IRGC controls not only around one hundred commercial enterprises, which account for a large proportion of domestic production, but also banks, airports, and seaports, which allow it to control imports. These companies have a disproportionate economic influence due to their close political ties. The Khatam ul-Anbiya—a construction company that employs 55,000 members of the IRGC—has more than seven hundred holdings and earns an estimated $7 billion. It was awarded a $1.3 billion contract within a year of Ahmadinejad's election.[47] Another IRGC company, Sepasad, won a no-bid contract to construct a line in the Tehran metro in 2006.[48] The IRGC has largely been able to expand its business interests as a result of the retreat of international firms during sanctions.[49]

In addition to raising institutional obstacles to competitors, the IRGC is able to undermine competition by linking economic decisions to political and security concerns. This is exacerbated by the provision of an explicit role for the military in the economy in Article 147 of the constitution, which reads:

> In time of peace, the government must utilize the personnel and technical equipment of the Army in relief operations, and for educational and productive ends, and the Construction Jihad, while fully observing the criteria of Islamic justice and ensuring that such utilization does not harm the combat-readiness of the Army.[50]

The IRGC, for example, famously shut down in May 2004 the newly built Khomeini Airport in Tehran because its construction tender had been awarded to a Turkish-Austrian consortium. It acted in a similar way in October 2007 when a mobile phone network tender was awarded to Turkcell. Both these actions were justified on national security grounds.[51]

Political rentier behavior is problematic for two reasons. First, it impairs Iran's ability to attract foreign investment by undermining private property rights, accountability, and the fairness of the market. Second, it damages economic productivity and efficiency because politically acquired businesses are isolated from market competition, operating in an artificial "bubble" largely financed from the state budget. They are also sheltered from competitors even before bidding, which gives them a disproportionate advantage and creates a major disincentive for foreign investors. The combination of both factors has provided the conditions for a redistribution of wealth in a manner that increases inequality. At the same time, predatory rentier practices undermine the development of legitimate business and the private sector in many areas, leading to a brain drain as skilled and educated workers leave the country while creating long-term structural imbalances that are offset only by oil rents.

OIL RENTIERISM

The Iranian economy is still highly dependent on oil, which accounted for 33 percent of government revenues and 24 percent of GDP in 2014.[52] Historically, volatility in oil prices has had a significant effect on the economy. Under Ahmadinejad, for example, falling oil prices, combined with a decrease in production (due to aging infrastructure and the impact of oil-related sanctions) led to significant losses that, combined with sanctions, cost the government $41 billion in oil-related revenues between 2011 and 2013.[53]

Dependence on oil has two effects. First, the abundance of energy resources—together with populist policies—has encouraged increased and inefficient consumption. It is exacerbated by Iran's lack of refining capacities, which has resulted in the country importing refined oil to meet domestic demand. Because this form of energy is subsidized, consumers have no incentive to use it more efficiently. This became evident when import controls were removed after the Iran-Iraq War, which led to major increases in oil consumption. Moreover, this inefficiency extends to industry. Iran's energy-intensive sectors, such as oil, steel, aluminum, and petrochemicals, use two to three times more energy than in other parts of the world.[54] Due to energy subsidies, Iran has the highest consumption among members of the Organization of the Petroleum Exporting Countries. All told, an estimated $30 billion a year is lost as a result of energy waste.[55]

Second, oil rents are distributed, both through state enterprises and populist policies such as cash handouts to low socioeconomic groups, price subsidies, and price controls. Using these rents allows the state to "buy" the support of targeted sections of the population while also fostering particular expectations about the role of the state and reinforcing statist and protectionist tendencies. Further, they make the state dependent on fluctuating oil prices for revenue, allowing it to neglect the development of other sources of income, notably taxation.

The Islamic Republic's political system and rentier economy have seriously impeded the development of an effective progressive tax system. The country's inefficient taxation has developed more on the basis of political/ideological expediency than of practical needs. In 2014, taxes accounted for only 6.4 percent of GDP, a figure projected to rise to 7.8 percent in 2017.[56] One Iranian tax official stated that Iran was losing 20–25 percent of GDP ($12–$20 billion) each year from tax evasion and avoidance.[57] By comparison, US tax revenues in 2016 accounted for 26 percent of GDP.[58] In the face of ongoing fiscal inefficiency and declining oil revenue, Rouhani decided in 2014 to raise taxes and cut government expenditure. In December 2014, the Majles adopted a law to tax *bonyads* and military-linked companies. The new law was projected to raise about 10 billion rials, or $377 million, on an annual basis.[59] While part of the tax revenue was earmarked for spending on building schools in disadvantaged areas, it could not make up for the government's falling oil revenues.[60]

CAPABILITY

Iran's economy has defied the many predictions of its collapse from war, sanctions, poor economic management, and fluctuating oil prices. The country has several strengths in facing its future prospects: a large, well-educated, young labor force, a relatively diverse economy, and a strong endowment of natural resources. In particular, the lifting of sanctions, should it materialize in full, offers new opportunities. In addition to increasing oil production and revenues, it will provide Iran access to some of the assets that have been frozen overseas since the revolution. In the long term, however, it could signal Iran's progressive reintegration into the global economy. If all goes according to the reformists' plans, that should translate into increased foreign investment and greater international involvement in Iran's economy, especially in light of the 2007 amendment of Article 44 of the constitution that forbade foreign ownership of oil assets and the introduction of the new model of the Iran Petroleum Contracts in 2016, which allows more liberal foreign ownership and more stringent transfer of know-how. This would also help build support for Iran's bid to join the World Trade Organization. However, one cannot be too optimistic about all this as long as the US remains opposed to Iran.

Iran's labor force is large and well educated. Its baby boom generation is now entering the workplace which, combined with higher investments in education and health (which reduced rates of child mortality from 281 per 1,000 in 1960 to 42 per 1,000 in 2001), has contributed to a demographic "bulge" of a larger, younger generation.[61] Literacy is nearly universal (98 percent among those aged 15–24), and university graduates account for 13.3 percent of the working population (compared to 11.7 percent in Brazil and 6.9 percent in Indonesia).[62] However, the quality of Iranian education is unexceptional and its methodologies questionable—favoring rote learning and formalized testing. The result is that the Iranian education system is too focused on producing graduates with diplomas rather than providing them with necessary and relevant skills.[63]

Despite the state's dependence on oil, 50 percent of Iran's economy is in services, compared to 41 percent in industry (of which around 20 percent is oil and gas) and 9 percent in agriculture in 2015.[64] Iran's economy is relatively diverse by the standards of other oil-producing states: mining (including oil) accounts for 40 percent of GDP in Saudi Arabia and Oman, 30 percent in the UAE, and almost 50 percent in Qatar.[65] Iran has the potential to attract the investment it needs to upgrade and develop its existing industries. In particular, Iran's automobile industry is well developed and supports a wider manufacturing industry around it. In 2011, before enhanced sanctions took effect, Iran was the thirteenth-largest global producer of automobiles and, at 1.65 million cars a year, produces more of them than the UK.[66] FDI inflow has gradually grown since 2010, as political stability has led to increased investment.[67] If all the sanctions are lifted over the next ten to fifteen years, provided the JCPOA survives and no further sanctions are imposed on Iran, growth is projected to reach as high as 8 percent per year.[68]

Oil has been not just a weakness for Iran but also a lucrative source of income capable of generating capital for investment in other sectors of the economy. Iran has the fourth-largest oil reserves and the second-largest gas reserves in the world. However, 90 percent of the gas produced in Iran is currently consumed domestically as a replacement for oil. Furthermore, the potential for gas as a resource for export is limited due to the costs of building the infrastructure (pipelines) to extract it as well as to geographical considerations. However, if the development of the South Pars offshore gas field (one of the largest in the world) comes to fruition, Iran is set to become a major gas exporter.[69] On broad macroeconomic levels, Rouhani's reforms have already produced some positive results. There is a consensus that Iran's economy has lately undergone a broad process of recovery and redevelopment across many sectors.[70] However, there is a popular perception that the economy has not substantially improved under Rouhani, which may prove especially disappointing given expectations that the July 2015 nuclear deal would bring immediate and tangible benefits. In a poll conducted by the Center for International and Security Studies in 2016, 74 percent of respondents said that living conditions had not improved because of the nuclear deal, with 13 percent saying they had improved only a little. Only 12 percent responded that conditions had improved, either a lot (2 percent) or somewhat (10 percent).[71] Similarly, only 13 percent believed that the economic situation had gotten better since 2015; 34 percent stated that things had gotten worse, while 49 percent believed things had stayed the same. Yet when interviewed the previous year, 63 percent had stated that they expected "tangible improvements in people's living conditions within a year."[72] Indeed, in August 2016 the Supreme Leader asked, "Are we witnessing any tangible impact on people's lives after six months?" This question echoed conservative opposition to Rouhani's reformist policies and was probably designed to place pressure on his administration.[73]

The Military

The Islamic Republic's military doctrine, strength, and capability exhibit both complexity and vulnerability. It has developed as largely defensive, with preference given to skills and tactical prowess focused on asymmetrical warfare. It is sizable in manpower but too short on internal cohesion and firepower to rival the militaries of other regional actors, for example, Turkey and Israel. The Republic's military and security structures are bifurcated, like its two-tier system of governance: in this case, between the conventional military and the ideologically mandated IRGC. While it has developed a strong missile capability, for all practical purposes, Iran lacks an effective air force or other conventional capabilities. As such, the Republic's capacity to project military power remains limited. Yet, this does not mean that the Republic is a "pushover." In conjunction with its other resources, including, most importantly, the use of proxy forces, the Islamic Republic has designed its military capability in such a manner so as to make any attack on Iran as costly as possible for the perpetrator.

DOCTRINE

The Islamic Republic's military doctrine has been primarily defensive, with a focus on the country's national defense alongside a regional security structure. It has had two main aspects: deterrence and denial. The country's two primary strategic concerns have been the US and Israel, and these priorities have also driven Iran's efforts to prevent the US-backed Arab countries from posing a threat to its regional security interests. In February 1991, the First Gulf War demonstrated to the Iranian authorities the futility of trying to defeat US forces in conventional battle. By the same token, the difficulties experienced by US forces in Iraq and Afghanistan—and the problems they had in fighting insurgencies—have largely underpinned Tehran's strategic shift toward asymmetric warfare. The logic is that although Iran cannot defeat the US or, for that matter, Israel, in conventional combat, it can make use of its geographical positioning, guerrilla tactics, proxy forces, and committed manpower to inflict costs significant enough to deter its adversaries from attacking it. This strategy, which is consonant with Iran's position as a "middle power" (as detailed in chapter 1), has sought to use political pressure to compensate for shortages in the country's hard power.

To this end, Iran's rhetoric stresses two themes: Iran is defensive and will not engage in aggressive military action; but if any action is taken against it, it will inflict heavy losses on the aggressor. In August 2014, for example, Rouhani stated:

> [Iran's] military doctrine is based on defense and we don't design any weapon for aggression; we don't carry out any research on how to occupy the regional states. All our researches are based on this defense principle of how we can defend ourselves or how we can stop the enemy.[74]

Shahram Chubin notes how "[Iran's] threats are often bellicose and apocalyptical, but they are defensive, issued as counter-threats that indicate how it would respond to an attack."[75] In a speech in 2005, the Revolutionary Guard commander, Major General Yahya Rahim

Safavi, declared that with "a spirit of jihad and martyrdom-seeking," the IRGC was ready for "an endless defense and long-term warfare on land, air, and sea."[76] Iran's military strategy is therefore centered on offsetting technological and material weaknesses by adopting unconventional tactics and asymmetrical warfare. This makes the Iranian army "exceptional among the world's armed forces: a regular army characterized by an asymmetric quasi-guerilla [sic] buildup."[77] Its strategy is built around disruption, hit-and-run tactics, and attrition and is specifically designed to counter the US and its regional allies' military advantages.

This strategy was codified in the 2005 Mosaic Doctrine, an approach whereby command is decentralized and symmetrical combat avoided so that invading forces face multiple, continual "layers" of resistance. Occupying forces become bogged down in localized urban-based insurgencies that negate their technological and air superiority. The Mosaic Doctrine reflects Iran's strategic prioritization of attrition as a form of deterrence. As part of this strategy, thirty-one regional commands, under the control of the IRGC, were created in 2008 (one for each province and two for Tehran), with each able to operate independently during wartime.[78] The architect of this doctrine—Major General Mohammad Ali Jafari—currently serves as the head of the IRGC.

The focus on denial and attrition is integrated into all branches of the military. One of Iran's greatest assets is its large population and the sheer size of Iran's army—the largest in the MENA region, providing Iran with a strategic advantage commensurate with its geopolitical position as a regional actor. While technologically limited, Iran's substantial manpower gives it a defensive advantage and complements its commitment to defensive asymmetrical warfare.[79] The decision in 2009 to establish the Air Defense Force as a separate branch of the military reflects this defensive approach. Through this new organ, Iran aimed to better defend nuclear sites, improve air force capabilities, combine information collection and air defense, and improve maneuverability. To this end, it is focused on deploying ground-to-air missiles and anti-aircraft artillery in key strategic locations.[80]

A similar approach has been adopted for Iran's naval strategy, which is anchored on the use of small, fast vessels to disrupt supply and ship movements, the use of mines and ambushes at geographic chokepoints, and, increasingly, the use of submarines.[81] The Strait of Hormuz, through which 20 percent of the world's total oil exports travel, would be a major target in the event of any conflict. Tehran has intimated in the past that in a major confrontation with the US, it would block the strait as a tactic to disrupt global energy supplies and internationalize the conflict, and thus rely on diplomatic pressure to force a favorable political settlement.[82] However, it would do so only in critical conditions, because disrupting oil exports would also inflict enormous damage on Iran's economy. In response, Washington has declared that it will never tolerate a blockage of the Strait of Hormuz.

POWER

Iran's military forces, like its political structures, are distinct because they are bifurcated. The Artesh (army), established under the Pahlavi dynasty, is charged with the defense of Iran's territorial sovereignty, while the IRGC is charged with the "defense of the revolution," the Islamic order, and national security. With a focus on asymmetrical warfare, the IRGC has separate land, air, and naval forces that parallel those of the Artesh. Although initially independent, since 1980 the Artesh has largely been subsumed under the control of the IRGC even in the conduct of Iran's territorial defense.[83]

Iran's defense expenditure is relatively low—around 2 percent of GDP, well below the MENA average of 6.48 percent in 2015. This percentage reflects both the impact of sanctions, limiting access to military technology and equipment, as well as the emphasis on self-sufficiency and unconventional tactics that these sanctions have entailed.[84] Indeed, Iran accounts for only 7 percent of the total defense expenditure in the MENA region, compared to 41.8 percent in Saudi Arabia, 7.4 percent in the UAE, and 5.1 percent in Oman.[85] Nonetheless, Mohammad Reza Farzanegan finds that military expenditures do respond to changes in oil prices,[86] which supports the contention that Iran is investing more in both conventional and asymmetrical military capabilities as its economy strengthens. The sixth Five Year Development Plan (2016–21), for example, commits $40 billion to military modernization, with a particular stress on improving technology. Let us now look at the profile of each of the armed forces and security branches as a prelude to evaluating Iran's military capability.

The Artesh functions like a regular, conventional military. It is composed of four branches, which as of 2016 possessed the following forces: the army (350,000–420,000 regulars, 220,000 conscripts), navy (18,000, including 2,600 marines), air force and the air defense service (30,000 total, 12,000 in air defense).[87] Because of technological and material constraints, the Artesh has limited capabilities and is typically deployed to Iran's borders. The conventional military is complemented by the Ministry of Intelligence and Security (MOIS), which is responsible for Iran's clandestine intelligence activities overseas.

The IRGC's divisions parallel those of the Artesh: ground forces (100,000), naval forces (20,000, including 5,000 marines), and an air force (which controls strategic and ballistic missile forces and is responsible for missile development). It also has two additional branches—the Quds Force and the Basij Resistance Force (Niru-ye Muqavemat-e Basij). The Quds Force, commanded since 1998 by General Qasem Soleimani (known as Iraq's Viceroy), undertakes covert military activities outside the country. It builds and maintains networks with subnational ethnic, religious, and political groups, establishing relationships that can further Iran's strategic interests. Furthermore, it provides Iran with "boots on the ground," delivering material assistance—weapons (especially rockets), supplies, expertise, and sometimes even soldiers—to its regional allies and proxies in areas of strategic interest outside Iran's borders.[88] Notable examples of this include, most prominently, Iran's close military relationship with Hezbollah in Lebanon, as well as its assistance to the embattled Bashar al-Assad regime in Syria, the Houthis in Yemen, and various Palestinian groups, especially in Gaza. The Quds Force has also been heavily involved in Iraq. Since the 2003

US-led invasion, it has backed Shia militia and paramilitary groups, including Muqtada al-Sadr's Jaish al-Mahdi (Mahdi Army), seeking to maximize coalition losses until their withdrawal by the end of 2011.[89] Although its involvement in Iraq was considerably curtailed following a series of raids by US forces, the Quds Force has nonetheless grown to be a significant player in the Iraqi and Syrian conflicts.[90] It is also the parallel institution to the MOIS, which operates formally under the direction of the president in performing covert intelligence activities but which is monitored very closely by the office of the Supreme Leader. The Basij Resistance Force is a paramilitary militia initially set up to protect the revolution from internal challenges and to meet Khomeini's call for a twenty-million-strong Islamic army. Its volunteer militia played an important role during the Iran-Iraq War, conducting raids and compensating for the incapacitated army, which was crippled by purges.[91] It has 90,000 soldiers, with reserves of up to 300,000 and a total mobilization capacity of one million. There have been talks in Tehran about merging the Basij with the IRGC ground forces.[92]

The bifurcated nature of the armed forces reflects the historical lessons of the wartime revolutionary period. In contrast to Artesh, the IRGC has two roles: maintaining internal stability—that is, protecting the Islamic regime from domestic challenges—and serving as a combat force in Iran's national defense. Shortly after the revolution, the IRGC was involved not only in eliminating the Islamic order's political opponents and suppressing local revolts in Kurdistan, West Azerbaijan, and Khuzestan, but it also participated in the war with Iraq.[93] It has continued to grow in the context of these two intertwined functions. During his presidency, Rafsanjani had attempted to integrate the IRGC into the Artesh, but by then the former had become strong enough to resist his efforts. Ever since, the IRGC has developed as the most instrumental and powerful force in the Islamic Republic's security architecture, having a significant share in the political, economic, and cultural life of the nation.

The IRGC also oversees one of the main features of Iran's military research and development: its ballistic missile program. Missile technology is a major component of Iran's defense expenditure and accords with the Islamic Republic's defensive military priorities. The focus on ballistics was initially inspired by Iraq's missile war against Iran's cities—the "war of the cities"—that demonstrated the viability of missiles for conducting retaliatory strikes. Iran's capacity to manufacture ballistic missiles domestically has also helped to make it a centerpiece of the country's defense policies.[94] Finally, missiles are more cost-effective than other defensive measures and are cheap enough to be deployed en masse—one strategy is to launch multiple salvos of missiles in order to "overwhelm missile defenses."[95] This factor underpins the continued importance of missiles to Iran's defense policy, although Israel and Saudi Arabia and some of its GCC partners have also invested in the development and purchase of more advanced missile shields to guard against a potential Iranian missile attack.

Since the 1990s, and with significant assistance from China, Iran has made considerable progress in missile production.[96] Indeed, Iran currently has the largest arsenal in the Middle East.[97] Most of these are short-range (500 km or less), but Iran has also developed mid-range ballistic missiles capable of hitting targets within a 2,000-km radius—a range that covers most of the Middle East, including Israel, and American bases in the region.[98] However, the effectiveness of Iranian missiles is unclear, and their accuracy is reportedly limited. Furthermore, although missile strikes have some tactical and political value, it is unclear whether they are strategically effective.

Another important feature of Iran's military power is the country's nuclear program. Iran has achieved sufficient nuclear capability for peaceful purposes and possesses the expertise, technology, infrastructure, and uranium enrichment necessary for the production of nuclear energy. By all accounts, it has never crossed the threshold to produce and deploy nuclear weapons, as the United States and its allies have fretted it might. The July 14, 2015 JCPOA that Iran signed with the five permanent members of the UN Security Council plus Germany, placed Iran's nuclear program under strict IAEA supervision and halted the country's ability to produce fissile materials for military purposes in return for the lifting of sanctions.[99] However, Iran has been allowed to keep all of its nuclear technology and limited enrichment capability and remains in a "semi-threshold state," since it still has the potential to develop nuclear weapons should the need arise, albeit in a longer time frame.

There is a group within the conservative cluster that is strongly in favor of nuclear weapons as a deterrent to potential attackers and as a symbol of national pride. At the same time, there are those from the pragmatist and reformist camps that see Iran's military nuclearization as providing a pretext for Israeli military aggression and a regional arms race, with Saudi Arabia taking the lead, possibly assisted by the US and Pakistan. The dispute over Iran's nuclear program, the negotiations leading to the JCPOA, and Iran's nuclear future are discussed in the context of the country's international relations in chapter 6.

Iran has also recently focused on "soft war," primarily in cyber defense. The objective of soft war is to counter Western culture and ideology disseminating messages that might undermine the regime. It is also to protect Iran's nuclear facilities, which were subjected in 2010 to the Stuxnet Worm cyberattacks, allegedly carried out by the United States and Israel. Those attacks are said to have set Iran's nuclear program back by a year. Cyber warfare, disseminated through the Internet and traditional media, has since become a major part of government policy, as reflected in the establishment of Iran's Cyber Defense Centre in 2015.[100]

CAPABILITY

A 2009 report produced for the US air force by the RAND Corporation concluded that Iran's military is "beset with structural, organizational, and capacity problems that prevent it from completely operationalizing Tehran's doctrinal ambitions."[101] It is widely acknowledged that the Artesh and the IRGC would be of limited effectiveness in conventional warfare but that they possess considerable capabilities in a defensive, asymmetrical combat situation. Its military lacks the level of technological and modern weapons systems that could enable it to successfully project its power beyond Iran's borders. Iran's geographic and economic size, its people's historical sense of fierce nationalism, combined with the Shia heroization of sacrifice and martyrdom, and its sheer numbers in terms of military manpower may enable it to offset some of these technological weaknesses. Nevertheless, Iran's military is "a shoestring enterprise in comparison to those of its Arab neighbours," being "robust and functional, without being a major challenge,"[102] and appears particularly weak when compared to that of some of the other regional actors. This has been demonstrated in the Iranian deployment in Syria, where it has provided military support for Assad's regime since the beginning of the conflict in 2011. When Iran and its allied Hezbollah could not tip the strategic balance in favor of the regime, Russia accomplished just that through massive air operations against the divided opposition forces. The same has proven to be the case with Iranian military involvement in Iraq, as discussed in chapter 7.

Notwithstanding Iran's strengths in asymmetrical warfare and manpower, three issues have limited the country's military capability. The first is institutional competition. As in the political system, the bifurcation of the military between the IRGC-Basij and Artesh undermines effectiveness by creating duplication, waste, and competition over resources. The IRGC is typically more successful in gaining resources and funding because of its close political connections to both conservatives and the Supreme Leader and its responsibility for the asymmetrical—and more effective—aspects of Iran's military policy.[103] In addition, the IRGC's resistance to professionalization creates problems with coordination and interoperability in relation to the Artesh. The institutional friction and competition resulting from parallel organizations is also evident in Iran's other security organs. In intelligence, for example, differences between Khatami and Ali Khamenei extended throughout state institutions and prevented cooperation and information-sharing between MOIS and the IRGC Intelligence Organization, which the Supreme Leader had in fact created in 1997 precisely to counter Khatami's influence over MOIS.[104] The conflicts arising from this bifurcation have undermined agencies in the performance of their roles. As Michael Wahid Hanna and Dalia Dassa Kaye conclude, having "multiple and redundant defense structures may be useful in protecting the regime's survival, but have created significant impediments to military effectiveness."[105]

The second issue is the quality of its forces, which is a matter surrounded by uncertainty. A large proportion of that military consists of poorly trained and ill-equipped conscripts. Even the combat quality of the IRGC and local militias is questionable—it is likely that a good portion are not adequately trained or equipped. Because promotions are often politically driven rather than based on merit, questions have also been raised about the effectiveness of leadership coordination.[106]

The third is the issue of technological and material deficiencies. Many seasoned analysts consider the biggest weakness of Iran's military to be its outdated technology and resources, which are in dire need of modernization. Long years of sanctions, a weak, oil-dependent economy, and material losses in the Iran-Iraq War, as well as the more recent engagements in Iraq and Syria, have combined to take a heavy toll on Iran's supply of military equipment and assets. Consequently, in every field, Iran's military is using at least partly old, obsolete equipment. The sheer size of Iran's military does not translate into a strategic advantage when its soldiers are bereft of state-of-the-art weapons and support technologies. In fact, with the notable exception of the delivery of the Russian S-300 surface-to-air missile systems in late 2016, "Iran has not imported major combat systems since the early 1990s."[107]

The Islamic Republic's air force has been particularly affected by a lack of parts and technology. It has 334 combat-ready aircraft, comparable to Saudi Arabia (325), but significantly less than Egypt (584).[108] However, unlike its Arab neighbors, Iran's air force is largely obsolete. Over half of its combat-ready aircraft consist of what it acquired from the Shah's air force, on which he had lavished the oil profits of the 1970s boom. Most of these are antiquated US aircraft, such as the F-4 Phantom II, the F-5E Tiger II, and the F-14A Tomcat. Recent Russian imports, notably the MiG-29 Fulcrum and the S-300 PMU-2 long-range surface-to-air missiles, with an effective range of 195 km, have changed the situation to some extent.[109] Even so, compared to Saudi Arabia, which operates F-15C and F-15S fighters and the Eurofighter Typhoon, or to Israel, which has acquired F-35 joint-strike fighters, Iran faces a considerable technological deficit and would most likely struggle to deny air superiority in the event of an attack.[110]

Similarly, its navy is of limited effectiveness. Iran produces midget submarines domestically, and has three Russian Kilo-class submarines, which can lay smart mines and fire long-range homing torpedoes. Outside of these assets, the majority of Iran's navy is likewise inherited from the Shah's era.[111] However, its focus on asymmetrical warfare means that any small vessels could be converted to serve a military purpose. Technology will remain the biggest hurdle for Iran's military as it transitions from its traditionally defensive role to take on more assertive actions that require greater force projection. Iran's military spending continues to fall considerably short of its Gulf neighbors: in 2014 Iran spent $16 billion on defense, just over one-tenth of the GCC's $113 billion.[112]

Under the circumstances, Iran has had to indigenize its arms production. It has concentrated on developing domestic production of light arms and ballistic missiles, alongside other weaponry designed for asymmetric warfare, such as improvised explosive devices and land mines. It currently makes "approximately 50 types of small arms and artillery ammunition, including tank ammo and missiles," while also "[producing] the majority of its light weapons, including handguns, rifles, antitank weapons and mortars."[113] Here, Tehran learned the lesson from America's experiences from the Iran-Iraq War and the Gulf Wars of 1991 and 2003, which demonstrated that technological superiority is not the only way—or even the surest—of developing and projecting military power.

Soft Power

Iran's soft-power capabilities, particularly its ties to subnational groups and transnational networks, have played a major role in expanding both Iran's real and perceived influence in the region.[114]

One of the most important documents outlining Iran's soft-power ambitions is its 2005 Twenty-Year Vision Document, which laid out the Islamic Republic's strategic path for the future. While hard power remains a central part of the Republic's foreign policy, the focus of this vision was also on consolidating and furthering Iran's regional and, for that matter, wider reach through the use of "smart power"—a coordinated policy of combining soft and hard power. The document states that Iran's future soft-power measures should stem from the "strengthening of Islamic-Iranian identity," "deepening the spirit of knowing the enemy" (resistance), and promoting the "political, cultural, and economic achievements and experiences of the Islamic Republic and a rich understanding of Persian culture, art, and civilisation and religious democracy."[115] In order to achieve this vision, Iranian soft power has targeted particular groups in three regions: Persian-speaking groups in Central Asia (particularly in Tajikistan and Afghanistan); Shia minorities in the Gulf States; and various religiously or ideologically amenable groups in Iraq and the rest of the Levant, including Palestinian groups resisting Israeli occupation.[116] In all three regions, Iran is drawing on its soft power to further its regional influence and achieve its goals.

SOURCES OF IRANIAN SOFT POWER

The Islamic Republic has primarily relied on four sources of soft power, the first of which is its Islamic revolutionary ideology. Khomeini's Islamic mode of political discourse upheld the Islamic Republic as the protector of the "oppressed" and "downtrodden" and the leading light for Islam in the world. Khamenei has continued this line, stressing that "the world [is] divided between the powerful and the powerless" and declaring that "the rise of the Islamic Republic of Iran [has] challenged this false and unjust division."[117] The main idea here is that the Islamic revolution has provided a liberationist model that oppressed people could follow to overthrow their oppressors. The Islamic Republic, even after tempering its efforts to export the revolution, has made clear that it is there to assist such elements.

Khomeini therefore established a discursive paradigm of political resistance and defiance that could appeal to those in both Muslim and non-Muslim states under corrupt and oppressive governments, especially the ones backed by a major power, such as the United States. This has continued to be a recurrent theme of the post-Khomeini order, and one that the Islamic Republic's leadership has constantly touted as a major ideological selling point. Certain groups have taken inspiration, either directly or indirectly, from the Iranian experience, and Tehran has justified its support for them on these grounds. These elements include not only the ruling Alawites in Syria, and Shia groups in Iraq, Afghanistan, Yemen, and Lebanon but also the Sunni Palestinian group Hamas, demonstrating the potential of Iran's revolutionary ideology to cross sectarian lines. The subnational allies have provided the Islamic Republic with a degree of proxy power that has enabled it to push for its ideological and geopolitical objectives beyond Iran.

Khomeini's concept of Islamic revolution contained not only a religious dimension—affirming the supremacy of Shia Islam while idealizing pan-Islamist solidarity—but also an anti-hegemonic posture, which emphasized Islam as a "third way" against the dual hegemony of the two Cold War superpowers.[118] The second source of Iran's soft power is this anti-hegemonic rhetoric that also potentially appeals to non-Muslims in the Global South because it challenges the prevailing US-led order. Here, Iran's history reflects the experiences of a number of postcolonial countries. Its political rejection of the status quo is increasingly seen as legitimate, especially as dissatisfaction grows with the current neoliberal paradigm. As Shahram Chubin notes, the revolutionary ability of the Islamic regime to resist the West in the past has been used to demonstrate that the downtrodden can stand up for themselves.[119] This appeal transcends religious affiliation and taps into political dissatisfaction with the dominant US-led orthodoxy. Iran's message has gained some support among countries in the Global South, particularly in Latin America, such as

Venezuela, Bolivia, and Cuba. In 2009, Ahmadinejad placed particular emphasis on "peripheral countries" in Latin America and Africa and became the first Iranian president to visit Brazil since the 1960s.[120] Iran's increased focus on the Latin American region is reflected in the creation of a Hispanic-language channel, HispanTV, in 2011 that broadcasts to Spain and Latin America.[121]

The third source of the Islamic Republic's soft power is its *velayat-e faqih* model of Islamic governance, which it has promoted as a model of emulation for the wider Muslim world. In the first few years following the revolution, Iran's Islamic system was highlighted as an original synthesis reconciling divine with popular sovereignty. This is a recurring element in Iranian leaders' political discourse rooted in Shia doctrines. For example, the foreign minister, Mohammad Javad Zarif, writes:

> In light of the increasing importance of normative and ideational factors in global politics, the Islamic Republic is well suited to draw on the rich millennial heritage of Iranian society and the significant heritage of the Islamic Revolution, particularly its indigenously derived and sustained participatory model of governance.[122]

The Republic's leadership has never failed to underline the success of Iran's two-tiered model for bringing stability and security to its people. While no Muslim country has adopted the Iranian model, some in the Islamic Republic leadership believe that their model still carries the potential to take root in the Arab world, particularly given the latter's political volatility, which may create conditions for some of Iran's subnational allies in the Muslim world to generate their own forms of Islamic governance.[123]

The fourth source of soft power is Iran's long and extensive historical and cultural ties with neighboring countries. Most notable in this respect is the network of Shia religious institutions between Iran and Iraq, whose formation predates the establishment of the two nations' current political borders. Tehran has been increasingly very active on this front, having the clear objective of carving out niches of influence. It has targeted those groups that have become receptive to Iranian overtures for one reason or another with great effect. They most prominently include Afghanistan, Tajikistan, and the countries to the west of Iran in the Levant.

CAPABILITY

The Islamic Republic projects its soft power to foster pro-Iranian foreign policies, especially in its neighborhood, through a variety of official and related instruments and methods. They include most importantly the *bonyads*, the Sazman-e Farhang va Ravabet-e Eslami (Islamic Cultural and Relations Organization, or ICRO), and a host of other cultural, welfare, economic, philanthropic, humanitarian, and foreign aid means. The financially and economically resourceful *bonyads* function as a key element of Iran's soft power.[124] As noted in chapter 3, *bonyads* are religious charitable foundations designed to provide social services. They have significant economic power and networks that distribute patronage and ensure loyalty among the conservative cluster. They are estimated to control up to 20 percent (some estimates say up to 30 percent) of Iran's GDP[125] and function as major economic actors with privileged status. Importantly, they operate largely outside of government supervision, accounting only to the Supreme Leader.[126] They run cultural, sectarian, construction, philanthropic, and humanitarian projects in the region and beyond.

For example, in Lebanon, Iran has backed Hezbollah not only through military resources and expertise via the Quds Force but also through extensive involvement in social services and reconstruction, especially following the 2006 Israeli-Hezbollah War. The Bonyad-e Shahid (Martyrs Foundation) funds social welfare projects such as the Rassoul al-Azam hospital in Beirut (where health care is free for families of soldiers killed fighting Israel and is subsidized by the foundation).[127] The US Treasury estimates that Hezbollah receives $100–$200 million a year from Iran.[128] Barbara Slavin writes that within a year after the 2006 war, "Iran had rebuilt 504 roads, 19 bridges, 149 schools, 48 mosques and churches, and 64 power stations."[129] In addition, in the two decades prior to 2007, Iran constructed around 330 schools teaching a total of around 700,000 students, 20 hospitals and clinics, and 550 miles of roads in Lebanon.[130]

Similarly, the IKRC collects donations and religious alms and distributes the proceeds both domestically and internationally. It receives state funding and maintains an extensive network of offices that provide welfare, cultural, and educational services in several countries in the region. As of 2012, it had offices in Afghanistan, Azerbaijan, Iraq, Lebanon, Syria, and Tajikistan, providing services to over 30,000 "welfare-seeking" households and over 94,000 individuals.[131] In Afghanistan alone, the IKRC employs 30,000 people and sponsors events such as Quds Day rallies.[132] An estimated 34,000 Afghans are enrolled in the committee's aid and educational programs.[133] Iran also supports several Shia religious and educational institutions in Afghanistan, such as the Khatam al Nabyeen University (Iranian donations account for support of 80 percent of its library). The university is run by Grand Ayatollah Asif Mohseni, the spiritual leader of Afghanistan's Shia minority, who form about 15 percent of the country's population. Mohseni has close ties to the clerical establishment in Iran and runs a television and radio channel called Tamaddon (Civilization), as well as a sizable Shia educational complex, built with Iranian assistance, in Kabul.[134]

Iran also runs, through various *bonyads*, charitable campaigns on specific "hearts and minds" issues. It has orchestrated a number of special campaigns to aid those who have suffered from attacks by Iran's enemies, including the victims of Israel's 2012 military attack on Gaza and Iraqi refugees displaced in 1991 and 2003. William Jenkins writes that "*bonyad* philanthropy is efficiently targeted due to the low bureaucratic overheads and existing *bonyad* integration in target communities."[135] Nadia von Maltzahn agrees, arguing that the success of Iran's cultural activities stems from their contextualization and specificity to local audiences; in this way, they "react to local characteristics, by studying to whom it can reach out in each region [and] finding points of commonalities."[136]

In culture and the arts, the Farabi Foundation and the Islamic Propagation Organization promote cinema, through which they act as "powerful vehicles for disseminating Islamic ideology [as] energetic partisans fulfilling the revolutionary mandate to promote a more just society."[137] Similarly, the Astan-e Quds-e Razavi *bonyad* (Astan Quds Razavi Foundation) in Mashhad owns and looks after the Imam Reza shrine, a complex that runs several libraries and museums and publishes Islamic materials in English, Arabic, Persian, Urdu, and Turkish. These efforts have yielded some concrete soft-power results: the Sultan of Brunei in the mid-1990s, for example, contracted the Marashi Library in Mashhad to trace his lineage to Prophet Mohammad—a service that was likely to have produced some diplomatic goodwill.[138]

The work of *bonyads* is complemented by the ICRO. This organization is nominally under the Ministry of Culture and Islamic Guidance, but in actuality it is funded by and directly linked to the office of the Supreme Leader. It is responsible for appointing cultural counselors in Iranian embassies abroad that liaise with formal and informal networks internationally to promote Persian language, culture, and history through supporting a variety of educational and religious events and artistic exhibitions. Its primary focus is on improving relations with Muslim and non-Muslim countries, although some have argued that its activities are at least partly directed at promoting the "export of the Revolution."[139] ICRO also runs the al-Hoda publishing house, which produces materials on Iranian culture and the Islamic Republic in twenty-five different languages.[140] The *bonyads* and ICRO have grown to be the main instruments of Iran's public diplomacy.

Tehran operates a number of media outlets and cultural organizations designed to promote cultural and political issues. The Seda va Sima-ye Jomhuri-ye Eslami-ye Iran (Islamic Republic of Iran Broadcasting, or IRIB) runs television and radio channels in several languages. PressTV, for example, is a twenty-four-hour English language international news channel that seeks to present the state's view of issues to foreign audiences. In doing so, it seeks to counter the anti-Iranian narratives in the international media. In particular, it emphasizes Islamic resistance and anti-American and anti-Israeli themes. It also has two Arabic-language outlets: al-Alam, a twenty-four-hour Arabic language news channel aimed at Iran's Arabic neighbors, notably Iraq, Lebanon, and Palestine, that seeks to challenge "the West's one-sided news imperialism,"[141] and al-Kowthar, a religious channel appealing to Shia communities in the Middle East.[142] Furthermore, the IRIB supports Hezbollah's television station al-Manar by providing programming.

In addition, the Islamic Republic has extensive economic and foreign aid involvement in the region. Since the overthrow of Saddam Hussein's regime, Iran has made a huge investment in Iraq, which has become Iran's second-biggest trading partner, with bilateral trade amounting to an estimated $12 billion in 2015.[143] To give just a few examples, *bonyads* have become extensively involved in the country's postwar reconstruction, providing social services and investing in businesses. In 2008, the governor of Najaf province claimed that the Iranian government provided $29 million for construction projects, particularly in tourism, while also promising to contribute $1 million toward a new power plant.[144] Iran also provides Iraq with electricity from its own grid to the amount of 470 megawatts across various regions, and regional energy export is a major strategic priority outlined in the Twenty-Year Vision Document.[145] Both countries share similar energy export policies, having a common interest in keeping oil prices high.[146] Iraq, both through its legitimate economic exchanges and black market trade with Iran, has allowed Tehran to circumvent sanctions to an extent.[147]

Iran's economic involvement in Afghanistan is also significant. Iran has been the fifth-largest contributor, after the United States, the European Union, Japan, and India, to Afghanistan's post-Taliban reconstruction[148] and has paid for the building of the electricity grid in Herat.[149] Iranian exports more than doubled, from $800 million in 2008 to $2 billion in 2011, while more than two thousand Iranian firms currently operate in Afghanistan, investing in mining, industry, and agriculture.[150] Importantly, the proportion of trade is not balanced—Iran accounts for 75 percent of the total volume of trade between the two countries. It also donated an annual substantial amount of cash to President Hamid Karzai (2001–14), ostensibly for the expenses of his office, although other sources intimated that it was to help the president maintain his patronage in return for being favorably disposed toward Tehran. One local official described the situation in this way: "Iran has influence in every sphere: economic, social, political and daily life. . . . When someone gives you so much money, people fall into their way of thinking. It's not just a matter of being neighborly."[151]

The Islamic Republic has also drawn heavily on a linguistic and cultural heritage shared with other countries in the region, especially in Afghanistan and Tajikistan, to advance its status as the center of the Persianate cultural world. Edward Wastnidge notes that "Iran regularly draws on cultural commonalities," such as *Nowrooz* (Persian New Year), a pre-Islamic event, as soft-power tools. In 2010, Iran hosted the first international celebration of *Nowrooz*, and several regional heads of state were invited. Similarly, Ahmadinejad established the Union of Persian Speaking Nations (between Afghanistan, Tajikistan, and Iran), which sought to "[draw] on cultural linkages as a means of furthering cooperation and making use of . . . common Persian bonds."[152]

Soft War

In addition to developing its soft-power resources regionally and internationally, the Islamic Republic has been working on countering the dominance of Western soft power. To this end, it is engaged in a *jang-e narm* (soft war)—a term that has become a central issue for the Iranian leadership after the Green Movement of 2009. According to Safavi, former head of the IRGC, soft war seeks to "block the enemy's cultural onslaught by using our own culture."[153] The focus on soft war stems from fears that direct US support for human rights and democracy promotion, combined with the prevailing liberal norms of the international system, are part of a deliberate US policy to undermine the regime and overthrow it by inciting popular uprisings, in a repeat of the Velvet Revolution in Czechoslovakia. To Iran's political elites, domestic unrest was the result of a "concentrated, directed and strategic series of information-related actions . . . by the United States and the West."[154] In response to the Green Movement protests, in June 2009 Khamenei declared that Iran was now "confronting a huge war, but a soft war":

> The goal is the defense of the Islamic system and the Islamic Republic in the face of a comprehensive movement relying upon force and deception and money and huge, scientifically advanced media capabilities. This Satanic current must be confronted.[155]

The focus on soft war reflects the shift in Iran's threat perceptions away from fears of US military involvement toward a growing consensus of the importance of its soft power in shaping Iran's domestic politics, particularly given the contentious 2009 election and the economic and political stagnation that has fed growing dissatisfaction among the younger generation.

Nevertheless, Iran has approached the issue of soft war from a conventional military perspective. It has tellingly labeled the concerted effort to propagate Western values as a "cultural NATO" that seeks to "force the system to disintegrate from within."[156] Accordingly, the Islamic Republic's leadership perceives itself as under threat from several sources: NGOs, particularly pro-democracy organizations such as the Near East Regional Democracy Fund (an issue that is discussed in chapter 7); the international media; and Western content delivered through the Internet. The launch of the BBC's Persian service in 2009, for example, was viewed by Iranian experts as an outlet for anti-regime propaganda[157] and labeled by the Iranian government as another tool through which foreign powers incite conspiracies against its rule.

To this end, the military created the Permanent Bureau for Soft War in December 2012, along with a host of other organizations, such as the Specialist Center for Soft War, the Center for Soft War and Psychological Operations, and the Center for Information Dominance and Strategic Insight.[158] The role of these organizations is to conduct "soft operations" that promote cultural activities while also engaging in "psychological operations" that aim to "confuse and [disrupt] foreign-organized soft attacks."[159] Particular emphasis is being placed on cultivating state ideology and revolutionary ideals among the younger generation, particularly through educational measures such as the institutionalization of *basij* centers in primary schools.[160] Iran's aforementioned activities in broadcast media and cyber warfare are also key weapons in the waging of its soft war. By expanding the number of media outlets that can provide counter-narratives to international media, Tehran aims to "neutralize the effect of anti-Islamic Republic media."[161] To fight the soft war on the Internet front, the regime created a cyber-police division in 2011 to monitor online content and crack down on online activists and banned content. Tehran also uses firewalls and other preventive technologies to block domestic access to specific sites.[162] In the process, the regime has attempted to impose a ban on all foreign media that it regards as hostile.

While *bonyads* and several similar outlets act as effective conduits of influence in relatively diverse arenas, the government's explicit links to these instruments compromise its projection of its soft power abroad in three respects. First, its "top-down" approach to cultural production and censorial interference undermines its ability to generate cultural exports that could be considered "authentic."[163] Second, these ties encourage suspicions of the political agenda behind what are purported to be purely humanitarian and cultural activities. The government's explicit links to its soft power means that there is a widespread perception that the latter are geared toward spreading the Iranian Shia Islamic ideology and exporting its Islamic revolutionary influence in the region. Third, the theocratic aspect of the Islamic Republic also limits its ability to draw on the cultural production of its diaspora, who are often critical of the state.

The other major challenge to Iranian soft power is sectarianism. While sectarian divisions have historically always been present in the Sunni-dominated region, they have intensified significantly, largely as a product of growing Saudi-Iranian geopolitical competition. Sunni-Shia divisions have become particularly acute since the 2011 Arab uprisings, dubbed the Arab Spring. While Iran initially sought to position itself as an instigator and guardian of the uprisings, which it called an Islamic awakening in allusion to its own 1979 revolution, its continued support for the minority Shia-linked Alawite-dominated regime of Assad quickly became a major liability, severely tarnishing its reputation in the region.[164] Iran's involvement in Syria has also been economically costly—it has spent an estimated $6–$15 billion annually over the last few years on support for the Assad regime. This is in addition to the materiel and military assistance that its Quds units have provided to the regime's forces.[165] Iran's role in Syria is discussed in more detail in chapter 6.

Iran's championing of Shia interests inherently limits its appeal to non-Shia Muslim groups, but this obstacle has become especially great in light of the growing sectarian divisions in the region. Shireen Hunter notes that while scholarships to Iranian religious universities, notably Qom, are a popular and effective means of projecting soft power among Shia Muslims, Iran struggles to attract non-Shia students, particularly given that it is in competition with prestigious Sunni institutions such as Al-Azhar University in Cairo. This provides one example of the difficulty Iran has faced in overcoming the sectarian limits to its soft power.[166]

The appeal of culture has also had its limits, even among those neighborly states that share a great deal with Iran in this respect. For example, in December 2013, despite extensive lobbying and financial incentives aimed at persuading the US-backed Afghan government, Tehran did not succeed in securing a "no" vote from members of an Afghan *Loya Jirga* (grand assembly). The assembly unanimously voted, against Iran's wishes, to sign a strategic agreement with the US allowing it to keep its troops and military bases in Afghanistan until 2024.[167] Tehran's concern was that these bases and troops could be used against Iran in the event of a conflict between the two sides.

The Islamic Republic of Iran has come a long way since its early years of postrevolution turmoil and disintegrated resources capability. When assessed against the backdrop of the consequences of the war with Iraq, international sanctions, hostilities with the United States and Israel, and regional apprehension—especially from the Gulf Arab states—the Republic has managed to sustain a largely resilient if rentier economy and to build relatively robust hard- and soft-power capabilities within a strategic vision that could enable it to act as an influential player in its region and beyond. As such, it has acquired the necessary resource capabilities to merit consideration as a middle power.

However, that does not mean it has achieved sufficient power capabilities to act as an offensively dominant regional actor. Its economic base of power remains weak, undermined by ideological and political domination as well as by patronage and corruption, and this is also largely true of its military and soft-power resources. It has therefore so far built a limited but not immaterial capacity to persuade other regional states to take note of, but not to embrace, its ideological or geopolitical preferences. The area in which the Republic has scored well is in the field of having cultivated a specific image of itself as a Shia power and building transnational Shia or Shia-linked proxy forces and networks in support of its security interests. This has provided it considerable leverage across the region—in Afghanistan, Bahrain, Iraq, Lebanon, Syria, and Yemen. The success of its Shia appeal stems partly from the fact that Shiism is multiethnic and multinational, and its networks are necessarily transnational because of the "cross-border geographical (and sectarian) distribution of core shared symbols and places."[168] Yet the Islamic Republic's success in this area has also contributed to inflaming sectarian and geopolitical tensions in its predominantly Sunni neighborhood. Apart from Iraq and Bahrain, all other regional states (notwithstanding secular Azerbaijan) are Sunni-dominated Muslim countries, albeit with Shia minorities. Here, Iran faces competition from Saudi Arabia, which claims the leadership of the Sunni Muslim world.

6

Regional Relations

As a whole, any state's regional and foreign policy is primarily a reflection of its domestic politics. The Islamic Republic of Iran is no exception in this respect. The feature that distinguishes the Republic from most other states is the extent to which the confluence of internally and externally generated factors has influenced its regional behavior. In the course of crises and opportunities, the Republic's foreign policy has remained one of defiance on the one hand and pragmatic reflexivity on the other. In this, it has kept very much within the tradition of Ayatollah Ruhollah Khomeini's *jihadi-ijtihadi* approach and so has spawned a pattern of foreign policy conduct that can be described as resistance, negotiations, and agreement. In order to enable it to act as a major regional player, the Islamic regime has often looked for a workable nexus between its domestic situation and foreign policy objectives. It has done so despite its broad-based but top-heavy foreign-policy-making process and the challenges that the Republic has faced since its inception.

The Iranian Revolution brought about distinct ideological and political shifts that fundamentally altered the regional balance of power and Iran's relations with its neighbors. Under the Shah's pro-Western secularist rule, Iran's political relations with its mostly

Sunni Arab and non-Arab neighbors were still colored by historical differences and geopolitical rivalry. However, they were also defined by a degree of shared regional interests and constraints in the relatively stable regional setting generated by Pax Americana in the bipolar context of the Cold War. Khomeini's Islamist politics radically reoriented Iran's foreign policy objectives away from the West in favor of a "third way" that was "neither East, nor West, but Islamic," also a motto for the "export of revolution" in defense of the downtrodden.[1] Initially, the ruling clerics had high hopes that their revolutionary ideals and model of *velayat-e faqih* governance would attract widespread support in the region. In reality, however, they were soon confronted with challenges that required them to be less ideological and more pragmatic in their policies. As such, their pursuit of "export of revolution" was gradually deprioritized except where it had already borne some fruit.

Iran's standing has benefited, more than anything else, from several recent events in the region—America's faltering 2001 intervention in Afghanistan, its 2003 invasion of Iraq, and its decisive inaction in Syria and the rise of the Islamic State of Iraq and Syria (ad-Dawlah al-Islamiyah fī 'l-'Iraq wa-sh-Sham, or Daish, commonly known as ISIS), which declared a *khilafat* (Islamic government) across large swathes of Iraqi and Syrian territories on June 29, 2014. These issues have led to a major reconfiguration of the status quo and the creation of power vacuums that Iran—along with its allies in Iraq, Syria, Lebanon, Yemen, and, since late 2015, Russia—has exploited to its advantage. By the same token, these developments, coupled with Iran's nuclear program, have alarmed Israel and the Saudi-led GCC, which have come to cooperate in a broad front against Iranian regional influence well beyond their parallel interests. Saudi Arabia and its GCC allies have become more concerned about the Islamic Republic as a major sectarian and geopolitical threat in recent years, especially as their confidence in the United States as the bedrock of their security declined, particularly under the US administration of President Barack Obama (2009–17). However, not all GCC states share this view; Oman, Qatar, and Kuwait have consistently favored good working relations with Iran. Meanwhile, Israel has treated Iran as a mortal enemy, buttressed by statements of various Iranian leaders calling for the destruction of the Jewish state. The result has been intensified Iranian-Saudi rivalry and proxy conflicts, especially in the Levant and Yemen, as well as a concerted Israeli effort to ensure that Iran and the US remain locked in hostility, in which it finds common cause with concerned Arab states.

Policy Objectives

Two interrelated objectives have governed the Islamic Republic's regional relations, reflecting both revolutionary ideological influences and realpolitik considerations—that is, preserving the regime and building the regional security architecture necessary to support and defend it. As its first priority, Tehran's regime survival efforts have taken both diplomatic and military dimensions. Despite its emphasis, particularly under Khomeini's leadership, on the universality of Islam as a religion that transcends all boundaries, the Islamic Republic was alert from its early days to the need to safeguard itself and maintain its sovereignty and territoriality in the face of a perceived threat from the United States and Israel—a perception deepened by the war with Iraq, against which the regime was literally fighting for its survival. It found it increasingly expedient to downplay the universality of Islamic revolution in favor of defending the Islamic Republic, thereby mobilizing even nonrevolutionary parts of Iranian society in support of the war and new Republic. As elaborated in chapter 5, it developed a defensive foreign policy and military posture focusing on asymmetrical capabilities in order to maximize the costs of an invasion to any larger, technologically superior adversaries.[2] This position, combined with the international ostracizing of the Islamic Republic, proved critical in shaping Tehran's perceptions and policies toward its neighbors, at least until 2001, when the US Afghan and Iraqi military campaigns, and the subsequent outbreak of the Syrian conflict and emergence of the so-called Islamic State (IS), changed the regional landscape. In order to work the new regional situation to its advantage, the regime was forced to sharpen its policy actions on the one hand and moderate its revolutionary rhetoric on the other.

While moving toward a forward defensive foreign policy posture, the Islamic regime enhanced its efforts in using diplomacy to reintegrate itself into the regional and international systems and function as an acceptable "normal" state. This tendency was evident to a degree under President Akbar Hashemi Rafsanjani's pragmatism, but it was more notable during President Mohammad Khatami's reformist presidency. Khatami's pursuit of the "dialogue of civilizations" saw Iran seeking friendly relations with all the neighboring countries, including the Gulf Arab states, as the main pole of its foreign policy. It did not oppose the US military campaigns in Afghanistan and Iraq and played a very constructive role in the post-Taliban political settlement of Afghanistan under the auspices of the United States and the United Nations. In a meeting shortly after assuming the presidency in 1997, Khatami declared:

> Our strategic policy is expansion of friendship with all regional countries. We believe that existing problems in the region can be solved by wisdom, negotiation and understanding and whenever the regional countries become close together they can prevent foreign interference in the region, which would lead to [the] creation of peace.[3]

While the Mahmoud Ahmadinejad presidency shifted Iran's domestic and foreign policies to the right, President Hassan Rouhani sought once again to redirect them to the path pursued in the Khatami era. Moderation and pragmatism were central emphases of his 2013 election campaign, as he said that "what I truly wish is for moderation to return to the country. This is my only wish, extremism pains me greatly."[4] Subsequently, his foreign minister, Mohammad Javad Zarif, outlined their vision of Iran as a "solid regional power" contributing positively to regional stability through a foreign policy based on pragmatism and "prudent moderation."[5] Importantly, this moderation was built on "realism, self-confidence . . . and constructive engagement."[6] In January 2017, Zarif said that this was entirely in accord with Khomeini's principle of neither "East" nor

"West." He claimed that Khomeini had intended by this policy that Iran must never be under the influence of any power but should have good relations with all countries that do not threaten it.[7]

The Islamic regime's second priority has been to shape a regional security structure in support of its domestic order, national stability, and security. To achieve this priority, it has used both ideological motivations and pragmatic actions as required in order to establish itself as a champion of Shia Muslims and their advocate in the region. Whenever appropriate and expedient, it has accused the conservative Gulf Arab monarchies of being "reactionary" governments propped up by the hegemonic United States. In the same vein, Iran has developed relations with those states and groups in the region that have not been part of the dominant Western-backed system. A prime example of relations with a receptive regional state has been that of Syria. The Iranian-Syrian strategic partnership (or as it is often called, "alliance") emerged shortly after the advent of the Islamic government in Iran, which brought about a confluence of interests. Both were regionally isolated, although to different degrees and for different reasons, and opposed to the US and Israel.[8] Syria was one of only two Arab countries not to support Iraq in the war with Iran; in fact, it helped Iran block the trans-Syrian pipeline that was central to distributing Iraq's oil exports. In return, Iran provided oil at discounted prices, instituting an arrangement that continues to this day.[9] Regional Sunni Arab aversion to the Islamic Republic interacted favorably with Damascus's disenchantment with the Arab states for not supporting it against a Sunni Islamist uprising in the Syrian town of Hama in 1982. This aversion also played its part in solidifying an enduring Iranian-Syrian partnership in which Iran has increasingly become the senior partner over time.[10] The Islamic Republic's close ties with sub-state actors, whether purely political or paramilitary, ranging from Hezbollah to various groups in Iraq, Yemen, and Afghanistan, as well as Palestine, have enabled Tehran to give expression to its revolutionary rhetorical legitimacy on the one hand and to build a regional structure of political and security influence for itself on the other.

The Islamic Republic could scarcely have hoped for better opportunities to widen its regional influence than the ones that have materialized since the turn of the twenty-first century, primarily as a result of regional US policy. Openings for Iranian ascendancy have come about largely due to the effects of US intervention—the deposition of both the medievalist Sunni Islamic regime of the Taliban and the anti-Iranian Arab dictator Saddam Hussein; its subsequent failure to bring peace and stability to the countries it had invaded; its inability or unwillingness to play a decisive role in securing a resolution of the Israeli-Palestinian and Syrian conflicts; the emergence of IS as a violent, Salafist anti-Shia force; and America's response to the rise of IS. These developments, combined with Iran's strategic links to the Syrian regime and the Lebanese Hezbollah, provided Tehran with unique opportunities and means to pursue several interrelated objectives. In Afghanistan and Iraq, Tehran was able to fill the power vacuum and build its influence. In Syria, it found it imperative to launch a direct but undeclared military intervention. It brandished IS as an example of the evil that the Saudi Sunni Wahhabi/Salafist (in contrast to the Shia) brand of Islam could unleash and stressed its own standing as an anti-extremist force by making common cause with the international community in the fight against terrorism.

Since the turn of the century, Tehran has played a key role in generating a predominantly Iran-led Shia strategic entity stretching from Afghanistan to Lebanon in a territory shaped like a crescent moon over the north of the Arabian Peninsula. Tehran's support for the Shia Houthi rebels against the Saudi-backed government in Yemen, as well as its advocacy and support for the rights of the Shia majority population of Bahrain and for the Palestinian cause, have helped to widen its regional reach. In 2015, Ali Younesi, the former head of intelligence under Khatami, stated that "since its inception Iran has [always] had a global [dimension]. It was born an empire. Iran's leaders, officials and administrators have always thought in the global."[11] Iran's burgeoning regional standing, however, has not come without its costs and challenges. To make sense of this, it is now important to turn to a discussion of Iran's relations with its neighbors.

Policymaking

The Islamic Republic has conducted its regional relations within a paradigm characterized by defensive resistance, pragmatic compromises, and assertive postures according to changing circumstances. In the process, it has from time to time exhibited confusion, contradictions, and anomalies, with a disconnect between policy intentions, pronouncements, and outcomes. The Islamic Republic's system of governance, which has produced separate centers of power with different, often conflicting, interests and priorities, is largely responsible for this.

On the one hand, the Supreme Leader acts as the ultimate state policy arbiter and determinant.[12] As the leading guardian of the revolution, he is constitutionally empowered to declare war and peace, dismiss elected governments, and vet and decide on all significant policy issues. In foreign as in domestic policy, he is tasked with ensuring the compliance of all decisions with the overall framework of Islamic government. Shireen Hunter argues that because political legitimacy is built on fidelity to revolutionary ideology, policy formation must take place within the limitations set by revolutionary Islamic discourse.[13] To be successful in this, however, the Supreme Leader needs to foster and maintain a balance between his appointed position as the embodiment of the "sovereignty of God," and the elected presidency and legislature representing the "sovereignty of the people," whose policy agenda or political desires have not always been in full conformity with his own. The elected bodies have mostly been congruent with the powers of the Supreme Leader but at the same time have had electoral obligations to fulfill, raising the potential for conflict between the two tiers, as examined in chapter 4.

Two foreign policy apparatuses have come to feature in the Iranian system, again mirroring Iran's two-tiered system: one is centered in the Beit-e Rahbari and another in the elected government. Advising the Supreme Leader on international affairs are a number of prominent and sometimes controversial figures from diplomatic and military backgrounds. A leading figure among them has been the conservative-leaning Ali Akbar Velayati, who is said to be especially close to the Supreme Leader. Velayati (born June 1945 in Tehran) has a degree in medical sciences from Tehran University and completed his specialty in infectious diseases under a fellowship from Johns Hopkins University. He joined the National Front as an opposition activist during the Shah's rule. Following the revolution, he served as a deputy health minister for a short period before being appointed as minister of foreign affairs in President Ali Khamenei's cabinet in 1981—a position he held for sixteen years. In 1997, he was appointed as a foreign policy advisor to the Supreme Leader while also serving as an active member of both the Expediency Council and Supreme Council of Cultural Revolution. Velayati, along with a number of other Iranian leaders, including Khamenei and Rafsanjani, was subject to an arrest warrant issued by an Argentinian judge in November 2006 for his alleged involvement in the planning of an Iranian bombing of an Israeli organization (Asociacion Mutual Israelita Argentina) in Buenos Aires.[14]

Joining Velayati as foreign policy advisor on security issues to the Supreme Leader is the former rear admiral Ali Shamkhani. Of Arab-Iranian origin, Shamkhani has held senior military and security positions, including as minister of defense. The Supreme Leader also consults two other foreign ministers and veterans of the anti-Shah revolution: Ali Akbar Salehi, who has been the head of the Atomic Energy Agency of Iran since 2013 and a heavyweight in Iran's nuclear negotiations ever since, and Kamal Kharazi. Whereas Salehi served in Ahmadinejad's cabinet (2010–13), Kharazi, together with Shamkhani, were in Khatami's cabinet (1997–2005). Kharazi also heads the Shurai-e Rahbarde Rawabit-e Kharij-e (Strategic Council on Foreign Relations), which Khamenei established by a June 2006 decree to serve as a think tank and advisory body to the Supreme Leader. Its objectives and functions, as stated in its publicity pamphlet, are to "engage and assume a role in major policymaking, open up new horizons in the era of foreign relations, benefit from the elite, and develop indicators with the aim of realizing the objective of the Iran Outlook Plan." In addition to Velayati and Shamkhani, the councils include Saeed Jalili, the former nuclear negotiator under Ahmadinejad, and Mehdi Mostafavi Ahari, a foreign policy advisor to Khamenei's office, both of whom are closely associated with the conservative camp.[15] These examples demonstrate how the Supreme Leader has collected a range of foreign policy advisors and analysts from across the ideological and political spectrum to advise him. The Islamic Culture and Relations Organization, discussed earlier in chapter 5, also operates as a foreign relations arm of the Beit-e Rahbari.

On the other hand, the foreign policy apparatus that exists primarily to serve the elected "republican" sections of the government is the powerful Supreme National Security Council (SNSC). Established under Article 176 of the 1989 revised edition of the Islamic Constitution, the council is entrusted with the defense of the Republic's Revolution, sovereignty, and territorial integrity.[16] It is supervised by the president, who also selects the SNSC's secretary. This position was held by President Rouhani from 1989 to 2005; since 2013, it has been occupied by Shamkhani. The other eleven members of the council include the chief justice, the Speaker of the Majles, the representatives of the Supreme Leader's chiefs of the general staff, the chief of army, the chief of the Islamic Revolutionary Guard Corps, the ministers of foreign affairs and of the interior, and the minister of intelligence. Information and analysis are fed to the council from the ministries of foreign affairs, interior, defense, and intelligence.

While every decision of the council is subject to the Supreme Leader's confirmation, this does not mean that differences have not arisen between it and the Beit-e Rahbari. Indeed, the SNSC has shown itself generally more inclined to pragmatism than the latter, which has resulted occasionally in political and institutional competition, producing policy inconsistencies and confusion in Iranian foreign-policy making during all presidencies, from Rafsanjani to Ahmadinejad.[17] Rouhani has not been immune from this conflict either; while Khamenei initially endorsed *ijtihadi* innovation to allow Rouhani to secure the landmark July 2015 JCPOA, primarily to improve economic conditions, at the same time he urged resistance to the United States as a hegemonic and distrusted power (see chapter 7 for details).[18]

This complex interaction of domestic forces within Iran's dual foreign policy–making apparatus underpins the country's regional relations and has produced policies defined by a combination of both *jihadi* and *ijtihadi* tendencies. In some cases Iran has sought to prioritize stability over conflict, whereas in others, it has acted as a catalyst in shaping instability according to its changing interests. This has been particularly prominent in the conduct of Iran's relations with its neighboring countries in the region.

Eastern Neighbors

In Afghanistan, Iran has had two main ideological and geostrategic objectives. The first is to foster stability within the country, in order to protect the Shia and Persian-speaking segments of the Afghan population, prevent Afghanistan's troubles from spilling over the Iranian border, and support a functioning state within which Iran could expand its influence. The second is to counter and limit any enduring US presence in Afghanistan that might threaten Iran's regional influence or even its own territory. The Taliban's rule (1996–2001) seriously perturbed the Islamic Republic and heightened its alertness to the threat of Sunni Islamic extremism of any variety. Although Pakistan bears much of the responsibility for the rise of Islamic extremism in Afghanistan from the early 1980s, Tehran is aware that continued conflict and insecurity in Afghanistan carries the potential for the country to become once again a hub for violent Sunni extremism. To this end, Iran has played a very active role in Afghanistan's reconstruction process in pursuit of promoting an effective, stable, and friendly government in Kabul. In the process, it has been one of the country's most generous donors. At the 2002 Tokyo Afghanistan donor conference, Iran pledged $560 million for reconstruction—the largest of any country outside the Organisation for Economic Co-operation and Development

(OECD).[19] It added another $100 million to this amount in 2006 and $50 million in donations, plus $300 million in loans, in 2008.[20] It has invested heavily in infrastructure, schools, and social services, while expanding its cultural, religious, and economic ties. Between 2007 and 2013, it contributed $50 million a year for counternarcotics operations alone.[21]

Since the 2001 US intervention, Iran has become Afghanistan's largest trading partner, with a balance of trade that weighs overwhelmingly in Iran's favor. The total volume of trade in 2015 between the two countries reached $2.4 billion, $2.3 billion of which was Iranian exports. Afghan imports to Iran accounted for only $10 million and comprised mostly seeds and plants.[22] Most of Iran's development aid has been channeled into projects in Afghanistan's western provinces along the border with Iran. Many cities and regions of these provinces have become dependent on Iran for electricity, fuel, and cross-border trade—in sum, for their general economic well-being. Because Pakistan's relations with Afghanistan have remained tense—largely due to the former's support of the Taliban—Iran has granted landlocked Afghanistan permission to use its Chahbahar port on the Gulf for transit purposes. It has also funded and constructed expensive infrastructure, including a bridge and a major road to link Chahbahar to the Afghan border. Pakistan's regional archenemy, India, has strongly supported this development, due to its longstanding desire to bypass Pakistan in order to secure safe transit access to Afghanistan and Central Asia.[23] Afghanistan is now linked to India by a road to Chahbahar constructed between Zaranj and Delaram, a trade route that rivals the China-Pakistan Economic Corridor and Gwandar Port in Balochistan. Chahbahar symbolizes Iran's and India's shared strategic interests in cooperating on antiterrorism, fighting the spread of religious extremism in the region, and containing Pakistan's influence in Afghanistan.[24] To this end, Kabul has also been very keen on expanding infrastructural links between India and Iran—an issue detailed later.

On the political front, Iran has secured allies among the estimated 15–20 percent Shia segment of the Afghan population, as well as the remaining elements of the United Islamic Front for the Salvation of Afghanistan, or the so-called Northern Alliance (Jebheh-ye Mujtahed-e Islami Bara-ye Nejat-e Afghanistan, or JMIBNA). Under the leadership of the legendary late Afghan Mujahideen commander, Ahmad Shah Massoud, the JMIBNA fought the Soviet Union and its surrogate government in Kabul in the 1980s and subsequently the Pakistan-backed Taliban. Massoud was assassinated by al-Qaeda agents two days before the group's September 11, 2001, attacks on the United States. Iran had supported the JMIBNA against the Taliban in the 1990s[25]; later it also provided cash assistance to President Hamid Karzai for his "office expenses," as discussed in chapter 7.[26] Further, Iran's efforts have involved securing ties with various receptive Pashtun groups, an ethnic cluster that has historically formed the largest and politically dominant segment, but not the majority, of Afghanistan's mosaic population. In the past, friendly Pashtun groups included the Hezb-e Islami-ye Afghanistan (Islamic Party of Afghanistan under the leadership of Gulbuddin Hekmatyar), with which Tehran maintained good relations in the 1980s.[27]

As of late, Tehran has also pursued relations with another Pashtun cluster, the Taliban. Although US sources accused Iran of sponsoring the Taliban as far back as 2005, events have made it clear that Tehran has intensified its efforts to cultivate ties with elements of the cluster in recent years.[28] The first proof of burgeoning, clandestine ties between the two sides came on May 20, 2016, when the former Taliban leader, Mullah Akhtar Mansour, was killed by an American drone strike just inside Pakistan after crossing the border from Iran. Mansour was the successor of the Taliban's founder, Mullah Mohammed Omar, whose death was announced by Afghan intelligence in July 2015, two years after his actual passing in a Karachi hospital. Later reports suggested that this was one of several visits that Mansour had made to Iran. Mansour's final visit to Iran confirmed a long-standing suspicion about Tehran's ties with the Taliban. The Iranian foreign minister Zarif confirmed his country's contacts with the Taliban while stressing that this was in no way designed to undermine Afghanistan's National Unity government under President Ashraf Ghani and Chief Executive

Abdullah Abdullah, which had been formed through mediation of the former US secretary of state John Kerry and the European Union following a messy presidential election in 2014.[29]

The Islamic Republic has not always looked favorably on the Taliban. The group's radical Sunni extremist ideology is anathema to the Shia revolutionary theology of the Islamic Republic. In 1998, Tehran came close to declaring war with them, after they killed eleven Iranians, ten of them diplomats, in the country's consulate in the Afghan city of Mazar-e Sharif. However, a number of emerging factors have impelled a pragmatic revision of Tehran's policy attitude toward the Taliban, especially since 2016. The first is the need to counter IS, whose forces have infiltrated Afghanistan. While some Taliban elements have been attracted to IS, their core body views the group as a rival that must be prevented from carving out a niche on the Taliban's turf in Afghanistan. The second relates to Tehran's ambitions to shape the country's post-NATO political future. Kabul's and Washington's decision to seek a political deal with the Taliban has indicated to Tehran that the cluster could eventually play a greater role in the future of the Afghan state than had previously been thought. As a result, Tehran considers it in its interest to cultivate ties with those Taliban elements with whom it could work.[30] The third is that Tehran has found in the Taliban and their associates a useful counter to the US presence in Afghanistan, as well as to Pakistani and Saudi ambitions in the country. Not only Washington but also the Afghan security forces now claim that Iran has increased military and logistical support to some Taliban forces.[31] This strategy stems from Iranian fears that America's military bases in Afghanistan may become permanent, providing the US with the capacity to launch attacks on Iranian nuclear facilities in the event of a conflict.[32] These strategic efforts, together with Iranian media and cultural activities, have served as valuable tools to advance Iran's position at the highest political level in Kabul and across Afghanistan for multiple possible outcomes.[33]

While Iranian-Afghan relations have overall been positive, they have not been free of certain challenges, some quite persistent. Disputes over water allocation and the delineation of boundaries affecting the Helmand River and the Harirod-Murghab basin in Afghanistan have been the source of multiple tensions since the nineteenth century. Given that both countries suffer from water shortages, this will continue to be a major point of contention. In particular, Iran's Sistan-Baluchistan province, the driest and poorest region in the country, is heavily dependent on the water flow from the Helmand River. Over one million Iranians live near Hamun Lake and the surrounding wetlands, which are fed by the 1,150-km long river. The two countries signed the Helmand River Treaty in 1973, which established a formal agreement on the division of water. However, the Iranian side has claimed that it has not been fully implemented. In 2001, a drought forced the abandonment of over 124 villages that depended on the lakes for their water supply.[34] The prospect of new dams, combined with overuse of water on the Afghan side, is an additional source of contention. Afghanistan currently plans to build twenty-one dams to boost agricultural production and produce electricity.[35] It has accused Iran of attempting to sabotage and block its dam projects. In 2011, a captured Taliban official claimed that he had been offered $50,000 to sabotage the Kamal Khan Dam in the Afghan province of Nimroz.[36]

Afghanistan's many refugees have been another contentious issue between the countries. Although there is no accurate figure for the number of Afghan refugees in Iran, the country is widely believed to host some 2.5–3 million of them—the second-largest number after Pakistan. However, only about 950,000 are UN-registered, as the Iranian government has refused to provide all Afghan refugees with the opportunity to legally claim asylum.[37] In 1991–92, more than 3 million Afghans sought refuge in different ways and were spread throughout Iran. They were initially well treated and given access to generous social security programs.[38] However, the plight of refugees has generally deteriorated as economic difficulties have prevented the maintenance of this support and stoked anti-refugee sentiments against a population increasingly viewed as a drain on the state's resources.[39] Iran has also used the refugee issue to gain political leverage against the Afghan government, with Tehran threatening to deport refugees en masse to Afghanistan on several occasions. Although some analysts thought it unlikely that Tehran would follow through with its threats, given the negative impact of such an action on Afghanistan's stability,[40] Tehran nonetheless forcefully repatriated almost 195,000 Afghan refugees in 2016, with the total number sent back to Afghanistan throughout the year numbering over 440,000, an 18 percent increase from the previous year.[41]

A further point of contention between the two countries concerns cross-border drug trafficking from Afghanistan into Iran. Because Afghanistan does not have sufficient security, border, and customs forces to control the crossings from its side, Iran has had to deploy a substantial and costly border guard to combat drug trafficking, costing the lives of many of its security personnel over the years. In 2016, Iran accounted for 75 percent of opium, 61 percent of morphine, and 17 percent of heroin seized globally.[42] Despite these efforts, Iran now has one of the largest numbers of addicts in the region. Although officially Tehran has claimed that there are an estimated two million addicts in Iran, unofficial sources put it at six million or more, entailing huge health and social problems for the country.[43] While Tehran wants Kabul to do more to stem the flow of opiates into Iran, the Afghan government has little capacity to do so. Afghanistan is one of the largest poppy-growing and heroin-producing countries in the world, accounting for two-thirds of the total global area of opium poppy cultivation (201,000 hectares) and producing around 80 percent of the world's opium.[44] The illicit opiate industry in Afghanistan was worth $2.8 billion in 2014, equivalent to 13 percent of its gross domestic product.[45] The country's drug industry has been widely linked to international cartels, and benefits both government officials and insurgents.[46]

The fourth factor complicating Iranian-Afghan relations is Tehran's distrust of nuclear-armed Pakistan, which has a long history of intervention aimed at countering Indian influence and preventing Iran from gaining the upper hand in Afghanistan. Pakistan is a predominantly Sunni Muslim state, with Shias forming around 20 percent of its population of some 200 million. Although Tehran and Islamabad have maintained the semblance of good neighborly relations, Tehran harbors serious reservations about Pakistan on four key issues.

The first and most long-standing is Islamabad's leveraging of the Taliban and their radical Sunni affiliates to maintain a determining influence in Afghanistan. A second is the widespread discrimination against Pakistan's Shia minority and the resultant intersectarian conflicts and killings, all of which challenge Tehran's position as the champion of Shia Muslims. The third is Pakistan's long-established strategic relationship with Iran's major regional rival, the Kingdom of Saudi Arabia. Pakistan's production of tactical nuclear bombs and their potential acquisition by Saudi Arabia are a matter of serious concern for Tehran. The fourth is the rise, over the last one and half decades, of Sunni insurgent groups in the Iranian Sunni-dominated province of Sistan-Baluchistan, which borders the Pakistani province of Balochistan. The most militant of these groups is Jundallah (Soldiers of God), which was established in 2002 and promotes itself as fighting for equal rights for the Iranian Baluchi and Sistani Sunnis, possibly with the long-term objective of gaining autonomy or independence. The group has carried out a number of violent operations against Iranian security and civilian targets, some of them extremely deadly. A 2010 suicide bombing in Chahbahar, for instance, claimed thirty-nine lives, prompting Tehran to reprimand Pakistan for its hosting of Jundallah terrorists for a second time since October 2009.[47] Iran captured and executed Jundallah's leader Abdolmalek Rigi in 2010, but the group has continued to remain active under the command of his successor, Muhammad Dhahir Baluch.

Tehran has alleged that Pakistan, in possible complicity with Saudi Arabia and the United States, has provided cross-border sanctuary and logistical support in Pakistani Balochistan for Jundallah and another Salafi extremist group, Jaish al-Adl (Army of Justice), which was founded in 2012 and fights for the same cause as Jundallah.[48] Although Islamabad has denied any involvement, Tehran continues to see Pakistan as responsible for the rise of what it considers to be designated terrorist organizations. This has considerably affected Iranian-Pakistani relations.

Western Neighbors

The 2003 US invasion of Iraq has significantly changed the situation to the west of Iran in its favor. Historically, Iraq's national identity had been forged within a pan-Arab paradigm, and since the late 1950s the country had increasingly been seen as an Arab front against Iranian regional influence. Chapter 3 described how, during the Iran-Iraq War, Saddam Hussein projected himself and his country as a Sunni Arab bulwark against Iran's Islamist expansionism, bolstering this with fiery anti-Persian, pan-Arab rhetoric. The experience and memory of this conflict played a defining role in shaping Iranian foreign policy, emphasizing to its leadership the paramountcy of developing Iran's defensive capabilities and cementing its paranoia of encirclement by hostile Arab regimes.

The US invasion altered this strategic calculus. It removed the Iraqi dictator and transformed the politically and socially divided country from a strong dictatorial state with suppressed societies into a weak state with strong but rival societies. In the process, it also empowered the marginalized Shia majority (who form 60 percent of Iraq's population) vis-à-vis the Sunni and Kurdish minorities,[49] opening the way for Iran to strengthen its affiliation with Iraq's Shia majority and dramatically shifting the regional power balance to Iran's advantage. At the same time, the invasion brought the threat of American troops enclosing Iran on two fronts. In addition to a strong military presence in the Gulf, the US had begun establishing military bases in some of the former Soviet Central Asian republics as part of the so-called war on terror, and also as a means of deterring Russia from its ambitions to regain its former influence in those republics during the Soviet era. While Tehran could rejoice over the removal of the two hostile neighboring regimes of Saddam Hussein and the Taliban, it now also had to fear an American encirclement, especially with the resurgence of right-wing forces in the US advocating the overthrow of the Islamic Republic.

Tehran decided on two policy goals in this context: preventative and promotional. The first was to preclude the US from making any gains in the region that would enable them to harm or threaten the

Islamic Republic in the future. In this, it was enormously assisted by the lack of a viable American strategy to effectively manage post–Saddam Hussein Iraq. As the latter rapidly descended into internecine conflicts, it was simultaneously transformed into a zone of competition between various regional powers—Iran, Saudi Arabia, and Turkey in particular—with each seeking to shape the post-invasion political scene. Iran had been covertly supporting various armed Shia insurgents ever since the beginning of the Iran-Iraq War, with the aim of instigating an insurgency against Saddam Hussein. This paralleled the Iraqi dictator's call on Iran's Arab minority, who form about 2 percent of the population and is largely concentrated in the oil-rich province of Khuzestan, to rise up against the Islamic regime. Neither side's expectations materialized as long as Saddam Hussein was in power. However, in the wake of the US invasion, Iranian involvement has paid very handsome dividends. The invasion not only provided a defensible niche for the Supreme Council for Islamic Revolution in Iraq to emerge as a major pro-Iranian political force in Iraq, it also enabled Tehran to fund and equip Shia militias such as the Badr Corps and the Mehdi Army to engage in a localized insurgency against the coalition forces. Tehran now had an opportunity to send members of its secretive Quds Force to assist and fight with these militias as part of a broader strategy of "bleeding" out coalition forces and forcing a political withdrawal by maximizing losses.[50] It is estimated that weapons and explosives provided by the Quds Force to the militias were responsible for 20 percent of US combat deaths.[51] When the US finally withdrew its forces at the end of 2011, it left behind a broken Iraq under a predominantly Shia, pro-Iranian government. Iran had never been better positioned to influence the country's political direction.

The second goal has been to advance broader Iranian political and strategic interests. Iran has several advantages over its regional competitors in Iraq, the most important of which is the country's Shia majority. Many members of Iraq's Shia political and religious elites, including such influential figures as Ayatollah Ali al-Sistani, Nur al-Maliki, and Moqtadr al-Sadr, had lived in exile in Iran, taking shelter there to escape persecution under Saddam Hussein's rule.[52] As discussed in chapter 5, Iran has pursued a concerted soft-power strategy in Iraq, developing close relations with Shia political parties, coreligionists, and the political elite. It has backed these allies within, rather than against, the American policy of democratization, which has enabled the Shia majority to dominate the Iraqi government. The two countries have signed more than one hundred cooperation agreements since 2003, including agreements in 2015 on taxation and customs.[53] Iran has become Iraq's largest trading partner, with trade reaching $12 billion in 2015, and plans to expand it to $20 billion by 2018.[54] Iran has also forged extensive links with Shia networks and communities by investing millions of dollars in infrastructure and tourism, particularly around Iraq's two largest holy Shia sites—Najaf and Karbala.[55] In 2015, Iran spent $13.5 million rebuilding and renovating holy shrines, double the amount spent the previous year.

Iran's growing ties and influence in Iraq have complemented its friendly relations with Bashar al-Assad's Syrian regime. It is important to note that the Islamic Republic's close relationship with Syria is largely strategic, being sectarian and ideological only to a marginal extent. Syria's strategic position has provided Iran with a critical link to Lebanon (that is, to Hezbollah), as well as port access to the Mediterranean. As such, the Islamic Republic has persistently viewed Syria as a central element in its foreign policy and regional security architecture and in its efforts to build a "forward defensive posture."

The Iranian-Syrian relationship has a sectarian dimension, but in a narrow and largely negative sense. The ruling Assad clan are members of the minority Alawite sect—a subgroup with secretive traditions that was only formally recognized as part of the Shia community in 1973.[56] However, unlike the Iranian system, the Assad regime's ideology has been strictly secular, a result of not only its Ba'athist and Arab socialist politics but also the diversity of Syria's religious landscape. Alawites have historically constituted only 12 percent of Syria's population, but they have ruled over the 70 percent Sunni majority, although in close alliance with Christian and Druze minorities, since Hafez al-Assad's accession to the presidency in 1970.[57] The popular revolts against the Assad regime that followed the advent of the Arab uprisings in late 2010 were largely spearheaded by the suppressed Sunnis, enabling the regime to ascribe the uprisings to the specter of Sunni "extremism" and "terrorism" and to appeal to ethnic and religious minorities for support.[58] Iran's virtually unqualified backing of the regime has largely underwritten its survival against the Syrian opposition, which the regime, instead of pursuing negotiations for a peaceful outcome, resolved to crush from the outset. There is no available source that would allow us to quantify Iranian assistance to the Assad regime, but it is widely believed to have included a substantial amount of military materiel and a sizable contingent of troops from the Quds Force, as well as Afghan, Iraqi, and Pakistani Shia fighters whom Tehran has recruited and deployed as "volunteers."[59] Early evidence of Iran's military involvement came in July 2012, when forty-eight Iranian nationals were captured by the Free Syrian Army, who claimed that they were on a "reconnaissance mission in Damascus."[60] In 2013, Tehran approved the entry of five to seven thousand Hezbollah troops from Lebanon to bolster the Assad regime's fighting capacity.[61] Indeed, one Syrian official stated in 2014 that "if it had not been for Iranian support we could not have survived the crisis."[62]

However, in the process, Iran has incurred high human, political, and financial costs. Although no reliable data are available on Iranian casualties, Iranians have borne witness to a procession of body bags returning to the country. Fatalities have included several high-ranking Iranian generals from the elite Revolutionary Guard, most importantly Brigadier General Hossein Hamadani, who was killed on October 8, 2015, and Brigadier General Mohsen Ghajarian, who reportedly lost his life on February 5, 2016.[63] In the financial dimension, it is estimated that Iran has helped maintain the regime to the tune of more than $6 billion annually, on average, since 2011.[64] Part of this has been in the form of massive loans; in 2013 alone, Iran extended a $3.6 billion line of credit to the regime, as well as an additional $1 billion for non-oil-related products.[65]

Iran has also successfully broadened its involvement to include conflicts that appear to have no direct relation to its national security but will give it the opportunity to strengthen its strategic reach in the region. This is most evident in Iran's activities in Yemen, where it has supported the Zaidi Shia Houthi insurgents, who seized Sana'a in 2014, against President Abdrabbuh Mansour Hadi, who is backed by Saudi Arabia, the GCC, and the West. Yemen, which remains a largely underdeveloped, tribal country, became unstable and conflict-ridden following the mass uprisings of 2011 that put an end to the authoritarian presidency of Ali Abdullah Saleh (1990–2012). The Houthis, most of whom inhabit the poor and marginalized regions of north Yemen, have opposed foreign interference and Riyadh's support of Hadi as well as the rise of Wahhabi groups, most prominently Al-Qaeda in the Arabian Peninsula (AQAP).[66] Foreign intervention has magnified the scale, duration, and intensity of the conflict, whose initial causes were primarily local. Indeed, some analysts have noted that the growth of the Houthis' organization as an effective military militia could not have occurred without Iran's assistance.[67] The Houthis were also backed by Saleh and his supporters. Ironically, Riyadh and Washington had backed Saleh for years despite his growing autocratic tendencies, largely because of his cooperation in anti-terror campaigns (directed primarily against AQAP). The success of IS in establishing a base in Yemen since 2015 has given Iran further reason to remain an active supporter of the Houthi cause. In this it shares a common interest with many regional and international actors, including even the United States.

Northern and Northeastern Neighbors

Among its neighbors to the north, Iran maintains a friendly working relationship with Turkey, despite the two countries' opposing interests in the Syrian conflict and wider foreign policy differences. Indeed, Turkey has publicly supported Iran's nuclear program for civilian purposes, to which end it has acted as a mediator between Iran and the West. Although political relations have proceeded cautiously due to mutual strategic and geopolitical wariness, Ankara and Tehran have displayed a strong willingness to build economic ties.[68] In 2011 and 2012, Turkey helped Iran circumvent financial sanctions by exporting gold to Iran in exchange for goods.[69] Trade between the two countries in 2015 was worth $10 billion, with both sides pledging to increase it to $30 billion by 2020.[70] Iran was also Turkey's seventh-largest export partner and eighteenth-largest import partner in 2017,[71] accounting for a quarter of Turkey's total energy imports.[72] These economic interests, combined with the two countries' shared concern to prevent Kurdish independence, have led them to try to compartmentalize their relations by "fencing off their geostrategic differences."[73] Of course, it remains to be seen whether this will actually work. Much depends on whether the preservation of the Assad regime remains a key component in determining the fate of Syria, which both countries see as central to their strategic interests. The Qatar crisis, erupting in June 2017 with Saudi Arabia, the UAE, Bahrain, and Egypt imposing a blockade of the country, has provided Tehran and Ankara with another common cause, which is discussed below.

Iran's ties with three of its other northern neighbors—Armenia, Azerbaijan, and Turkmenistan—are of a variable nature. Iran and Azerbaijan have had strained relations ever since the latter's independence in the wake of the Soviet Union's breakup in 1991. This can be largely attributed to two factors. First, much of Azerbaijan was once part of Iran but was lost to tsarist Russia in the Russo-Persian War of 1808–14. As a result, there are currently thirteen million ethnic Azeris in the contemporary territory of Iran, more than the entire population of Azerbaijan. Issues of national identity have frequently affected the relationship between Baku and Tehran. The status of Iran's sizable Azeri minority has been a recurrent issue for the Islamic Republic, underpinning its geopolitical approach to its northern neighbor to a considerable extent.[74] In 2012, Iran withdrew its ambassador from Azerbaijan after protesters outside the embassy allegedly insulted Islam.[75] In 2015, a children's television program in Iran sparked protests among Iranian Azeris after it made offensive jokes and mocked the Azeri accent.[76] Ever since its independence, Azerbaijan has vigorously sought to establish its own national identity on ethnic grounds, thereby distinguishing itself from Iranian influences. Second, Azerbaijan, although predominantly Shia, is a secular authoritarian state. As such, its ideological and political texture is in total variance with Iran's theocratic political makeup. These differences are reflected in its policy attitudes. Azerbaijan regards Turkey as a natural ally in a broadly defined pan-Turkism. It has also forged close ties with Israel. In 2012, Azerbaijan and Israel signed a $1.6 billion defense deal, with rumors that Baku had given Tel Aviv access to its airfields in the event of an Israeli strike on Iran's nuclear facilities.[77] In this respect, Azerbaijan's foreign policy position puts it plainly at odds with Iran.

In contrast, Iran has developed warmer relations with predominantly Christian Armenia. It has pursued a muted policy toward the Azerbaijan-Armenian conflict over Nagorno-Karabakh—an Armenian enclave inside Azerbaijan, which claims the enclave as part of its territory. Tehran's historically close relationship with Yerevan stems from a "strategic partnership" that demonstrates the pragmatic dimension of its foreign policy. Armenia, as a member of the Eurasian Economic Union, is an important access route for Iranian energy exports and trade. Iran is also Armenia's fourth-largest trading partner, with bilateral trade amounting to $300 million in 2015.[78] At the same time, Armenia's adversarial relationship with Turkey aligns with Tehran's geopolitical interests.

Iran-Turkmenistan relations have been stable, with a considerable degree of cross-border economic and trade activities between them. These ties are underpinned by their mutual international isolation as well as by shared economic and energy interests, particularly in the development of hydrocarbon resources in the Caspian Sea.[79] Furthermore, Iran is Ashgabat's only connection to the Persian Gulf and its lucrative export routes, while Turkmenistan provides Iran with an important access route to the rest of Central Asia. Annual Iranian exports to Turkmenistan were worth $1 billion in 2015. The following year, Turkmenistan contracted to import $2.5 billion worth of engineering equipment, materials, and services from Iran, while Tehran announced plans to import more than $30 billion worth of gas from its northern neighbor over the next decade.[80] However, while energy and economic interests have produced favorable relations thus far, Iran and Turkmenistan are likely to become energy competitors in the gas market in the future. Indeed, in January 2017, Turkmengaz, the state-owned gas company, cut supplies to Iran because of $2 billion worth of unpaid debts that Iran had incurred while under international sanctions.[81] Moreover, despite good relations, the reclusive nature of Ashgabat's secular government has prevented closer ties.

It is important to bear in mind that Iran's relations with adjoining states are characterized by a strong element of mutual reactiveness. Nowhere has this been more evident than in the Islamic Republic's relations with its geopolitical and sectarian archrival, Saudi Arabia. Nevertheless, the pattern of mutual reactiveness has also affected Iran's ties with other regional states to varying degrees. To illustrate this, we now turn to a consideration of Iran's relations with the Arab Gulf states, including how the latter have perceived and responded to the former's policy behavior.

The Gulf Neighborhood

The Saudi-led Gulf Arab states have viewed Iran's forward regional posture and nuclear program with growing alarm, especially as they perceived a diminishing assertiveness of America in the region under President Obama. They have accused Tehran of expansionism in the Levant, of playing a subversive and politically treacherous role, supporting "terrorism"—with clear reference to Hezbollah and the Houthis—and of fueling conflicts in the region for the purpose of regional supremacy and domination. In an October 2015 interview, the Saudi foreign minister Adel al-Jubeir claimed that Iran "is the biggest sponsor of terrorism in the world, and it is working on destabilizing the region."[82] Saudi Arabia and its allies have opposed the JCPOA and the lifting of sanctions on Iran, arguing that this could only enrich Tehran with more resources and embolden it to continue its aggressive and destabilizing policies—an argument that Israel has also advanced, in even stronger terms. Indeed, following the deal, al-Jubeir wrote that "Iran is the new great power of the Middle East and the US is the old."[83]

In view of Iran's military involvement and soft-power influence in Iraq and Syria, as well as its intervention in Yemen and alleged meddling in Bahrain, Saudi Arabia has strenuously sought the GCC to adopt a united defiant stance against Iran, with more defense expenditure and coordination to develop a unified military command of the GCC's forces. However, this goal has eluded the organization for years due to problems of interoperability and political differences.[84] Not all of the GCC's members have been inclined to embrace Riyadh's leadership or, for that matter, its demonization of Iran. The Sultanate of Oman has been on amiable terms with Iran since the advent of the Islamic Republic. In fact, contrary to Saudi wishes, Muscat played a critical role in hosting the secret, high-level US-Iranian talks that led eventually to the conclusion of the JCPOA.[85] Similarly, Kuwait and Qatar have consistently preferred a policy of engagement to confrontation with Iran. The best Riyadh has been able to elicit is full support from the UAE and Bahrain. This has left Saudi Arabia—the largest and most resource-rich GCC member, given the size of its wealth, population, political, and religious leverage and the length of its de facto alliance with the West, more specifically the United States—to take the lead in meeting Iran's challenges to the Arab states of the Gulf.

Riyadh has pursued multiple strategies and means to counter Iran's geopolitical and sectarian influence. First, it has steadily expanded its defense budget and capability by substantially enlarging its military and equipping it with state-of-the-art weapons systems. The Saudi defense budget almost doubled, from $48.5 billion in 2011 to a staggering $87.2 billion in 2015.[86] As such, during this period, it spent nearly six times as much on defense as Iran, accounting for 41 percent of the total defense expenditure in the Middle East and North African region compared to Iran's 7 percent.[87] The Saudi defense expenditure constitutes the largest share of the GCC's total military spending (well over $120 billion in 2015), which in turn accounted for more than half of the total military expenditure of the entire Middle East ($200 billion).[88] Riyadh's signing of a $110 billion arms deal with the United States on May 22, 2017, has steepened the trajectory of Saudi Arabia's astronomical military buildup, as discussed later. The country is currently the world's second-largest arms importer after India.[89]

Against this backdrop, the Saudi kingdom took the lead in establishing an Arab military coalition, with contributions from four other GCC members (the UAE, Kuwait, Qatar, and Bahrain), to launch the Operation Decisive Storm military campaign (later renamed Operation Restoring Hope) in March 2015 against the Iranian-backed Shia Houthi rebels in Yemen. The coalition was supported by the United States and some of its NATO allies, Britain in particular. This unprecedented initiative was designed not only to restore the Saudi-sponsored Hadi to power but also to send a loud message to Iran that it no longer was prepared to tolerate its "interference" in Arab affairs.[90] The campaign could not achieve its objectives in the short run; instead, it has involved Saudi Arabia and its allies in a costly, protracted Yemeni conflict, resulting in high human and material costs, and also in the widespread destruction and killing of civilians, as well as severe shortages and contamination of food and water that precipitated in 2017 the worst outbreak of cholera in modern history. By early 2016, four hundred Saudi soldiers and four hundred Saudi civilians had been killed in attacks along the border with Yemen alone.[91] Similarly, the UAE had lost more than eighty troops, including forty-five soldiers to a rebel missile strike that was the single deadliest attack on its military in the country's history.[92] Meanwhile, the UN has estimated that the total death toll of the conflict reached 10,000 by February 2017, including 3,799 civilians, with three million persons displaced. The Saudi-led coalition was responsible for 60 percent of Yemeni civilian deaths.[93] This prompted the Obama administration to distance itself from the coalition operations in August 2016—much to the Saudis' annoyance. However, Obama's controversial, populist Republican successor, Donald Trump, upon assuming office in January 2017, reversed this policy. He declared his full support for the Saudi-led intervention and condemned Iran as subversive for its backing of the Houthis. Shortly thereafter, he approved a covert US intelligence raid targeting AQAP, which resulted in the death of a US navy seal and an estimated twenty-five civilians.[94]

To further strengthen its anti-Iranian posture, the Saudi leadership very warmly welcomed President Trump on a state visit to Riyadh during May 20–22, 2017. The objective was not only to revitalize Saudi-US strategic ties in the strongest public terms possible. It was also to have Trump restate his condemnation of Iran on a shared platform with the Saudi leadership. This he did in the presence of all GCC leaders as well as more than thirty heads of predominantly Sunni Muslim states that Riyadh had invited in a show of confessional unity. By injecting more substance into Saudi-US ties and sending a message to Tehran, Riyadh signed on for a whopping $350 billion economic and trade agreement, including $110 billion for American arms, as mentioned earlier.

Following this, the Saudi leaders and their Emirati and Bahraini counterparts, plus the Egyptian military-general-turned-politician, President Abdel Fattah al-Sisi, were so emboldened that they not only stepped up their rhetorical ravaging of Iran and made common cause with Israel but also, more importantly, accused one of their GCC partners, the tiny but oil- and gas-rich Emirate of Qatar, of funding and supporting terrorism in the region. They castigated Qatar for its past sympathy for the Muslim Brotherhood, which won a democratic election in Egypt in 2012 following the fall of the Egyptian dictator Husni Mubarak in the wake of the revolution in 2011. The Brotherhood was overthrown only a year later in a counterrevolution led by al-Sisi with support from Saudi Arabia and the UAE. They also censured the small emirate for providing financial and material assistance to the Gaza Strip (under Israeli blockade since 2007) through the Palestinian Islamist group Hamas and more pointedly for its working relationship with Iran. Led by Riyadh, the four countries broke off all relations with Qatar on May 8, 2017, putting it under a virtual blockade from land, air, and sea to punish it for not toeing their line on regional policy. This confronted the Trump administration with a serious dilemma in light of Qatar's very close economic, trade, and military ties with the United States—the country hosts America's largest airbase in the Middle East, which is therefore crucial for US operations in Iraq, Syria, Afghanistan, and Yemen. However, given the contradictory nature and ad hoc policymaking decision of the Trump administration, the president declared his support for the Saudis and their allies while his secretary of state, Rex Tillerson, called for dialogue and a resolution of the dispute and unity of the GCC in the fight against terrorism.[95] Doha has characterized all allegations that it supports terrorism as baseless and vowed not to compromise the distinct national identity and foreign policy that it has developed since its independence from Britain in 1971.

In response, Turkey, under the moderate Islamist president Recep Tayyip Erdoğan, joined the Islamic Republic of Iran in declaring their support for Qatar. Although the two countries have been backing opposing sides in Syria, they found it opportune to adopt a common position in relation to Qatar as they had in other geopolitical areas. Ankara, which has had close relations with Doha for both ideological and economic reasons, decided to send troops to Qatar, presumably to defend it in the event of a Saudi-led invasion, while Tehran dispatched planeloads of emergency food supplies to compensate for the severing of Qatar's usual supply lines from Saudi Arabia. Moscow also received the Qatari foreign minister and gave him a sympathetic hearing. No doubt Russia has found it expedient to keep an eye on Qatar in order to gauge how to make use of the dispute to work with friendly Iran and, increasingly, amenable Turkey, to advance its interests in the region. This is not the only diplomatic crisis to hit the Gulf in recent years. Qatari support for the Arab Spring uprisings resulted in Saudi Arabia, the UAE, and Bahrain withdrawing their ambassadors from the emirate in 2014, and Qatar's relations with Egypt and Saudi Arabia had been growing tense ever since. This time, however, the rift precipitated a deeper crisis, with serious regional and international dimensions. In all probability, it marked the end of the GCC as a united Arab front—much to the delight of the organization's adversaries, Iran in particular.

Saudi Arabia has simultaneously intensified its religious rhetoric, seeking to portray the Islamic Republic of Iran as a sectarian menace and to project itself as the leader of the Sunni world.[96] Although no prominent members of the Saudi royal family have publicly attacked or disparaged Shia Islam, the same cannot be said about their allies in the religious establishment. Many Saudi clerics have long denounced Shias as "heretics" and "false," and this has been amplified in recent times.[97] In December 2016, the kingdom's Grand Mufti, Abdul Aziz al Sheikh, controversially opined that Iran's political elite "are not Muslims" and that "they are the son of the Magi [followers of Zoroastrianism] and their hostility towards Muslims is an old one, especially with People of the Tradition [Sunnis]."[98] This was part of an attempt to counter the Iranian regime's insistence on Shiism as the authentic path of Islam and to cast doubt on the religious legitimacy of its theocratic order.

Riyadh has also reacted to Iran's rising influence by stepping up its surveillance and suppression of its own Shia minority, which constitutes 10–15 percent of the kingdom's population. It has viewed its Shias as internal security threats acting as a fifth column for Iran. Tehran has loudly condemned the Saudi treatment of its Shias, especially pilgrims, as purposely discriminatory. In January 2016, tensions between Iran and Saudi Arabia escalated following the Saudi government's execution of a leading and popular Saudi Shia cleric, Sheikh Nimr al-Nimr, on terrorism-related charges. Nimr was outspoken in his criticism of Riyadh's behavior toward the kingdom's Shia minorities and had backed anti-government protests in the Shia-majority Eastern province.[99] Nimr's execution led to further protests not only in the Eastern province but also in Iran, Lebanon, Bahrain, and Yemen. In Iran, protesters attacked the Saudi embassy in Tehran and the consulate in Mashhad. In retaliation, Saudi Arabia severed all relations with Iran. Bahrain and Sudan followed suit, but other GCC members only downgraded their missions in muted deference to Saudi Arabia. In September 2016, Iran banned its pilgrims from undertaking the Hajj, ostensibly to avoid the loss of Iranian lives following a stampede that killed 2,426 people the previous year. Iran, which lost 464 of its citizens, including some prominent clerics, blamed the incident on Saudi negligence.[100] Three months later, Saudi Arabia sentenced 15 Shia citizens to death on charges of spying for Iran.[101] Ties have plummeted to their lowest level since the massacre in Mecca in 1987, when over 200 Iranian pilgrims chanting anti-US and anti-Israel political slogans and brandishing portraits of Khomeini were killed in clashes with Saudi security forces.

Moreover, Riyadh has made efforts to expand its regional engagements to counter Iranian influence. It has focused on strengthening strategic ties with the nuclear-armed and predominantly Sunni Islamic Republic of Pakistan. The two states have shared a historically close relationship dating back to Pakistan's creation from the partition of British India in 1947. Pakistan's founding father, Ali Jinnah, proclaimed a national Islamic identity for his country and sought close ties with the Muslim world as well as the West. This foreign policy sought to strengthen Pakistan's position in two arenas. First, it aimed to counter the international and regional influence of India, in the context of the countries' entanglement in serious border disputes in the wake of a contested partition process, especially over Kashmir. Second, Pakistan pursued close international relations in order to compensate for the infrastructure deficit that it had inherited from the British partition plan, which had given India the lion's share of institutional, economic, and industrial assets. Saudi Arabia and Pakistan found comfortable bonds with one another as two fellow Sunni states. In the early 1970s, Pakistan provided Saudi Arabia a military contingent on a "special mission," essentially to protect the ruling Saudi family. In exchange, the oil-rich kingdom grew to be a major financial donor to Pakistan, funding various development projects, including its secret nuclear program.[102]

Pakistan-Saudi relations were cemented with the rise of General Zia ul-Haq (1977–88), who made the Islamization of Pakistan and the frontline status of his country against the Soviet invasion and occupation of Afghanistan for a decade from December 1979 the mainstay of his policy. Riyadh provided a large amount of financial assistance to the main Sunni Afghan Islamic resistance forces (the Mujahideen) to the Soviet occupation, and to Pakistan as their main state backer. It also allowed many of its citizens—including Osama bin Laden, the subsequent leader of al-Qaeda, and many of his operatives—to join the Mujahideen's declared *jihad* to liberate

Afghanistan from Soviet communist rule. Expelling the Soviets from Afghanistan was also the main objective of the United States and its allies. Foreign resistance fighters thus made their way into Afghanistan through Pakistan under the watchful eyes of not only Pakistan's powerful Inter-Services Intelligence but also its American counterpart, the CIA, which jointly guided and supported various Mujahideen groups and coordinated their activities. Saudi Arabia, in close collaboration with the United States, funded many *madrassas* (Islamic schools) in Pakistan that recruited and trained fighters from among the Afghan refugees for the Mujahideen. According to the former Saudi Chief of Intelligence, Prince Turki al-Faisal, Saudi assistance to the Mujahideen and, later on, to the Taliban, amounted to $24 billion during the 1980s and 1990s.[103]

In recent years, Riyadh has deepened its defensive and strategic ties with Pakistan. During February and March of 2014, the then crown prince, Salman ibn Abdulaziz, accompanied by the foreign minister, Saud al-Faisal, visited Pakistan. Meanwhile, Saudi Arabia hosted a visit by Pakistan's new army chief, General Raheel Sharif, who met with King Abdullah and top Saudi commanders to discuss and bolster defense, economic, and cultural cooperation between the two countries.[104] These exchanges resulted in two agreements. The Saudis offered Pakistan a $1.5 billion grant, [105] reportedly out of a promised $3 billion, which the Pakistan authorities described as an "unconditional" and "friendly gift"[106] to help Islamabad stabilize its declining currency, boost its foreign exchange reserves, "meet [its] debt-service obligations and undertake large energy and infrastructure projects."[107] The two sides also signed a weapons deal to enable Saudi Arabia to purchase Pakistani arms. Although Pakistan, which has the sixth-largest army in the world, is a net arms importer, it also sells jet fighters, anti-tank missiles, armored personal carriers, and small arms to Sri Lanka, Iraq, and Malaysia. Reports in the Pakistani and international press contend that the deal's main objective was to enable Saudi Arabia to send Pakistani arms to Syrian rebels in order to counter Iran and Hezbollah's support for the Assad regime.[108]

Saudi-Pakistani connections grew at an unprecedented rate under Prime Minister Nawaz Sharif (2013–17), who spent seven years in exile in the kingdom after being ousted from office in a military coup led by General Pervez Musharraf in 1999. Sharif's relations with the kingdom can be gauged by the Saudi magnate Prince Al-Waleed bin Talal's description of him as "our man in Pakistan."[109] Close Saudi-Pakistani ties, amounting to a de facto alliance, are also designed to help the two sides coordinate their involvement in the post-2014 political landscape in Afghanistan. In this, one of their main objectives is to hinder Iran from playing a determining role in the country. According to some Washington insiders, Pakistan has been producing significant quantities of small tactical nuclear weapons that can be loaded onto conventional cruise missiles.[110] The Saudis may well have an interest in procuring either some of these weapons or at least a Pakistani pledge of support in the event that Iran acquires military nuclear capability.

However, Saudi-Pakistani strategic cooperation has not been without its problems, because Islamabad's interests have not always coincided with those of Riyadh. For example, when Saudi Arabia assembled the Arab coalition force against the Houthis and requested contributions from a number of Muslim countries, the Pakistani parliament declined, despite the initial positive response of Prime Minister Sharif's leadership. The parliament argued that because the "Haramain wa Sharafain" (the two holy sites of Islam in Mecca and Medina) had not been attacked, Pakistan had no justification to participate in the Saudi-led operations in Yemen. To placate Riyadh's deep dismay, Pakistan's chief of army staff, General Sharif, and Prime Minister Sharif paid urgent visits to reassure the Saudi leadership of Pakistan's commitment to the kingdom.

General Sharif retired from Pakistan's top military position in November 2016. Only five weeks later, Riyadh invited him to head another Saudi extraregional initiative: the Islamic Alliance to Fight Terrorism, with membership from thirty-nine Sunni Muslim countries and headquarters in Riyadh. General Sharif accepted the position with the Pakistani government's backing, another development in the deepening of Saudi-Pakistan strategic relations.[111] Sharif's appointment and Pakistan's involvement in this explicitly sectarian initiative sparked debate in the country, given the fact that 20 percent of Pakistan's population is Shia (albeit of a South Asian variety not recognized as orthodox by Saudi Wahhabis). It also prompted Iran to raise serious objections, arguing that it could "impact the unity of Islamic countries"[112] and therefore solidify Tehran's distrust of Pakistan.[113]

Meanwhile, Riyadh has made sure to maintain strong leverage against Hezbollah and Iran by backing the Sunni Future Movement as the core of the March 14 Alliance, led by Saad Hariri, in Lebanon. The Future Movement in general (and the March 14 Alliance in particular) views Hezbollah as a subversive influence responsible for the instability and political gridlock plaguing Lebanon. In their eyes, the Iranian-backed Assad regime bears the blame for many of the crises afflicting Lebanon and the region. They are therefore deeply opposed to Iranian influence. Lebanon was without a president for twenty-nine months from May 2014 due to disputes between different political factions, including Hezbollah and the Future Movement.[114] The issue was finally resolved not by an internal settlement but rather by Tehran and Riyadh, which came to an agreement on the choice of the Maronite general Michel Aoun, who assumed the Lebanese presidency on October 31, 2016. Aoun is allied with Hezbollah, which continues to be the strongest political and military force in Lebanon. Hezbollah has been described as a "state within a state" that is arguably more powerful and influential than any Lebanese political group and army.[115] In March 2016, Riyadh cut off $4 billion in military aid to Lebanon's security services in protest against Hezbollah's political obstructionism, a counterproductive move since it turned out to undermine the military vis-à-vis the paramilitary Hezbollah.

In Syria, Saudi Arabia has countered Iran and Hezbollah by providing funding and arms to the al-Mu'aradah al-Suriyah (Syrian Opposition). The assistance from Saudi Arabia, together with some of its GCC partners, Kuwait and Qatar in particular, has primarily been directed to the Syrian National Coalition and associated groups. However, at least initially, a great deal of this assistance also benefited the al-Qaeda–linked radical Salafist Jabhat al-Nusra (the Victory Front), which changed its name to Jabhat Fattah al-Sham (Front for the Liberation of the Levant) in 2016 and again to Hay'at Tahrir al-Sham (Levant Liberation Committee) in a move to distance itself from al-Qaeda. Yet due to the divided nature of the Syrian Opposition, which is composed of a broad spectrum of Islamist and secular groups that lack a unified political program, Riyadh made little progress in its anti-Assad and anti-Iranian objectives in Syria.[116] As such, its support did not translate into increased Saudi influence or control over the situation on the ground. On the contrary, Saudi Arabia's sponsorship of certain groups exacerbated factionalism within the Islamist opposition, resulting in the growth of Jabhat al-Nusra and its successors, including factions that would later become IS.

The emergence of IS in mid-2014 presented Saudi Arabia with a policy conundrum. Consolidating from 2012, IS had its genesis in the anti-Shia Al-Dawlah Al-Islamiyah fi Iraq (Islamic State in Iraq), which had been declared in 2005 by the Jordanian-born, al-Qaeda-linked (at least initially) Abu Musab al-Zarqawi. Although al-Zarqawi was targeted and killed by the US in 2006, his concept of an "Islamic state" as an extremist Salafist-Wahhabi–rooted political and territorial entity continued to survive in the minds of many of his cadres. These included Abu Bakr al-Baghdadi, the man who would later assume the leadership of IS and claim for himself the title of *khalifa* (or caliph, the leader or deputy to Prophet Mohammad) and Amir al-Mu'mineen (Commander of the Faithful). The outbreak of the Syrian conflict and the ongoing turmoil in post-invasion Iraq provided al-Baghdadi with the space and opportunity to exploit the grievances of Sunnis, including the disenchanted supporters of Saddam Hussein, in the Levant. In 2013, it succeeded in turning the Syrian city of Raqqa into its headquarters and conquering Iraq's second-largest city, Mosul, and declaring his Islamic State (IS) or *khilafat* on June 30, 2014.

From that point, while declaring a *jihad* and calling on all Muslims to follow and obey al-Baghdadi as *khalifa* and to combat infidels and misguided Muslims, IS rapidly consolidated its hold on most of the Sunni-populated western Iraqi province of Anbar and northern Syria through a politics of brutality and terror. It not only posed an existential threat to Iraq, Syria, and their neighbors but also alarmed the US and its allies, which saw their security and regional interests in jeopardy. The United States, backed by an array of regional and international forces, took the lead in containing, degrading, and destroying IS as a terrorist phenomenon. Thus, Saudi Arabia and Iran found themselves on opposite sides in relation to IS. Riyadh viewed IS with ambivalence: on the one hand, it posed a threat to Riyadh's claim of the Sunni leadership of Islam, but on the other, it had proved a useful force for Riyadh's objective of weakening Iran. Saudi Arabia joined the US-led coalition yet remained lenient toward IS. No neighboring state was placed more in IS's firing line than Iran, given the entity's anti-Shia and anti-Iranian stance. Tehran found itself compelled not only to act against IS—thus aligning itself with the US and its allies on this issue—but also to make use of the group's rise as another opportunity to enhance its influence in the Levant.

Saudi-Iranian relations have nose-dived to what appears now to be an irreconcilable rivalry and enmity. Although Tehran lifted the ban on Iranians making pilgrimage to Mecca and Medina in early 2017, the two rivals remain at perhaps the highest level of mutual distrust in their history. This situation has been compounded by, and is a function of, the two sides' unprecedented entanglement in proxy conflicts, which have seen Saudi-Iranian hostility playing itself out in many tragic scenes. The Trump leadership's strong stance against Iran and its expression of deep camaraderie with Saudi Arabia and some of its GCC partners as well as Egypt and Jordan, have substantially diminished the prospects for Saudi-Iranian detente for the foreseeable future.[117] A number of Muslim countries, including GCC members Oman and Kuwait, have been trying to deescalate the situation, but so far without success.

Drawbacks

A very potent regional policy complication facing the Islamic Republic is the escalation of geopolitically driven sectarianism. It is impossible to overstate Tehran's role in the generation of this development, as evidenced in its handling of some of the regional issues. Iran had gained some popularity on the "Arab street" until late 2010 due to its revolutionary rhetoric, its fierce opposition to the US and Israel, and its support of the Palestinian cause. Iran made major strides in its soft war in the Arab world through Hezbollah's resistance to Israel, which prompted the Jewish state's "strategic retreat" from Lebanon in 2000 and its successful defiance of the Israeli military campaign to destroy it in the 2006 Lebanon War. These victories earned Hezbollah, and by extension its Iranian patron, the veneration of the Arab peoples (though not of their governments). Similarly, while caught off guard by the Arab Spring popular uprisings in Tunisia and Egypt, Iran quickly decided to back the protests. It also reached out to several Islamist groups in the opposition, in particular the Muslim Brotherhood, which it backed when it came to power in Egypt in 2012.

However, when the uprisings spread to Syria and it became clear that the wave of Arab revolutionary movements now threatened to wipe out the Assad regime, Iran's alleged solidarity with the Arab protestors showed its limits. Within a year of the outbreak of the Syrian conflict, the Islamic Republic declared its unconditional commitment to the Assad regime's survival. It sought to discredit *all* Syrian opposition groups by lumping them together as Islamic extremists linked to al-Qaeda, accusing the entire Syrian opposition of harboring a dangerous anti-Shia agenda bankrolled by the West and the Gulf Arab states.[118] In direct contradiction to its narrative of supporting an "Islamic awakening," it furnished political and material support for the Assad regime's massive repression and killings of the opposition. Doing so tarnished Iran's image, eroded its legitimacy in the eyes of the Arab revolutionary movements, and undermined its rhetorical and political strategy. Whatever earlier appeal it had achieved on the "Arab street" was lost as Iran revealed itself to be as responsible as its Gulf Arab counterparts for fueling Shia-Sunni sectarian divisions and state repression in the region.

The result has been a dramatic widening of the Sunni-Shia fault line, which has added to the host of other issues besetting the region. Although Tehran has often tried to emphasize its pan-Islamic credentials, its disproportionate support of Shia groups and its commitment to the Assad regime compromise its ability to project itself as the premier champion of all Islam.

Meanwhile, the rise of IS presented Tehran with security challenges closer to home. Instead of dealing with IS as an aberrant phenomenon, Iran made countering Sunni extremism a policy priority. For example, in an Eid sermon in 2014, Khamenei declared that

> Shiites and Sunnis should not help the enemy by insulting each other's sanctities. Anyone who fuels the Shiite–Sunni conflict is helping the United States, the Zionist regime and the evil United Kingdom, which are responsible for creating IS and al-Qaeda in the first place.[119]

Similarly, at the 2015 International Islamic Unity Conference, Rouhani emphasized that "both Shiite crescent and Sunni axis are wrong. Shiites and Sunnis are brothers and followers of Islam and the manner of the great Prophet [Muhammad]."[120]

In a similar vein, while opposed to the Iraqi Kurds' desire for an independent state, Tehran showed no qualms in adopting a dual strategy of supporting Sunni Kurdish militias, such as the Patriotic Union of Kurdistan, and Shia groups to fight IS. Most notably, it revoked its support for a close Shia ally, Prime Minister Nouri al-Maliki, in the wake of the establishment of IS and joined regional and Western calls for him to step down in favor of Haider al-Abadi. This was a crucial development, given the incredibly sectarian nature of al-Maliki's government, which Tehran saw as a long-term destabilizing force for Iraq.[121] Yet under the premiership of al-Abadi, Tehran has not necessarily prevented some protégé Shia militias and groups from combating Arab Sunnis in Iraq when it has served its interests.

In the end, Tehran has managed to gain little popularity in the region, even where it has made the most investment. In Afghanistan, there is little or no support for an emulation of the Iranian system of governance, and Iran remains unpopular among the country's Sunni Pashtun ethnicity. Even among non-Pashtun segments, including Shia Muslims, there is skepticism about Iranian interference in Afghan affairs.[122] This view was reflected in Kabul's refusal to bow to Iranian pressure not to sign the 2012 Strategic Partnership with the United States, as well as Kabul's decision to maintain very close ties with the US and its allies. Tehran's establishment of relations with the Taliban can only add to the Afghan government's skepticism toward Iran.

Although there has been much noise made over the emergence of a so-called Shia crescent, the importance of Iran's sectarian influence in Iraq should not be overstated. While Shia communities in both countries share common links, this does not necessarily translate into extensive political leverage or loyalty. In fact, Najaf and Qom have historically competed for the status of being the center of Shia theological traditions. Indeed, one of the greatest challenges to Iran's pretensions to leadership of the Shia world comes from the widely popular Najafi cleric, Ayatollah al-Sistani, who has been a critic of the *velayat-e faqih*. In the course of its involvement in Iraq, Iran has made several missteps and statements that have compromised its reputation among all Iraqis, including Shias. In a 2010 survey, 48 percent of Iraqi Shias held negative views of Iran's ties to Iraq's political elites (compared to 18 percent who held positive views).[123] While another survey by the University of Aberdeen conducted in 2014 found that these views were drawn along sectarian lines, almost 39 percent of Shia respondents nevertheless saw Iran as a factor of instability (compared with 90 percent of Sunni respondents).[124]

In the Iraqi and Syrian conflicts, Iran has proved unable to prevail on its own. The United States and its Western allies had to provide enormous assistance to the Iraqi government, and indirectly to their Iranian supporters, to get the job done in the fight against their common enemy, IS. Similarly, had Russia not come to the aid of the Assad regime from late 2015, Iran would not have proved capable of saving the regime on the basis of its massive human and material investment alone. In fact, Russia's escalation of its military involvement was prompted by the fact that the Assad regime was on the verge of a collapse that Iran was powerless to prevent. Thus, while Iran faces and rises to many challenges to expanding influence in its neighborhood, recent tests of its hard and soft capabilities have put its geopolitical limits in plain sight, even for those in its own region.

The Islamic Republic of Iran's regional policy behavior has concentrated above all on forging a regional security structure in support of regime and state survival. Iran's Islamic leadership has not always allowed the ideals that it so actively publicizes to stand in the way of its interests. On the contrary, while it has deployed Islamic revolutionary rhetoric to justify policy actions, the latter have been influenced more by pragmatic than by ideological considerations. This is reflected in the fact that the Republic has, by and large, adjusted its regional relations according to its changing internal and external circumstances. From the largely defensive posture it adopted in its first two decades, the Islamic Republic has come to favor a policy that is both reactive and assertive. It has managed not only to counter, endure, or neutralize the regional challenges facing it but also to exploit them. Despite the Islamic Republic's contradictory policy behavior and the unremitting hostility of several of its US-backed neighbors, the Republic has succeeded in converting regional debacles into favorable opportunities to advance its ideological, political, and security agendas.

7

Relations with Major Powers

Ever since the advent of the Islamic regime plunged Iran into unrestrained animosity with the United States and Israel and strained its ties with the Gulf Arab states, the regime has continued the two-pronged *jihadi-itjihadi* approach of its founder Ayatollah Ruhollah Khomeini in the conduct of Iran's relations with world powers. One has followed a path of perseverant but flexible resistance toward its adversaries, and another has aimed at pragmatic friendship toward receptive powers—that is, Russia, China, and India as well as key member states of the EU, although the latter's dealings with the Islamic Republic have occasionally been restrained by their relations with the United States. Through this two-pronged approach, Tehran has sought to deflect and counter the US and US-allied pressure on the one hand and, ostensibly, to demonstrate its loyalty to Khomeini's "pro-Islamic foreign policy" on the other. Reconciling these two approaches has often confronted the Islamic regime with foreign policy dilemmas and contradictions, especially in light of its bifurcated and factionalized political system. One significant dimension in which these contradictions have manifested is in frequent ideological and realpolitik clashes between Tehran and the United States. The US-Iranian enmity has been central in shaping not only the two sides' policy attitudes toward one another but also Iran's international relations in general. Indeed, Iran's ties with other powers largely flow from this variable. Nonetheless, it is within this paradigm that the Islamic regime has managed to steer its way through a complex set of foreign policy complications to date. Let us now turn to assessing the nature and extent of Iran's relations with major powers.

The US-Iran Conundrum

The bilateral relationship—or the lack thereof—between the Islamic Republic of Iran and the United States has proved extremely volatile, challenging, and costly for both sides over the last forty years. The Islamic Republic has viewed the US as an arrogant hegemonic power intent on, at best, limiting and, at worst, destroying the Iranian Islamic government. The US, on the other hand, has denounced the Islamic Republic as a repressive theocracy and treated it as a regional menace and sponsor of international terrorism, and thus a threat to America's interests in the Middle East and beyond. Both sides have engaged in a defensive build-up against the other and a persistent campaign of demonizing and discrediting one another. Despite this state of affairs, neither side has so far found it in its interest to escalate this cold war into a direct hot war. In fact, both states have restrained themselves from responding militarily to each other's provocations on many occasions, including the incident of July 1988, when the US shot down an Iranian civilian passenger plane, resulting in the deaths of 290 passengers. President Ronald Reagan (1981–89) called it "a human tragedy" but declared that there would be no change in America's commitment to protecting the shipping lanes through the Strait of Hormuz and to safeguarding US interests in the Middle East.[1] Tehran described it as an act of premeditated murder, with Ayatollah Khomeini urging his people to wage a war against the United States.[2] Even so, in spite of the mutual recrimination, the situation did not escalate into full-scale war.

By the end of the presidency of George W. Bush (2001–9), America's policy of sanctioning, isolating, and containing the Islamic

Republic failed to bring Tehran to its knees or to make it fall in line with American geopolitical priorities. Similarly, the Iranians proved unable to make the US embrace the Islamic regime's legitimacy or even to recognize it as "normal." President Mohammad Khatami made a serious effort toward this, but (as explained in chapter 4) he was very much limited by domestic factional opposition to a thaw in US-Iranian relations and by Washington's unwillingness to trust him as the man in charge. Given this gridlock, the antagonists eventually found themselves with little choice but to opt for a policy of relative detente. The initiative had to come from the American side, and it materialized with President Barack Obama (2009–17), who, during his presidential campaign in 2008 and afterward, voiced a strong preference for diplomatic engagement over military options (which were kept open as a last resort). Obama saw this approach as expedient in order to reduce misunderstandings with Iran and to reach a negotiated settlement of some of the fundamental issues underpinning US-Iranian hostilities.

Although Obama could not advance his diplomatic aims during the hard-line presidency of Mahmoud Ahmadinejad, he found a receptive partner in the latter's successor, the moderate Hassan Rouhani. The Obama-Rouhani combination proved effective in bringing about a thaw in the US-Iranian relationship. However, the election of the conservative, protectionist, and divisive President Donald Trump, who has taken a strident pro-Israeli and pro-Saudi Arabian stance and anti-Iranian posture, has once again changed the situation. He has lambasted Iran as a dangerous actor and for its ballistic missile tests—a reason that Tehran considers entirely invalid.[3]

Over the last forty years, four salient issues have come to define US-Iranian relations. The first is Iran's nuclear program. Concerns about Iranian nuclear proliferation have been a consistent fear in Washington and among its allies ever since the early 1990s, when Iran began seriously developing its nuclear program on the foundations of Pahlavi-era nuclear infrastructure (which the US had endorsed) and began receiving technical and material assistance from China and Russia.[4] The US believes that Iran harbored ambitions to acquire nuclear weapons, in violation of its obligation as a signatory to the NPT. This fear has been exacerbated by Iran's virulently anti-Western posture, its militant rhetoric against Israel, and criticisms of Saudi Arabia and some of its GCC allies.

The second is Iran's support for various subnational groups in the region, most importantly Hezbollah, and some Palestinian factions and other friendly entities that oppose the US-backed status quo in the region. The US and its allies have classified Hezbollah, along with Hamas, as terrorist organizations and hold Iran's sponsorship of such groups largely accountable for the spread of their activities at the expense of US interests in the region. Washington sees Iran's support for Shia groups in the Gulf area as endangering the security and stability of its key allies and fermenting sectarian discontent.[5] Beyond this, it is seriously discomforted by Iran's role in Iraq and Afghanistan, as well as in Syria, where Tehran's support for the Bashar al-Assad regime has undermined the US's position and influence and demonstrated America's increasing impotence to shape the region in the face of changing circumstances. Iran's support for the Houthis in Yemen has added to the plethora of US and Saudi-led Arab concerns.

The third is the Israeli-Palestinian conflict. The Islamic Republic has persistently viewed the US's continuous unconditional support for Israel as part of an aggressive, imperialist design for regional domination. Israel and Iran are strategic and ideological rivals, each seeing the other as an existential threat. Conversely, the US has seen the Islamic Republic's regional activities, and its rhetorical rejection of Israel as a Zionist expansionist state, as responsible for causing roadblocks on the path to securing a viable resolution of the Israeli-Palestinian conflict.[6]

The fourth is Iran's Islamic system of governance and its human rights record. The US objects to the Iranian regime's use of force to repress dissent, which it regards as emblematic of the autocratic and corrupt nature of the system as a whole. The government's suppression of the 2009 Green Movement was taken as unambiguous evidence of the Islamic Republic's fundamental incompatibility with the human rights and democratic standards that the US claims to champion as universal values, although in relation only to its adversarial states in the Middle East. For its part, Tehran feels perennially threatened by Washington's rhetorical and material support of democracy and human rights, which it sees as hypocritical in light of its conduct in the region; by its sponsorship of NGOs promoting these values; and by congressional funding for intelligence and nonintelligence activities to destabilize the Iranian regime. The controversial Iran Democracy Fund, created by the Bush administration in 2006, was interpreted in this light. The fund was even criticized by Iranian civil society groups, which claimed that it "tainted" their image and left them open to accusations of collaborating with the US toward regime change, ultimately undermining their work and leading to increased persecution in Iran.[7] In a separate case, in 2010, Iran's Ministry of Intelligence and Security labeled sixty media groups, think tanks, and NGOs as "Soft War agents," prohibiting any Iranians from receiving funds or working with these organizations.[8] Tehran views Washington's sponsorship of democracy and civil society as shorthand for US support of dissidents and regime change—akin to the CIA-organized coup that removed Prime Minister Mohammad Mosaddegh from power in 1953. In May 2016, Ali Khamenei warned about the effects of foreign efforts to "weaken the system from within," stating that "Iran's enemies try to influence decision-making centers, alter Iranian officials' positions and change people's beliefs. . . . We should be strong and empowered [in the face of these]."[9]

Of these four issues, the most important for both Obama and Rouhani was a negotiated resolution of the dispute over the Iranian nuclear program. Each side had its own reasons for moving in this direction as speedily as possible.

Iranian Motivations

Rouhani was elected on what essentially amounted to a reformist platform (see chapter 4). He had promised to make improving the economy and social services as his most urgent priority, but it was clear to him that achieving this would not be possible without first bringing an end to United Nations (UN) and, more important, US-led sanctions. For him, the removal of sanctions was central to tackling the myriad economic challenges that faced the country and to securing the foreign investment and technology that Iran badly needed to overhaul its aging oil infrastructure and modernize its economy. Khamenei and the conservative religious establishment, which did not oppose Rouhani's election, by now also recognized the urgency of improving Iranians' economic and living conditions. They had grown concerned about the possibility of the reemergence of the 2009 Green Movement, which had threatened their base of power.[10]

The wide-ranging sanctions had seriously impacted Iran's economy, particularly after 2012, when Iran was placed under a joint US-EU oil embargo and disconnected from the Society for Worldwide Interbank Financial Telecommunication (SWIFT) network. The imposition of these new sanctions led to a drop in oil revenues from $9.8 billion in July 2011 to $2.9 billion in July 2012,[11] causing a 9 percent contraction of GDP between 2012 and 2014.[12] Ahmadinejad described the sanctions as "the most extensive . . . ever," claiming that they were "the heaviest economic onslaught on a nation in history . . . every day, all our banking and trade activities and our agreements are being monitored and blocked."[13]

However, Rouhani's election and Obama's incumbency created a unique convergence of interests, placing conciliatory governments at the helm concurrently in both countries for the first time since the revolution.[14] Rouhani and, for that matter, the Supreme Leader by now felt quite comfortable to pursue the path of negotiations to resolve the nuclear dispute for two main reasons. First, Iran had achieved in its nuclear program what it had intended in terms of know-how and technological, infrastructural, and enrichment capabilities. Second, its hand had been strengthened by the leverage it had acquired in neighboring states—Afghanistan, Iraq, Syria, and Lebanon. Tehran knew that the US needed Iranian cooperation if it wanted to play a constructive role in resolving conflicts and improving its regional standing.

US Incentives

The Obama administration had several good reasons to become receptive toward Iran. First, a possible rapprochement with Iran could improve US security and foreign policy in the Middle East at a time of waning US influence in the region. Bush's invasions of Afghanistan and Iraq created two costly wars that had caused widespread regional instability and fed the rise of anti-US, Sunni extremist groups and their sentiments.[15] Western intervention in Libya and Obama's prevarication in regard to the Arab uprisings (the Arab Spring) had further eroded America's standing in the Middle East. Initially, Obama adopted a haphazard and ambivalent approach toward the uprisings. While giving verbal support to the pro-democracy movements, he simultaneously backed long-standing Arab autocracies and ultimately embraced Egypt's return to authoritarian rule under Abdel Fattah el-Sisi. This, together with his failure to implement the "red line" he had drawn on the Assad regime's use of chemical weapons in Syria in 2013 and to secure a resolution to the long-running Israeli-Palestinian conflict in the face of Israel's intransigence, underlined the US's weakening ability to dictate favorable outcomes in the region.[16]

Iran's cooperation, which had been missing from US strategic calculations since 1979, had nevertheless become more and more essential for its ability to resolve conflicts in the region. This was especially true in those cases in which Iran had been directly or indirectly involved—an involvement that Iran had assumed in part because of US policy failures. Roman Muzalevsky notes: "Some of Iran's wins are really US geopolitical mistakes."[17] He also aptly states:

> While Iran's regional position has strengthened vis-à-vis the United States following the toppling of the Taliban in Afghanistan and Saddam Hussein in Iraq, Iran has proven unable to force game-changing outcomes. By the same token, the United States, while still the most formidable military power, is no longer in a position to force regional dynamics without substantially damaging its already weakened regional standing. Neither Iran,

> nor Washington today is able to address effectively—certainly not alone—the numerous security challenges emanating from Afghanistan, Iraq, Libya, Syria, Lebanon, and Yemen, among other states.[18]

A possible breakthrough in US-Iranian relations could offer a potential avenue to improve regional stability by allowing cooperation in key areas of common strategic interest. In Afghanistan and Iraq, for example, the US and Iran shared the goal of maintaining stable and functioning central governments, although they competed over who would have the greater influence in them.[19] Both in and beyond Afghanistan, the subsequent emergence of IS and the rise of Sunni extremism (and sectarianism) became a common security threat for both Iran and the US.

The issue of Iran and weapons of mass destruction (WMD) had been a recurring theme in US political security discussions. Reaching a deal through diplomacy represented an attractive solution that could be achieved via multilateral cooperation within international norms without producing instability or further conflict. This was particularly important given the fragile state of the US economy following the global financial crisis of 2008, as well as the public's limited appetite for military action after several years of stagnation in Afghanistan and Iraq, which had made it very difficult for Washington to sustain multiple, costly foreign interventions.[20] Moreover, improved relations with Iran raised the possibility of changing the regional dynamics in such a way as to allow the United States to extricate itself from Middle Eastern crises and shift resources to bolster one of Obama's strategic moves: America's "pivot to Asia"—a policy that has also underpinned Trump's calls to counter China's expanding power.

A thaw in relations with Iran could also unlock potential economic benefits for the US, given Iran's immense natural resources and sizable economy as well as its investment opportunities. As mentioned in chapter 5, Iran's economy is also relatively diverse—oil and gas accounted for around 15 percent of GDP in 2016.[21] By comparison, in the same year, oil in Saudi Arabia accounted for 87 percent of government revenues, 42 percent of GDP, and 90 percent of export earnings.[22] This diversification means a wider range of opportunities for investors, particularly given Iran's large, educated, young population and its broad-based growth prospects. Iran's reintegration into the world economy could offer the US access to a highly lucrative new market beyond its established regional and global trade partners.[23]

Further, a rapprochement could lead to broader US political and strategic gains. Iran's strength in hydrocarbons and its geostrategic location put it in a good position to act as an energy corridor to both Asia and Europe. Iran's relative stability, in comparison with the volatility of its neighbors, makes it well placed to benefit as a major energy supplier. The country's return to the international system could be expected to bring "peace dividends" by encouraging the country to foster stability in its neighborhood. In other words, as Muzalevsky put it in 2015, "currently, energy, trade, and transit companies and developers shun Iran, forestalling the inter-regional integration of these areas on terms that Washington could shape were it to engage Iran."[24] The prospect of US commercial engagement with Iran was an especially attractive option as it could undercut Russian dominance in European and Eurasian markets. The removal of oil-embargo sanctions also meant that Iranian exports would increase, driving down or at least maintaining low oil prices, which could have significant effects not only on the Russian economy but also on US energy exports.[25]

The Nuclear Deal

By 2013, the two sides had compelling reasons to seek a resolution of the nuclear dispute as quickly and earnestly as possible. Rouhani moved swiftly to secure a breakthrough in responding to President Obama's long-standing overtures. After having secured the consent of the Supreme Leader and following the conclusion of a series of secret US-Iran talks in Oman (which had begun prior to Rouhani's assumption of the presidency), the Iranian president instructed his able and experienced foreign minister, Mohammad Javad Zarif, to formally engage world powers in Geneva. This included direct discussions with US Secretary of State John Kerry—the first of their kind since the advent of the Iranian Islamic regime. Rouhani followed this up by breaking another taboo: he made a telephone call to his American counterpart after leaving the UN General Assembly on September 27, 2013, to signal Iranian interest in resolving the nuclear dispute and ending sanctions.

On November 24, 2013, after intense negotiations in Geneva, Iran and the five permanent members of the UN Security Council, plus Germany (P5+1), settled on the Joint Plan of Action (JPA)—an interim agreement to halt parts of the Iranian nuclear program and introduce greater oversight while a comprehensive deal was worked out. Under the JPA, Iran retained the rights to nuclear enrichment and to continue its activities at its nuclear facilities (Arak, Fordow, and Natanz). However, it agreed to freeze uranium enrichment to 5 percent (and to dilute its stocks of 20 percent enriched uranium down to this level), while also allowing more inspections by the IAEA, in return for gaining access to $7 billion in foreign exchange currency held in frozen Iranian assets.[26] This was followed by negotiations that began in February 2014 for a comprehensive settlement. After missing the August and November deadlines, the negotiations were extended.

Finally, on July 14, 2015, the P5+1 and Iran signed the landmark JCPOA.[27] The deal involved serious compromises from both sides. Tehran moved from its original demand of no reduction in its uranium enrichment, accepting instead to limit it to a level demonstrably "for peaceful purposes." The US, on the other hand, abandoned its long-held insistence on a complete halt to the Iranian nuclear program. Both Obama and Rouhani praised the deal as historic and a triumph of diplomacy over confrontation. While the two sides gave differing interpretations of certain provisions of the agreement, primarily for domestic political purposes, the major features of the deal were as follows:

1. The expansion of IAEA oversight, monitoring, and inspections of Iran's nuclear facilities and program.

2. The production of highly enriched uranium and plutonium will be halted and the stockpile of uranium reduced from 7,500 kg to 300 kg, enriched to no more than 3.67 percent, for the next fifteen years.
3. The total number of centrifuges will be reduced from 19,000 to 5,060 IR-1 (first generation) gas centrifuges over the next ten years, the rest to be stored under IAEA supervision. More advanced centrifuge models will be phased out. A small number of IR-4, -5, -6, and -8 centrifuges will be allowed for research and development purposes for the next ten years.
4. Iran will limit uranium enrichment for research and development purposes for eight years, after which it will gradually introduce the "next stage of enrichment activities" for "exclusively peaceful purposes."
5. No heavy-water reactors will be used for the next fifteen years—the Arak heavy-water reactor will be redesigned to a new model that does not produce enriched uranium above 3.67 percent.
6. The Fordow nuclear facility will be converted into a nuclear, physics, and technology center with a maximum of 1,044 centrifuges for stable isotope production.
7. No fuel reprocessing will be carried out for the next fifteen years, except for the creation of medical and industrial isotopes.
8. An agreement to a "road map" for investigations into past nuclear activities that may have breached Iran's NPT commitments (including any military applications), particularly before 2004.

In return for this compliance, the UN, the EU, and the US agreed to

1. Lift all economic and financial sanctions related to the nuclear program. An arms embargo will remain in place for five years, and a ban on the transfer of missile technology will remain for eight years. No new sanctions can be enforced as long as there is compliance, and the US must work in good

faith to create the domestic legal conditions necessary (including repealing any law at the local or state level that prevents the removal of sanctions) for sanctions to be lifted.
2. Reintegrate Iran into the SWIFT network, allowing it to participate in international finance.
3. Make efforts to ensure that Iran has access to trade and peaceful nuclear technology and cooperation.

STRENGTHS AND WEAKNESSES

Proponents of the JCPOA have argued that the agreement is effective because it prevents Iran from acquiring nuclear weapons for fifteen years and increases the estimated breakout time—that is, the amount of time necessary for Iran to produce enough weapons-grade enriched uranium fuel for a single nuclear weapon—to between three months and a year (both would be significantly less if Iran continued to work on its nuclear program without the deal).[28] They have also contended that the verification mechanisms put in place are some of the most rigorous and invasive ever devised—they certainly go beyond Iran's commitments under the NPT.[29] Thus, if Iran breaches its obligations, the US will be better placed to take action because it will have verifiable evidence and will therefore be in a better position to muster the support of key players such as China, Russia, and the EU. Furthermore, even though conditions of the JCPOA are limited to ten to fifteen years, the conditions under the Additional Protocol are permanent. The Additional Protocol to the JCPOA is enforceable by the IAEA and provides "a safeguards agreement that provides additional tools for verification. In particular, it significantly increases the IAEA's ability to verify the peaceful use of all nuclear material in States with comprehensive safeguards agreements."[30] Finally, proponents of the agreement have contended that Iran's integration into the global economy provides significant economic benefits (through the opening of a large market and increased, more stable supplies of oil) as well as a political windfall since the removal of sanctions would improve living conditions and empower the moderate-reformist factions in Iranian politics to enact domestic reforms.[31]

However, critics of the deal have voiced serious concerns about its workability. They have argued that, first, the JCPOA does not dismantle the architecture of Iran's nuclear program, instead allowing Tehran to keep all of its nuclear technology, equipment, and infrastructure, including 1,044 functioning centrifuges at the Fordow facility.[32] In their view, the deal only postpones Iran's nuclear ambitions for ten to fifteen years, during which time it will remain in a "semi-threshold state" that will enable it to immediately resume its program after the deal ends from a stronger economic position.[33] Tied to this argument are the complaints that the deal makes too many concessions to Iran and that the US is not getting enough out of the agreement.[34]

Second, the critics have stated that the IAEA safeguards and verification mechanisms provided in the deal may not be stringent enough. Their contention is that Tehran has not been transparent about its nuclear program in the past, making investigations into its efforts to achieve nuclear weapons—"Possible Military Dimensions"—very difficult. They have claimed that a comprehensive monitoring of Iranian nuclear activities requires a rigorous inspection of all related military or strategically sensitive programs and facilities (notably at Parchin), which have been kept secret for a long time and were largely excluded from the nuclear deal itself, although Iran previously allowed inspections at such facilities, including Parchin.[35] Therefore, the deal on this score lacks accountability or the requisite depth to ensure Iran's past and future compliance across the full range of its nuclear activities and sites.[36] Another objection has been that allowing Iran to keep its nuclear infrastructure will encourage proliferation when the deal ends, raising the possibility of a regional nuclear arms race, given Saudi Arabia's resolve to counter Iranian capability.[37]

Third, objectors have protested that the deal only covers Iran's nuclear-related behavior and fails to address its human rights violations, sponsorship of international terrorism, and destabilizing influence in the region. In this view, the deal makes an arbitrary distinction between nuclear and nonnuclear sanctions, removing the bulk of sanctions while allowing Iran to pursue its nonnuclear strategic objectives.[38] Lifting sanctions will allow Iran access to up to $100 billion in frozen assets, which will empower it to develop its economy and become a stronger, more influential regional power which can then afford to increase its funding to organizations such as Hezbollah.[39] This concern has been expressed by Israeli prime minister Benjamin Netanyahu, who rejected the JCPOA as disastrous, arguing that Iran would use the increased funds "to pump up their terror machine worldwide."[40] These views have been echoed by some Arab governments, most importantly that of Saudi Arabia.

In the US, opposition to the deal has been largely drawn along partisan lines. Republicans in the Congress have strongly opposed the deal. John McCain, chairman of the Senate Armed Services Committee, has stated that the JCPOA

> will not only legitimize the Islamic Republic as a threshold nuclear state with an industrial enrichment capability, but will also unshackle this regime in its long-held pursuit of conventional military power, and may actually consolidate the Islamic Republic's control in Iran for years to come.[41]

Meanwhile, in March 2015, forty-seven Republican senators signed an open letter to Iran's leaders warning that the nuclear deal would face considerable opposition in Congress, implying that it would not survive the conservatives' obstructionism in the legislature.[42]

In Iran, the conservatives initially remained quiet about the deal, to which the Supreme Leader had given qualified support, on the condition that the US honored its end of the bargain.[43] However, shortly thereafter some of these *jihadi* elements protested the JCPOA, branding it an "American Trojan horse to infiltrate Iran,"[44] with many unable to find negotiating with the US in their interests.[45] When the promised economic improvements that the deal was supposed to deliver did not immediately materialize, it provided ammunition to opponents of the deal, who included elements of not only conservative factions but also the public. Since then, Khamenei has stated that the nuclear deal should not lead to improved relations with the US[46] and has sought to retain the power to call the deal off with the United States should he deem it necessary.[47]

The JCPOA was nonetheless implemented by its deadline of January 14, 2016. As of mid-October 2017, both sides had honored their commitments to the agreement, with the deal having had predominantly positive results, despite failing to fulfill the more dramatic expectations of its proponents and critics. On Tehran's side, the IAEA confirmed Iran's adherence to its obligations on six occasions. It also verified that the Arak heavy-water reactor had been filled with concrete and that the Fordow enrichment plant—previously fortified and bunkered—had been converted into an international physics facility.[48] Although there were some alleged violations, these were recognized as technical difficulties in the readaptation and drawing down of the Iranian facilities. Otherwise, there was no evidence that the deal had been breached, despite some critics' objections to the brisk manner in which the IAEA's investigation into Iran's potential military program had been concluded.

Thus far, while in full compliance, the Islamic Republic had nonetheless benefited substantially from the removal of the EU and US oil embargoes under the agreement. At the end of 2016, it was able to increase its oil production to 3.85 million barrels per day, similar to pre-2012 sanctions levels, and gained access to $55 billion in previously frozen assets and over $11 billion in foreign direct investment. By early 2017, Iran had also signed $150 billion worth of economic deals with European, Asian, and US firms,[49] resulting in a 43 percent increase in trade with the EU.[50] However, several issues remained that prevented Iran from receiving the full benefits of sanctions relief. Iran was unable to attract the levels of foreign investment that it had anticipated with the lifting of the sanctions, nor could it do away with the reluctance of major international financial institutions to process Iranian transactions. As a result, Iran could not access much of the foreign investment that it had already contracted.

Tehran accused the US Department of Treasury of dragging its feet by not clearly outlining the rules and guidelines for American individuals and companies to do business in Iran—specifically relating to the lifting of nuclear sanctions and any financial or legal repercussions resulting from it.[51] The confusion, and the US delay, stem from an array of nonnuclear US sanctions that remain in place—including trade embargoes, a blanket ban on US persons (legal or natural) dealing with Iran, specific sanctions levied against alleged Iranian human rights abuses and support for terrorism, and sanctions targeting Iran's ballistic missile program and the IRGC in particular. The uncertainty around US policy on trade with Iran is part of the reason that major international banks have chosen to refrain from returning to Iran and even supporting business inclined to go into Iran.

Zarif has complained that

> [The US Treasury] goes out and tells these people that it's OK to do business with Iran, but . . . [then there are] five pages of ifs and buts. So at the end of the day, these banks say we'll take the safe road. . . . As far as the US government is concerned . . . [it] took six or seven months to give the license to Airbus to sell 17 out of 118 they requested [to sell to Iran].[52]

The nuclear deal contains a "snapback" provision that also heightened financial uncertainty around the Iranian economy. Under this provision, members can refer any perceived noncompliance to the UN Security Council, which will then resolve to retain the sanction's waivers under the agreement or to reapply sanctions. If the resolution is not passed within thirty days, previous sanctions and resolutions relating to the nuclear issue will be reimposed. The snapback provision raises the prospect of sanctions being reinstated at any time, depending on political events—thereby chilling long-term investment confidence. Even with the economic and trade agreements that have been concluded, US businesses face considerable difficulties in trading with Iran. The December 2016 Boeing deal to sell eighty commercial airplanes to Iran at the cost of $17 billion, for example, faced opposition from Congress.[53]

Meanwhile, Tehran has stated that the snapback provision works both ways, warning that it will halt the implementation of the deal if the US violates the JCPOA and enacts legislation expanding the Iran Sanctions Act.[54] Zarif has insisted that "if they [the US] return to sanctions, we will not remain committed to the agreement"[55] and confirmed to the author that Iran will not only return its nuclear program to its pre-JCPOA state but will also install an even more advanced generation of centrifuges.[56] However, despite the Congress's unanimous vote to renew the Iran Sanctions Act on December 1, 2016, Tehran did not take any definitive action to recommence its nuclear program or exit the deal.

Iran's ballistic missile program also remains a major point of contention. The deal does not explicitly prohibit Iran from developing its missile programs, except for missiles that could carry WMDs. While UN Security Council Resolution 2231 "calls upon" Iran to refrain from any ballistic missile activity until 2023, the language is nonbinding.[57] Tehran claims that missile testing and research is for defensive purposes and is a legitimate and central part of its military strategy. However, since the conclusion of the JCPOA, every time that Iran has carried out a ballistic missile test, the US has denounced it and imposed new sanctions.[58] This was the case under Obama, and it has intensified under Trump.[59]

In his campaign for the White House, Trump had declared total opposition to the JCPOA, calling it "the worst deal ever" and promised to scuttle it.[60] Upon assuming the presidency, he remained adamant in his bellicose posture and condemnation of the Islamic Republic. In the wake of Iran's ballistic missile test on February 1, 2017, he unreservedly blasted Tehran in a series of tweets, reinforcing the warning issued by his short-lived national security advisor, Michael Flynn, that Iran was on "notice." He slapped new sanctions on a dozen companies, including Chinese businesses suspected of supplying parts for Iranian missiles, and thirteen individuals linked to supplying Iran's missile industry.[61] Tehran declared the sanctions "illegal" and in violation of the JCPOA. Zarif maintained that the missile tests were outside the scope of the JCPOA and consequently did not violate Iran's commitments under the deal, stressing the program's defensive nature and adding that the missiles were "not designed for the capability of carrying a nuclear warhead."[62] Meanwhile, Tehran retaliated, imposing legal restrictions on American individuals and entities alleged to be assisting "regional terrorist groups."[63] Although the Iranian countersanctions could not inflict much damage, the tit-for-tat approach marked a downward slide in US-Iranian relations. In mid-April 2017, the Trump administration once again accused Iran of "bad behavior." The US secretary of state, Rex Tillerson, castigated Iran for its "alarming and ongoing provocations" and described the country as "the world's leading state sponsor of terrorism." He also warned that an "unchecked Iran has the potential to travel the same path as North Korea."[64] These accusations happened even though the IAEA's reports kept confirming Iran's compliance[65] and the Trump administration approved of these reports by recertifying the JCPOA to the Congress not only in April but also again in July 2017, as it was required to do every three months as part of US domestic politics.

President Trump, who has given total support to Israel and embraced Netanyahu's opposition to Iran as well as his antipathy to any possible improvement in US-Iranian relations, has the power to withdraw America's participation from the JCPOA. But he cannot nullify it altogether. The agreement is not between Iran and the US alone, but rather between Iran and the P5+1 as guaranteed by the UN Security Council. The other powers—all of which have lucrative economic and trade ties with Iran and, in the case of Russia and China, also military and security relations—have categorically stated that they will remain committed to the nuclear agreement in the event of a US withdrawal from the deal.[66] However, Trump still remained determined to do whatever he could to undermine the agreement as part of a policy of containing Iran, irrespective of other signatories' position and the rising regional tensions and resurgent Iranian-Russian security and military cooperation. This brings us to the next section of the chapter before discussing further Trump's actions regarding the nuclear deal in chapter 8.

Iran-Russia Axis

The Islamic Republic has sought to balance pressure from the United States and its allies by cultivating good relations with other powers. One is Russia as successor to the Soviet Union. Historically, Iran's ties with Russia have been fraught with contention. As elaborated in chapter 2, Iranians have maintained a deep suspicion and distrust of Russia due to the latter's occupation of parts of their country at different times in the nineteenth and twentieth centuries. During the Second World War, the Soviet Union occupied northern Iran and violated its treaty obligations by not withdrawing on the agreed-upon date. The 1979 Soviet invasion of Afghanistan in the context of the Cold War heightened fears of renewed Russian incursions into Iran. However, in spite of this and Khomeini's stress on pro-Islamic foreign policy, as the Islamic Republic faced increased US-driven international isolation Russo-Iranian relations took an upward trajectory, especially after the end of the Iran-Iraq War and the collapse of the USSR, at which point Russia became Iran's main arms supplier. In the wake of the Syrian conflict, Russo-Iranian relations have expanded to include a strong geostrategic dimension. Moscow's direct intervention in support of Iran's staunch ally, the Assad regime, has strongly been backed by Tehran, and the two sides have engaged in close coordination over military operations and diplomatic cooperation since September 2015. The two states' relations have been underwritten by pragmatic interests when these interests align—despite a historical undercurrent of distrust between them. This has been called "wary engagement"[67] and a "marriage of convenience."[68]

The growing Russo-Iranian strategic cooperation is underpinned by three factors. First, both countries share similar security objectives. From Russia's perspective, Iran is well placed to play a critical stabilizing role in the wider region—from the Gulf to the Levant to the Caucasus to Central Asia (particularly in Afghanistan).[69] Furthermore, Iran's Shia ideology is a potential foil to the spread of Sunni radicalism, which Russia is keen to prevent among Muslims living in its southern provinces. Moscow is especially concerned about some four thousand young, radical Muslims from the Central Asian republics and Chechnya who have joined IS.[70]

Second, the two countries share similar interests in Syria. For Moscow, Syria is a strategically important state that allows Russia to project and expand its influence in the region, in particular through its naval base at Tartus, which provides access to the Mediterranean, and the Syrian Khmeimim airbase in Latakia, from which the Russian Air Force operates. At the same time, Assad's regime is central to the regional alliance network created by Iran, serving as the nexus between Iran and Hezbollah, which assists Moscow and Tehran in pursuit of diminishing US influence. Russia's military involvement and cooperation with Iran, then, is the logical and natural outcome of a common strategic interest in maintaining the status quo, for both Russia and Iran have been keen to prevent radical Sunni forces or pro-US groups from taking control in Syria or, for that matter, anywhere else in the northern area of the Levant.

Third, cooperation with Tehran offers potential economic benefits for Russian exports of arms and nuclear technology. Russian arms transfers to Iran up to 2015 consisted of a wide range of weapons systems, including MiG-29 and Su-24MK aircraft and T-72S tanks.[71] No reliable statistics are available to quantify Iranian military purchases from Russia, but for the period 2012–15 alone they were estimated to be $600 million.[72] In 2016, Russia delivered a supply of its advanced S-300 surface-to-surface missile systems to Iran. Tehran is currently negotiating a $10 billion arms deal that includes artillery, aircraft such as the SU-30, and tanks such as the T-90.[73]

Russo-Iranian economic relations remained limited until recently, largely due to the international sanctions on Iran. In fact, bilateral trade decreased from $1.7 billion in 2014 to $1.3 billion in 2015. With the lifting of the nuclear-related sanctions in early 2016, however, economic and trade ties were expected to grow substantially. As an early sign, the volume of Russo-Iranian trade jumped by almost 80 percent in 2016, almost doubling to $2 billion.[74] With the Russian economy stagnating under the pressure of Western sanctions (imposed in 2014 in retaliation for Moscow's annexation of Crimea), a sanctions-free Iran offers increased economic benefits and, indeed, some lessons on how to weather a Western sanctions regime.

Both countries also have an interest in resolving territorial disputes over Caspian Basin oil deposits, as well as coordinating energy export policies. Although they dispute the allocation of the hydrocarbon-rich seabed, Tehran has been willing to acquiesce to Moscow's interests, for shared economic and strategic objectives. Iran opposes the classification of the Caspian Basin as a "sea," the legal implication of which would be to allow states to individually develop resources and construct pipelines without the consent of all five neighboring states. Tehran therefore aligns firmly with Russia in objecting to the proposed construction of the Trans-Caspian pipeline, which would connect Turkmenistan's energy supplies to Europe via Azerbaijan and potentially challenge Russia's dominance in the gas market.[75] Moscow and Tehran have also been keen to do whatever possible to minimize US and European influence in the area. At the Third Caspian Sea Summit in Baku in 2010, Russia and Iran successfully pushed through an agreement stipulating that only ships from the five states bordering the Caspian Sea (Azerbaijan, Iran, Kazakhstan, Russia, and Turkmenistan) have the right to sail in its waters. This has effectively cut off the possibility of US or NATO intervention.[76]

These strategic and economic considerations have driven Russia to position itself as a key party in negotiations over Iran's nuclear program. Russia's role in the process has helped to bring it closer to Iran than ever before. Iran's proposed membership of the Shanghai Cooperation Organisation, which Russia has consistently supported, underscores greater efforts to expand the arena of Russo-Iranian cooperation beyond bilateral ties to a wider multilateral basis. Both Moscow and Tehran view their close relations as an important bargaining chip in their negotiations with the West: first over its own sanctions and actions in Ukraine; and second in its dealings with foreign powers, especially the United States under President Trump.[77]

In further cementing their ties, Russian president Vladimir Putin visited Tehran at the start of November 2017—the first visit of its kind. He not only met with President Rouhani and some of his cabinet members but also with the Supreme Leader, Ayatollah Khamenei. During the meeting, Khamenei urged Moscow and Tehran to step up their cooperation to "isolate America," eliminate Sunni "terrorism," and bring stability to the region.[78] Meanwhile, the Russian oil producer Rosneft and the Iranian National Oil Company agreed to work on "strategic" projects worth up to $30 billion.[79] The level of talks and mutual support for each other's position, which involved Putin renewing Russia's commitment to the JCPOA, clearly signaled a deepening of strategic alliance between the two sides.

Against these shared interests, however, the two sides have several diverging political and strategic objectives that underpin the notion that their relationship is one of strategic convenience. First, even in areas where they have common interests, the two states harbor different objectives. For instance, while Russia is willing to support Assad in Syria, it does not view him as essential and has shown an inclination to accept an alternative government as long as its strategic assets (especially its access to airbases and the port) remain intact. Russia's position in this respect stems from its objectives as a major power. As Nikolas Gvosdev writes: "For Moscow, the key objective is to preserve the international state system and foster an ally in Damascus that would be conducive to Russian strategic interests."[80] Thus, Russia has reason to be willing to compromise to reach an international settlement that is acceptable to the United States in return for recognizing Russia's role as a major player in the Middle East, as well as its annexation of Crimea, and for lifting sanctions against it over Crimea. To this end, Russian strategic gains in Syria—notably the establishment of permanent air and naval bases—carry the potential to diminish Iranian influence in Syria in the long term.[81] For Iran, by contrast, Assad and his ruling clique are central to its regional security policy. Iran's penetration of Syria is deeper than that of Russia in terms of both its organic ties with the Assad regime and the elite political strata, as well as military and security commitments on the ground, including those of

Hezbollah. In November 2015, the commander of the IRGC, Mohammad Ali Jafari, highlighted this key point of divergence, saying that Russia "may not care if Assad stays in power as we do."[82]

Moreover, Russia still seeks positive trade relations with the West, particularly in oil and technology. Indeed, Russia privileges its relations with the US over those with Iran. Moscow's decision to join in the imposition of UN sanctions on Iran in 2010 was part of a broader Russian "reset" that sought to improve relations with the US.[83] Thus, for Russia, the West represents a more important market than Iran, which lacks the purchasing power to become a trading partner for Russia on the scale of Europe or the US. During the US-led sanctions on Iran, Moscow was careful not to deal with Iran in ways that could jeopardize its relations with the West. For example, it typically refused Iranian requests for more advanced, high-quality weapons systems. Despite having signed the initial contract for the sale of the S-300 missiles in 2006, it did not deliver them to Iran until the lifting of sanctions a decade later.[84] This, in addition to Russia's delay in the construction of the Bushehr nuclear reactor, which was finally finished in 2011, has served as a source of tension in bilateral relations.[85]

Second, Russia remains a major strategic competitor with Iran for influence in Central Asia and the Caucasus and to a lesser extent in the Middle East. In this sense, Russia's growing leverage, involving its permanent military bases in Syria, has not sat comfortably with Iran. Iran cannot fully embrace Russia as a strategic ally for domestic reasons as well. When it emerged that the leadership had signed a deal that allowed Russia to use the Iranian Hamedan airbase in late November 2016 to fly missions into Syria, the Majles and Iranian public expressed such intense criticism and outrage that the authorities had to terminate the deal after just one week.[86]

Third, Russia maintains positive relations with several US allies and Iran's geopolitical rivals in the region, notably Israel. The country's cooperation with Israel to combat Sunni terrorist activities in Syria, as well as its relative silence over its continued occupation of Palestinian lands, has caused chagrin in Tehran. While Israel is troubled by the deployment of Iranian forces in Syria, Moscow and Tel

Aviv have often coordinated military actions that run contrary to Iranian interests in that country.[87] In the wake of Russia's escalated military intervention in Syria in September 2015, Netanyahu urgently met with Putin to seek assurances about Russia's involvement. Four months later, Israeli president Reuven Rivlin was invited to Moscow to meet with Putin to discuss Russia's drawback in Syria.[88] Four years earlier, Putin had visited Israel, declaring that it "is in Russia's national interest to provide peace and tranquility in the Middle East, peace and tranquility to the Israeli people. It is not by accident that the Soviet Union was among the initiators and supported the creation of the state of Israel."[89]

As a major power with growing regional ambitions, Russia has also diversified its engagements with Iran's other traditional rivals in the region, most importantly members of the Saudi-led GCC. Although Russia's ties with Saudi Arabia and its GCC partners have typically been low profile, Moscow has dealt with them pragmatically to boost economic relations, attract investment, combat "Sunni extremism" within Russia, and score leverage against the US.[90] As two hydrocarbon giants, Russia and Saudi Arabia have shared interests in energy export coordination, with the potential for "transnational" deals, such as the December 2016 agreement between OPEC and non-OPEC oil producers to cut production by 500,000 barrels per day.[91] In late May 2017, President Putin very warmly received the Saudi defense minister (now crown prince) Mohammed bin Salman in Moscow, where both sides hailed the strength of Russian-Saudi relations. Salman declared that ties between the two countries were "seeing one of their best stages," and Putin yearned for King Salman's visit, despite their stark differences over Syria. Although Russo-Saudi bilateral trade amounted to about $1 billion in 2015,[92] the two parties promised to take their cooperation in this and other areas of mutual interest to a higher level.[93] In early October 2017, King Salman paid an official visit to Moscow, where he signed multibillion-dollar energy and defense contracts, involving a $3 billon arms deal[94]—something that could not have pleased Tehran.

Moscow has similarly been keen to court other GCC member states, which has paid off handsomely, for example, in its relations with the UAE. Trade between Russia and the UAE, where three hundred Russian businesses currently operate, reached $2.5 billion in 2015.[95] In February 2017, the two states announced plans to coproduce a fifth-generation Russian fighter plane in the UAE.[96] Moscow's approach to Saudi Arabia and its close GCC partners has been at odds with Iran's position as a rival to and target of the Sunni Arab bloc in the emerging regional "cold war." Putin has not found it in Russia's interest to solely support Iran's Shia-denominated "axis of resistance," especially given the fact that a majority of Russia's Muslim minority are Sunni. This indicates that the Moscow-Tehran-Baghdad-Damascus-Hezbollah axis that has emerged cannot be taken as static or given.

Iranian-Chinese Cooperation

The relationship between the People's Republic of China and the Islamic Republic of Iran is underpinned by two interrelated issues. First, Iran is critical to China's energy needs. China imports 55 percent of its oil, and the Middle East accounts for 50 percent of this amount.[97] China is Iran's largest importer of crude oil, accounting for around 31 percent of Iran's total oil exports in 2016.[98] Before the 2012 sanctions, Iran was China's third-largest oil provider (11 percent of total imports in 2011).[99] Following the embargo, this figure dropped to 8 percent, putting it in fourth place after Saudi Arabia (20 percent), Angola (15 percent), and Russia (9 percent).[100] In 2016, oil exports to China were worth $10.7 billion, making Iran China's sixth-largest supplier of oil.[101] In the same year, the bilateral trade between the two countries amounted to $31.2 billion.[102]

Second, China has also been a major arms provider to the Islamic Republic, especially since 1986. China began supplying arms first to the Republic in 1981 and accounted for 41 percent of all of its arms trade between 1980 and 1988.[103] During the Iran-Iraq War, Beijing furnished Tehran with a variety of weapons, notably HY-2 Silkworm anti-ship missiles.[104] Further, Beijing has played an instrumental role in Iran's ballistic missile program, providing technologies and designs that can be seen in Iranian surface-to-surface missiles like the Shahab-3 and Nasr.[105] The US and EU sanctions helped to deepen Sino-Iranian economic and strategic cooperation by creating an opening for investment in business and infrastructure that China readily filled. In 2010, China overtook the EU as Iran's largest trading partner.[106] Beyond this, EU reluctance to sell weapons to Iran created an easy market for Chinese arms exports.[107]

For Iran, China has been an indispensable economic partner. Trade with China has lessened the impact of sanctions, giving Iran access to desperately needed investment, infrastructure, and manufactured goods in exchange for its energy and mineral exports. After the imposition of more US sanctions in 2009, Chinese companies signed as much as $3 billion in deals to upgrade Iran's gas refinement infrastructure.[108] In 2010, as European involvement was dwindling, China continued to expand its economic engagement, investing $1 billion in infrastructure projects in Tehran alone, including expanding highways and updating its metro system, which was originally built with Chinese assistance.[109] With the lifting of sanctions, Chinese investment is set to increase, but at a slower rate due to increased competition from other international companies. In December 2016, the Commercial Bank of China proposed to contribute 85 percent of the $1.27 billion needed to develop the Mehran Petrochemical Complex,[110] while in February of the following year, Chinese companies signed a deal to provide $3 billion to upgrade the Abadan refinery.[111]

There have also been problems. Chinese firms operating in Iran during the sanctions period were often slow to deliver services and charged high prices.[112] In particular, Chinese involvement in oil and gas projects has become a point of contention with Tehran, which accuses Chinese firms of not delivering results on time. In 2013, Iran canceled a contract it had awarded to the China National Petroleum Corporation (CNPC) to develop part of the South Pars gas field in response to multiple delays.[113] In 2014, Tehran canceled, for the same reason, a $2.5 billion contract to develop the South Azadegan oil field with the CNPC, accusing the company of charging high prices for low-quality work.[114]

In 2013, Chinese president Xi Jinping launched his One Belt, One Road foreign policy, which is centered on fostering economic and developmental links between China, Eurasia, Europe, Oceania, and parts of Africa via both the Silk Road Economic Belt and the Twenty-First Century Maritime Silk Road.[115] The initiative is designed to further advance China's economic and strategic influence across multiple regions by encouraging greater economic integration through trade. Iran is an important factor in this initiative because of its geopolitical centrality, which Robert Kaplan calls the "Iranian pivot,"[116] and its ability to influence the development and stability of neighboring countries, especially Iraq and Afghanistan. To this end, China has routinely supported Iran by generally opposing sanctions while fostering economic ties, both of which have the additional advantage of undermining US regional dominance. During the visit of President Xi to Iran on January 23, 2016, President Rouhani "announced that China and Iran plan to build economic ties worth up to $600 billion."[117]

For China, Iran's capacity to promote regional stability is critical to its overall objective of ensuring the security of energy corridors and supplies, especially given the country's strategic location as the linchpin between the Middle East and Asia. Most of China's current oil imports are shipped through the Strait of Hormuz. In addition to energy security, Iran is also important in countering the rise of "Sunni extremism," which could affect China's restive Xinjiang province. Both countries have upgraded their military ties in recent years. The Chinese defense minister, General Chang Wanquan, and his Iranian counterpart, General Hossein Dehghan, signed a defense agreement in Tehran on November 14, 2016, pledging closer cooperation in military and counterterrorism affairs. The agreement called for intensification of bilateral military training and tighter interaction on what Iran sees as regional security issues, with counterterrorism and the Syrian conflict as top priorities. Dehghan declared that it represented an "upgrade in long-term military and defense cooperation with China."[118] The chief of staff of the Iranian

Armed Forces, Major General Mohammad Hossein Baqeri, said that Iran was ready to share with China its experience in fighting terrorist groups in Iraq and Syria.[119]

Chinese support for the JCPOA also fits in with its foreign policy of a "peaceful" ascendance and its noninterventionism, multilaterism, and commitment to nonproliferation.[120] Initially China played an important part in Iran's development of nuclear know-how and technology, including uranium enrichment. From 1985 to 1997, "China provided Iran with four small teaching and research reactors, including one utilizing heavy water—the key to producing plutonium and fissile bomb material [as well as] . . . uranium including for enrichment purposes and specific chemicals for the purpose of extracting plutonium."[121]

It also assisted the International Atomic Energy Agency in designing "a plant to be used during the uranium enrichment process" and with "other steps to develop self-reliant nuclear capability."[122] Like Tehran, Beijing has been concerned about the spread of Sunni extremism across its short border with Afghanistan into China's Xinjiang province, home of the country's restive Muslim Uighur minority. Beijing has reportedly deployed, albeit with the Afghan government's agreement, some security forces in Afghanistan's Wakhan corridor bordering Xinjiang in order to make sure that it remains free of radical Islamic elements, including the Taliban.[123]

China's approach to Iran has so far been to balance these strategic interests with the imperative of maintaining workable relations with the US. While Beijing has sought to support Tehran on issues such as trade and nuclear development, it has intentionally moderated its relations in order to avoid damaging US ties whenever deemed desirable. After the West raised issues about Tehran's nuclear intentions and after the UN imposed sanctions on Iran, China committed itself to respecting not only those sanctions but also the ones imposed by the US and the EU in 2012, despite opposing any additional sanctions. While China played a constructive role in the negotiations leading to the JCPOA and agreed to undertake the redesign of the Arak reactor under the deal, Chinese support for the imposition of UN sanctions demonstrates how Beijing prioritized its relations with the West over Iran at the policy level. In 2012, China also reduced its oil imports from Iran, primarily in order to maintain positive relations with the EU and the US but also as part of a broader campaign to convince Tehran to enter nuclear negotiations.[124] The result was that "neither Tehran nor Washington was completely satisfied with Beijing's balanced approach, but both were minimally satisfied."[125] However, the rise of President Trump has raised challenges for US-Chinese relations. Trump's call to rebalance trade ties in favor of the US, his dubious stance on the traditional US "one China" policy, his condemnation of China's assertive approach to the disputed islands in the South China Sea, and his declarations that China has not done enough to contain the nuclear ambitions of North Korea have been met with strong rebukes from Beijing. Should this trend continue, China, along with Russia, may increasingly act on their shared interests with Iran. This carries the potential for a Russia-China-Iran axis to counter the US. Yet, it is important to note that there is no certainty about the Trump administration's foreign policy behavior, because it has been contradictory and variable. At times he has lambasted China on a variety of issues, but at other times he has appeared conciliatory toward the country.

Iran-EU Engagement

The fourth power with which Iran's ties are most important is the multinational EU bloc, especially its formidable core member states: Germany, France, and Italy, as well as the United Kingdom until its forthcoming exit from the EU. While Iran's relations have varied with EU member states, they have primarily been defined by diplomacy, engagement, and economic interests within a policy of "constructive engagement." Unlike the US, Iran-EU relations do not have a history of mutual enmity, although Iran's ties with some EU member states have been difficult and uneven at times. This is most true of its relations with the United Kingdom, which, until the early 1950s, wielded much political and economic influence in the country and which the Islamic Republic has often blamed for Iran's historical woes and contemporary domestic unrest. The result has been the downgrading or breakdown of diplomatic relations between the two sides on several occasions since the rise of the Islamic regime, one of them being the Rushdie Affair (see chapter 3).

On the diplomatic front, the EU has typically sought to engage Iran—especially on the nuclear issue—in order to avoid military confrontation. While initially concerned about the revolutionary regime destabilizing the region (and therefore interrupting oil supplies), following the Iran-Iraq War, the EU sought to enhance diplomatic and economic ties with Iran, which at the time welcomed European technical assistance and investment.[126] Regarding nuclear negotiations, the EU has generally been able to approach the issue with a unified voice, represented initially by France, Germany, and the United Kingdom (the E3) and later by the high representative of the European Union for Foreign Affairs and Security Policy. Thus, despite individual member states maintaining bilateral ties with Iran (Germany, for example, has been a consistently significant trading partner), the EU's conduct of relations with Iran has commonly been based on an alignment of foreign policies, called effective multilateralism.[127] Of course, this is not to suggest that there is no disunity within the bloc. France's secular republic, for example, is naturally at odds with Iran's theocratic system, and human rights issues have negatively impacted the Islamic Republic's reputation in the eyes of countries such as Sweden and Denmark. Overall, however, member states have been able to contain their differences and maintain a consistent, unified policy on Iran at the EU level.

The EU's policy until 2006 had been to use diplomacy and economic links and incentives to encourage changes in Tehran's political behavior. Between 1992 and 1997 the policy took the form of "critical dialogue," whereby the EU engaged Iran on key issues. This engagement ended abruptly in 1997, when a German court found several Iranian officials to be complicit in the 1992 assassination of four Iranian-Kurdish dissidents in a Berlin restaurant.[128] The EU began a new phase of engagement—comprehensive dialogue—in 1998 following Khatami's election and diplomatic overtures to the West. This dialogue sought broader engagement with Iran on a wider range of issues, including terrorism, human rights, the Arab-Israeli conflict, and nuclear weapons, while also notably seeking to negotiate a trade and cooperation agreement.[129] The new initiative stemmed from an awareness that imposing sanctions would empower conservative hard-liners and undermine prospects for progressive reform and progress in Iranian politics.[130] However, the comprehensive dialogue ended in 2002, as more information about Iranian nuclear activities was uncovered.

After 2002, four issues took wider importance in EU-Iranian relations: human rights, terrorism, energy and trade, and the Iranian nuclear program. Early on, the EU had generally been resistant to imposing sanctions on Tehran. In fact, when the US Congress passed the Iran and Libya Sanctions Act in 1996 (renamed the Iran Sanctions Act in 2006), to prevent US and non-US businesses from investing more than $20 million in the Iranian petroleum industry, the EU opposed the move, considering it a violation of international law.[131] The nuclear issue assumed a central place only when an international investigation established that Iran was engaging in undeclared nuclear activities. That, combined with the election of Ahmadinejad and his hard-line approach to the nuclear issue and belligerent foreign policy rhetoric, led the EU to endorse UN sanctions for the first time. The E3 described Iran's decision to recommence uranium enrichment in 2006 as "a clear rejection of the process."[132] This led to a convergence of EU and US policies and to the referral of an Iranian nuclear file to the UN Security Council. Despite its adoption of the US-led sanctions approach, the EU never abandoned the diplomatic track in its relations with Iran. Between 2010 and 2013, the EU-led negotiations between the P5+1 and Iran eventually resulted in the JPA and then the JCPOA. Both of them brought credit to EU diplomacy, demonstrating the bloc's influence as a strategic, multinational actor.

The EU and Iran have three major overlapping interests. The first is Iran's centrality to the EU's desire to see regional stability in the Middle East. Given the proximity of major conflict areas to European borders, the EU has an interest in engaging with Iran over major strategic issues. In particular, the migration of millions of refugees toward Europe as a result of the conflicts in Afghanistan, Iraq, and Syria has demonstrated the proximity of the two regions. At the same time, the refugee crisis has generated fierce debate and socioeconomic and ideological problems within the EU.[133] Instability in Iran's neighborhood runs counter to Tehran's strategic and security interests.

The second is the EU's interest in Iran as a key player in combating terrorism and resolving regional conflicts. The emergence of IS and the intensified dissemination of its extremist ideologies have had real and tragic consequences in Europe, resulting in several high-profile terrorist attacks. The EU's high representative, Frederica Mogherini, who proved to be a key player in the nuclear negotiations since her appointment in November 2014, has stated that "the EU needs Iran's cooperation as a key and important power to resolve problems in the region,"[134] adding that "cooperation between Iran, its neighbours and the whole international community could open unprecedented possibilities of peace for the region, starting from Syria, Yemen, and Iraq."[135]

The third is the fact that Iran and the EU have major economic interests. Historically, the EU has been Iran's largest trading partner. Trade between the two sides reached €27 billion in 2008, before dropping to €7 billion following rounds of sanctions in 2010 and 2012.[136] Since then, the volume has risen to €13.7 billion in 2016 as the lifting of sanctions has allowed European companies to reenter the Iranian market.[137] Until the imposition of the 2012 sanctions, Iran was a major energy exporter to Europe, while the EU provided manufactured goods. Furthermore, Iran's strategic position makes it crucial to debates about energy-source diversification and pipeline construction (particularly away from Russian predominance), as well as energy security. This is especially important given that the EU currently imports 56 percent of its energy needs.[138] The JCPOA has offered new prospects for investment by European companies, which have already signed a number of business and economic contracts with Iran. Tehran was encouraged with the renewed strength of EU ties by its purchase of its first airbus, which arrived in January 2017.

While Iran's ties with some members of the EU—more specifically with the UK—have experienced a considerable amount of fluctuation over time, the same has not been the case with Russia and China. Since the dissolution of the Soviet Union on December 26, 1991, Russo-Iranian relations have steadily moved forward. Russia has become not only Iran's main arms supplier but also a strategic partner in Syria. Sino-Iranian ties have seen more or less a comparable trajectory. In spite of its ideological differences with Beijing, Tehran has persistently courted China as an important trading partner and aide in its nuclear program. The growth in Sino-Iranian relations has continued without interruption, even during the period of international sanctions. Beijing's role, like Moscow's, in the process of negotiations leading to the nuclear deal and its implementation, and its support for the joint Russo-Iranian operations in Syria, especially since September 2015, have been invaluable to Iran.

The Islamic Republic's relations with all major powers have primarily been influenced by its adversarial relations with the United States. The more the US has sanctioned, pressured, and isolated the Islamic Republic, the more the latter has found it politically, strategically, and economically expedient to forge closer ties with other major powers. Indeed, had it not been for the strategic rebalancing underlined by its pragmatically driven ties with Russia and China, the Islamic Republic may not have been able to achieve its current status as an influential regional player or have played so integral a role on the world stage.

8

Conclusion

The Islamic Republic of Iran has generated and endured many domestic and foreign policy anomalies and challenges through its very turbulent journey. Yet despite the internal opposition and external hostility it has faced, especially from the United States and some of its regional allies, it has managed to endure. The Islamic Republic now stands at a crossroads. It must either pursue further the *ijtihadi* liberalization of its polity or face a future that may turn out to be as tumultuous as its past. The presidency of Donald J. Trump has not only made the first option more difficult, it also means that a direct confrontation between Iran and its main regional rivals is potentially on the cards. The Islamic Republic has proved resilient in the face of adversity before, but domestic and international developments have presented it with new points of vulnerability. The intertwined imperatives of regime preservation and external-threat deterrence have historically shaped the Islamic Republic's internal development and security and foreign policies and are set to determine its future path.

A number of variables account for the resilience of the Islamic Republic since its inauguration. Its two-tier system of governance has provided the public with limited electoral participation in determining the choice of the president and legislators every four years within a parliamentary system—albeit one where all candidates are vetted by the Council of Guardians to ensure their loyalty to the principles of Islamic government and to the Supreme Leader. As such, the system provides for a form of political contestation and representative government, enabling the public to have a say in changing their elected leaders and governments. The polity's built-in elasticity to accommodate different shades of Shia political Islam within a *jihadi-ijtihadi* modus operandi has enabled the Islamic regime to be inventive and dynamic when required by domestic or international pressures.

Meanwhile, the Ruhaniyyat has used the state apparatus to gain control of coercive forces, means of mass communications, educational institutions, economic organizations, and public forums. This control has been tight enough to stifle any form of dissent and transgression that the regime perceives as threatening or subversive. The fate of the ruling stratum that established Iran's political system is intimately linked to that system's survival. Any serious disruption in the existing configuration and operation of the power structure poses a potential threat to their political and economic fortunes and security requirements. Iranian history contains many precedents to warn the dominant conservative forces that they should nip any sign of resistance in the bud.[1] As such, the regime's need for survival and continuity defines the conduct of Iran's national affairs.

The policy of other actors in the region has created space for the regime not only to consolidate but also to expand its influence. Washington's posture toward the Islamic regime has helped it in two important ways. The US's debacles in Afghanistan and Iraq, as well as its indecisiveness over the Syrian conflict and its complicity in Israel's ongoing settler colonial project, have helped Iran to take on a greater regional role and to shore up its rhetoric of defending the oppressed against the aggression of the more powerful. Thus, US hostility has also given the regime an existential threat that it has invoked to cement its political primacy. The same is true of the Saudi-led policy of countering the Iranian influence, which has not proved to be effective in the face of Tehran's more nuanced and well-calculated strategic actions in Iraq, Syria, Lebanon, and Yemen.

In critical moments, the regime has also made skillful use of what it has homogenized as traditional Iranian values and practices. It has successfully promoted a religious nationalism combining Shia political Islamism and traditional feelings of civilizational and cultural pride, both of which are deeply rooted in the identity and psyche of a majority of the Iranian people. This ideology has proved a remarkable means for the regime to mobilize the public against internal opposition and outside threats, often in combination with one another.

The Main Challenges

Despite this resilience, the Islamic Republic has been fraught with vital weaknesses, contradictions, and vulnerabilities on both domestic and foreign policy fronts. The two-tiered system of governance has not worked as well as its founder, Ayatollah Khomeini, had intended, giving rise to serious political bifurcation and factionalism, power and personal rivalries, patronage building, bureaucratic and administrative malfunctioning, and systematic corruption. The Islamic system has fostered unpredictable, ad hoc, and uneven processes of social and economic change, electoral irregularities, and state repression. It has, finally, caused a growing gulf between the ruling elites and the public, corresponding to a state-society dichotomy that has alienated many citizens, especially among the postrevolution generation, from the regime, its conservative clerical strands in particular. Although these outcomes have been accentuated since Khomeini's death, they have their foundations in the way that he structured and operationalized the Islamic Republic. As the Supreme Leader and his conservative supporters have maintained their grip on the levers of power and have compelled elected governments to defer to their authority, relations between the two tiers within the system have come into serious tension that has periodically given way to open hostilities.

The conflict between the conservative and the pragmatist and reformist clusters over the disputed result of the 2009 presidential elections clearly underlined this issue. Although the conservative forces prevailed in the crisis, its underlying causes went unresolved. While the anti-extremist and reformist president Hassan Rouhani—more than any of his predecessors—has enjoyed the support of the Supreme Leader for certain domestic and foreign policy reforms, his conservative opponents have not given him a wide berth for implementing his reform agenda.[2] They have continued to constrain Rouhani from shaking up their hold on power by blocking him from going beyond the most necessary of reforms. Although the president commands sizable (although not majority) support within two important institutions—the Majles and the Assembly of Experts—the real power lies with the Supreme Leader and his supporters, who control the bulk of the state's political, coercive, administrative, cultural, and economic structures. The Islamic system of governance is in dire need of streamlining. An obvious and effective way to reform is to allow the will of the people within the publicly mandated government to prevail at the cost of the powers of the Supreme Leader and the Ruhaniyyat stratum. However, this would challenge not only the latter's dominance but also the structures of the entire Islamic system.

The Islamic Republic's economic record poses another source of vulnerability. As it stands, the system has not proven to be conducive to a mode of social and economic development that could ensure that the growth of the Iranian polity accords with the enormous potential afforded by its human and natural resources. In many ways, its leadership has made it harder for the state to fulfill the expectations of a majority of the Iranian population. The Islamic Republic's processes of change and development have been marred by a heavy top-down approach, enabling the ruling clerics, *bonyads*, Sepah, and companies linked to these powerful forces to use their positions for personal, theological, political, and economic gains. Such patrimonial, nepotistic, corrupt practices, which have permeated the state and society in different ways,[3] have resulted in socioeconomic disparities and inequalities that rival the people's suffering under the Shah's rule, which Khomeini had promised that an Islamic government would alleviate. These imbalances have seriously affected the Islamic Republic's ability to develop its economic and hard- and soft-power capabilities to the maximum benefit of its citizens. Although there is no absolute poverty and the rural inhabitants (26 percent of the total population in 2016) enjoy better living conditions than under the monarchy, a substantial percentage of Iranians continue to live below the unofficial poverty line.[4] This is especially jarring in light of the abundance of natural resources (oil and gas), as well as the trained manpower, with which Iran is endowed.

The Islamic Republic has nevertheless achieved a level of defensive capability that provides extensive protection against vulnerability to foreign aggression. It has nurtured a military doctrine and regional security architecture that has equipped it to make an outside force's attack on it costly for its perpetrator. This objective forms the heart of Tehran's deterrence strategy. It has also acquired an ability to engage in a forward defensive policy, involving offensive actions for defensive objectives, but only occasionally and on a limited scale when special and compelling circumstances arise. The Republic's direct military involvement in Syria revealed that its offensive capabilities were not of a quality and extent to enable it to save the Bashar al-Assad's regime alone. Had it not been for Russian intervention and Tehran's tactical alliance with Moscow from October 2015, the Islamic Republic could have easily lost the central plank of its regional security architecture.

The Islamic regime's persistent fear of an outside aggressor and its direct military involvement in Syria and Iraq, and proxy actions elsewhere, have contributed to making threat and counterthreat, as well as mutual distrust, the defining patterns in the Islamic Republic's international relations.[5] The memory of foreign interventions and the hostility have instilled in the ruling cluster a siege mentality and sense of paranoia. Indeed, the regime's internal and external defensive measures have aimed primarily to guard against the threat of history repeating itself in another foreign-backed coup or military intervention, similar to the one in 1953. Its regional policy adventures—either directly or indirectly—have been in pursuit of an iron-clad resistance to political dissent at home and impenetrable national security and foreign policy posture.

Rouhani has sought to elevate the regime out of this predicament by attempting a series of *ijtihadi* economic reforms and, in conjunction with sensible foreign policy actions, expanding Iran's business and trade relations and attempting to attract foreign investment. In addition to his drive to tackle widespread state corruption and to bring transparency to state operations, since his reelection he has made a concerted effort to curb the excesses of the IRGC and its associated *bonyads*.[6] He has considered the special treatment of these forces and their substantial share in the economy and foreign policy and security operations as suppressing private sector development and causing public discontent.[7]

However, it is worth remembering that Rouhani is a product of the system and has reached the position of the presidency through its ranks. He and his inner circle of supporters are therefore as committed as their conservative counterparts to maintain the fundamentals of the Islamic system of governance. They strongly believe that the system contains sufficient liberal and participatory elements to make it highly suitable for Iran's unique conditions. They consider Iran's Islamic government capable of sustaining the country's regional position and sectarian networks and of fulfilling what Rouhani's reformist predecessor, Mohammad Khatami, called "Islamic democracy." Rouhani has alluded to it in his remarks that democracy can take different forms, as one size does not fit all. As such, he is not equipped or, for that matter, apparently inclined to change the system structurally.

Any effort on the part of Rouhani to engage in changing the structure of the system can bring stiff resistance from an alliance of the conservative forces, or *osul-garayan* (principlists), which operates in opposition to the *islah-garayan* (reformists), with which the president is closely identified. Every time Rouhani has taken a step that his opponents have found to be contrary to their interests, they have used different and often indirect methods to stonewall it. A prominent example is the conservatives' roadblocking of Rouhani's efforts to secure the release of political prisoners, which had been a significant promise of his first presidential campaign. The prisoners have included, most importantly, the two 2009 reformist presidential candidates, Hussein Mossavi and Mehdi Karroubi, who have been under house arrest since 2011. Given the opposition by the conservative judiciary and security apparatus to this action, Rouhani has found it expedient over time to become largely silent on the issue. In August 2017, after six years of around-the-clock surveillance in his own home by a dozen guards and cameras, Karroubi, then aged seventy-nine, went on a hunger strike, demanding a public trial and the removal of the guards and cameras. Fearing the public unrest that Karroubi's death could cause, the authorities removed the guards and cameras but only promised to "endeavor" to realize his request for a public trial.[8] Khatami, who is now viewed as the most popular leader of the reformist camp and who has backed Rouhani in his two presidential elections, has meanwhile remained subject to a media and foreign travel ban. Rouhani has only been able to mention his name respectfully and prominently in public on one occasion, in a speech on March 6, 2017.[9]

The conservatives' tactics have also included the occasional arrest of a prominent figure from the reformist camp or a Westerner, especially a US citizen, the targeting of reformist publications, and conducting missile testing at strategically sensitive and opportune moments in order to undermine Rouhani's attempt to strengthen his power base and improve relations with Iran's adversaries. A recent example of this was the arrest and jailing of Rouhani's brother, Hussein Fereidoun, in mid-July 2017, on charges of what the judiciary called "financial crimes."[10] Hussein, a senior presidential aide, had played a key role in the nuclear negotiations resulting in the July 2015 JCPOA. At about the same time, a Chinese-American citizen and doctoral candidate from Princeton University, Xiyue Wang, was sentenced to ten years' imprisonment for spying, although his university claimed that Mr. Wang was merely in Iran researching modern Eurasian history. The US government condemned the charges as fabrications and demanded Wang's immediate release.[11] Although Hussein was released on bail shortly after his arrest, Wang remains in prison at the time of writing.

The results of these various strategies demonstrate three main features of Iran's contemporary political scene. First, they show the continued tight hold of the conservative forces on the system and their ability to rein in the reformists whenever desirable. Second, they display the conservative camp's willingness to allow only those reforms that are necessary for regime survival and national security but that do not harm their political and economic interests and concomitant foreign policy objectives. Third, they illustrate that the growing rift between the conservative and reformist factions, which reflects the continuous tension within the two tiers of the Islamic system of governance, is very real and that it has widened rather than diminished with time.

Having said this, it must also be noted that Rouhani's emphasis on anti-extremism and reform and his success in concluding the JCPOA have generated more political moderation and foreign policy openness than Khatami managed to accomplish. This, together with some relaxation of social controls, which has allowed the youth to enjoy some freedoms in terms of political discussion and lifestyle within the limits set by the regime, has revived the humanist and constructive aspects of the Islamic regime's profile bequeathed by Khomeini's *ijtihadi* legacy.[12] Undoubtedly, Rouhani's slow progress with reforms has caused frustration, especially among many young Iranians, who form the potentially most restless and concerned body of the population. But at the same time, there seems to be a broad awareness among them that they are better off under the reformist camp than under the conservative, militantly isolationist opponents. Meanwhile, the conservative factions have learned from experience that the best way to maintain the Islamic system is to engage in reinventive politics in the conduct of national affairs from time to time.

In the short run, two issues are set to test the strengths and weaknesses of the Islamic Republic: the Supreme Leadership succession and the Trump administration's policy behavior toward the

Republic. Both will have a defining impact on the future direction of the Islamic Republic.

The Succession to the Supreme Leadership

The Supreme Leader Ayatollah Ali Khamenei is in his late seventies and has so far avoided anointing a successor. Article 107 of the constitution states that in the case of the demise of a Supreme Leader, the Assembly of Experts is tasked either to look for a *marja* who meets the qualifications as defined in Article 108 or, in the absence of such a person, to elect a qualified successor from among themselves. While the constitutional procedure is clear, applying it to achieve a viable and widely consensus-based outcome may turn out to be very complex.[13] The many choices of candidates and horse trading among various groups within the theocratic but politically pluralist system could produce a very controversial result.

The Islamic Republic has not faced the issue of the succession of the Supreme Leader since Khomeini used his enormous authority and popularity to endorse Khamenei, somewhat controversially, as his successor shortly before his death. This endorsement was crucial because it enabled Khamenei to win majority support in the Assembly of Experts and be elevated to the position of Ayatollah, as explained in chapter 4. Given the bifurcated and factionalized nature of the system and the persistent demands of the postrevolution generation to have a greater role in who should govern them (and how they should be governed), the process of appointing the next Supreme Leader will mark a watershed in the history of the Islamic Republic. There is no certainty that it will transpire smoothly, unless Khamenei designates a successor whom he can trust totally and who is capable of gathering sufficient support from within the system.

Khamenei has so far shown no sign of doing this. Speculation before the 2017 presidential election suggested that the running candidate from the conservative camp, Seyyed Ebrahim Raisi, might be the one to succeed him. While Raisi's poor performance in the election reduced his chances, he still cannot be ruled out of the race.

In the past, there have also been voices calling for Khamenei's son, Mujtaba, to succeed his father. However, given Mujtaba's accumulation of wealth through allegedly illegal activities, and given that the constitutional and clerical qualifications are not hereditary in Iran, his odds do not appear good either.

The leadership succession is critical for the Islamic Republic's future direction. If someone similar to Khamenei is chosen, he can be expected to follow in his footsteps. However, if someone with a more liberal view of the world and Iran's place in it is elected, the Islamic Republic could take a more moderate direction in both its domestic and foreign policy disposition. In all probability the successor will come from the ranks of the conservative clerics; but in either case, an element of uncertainty hangs over Iranian politics.

The Trump Administration

The Trump administration's attitude poses a greater and even more immediate challenge to the Islamic Republic than the Supreme Leadership succession. While reflecting the long-standing Republican Party's hard-line attitude toward the Iranian Islamic regime, Trump has evidently made it almost his holy mission to do whatever it takes to contain and diminish Iranian influence in the region. The former US Middle East envoy Dennis Ross has warned that the Trump administration is on a collision path with Iran.[14] Rouhani needs to navigate this path within the space available to him between his domestic opponents and Trump's provocative and confrontationist postures.

Invigorated by support from the Israeli and Saudi leaderships, Trump has persistently castigated the Iranian regime as "corrupt," a supporter of "terrorism," and the source of all menace in the Middle East. Since March 2018, together with his new hardline secretary of state Mike Pompeo, Trump has repeatedly vowed to see Iran tamed, with the ultimate goal of regime change, in ways that will support the US's historical hegemonic role and interests in the region. The US military operations, under Trump, against IS in Iraq and Syria has aimed at countering Iranian influence in those two countries, in addition to checking the growing Russian influence in Syria and, indirectly through Iran, in Iraq.[15] A further objective, corresponding with Trump's enthusiastic embrace of Israel, has been to alleviate Tel Aviv's growing concerns about the Iranian forces and their proxies, Hezbollah in particular, securing a presence on the Syrian side of the border.

In the event of a confrontation, the Trump administration can count on the backing of Israel and Saudi Arabia and some of its GCC partners, namely the UAE and Bahrain. However, the GCC has undoubtedly been weakened in the wake of disputes among its members that have erupted recently. In June 2017, Saudi Arabia, backed by the UAE, Bahrain, and Egypt, imposed a blockade on Qatar, with one of their significant demands being that Doha should downgrade or curb its close relations with Iran. Taking advantage of this development, Tehran promptly offered assistance to enable Qatar to circumvent the blockade. That action accords with Iran's policy of undermining the GCC, which was originally set up as a defensive measure against Iran. Tehran supplied the emirate with fresh vegetables and fruit to compensate for the loss of these products, which are normally transported overland from Saudi Arabia. In return, instead of retrenching its relations with Iran, Qatar redispatched its ambassador to Tehran (whom it had withdrawn in January 2016 in support of Saudi Arabia's breaking of relations with Iran) on August 25, 2017. The reestablishment of Qatar-Iran ties thwarted one of the main objectives of the Saudi-led blockade of Qatar and frustrated President Trump's efforts to boost regional opposition to Iran.[16]

The Qatar crisis also shifted the ground for the Turkish president Tayyip Erdoğan, who found it expedient not only to stand by Qatar and to beef up Turkey's military base in the emirate (in defiance of the Saudi-led quartet's demand for its removal) but also to draw closer to Iran despite the two sides' differences in Syria. These moves, along with Turkey's improved relations with Russia, has further altered the regional strategic landscape in favor of Iranian interests.

Against the backdrop of these developments, President Trump intensified his condemnation of the JCPOA. When it came to the

October 2017 round of recertification of the nuclear agreement, he acted against the strong advice of America's main European allies: Britain, France, and Germany. At the same time, he showed complete disregard for Russia and China and therefore all the signatories to the agreement.[17] He accused Iran of having a "corrupt regime" dedicated to spreading terror, violence, and instability in the region, and refused to reconfirm the agreement. He passed the decision to the US Congress either to reimpose sanctions on Iran or to change the deal according to his preferences within sixty days, threatening to cancel the agreement if it failed to act.

To drive home his opposition to the JCPOA and Iran's ballistic missile testing, Trump slapped more sanctions on Iran. A number of ostensibly Iranian companies and one Chinese firm were targeted because of their links with the IRGC, which Trump wanted to declare as a terrorist organization. Tehran warned that this would mean a declaration of war. A noteworthy exception was Azarpassilo, one of the several companies that the IRGC had set up to circumvent international sanctions. This company is reportedly led by IRGC veterans and has indirect business ties with the Trump Organization through a "notoriously corrupt" partner, the Mammadov family of Azerbaijan.[18] The Mammadov family had been accused of money laundering, which allegedly enabled the IRGC to "purchase crucial components for weapons of mass destruction." This points to an indirect business relationship between the Trump Organization and the IRGC that operated until 2016 and helps shed light on President Trump's contradictory postures.[19]

Trump's refusal to reendorse the JCPOA was applauded by Israel and Saudi Arabia but infuriated Tehran and received no support from any other country. President Rouhani condemned it as a provocation based on lies, deceptions, and misconstructions "against the Iranian people."[20] As before, he rejected any renegotiation of the agreement and vowed that the Iranian nation would never give in to US pressure. The high representative of the European Union for Foreign Affairs and Security Policy, Federica Mogherini, rejected Trump's action and asserted that the JCPOA was "working and delivering" with Iran's full compliance and that the agreement was not a unilateral but a multilateral deal and was "not in the hands of any one president to terminate."[21] This rejection was shared by all the other JCPOA signatories, who made a firm pledge to maintain their commitment, although the Iranian side reserved the right to pull out of the deal if its interests required. Even so, finally Trump withdrew the US from the JCPOA in May 2018, vowing to impose such severe sanctions as to cripple the Iranian economy and hopefully bring about regime change. When in late July 2018 Rouhani warned the Trump administration that, while peace with Iran is "the mother of all peace" and war with Iran is "the mother of all wars," Trump tweeted that Rouhani must never threaten the US, for otherwise Iran would face "consequences the likes of which few throughout history have never suffered."[22]

Trump's diabolical decision to withdraw from the JCPOA has entailed serious implications, four of which are worth emphasizing. First, it has constituted a mortal blow to the nonproliferation regime and to the credibility of the United States as a reliable and dependable negotiator. This setback could provide only more reason for a state like North Korea to remain distrustful of the United States in any negotiation with it over its nuclear status. It has sent a similar message to all other countries, including, most importantly, America's allies, which had already been bruised in different ways by Trump's rejection of multilateralism, as seen in his withdrawal from the Paris Climate Agreement and the Trans-Pacific Partnership Agreement.

Second, it has emboldened Iran's regional adversaries, most importantly Israel and Saudi Arabia and some of its GCC partners, to continue to treat Iran as the number-one enemy while obscuring their own hand in the ongoing volatility in the Middle East. The Gulf and its wider environs badly need a degree of regional cooperation in order to address the conflicts in Syria, Iraq, Yemen, and Afghanistan, which cannot be resolved without Iranian assistance. The division of the region between enemies and friends may suit the Trump administration's aim of creating loyal and dependent clients, but it is detrimental and destabilizing to the millions who inhabit it.

Third, Trump's action has created a serious rift between the United States and its allies, especially Britain, France, and Germany, which remain dedicated to the preservation of the JCPOA for their own collective security. Trans-Atlantic relations have never been at such a low point, widening the gap in world leadership, which adversarial powers, such as Russia and China, would be eager to fill, at a tremendous cost to the United States.

Fourth, it has the potential to affect the texture of the Iranian domestic political scene. The Supreme Leader and the conservative clusters, including the powerful IRGC, which Trump has especially targeted as an evil force, have all along been highly skeptical of the United States. Given their strong hold on the power structure, they are now in a position to remind their moderate and reformist counterparts that they had "told them so" and to push for a sterner attitude in response to Trump's provocative actions.[23]

The Trump leadership has set the US on a confrontational path with the Islamic Republic of Iran. Yet considered rationally and logically, the circumstances cannot be more unfavorable for President Trump to take on Iran militarily. First, any confrontation with Iran would not only be massively damaging to Iran, it could also prove to be very costly for the region and therefore American interests in the Middle East. Iran has the hard- and soft-power capabilities, as well as de facto strategic partnerships with Russia and China, necessary to turn any American, Israeli, or combined attack into a war of attrition beyond what its adversaries may envisage. Given the escalation of tensions, the conservatives have already edged toward restoring and accelerating Iran's nuclear program, which could introduce another highly explosive dimension to the confrontation. The Islamic Republic has built sufficient resources capability and a regional network of activist groups to turn the whole region into an inferno. Moreover, despite their political divisions, the Iranian public can be expected to unite behind the Islamic government against external intervention, as they have repeatedly shown throughout their history.

Second, the Trump administration has other, more urgent priorities than to engage in a costly war with Iran. They include the nuclear standoff with North Korea, increased rivalry with Russia and China, and the Qatar crisis, which has embroiled America's Arab allies in another potentially enduring divisive dispute. Added to the list is not only the interminable Syrian conflict but also the result of the September 2017 Kurdish referendum, which resoundingly favored independence from Iraq. The result was rejected by Iraq's central government and the country's neighbors. Even Washington, despite its long-standing commitment to the Iraqi Kurds as a very reliable ally and good fighting force in support of America's interests, could not support it at the cost of dismembering an already divided Iraq.[24] Although the Iraqi government forces, aided by Iranian-backed Shia militias, succeeded in regaining control of the oil-rich but multiethnic and multisectarian Kirkuk that the Kurdish forces had held until early October 2017, relations between Baghdad and the Kurdish regional government are critically low. Beyond the military defeat of IS, the issue of Kurdish independence is likely to become yet another critical factor contributing to Iraq's and regional long-term instability.

Third, the Trump administration's compounding domestic problems are unlikely to provide him sufficient leverage to launch another Middle East war. Most of these problems have been created by the president's impulsive, nationalist, and populist rhetoric and actions. He is increasingly faced with more internal criticisms than any of his predecessors, while under fire not only from a three-way investigation by the special prosecutor, Robert Mueller, the Congress, and the Federal Bureau of Investigation into him and his campaign team's preelection dealings with Russia, but also from a wide array of individuals and groups due to his treatment of a host of other issues—race relations, law and order, and immigration. Trump's alienation, even within the Republican Party, is likely to be exacerbated should some of his strong supporters cease to feel that it would be in their electoral interests to stand behind him. By the end of 2017, there were already signs of this in the growing tensions between the president and some senior Republicans inside and outside Congress. A similar trend pervaded Trump's cabinet, with the president publicly undercutting and humiliating Secretaries

Tillerson and Mattis and Attorney General Jeff Sessions in order to pull them into line with his way of thinking. The President's imposition of substantial tariffs, resulting in a trade war, especially with China and its European allies has only added to the president's preoccupations.

Fourth, President Trump is likely to encounter serious difficulties in getting all of the GCC, let alone most of the other Arab countries, on board for a military campaign against Iran. Qatar will not be part of it, and the Sultanates of Oman and Kuwait will be extremely hesitant to back such an action. These three states have found it beneficial to maintain good working relations with Iran and will be averse to any development that could make them an Iranian target in the event of a US-Iranian confrontation.[25]

While logically President Trump is not in a strong position to take on Iran militarily, he may well deem a confrontation with Iran to be a desirable foreign policy diversion that could help shore up his domestic position and raise his profile as a formidable and fearsome actor on the world stage. This prospect has already been on display with Trump's bombastic approach to North Korea's nuclear threat, his authorization of a cruise missile attack on Syria in April 2017, and his use of the CBU-43 bomb, the most powerful nonnuclear bomb ever deployed, in Afghanistan in June 2017. But this could equally be a very risky strategy to pursue. It may easily backfire by igniting a regional conflict from which the US may not be able to extract itself easily, as the US-led invasions of Afghanistan and Iraq have been.[26] As a further deterrent, the Iranian regime has repeatedly made it clear that in the event of a confrontation, all American assets and allies in the region will be potential targets.

The Islamic Republic of Iran has so far proved sufficiently resilient and adaptable enough to weather its internal and external challenges in the past, and this may well remain the case for the foreseeable future. The Republic has learned a great deal from its trials and tribulations. In times of crises, the forces upholding the Islamic system have closed rank to preserve their hold on power and the longevity of the Republic, with a close eye on both what is ideologically permissible and what is pragmatically achievable. The

Republic cannot be expected to have a less dramatic and tempestuous time ahead than what it has experienced so far or, indeed, than what Iran has experienced in different forms and shapes under mostly authoritarian rule over the last two and a half millennia.

The Islamic Republic is currently placed among three clusters: conservative Islamists, reformist Islamists, and those elements who want an accelerated pace of semi-secular changes. Whereas the first cluster wields considerable state power, the second cluster has nevertheless been able to move Iran in the direction of ideological and political moderation and a viable course of change and development. The third cluster is squeezed in by the first two, but there is little chance of returning Iran back to the secularist politics of the Shah's era. The future of the Islamic Republic is most likely to be influenced by a power struggle that has already been settled but nonetheless remains consequential: between the conservative, or *jihadi*, and the reformist, or *ijtihadi*, clusters. This struggle, as well as the outside world's treatment of the Republic, especially by the United States and its allies, will continue to shape the Republic's domestic politics and foreign relations. The *jihadi-ijtihadi* paradigm of change and development—an important aspect of Ayatollah Khomeini's legacy—will remain as relevant in influencing the evolution of Iran's politics and society in the coming years as it has been thus far. Yet as the Republic moves forward, the *ijtihadi* aspect is likely to gain ground as the postrevolution generations come of age. The more this feature is understood in the outside world, the better the chances of dealing with the Islamic Republic from an informed and realistic position.

Irrespective of the direction that the Iranian Islamic system may take, Iran's viability, integrity, and influence as a qualified middle-power remains paramount. Despite all its problems over the last forty years, the Islamic Republic has emerged as a critical actor in its region, with an important imprint on the global stage. There are few regional disputes and conflicts that can be expected to be resolved satisfactorily without its cooperation. Iran is a key player, with a capacity to promote stability and security (or, conversely, instability and disruption) in a strategically and economically vital part of the world. The US-led efforts to contain and isolate the Islamic Republic for four decades have not borne fruit. It is time for the alternative approach: to engage the Republic diplomatically as President Barack Obama had begun to do. A policy of engagement carries greater potential than Trump's gunboat diplomacy to generate favorable conditions for the forces that are dedicated to the cause of ensuring Iran's progress as a stabilizing regional actor and, for that matter, as a responsible player in world politics.

NOTES

Chapter 1. Introduction

1. Morello, "Iran Accuses US of Bullying."

2. For an overview of the politics of Iran under Khamenei, see Arjomand, *After Khomeini.*

3. For a comprehensive overview of the regional and international impact of the revolution, see Esposito, *Iranian Revolution.*

4. Israel's approach to the conflict is detailed in Alpher, "Israel and the Iran-Iraq War."

5. Moin, *Khomeini*, pp. 195–96.

6. *Faqih* essentially means "deputy to the last Imam of the Twelver Shia sect," who is believed to have gone into occultation in the tenth century, but who reappears before the end of the world to prepare and save it for the day of judgment, possibly in conjunction with Jesus Christ.

7. The term "polyarchy" denotes a system of formal, but not substantive, representative government. It allows free elections, but the choice is limited between competing elites only. It entails equality when it comes to process, because everyone can vote, but not in who actually gets power, with formal consent in voting only propping up the inequalities of the system. In all it is neither a dictatorship nor a democracy, therefore somewhere in between. See Dahl, *Preface to Democratic Theory*, pp. xviii–xix.

8. Bjorvatn and Selvik, "Destructive Competition."

9. Khomeini famously described the decision as "more deadly than taking poison." Pear, "Khomeini Accepts 'Poison.'"

10. See Nader, *Rouhani's Election.* For an analysis of the 2017–18 protests, see Asadzade, "New Data Shed Light."

11. Erdbrink, "Enigmatic Leader of Iran."

12. "Trump Administration Pledges 'Great Strictness.'"

13. Holland and Spetalnick, "Trump Adopts Aggressive Posture."

14. "Iran Deal 'Does Not Belong to One Country.'"

15. Perry, "James Mattis' 33-Year Grudge."

16. For a comprehensive discussion of Mattis's views, see Filkins, "Warrior Monk."

17. See Baig, "Steve Bannon's War with Islam."

18. Porter, "Untold Story of John Bolton's Campaign."

19. For an argument in support of a likely US-Iranian confrontation, see Ross, "Trump Is on a Collision Course."

20. Khan, "Saudi Prince Mohammed bin Salman's Warning."

21. Gradstein, "Israel Develops New Ties"; see also Irish and Shalal, "Saudi Arabia, Israel."

22. Trump, "President Trump's Speech."

23. Indeed, Russia is maintaining close ties with Israel as part of its policy of cultivating relations with all major powers in the region. Ahren and Surkes, "Rivlin in Moscow."

24. Ehteshami, "Iran as a Middle Power," pp. 54–55.

25. For a comprehensive historical overview of the middle power concept, see Ping, "Middle Power Statecraft," pp. 43–101.

26. Bélanger and Mace, "Building Role and Region," p. 154.

27. Ya'alon, "Why Iran Is More Dangerous."

28. For a detailed discussion, see Chapnick, "Middle Power."

29. Wight, *Power Politics*, p. 65.

30. Prys, "Variability of Regional Powers," pp. 9–11.

31. Treverton and Jones, *Measuring National Power*, p. ix.

32. Baldwin, *Power and International Relations*, pp. 70–72.

33. Cooper, *Niche Diplomacy*, p. 14.

34. Ping, "Middle Power Statecraft," p. 91.

35. Morgenthau, *Politics among Nations*, pp. 80–120.

36. Waltz, *Theory of International Politics*, pp. 192, 131.

37. Nye, "Soft Power," p. 167.

38. McClory and Harvey, "Soft Power 30."

39. Pallaver, "Power and Its Forms," p. 91.

Chapter 2. Revolution and Transition

1. Davis, *Typing Politics*, p. 186.

2. Tazmini, *Revolution and Reform*, p. 20.

3. Skocpol, *State and Social Revolutions*, p. 4.

4. See, for example, Pipes, *Russian Revolution*.

5. Bunyan and Fisher, *Bolshevik Revolution*, p. 79.

6. V. I. Lenin, "Transfer of Power and the Means of Production to the Toilers" [1917], quoted in ibid., p. 287.

7. Chen, *Making Revolution*, p. 501.

8. Fu, *Autocratic Tradition and Chinese Politics*, p. 171.

9. Deng Xiaoping, quoted in Pei, *From Reform to Revolution*, p. 13.

10. See, for example, Newman, *Safavid Iran*.

11. A. Conolly, quoted in Yapp, "Legend of the Great Game," pp. 180–81.

12. Verrier, "Francis Younghusband."

13. See Ghani, *Iran and the Rise of Reza Shah*.

14. Abrahamian, "Causes of the Constitutional Revolution," pp. 410–11.

15. The first Iranian Majles lasted just 20 months (October 7, 1906, to June 23, 1908) and the cabinet was changed nine times. Sohrab, "Historicizing Revolutions," p. 1416.

16. Saikal, *Rise and Fall of the Shah*, p. 15.

17. Kinzer, *All the Shah's Men*, p. 44.

18. Abrahamian, *History of Modern Iran*, p. 72–91.

19. During this time, the Soviet dictator Stalin was focused on consolidating his rule at home, while Britain was increasingly preoccupied with difficulties arising from the growing nationalist movements in its colonies, particularly in the Indian subcontinent.

20. Ghani, *Iran and the Rise of Reza Shah*, p. 12.

21. Churchill, *Triumph and Tragedy*, p. 90; Parsa, *Social Origins*, p. 37.

22. For a detailed discussion, see Saikal, *Rise and Fall of the Shah*, pp. 26–27.

23. Mohammad Foroughi served as prime minister from August 1941 until his death in November 1942. He had also served in such a post twice before: in 1925–26 and 1933–35.

24. Hess, "Iranian Crisis of 1945–46," p. 124.

25. Kinzer, *All the Shah's Men*, p. 45.

26. Winston Churchill in a drafted telegram to Stalin, in Churchill, *Grand Alliance*, p. 431.

27. Golan, *Soviet Policies in the Middle East*, p. 29.

28. Reported in Smith, *Moscow Mission, 1946–49*, p. 40.

29. Ibid., p. 31.

30. Sir Francis Shepherd, British ambassador to Iran, quoted in Abrahamian, "1953 Coup in Iran," p. 187.

31. Ebrahimi and Yusoff, "Aftermath of *Coup d'État*," p. 206.

32. These were precisely some of the same goals that the Constitutional Movement sought to achieve forty years earlier.

33. He once stated that "the moral aspect of oil nationalization is more important than its economic aspect." Mohammad Mosaddegh, quoted in Katouzian, *Mussadiq and the Struggle for Power*, p. 92.

34. Cooper, *Fall of Heaven*, pp. 70–72.

35. Yazdi, "Patterns of Clerical Political Behavior," p. 289.

36. US State Department, quoted in Elm, *Oil, Power, and Principle*, p. 112.

37. To resolve the oil nationalization issue, Washington proposed an international consortium, which became operational from late 1954, to be dominated equally by British Petroleum and five American oil companies to run the Iranian oil industry under the nominal tutelage of the National Iranian Oil Company. Ibid., p. 84.

38. Diba, *Mossadegh*, pp. 137–38.

39. In 2013, the CIA declassified documents that acknowledged its role in the coup, and in June 2017, a further tranche that demonstrated the motives and tactics in greater detail. Fakhreddin, "Unseating Mosaddeq."

40. "CIA Documents Acknowledge Its Role"; "Iran 1953."

41. Mohammad Mosaddegh, quoted in Elm, *Oil, Power, and Principle*, p. 334.

42. For an elaborate account of the Mossadegh period, see Saikal, *Rise and Fall of the Shah*, pp. 35–41.

43. Saikal, *Rise and Fall of the Shah*, p. 55.

44. After the coup, US oil companies gained a 40 percent share in the new oil consortium that was set up. Ghods, *Iran in the Twentieth Century*, p. 190.

45. For a detailed discussion, see Saikal, *Rise and Fall of the Shah*, chapter 2.

46. The kingdom was established in 1745 on the basis of a deal between the ruling Ibn Saud family and the religious clerical establishment. See al-Rasheed, *History of Saudi Arabia*.

47. Miglietta, *American Alliance Policy*, p. 19.

48. Summitt, "For a White Revolution," pp. 562–63.

49. Ibid., p. 565.

50. Six reforms formed part of the Shah's "six-point" program that was the White Revolution: land redistribution, the nationalization of forests, the sale of state factories, profit-sharing for the working class, the right to vote for women, and improving rural literacy. See Abrahamian, *Iran between Two Revolutions*, p. 424.

51. For a detailed discussion, see Saikal, *Rise and Fall of the Shah,* chapter 3.

52. Mohammad Reza Shah Pahlavi, quoted in Holliday, *Defining Iran*, p. 36.

53. Ibid.

54. Krasner, *Defending the National Interest*, pp. 122–23.

55. Quoted in Abrahamian, *History of Modern Iran*, p. 126.

56. Zonis, *Political Elite of Iran*, p. 13.

57. See Sadeghi-Boroujerdi, "Origins of Communist Unity."

58. Kamrava, *Revolution in Iran*, pp. 121, 119–21. They were also targeted because they were a class that was traditionally politically independent from the state. In fact, the strong ties between the *bazaaris* and the *ulema* (learned critics) were seen as a major political threat by the Shah.

59. This underpinned his desire to break up the traditional *bazaari*-clerical alliance through policies such as land reform, which sought to undermine the power of land owners, many of whom were part of the clerical elite. Ibid.

60. For a detailed discussion of these issues, see Saikal, "Islamism, the Iranian Revolution," pp. 114–21.

61. Abrahamian, *Iran between Two Revolutions*, p. 427. All dollar amounts cited in this book are in US dollars.

62. Keddie, *Modern Iran*, p. 163.

63. Amirahmadi, *Revolution and Economic Transition*, p. 18.

64. From 1972 to 1977, military imports from the US reached over $16 billion, while Iran's defense budget increased from $1.4 billion in 1972 to $9.4 billion in 1977. Ibid., p. 17.

65. Guerrero, *Carter Administration*, p. 20.

66. Adult literacy rates increased from 16 percent in 1960 to 36 percent in 1975. Maloney, *Iran's Political Economy*, p. 61.

67. For details, see Saikal, *Rise and Fall of the Shah*, pp. 153–54.

68. Similarly, the Fedayin-e Khalq during the same time had assassinated the chief military prosecutor and bombed a number of police headquarters and the British, Omani, and US embassies. Abrahamian, *Iran between Two Revolutions*, pp. 488–91.

69. See Yodfat, *Soviet Union and Revolutionary Iran*.

70. Similarly, the Shah also offered to support Pakistan in crushing the Popular Front for the Liberation of Pakistani and Iranian Baluchistan, which was supported by Afghanistan, another Soviet ally. Saikal, *Rise and Fall of the Shah*, pp. 139–47.

71. Bashiriyeh, *State and Revolution in Iran*, p. 97.

72. Carter, "Toasts of the President."

73. Carter, "Tehran, Iran Toasts."

74. Cooper, *Fall of Heaven*, p. 359.

75. Hiro, *Iran under the Ayatollahs*, p. 51.

76. Parsa, *Social Origins*, p. 190.

77. Khomeini, "Granting of Capitulatory Rights," p. 181.

78. Ibid., p. 184.

79. Nasr, *Shia Revival*, pp. 67–68.

80. See, for example, Bayat, "Iranian Revolution"; Adib-Moghaddam, "Introduction."

81. See Milani, *Eminent Persians*, p. 348.

82. See Khomeini, *Islam and Revolution I*, section "Islamic Government," pp. 27–68.

83. Khomeini often couched his political messages in Shia imagery. One typical example was when he compared the growing revolutionary spirit to the cleansing justice of Karbala, declaring, "Just as the pure blood brought to an end the tyrannical rule of Yazid, the blood of our martyrs has shattered the tyrannical monarchy of the Pahlavi's." Khomeini, January 15, 1979, quoted in Gholizadeh and Hook, "Discursive Construction," p. 180.

84. Khomeini, *Islam and Revolution I*, p. 64.

85. He also stated that "rule and command, then, are in themselves only a means, and if this means is not employed for the good and for attaining noble aims, it has no value in the eyes of the men of God." Ibid., p. 65.

86. Khomeini, *Islam and Revolution I*, p. 59.

87. Ibid., p. 62.

88. Ibid., p. 79.

89. "For the Imam forbade the Muslims to have recourse to kings and their appointed judges for the purpose of obtaining their rights." Ibid., pp. 98–100.

90. Ibid., p. 60.

91. Ibid., p. 61.

92. Ibid., p. 49.

93. Esposito, *Islam and Politics*, p. 14.

94. Bayat, "Iranian Revolution," p. 33.

95. Shariati, quoted in Kian, "Gendered Khomeini," p. 180.

96. Cottam, "Goodbye to America's Shah," p. 11.

97. "ANJOMAN (Organization)."

98. Beheshti was behind the assassination of Prime Minister Hassan Ali Mansur in 1965. Cooper, *Fall of Heaven*, pp. 252, 468–69.

99. Ibid., p. 290.

100. Khomeini, "Thirty Million Have Stood Up," p. 322.

101. Fattahi, "Two Weeks in January."

102. Deputy National Security Advisor David Aaron, quoted in ibid.

103. Ibid.

104. Ibid.

105. Ibid.

106. See Dehghan and Bowcott, "Thatcher Files."

Chapter 3. Khomeini's Theo-Political Order

1. An article by Farhad Nikukah, a low-ranking official in the Ministry of Information, argued that the Shah's modernization agenda was under threat from "red" leftists and "black" religious reactionaries. In particular, it also accused Khomeini of being a foreigner and an agent of British interests. The article sparked protests in Qum. Nikukah, "Iran and Red and Black Colonialism."

2. *Le Monde*, May 6, 1978; English translation published in *Manchester Guardian*, May 21, 1978; reprinted in Nobari, *Iran Erupts*, pp. 14, 15.

3. *Le Monde*, October 17, 1978, reprinted in ibid., pp. 19–20.

4. Parsa, *Democracy in Iran*, p. 144.

5. Sabet, "*Wilayat al-Faqih*," pp. 83–84.

6. For the reception of Khomeini's theory among the Iranian *ulama*, see Enayat, "Iran: Khumayni's Concept."

7. Ayubi, *Political Islam*, p. 114. He also used this discourse to discredit his political rivals. In the lead-up to the 1988 legislative elections, he urged supporters not to vote for candidates of "capitalist Islam." Baktiari, *Parliamentary Politics in Revolutionary Iran*, p. 147.

8. Harding writes that even during the Second World War, "Lenin refused outright to make the slightest concession to the near-universal patriotic infatuation of socialists and working people throughout Europe," arguing instead for pacifism—an unpopular position that seemed "beyond treasonous." He concludes that "Lenin . . . remained true to the fundamentalist Marxism he had always espoused. . . . To these fundamentals, Lenin stood firm to the time of his death." Harding, *Lenin's Political Thought*, pp. 37–38.

9. "Iran's 'Hanging Judge' Dies at 76."

10. The report covered the period January to December 1981. See Amnesty International, "Annual Report 1982," p. 323.

11. A detailed analysis of the constitution is provided in Schirazi, *Constitution of Iran.*

12. See Forozan, *Military in Post-Revolutionary Iran.*

13. See Esposito, *Oxford Encyclopedia*, vol. 1, sv. "*bunyad*," pp. 235–37.

14. Jenkins, "Explaining Iranian Soft Power Capability."

15. Rakel, "Conglomerates in Iran"; Samii, "Iranian Nuclear Issue."

16. See Jenkins, "Explaining Iranian Soft Power Capability."

17. Malek, "Elite Factionalism," p. 442.

18. Moghadam, "Socialism or Anti-imperialism?," p. 22.

19. "Rumors Confirmed."

20. "Enteshar-e fayl-e Ayatollah Montazari dar moured-e 'addamhai-e sali hazaro sisadi shastu haft."

21. For an English summary, see Gambrell, "Released Tape Rekindles Memory."

22. "Clashes Reported at Funeral."

23. Four hundred and ninety-seven political opponents were executed between February 1979 and June 1981. These included six former cabinet ministers, three SAVAK chiefs, and thirty-five generals. Over eight thousand more were executed in the next four years. Abrahamian, *History of Modern Iran*, pp. 181–82.

24. Khomeini, *Clarification of Questions.*

25. For an overview of the IRGC's involvement in the Iranian state, see Hen-Tov and Gonzalez, "Militarization of Post-Khomeini Iran"; Josef, "Iranian Revolutionary Guard Corps," p. 171; and Forozan, *Military in Post-Revolutionary Iran.*

26. Khomeini, "Announcement of International Quds Day."

27. Roy, *Islam and Resistance in Afghanistan*, pp. 23–26; also, Emadi, "Exporting Iran's Revolution."

28. "Imam Khomeini Advised Gorbachev."

29. Ibid.

30. Rizvi, "Ayatollah Denounces US Embassy."

31. Beeman, *"Great Satan" vs. the "Mad Mullahs,"* p. 65.

32. Murray, *US Foreign Policy and Iran*, p. 41.

33. In an interview, Yazdi claimed that the release of the hostages was authorized only after Ronald Reagan had won the US presidential election, to show that Iran had significant influence over the US political process (a reversal of roles of the 1953 coup). See Houghton, *US Foreign Policy*, p. 143.

34. The plan was also criticized for being convoluted and overly complicated. See Celmer, *Terrorism, US Strategy*, p. 68.

35. "Imam Khomeini Denounced US Operation in Tabas."

36. James Piscatori notes how the issue presented a challenge for Muslim jurists, raising challenges between Sunni and Shia jurisprudence on the question of the death penalty as an appropriate punishment for apostasy. See Piscatori, "Rushdie Affair," p. 782. See also Pipes, *Rushdie Affair*, pp. 146–52.

37. Crossette, "Iran Drops Rushdie Death Threat."

38. Marschall, *Iran's Persian Gulf Policy*, p. 44.

39. Moin, *Khomeini*, pp. 195–96.

40. The main causes of the decline in oil production and revenues were Iraqi attacks on Iran's oil infrastructure (particularly in the Gulf and its export facilities as part of the "tanker wars") and an increase in supply from Iraq's allies in the Organization of the Petroleum Exporting Countries (OPEC), notably Saudi Arabia. Maloney, *Iran's Political Economy*, p. 165.

41. Ibid., pp. 169–70.

42. For a full discussion, see "Iran-Iraq War (1980–1988)."

43. Abrahamian, *History of Modern Iran*, p. 147.

44. Bjorvatn and Selvik, "Destructive Competition."

45. Seifzadeh, "Landscape of Factional Politics."

46. See Ghamari-Tabrizi, "Contentious Public Religion"; as well as Akhavi, "Islam, Politics and Society."

47. Saikal, *Iran at the Crossroads.*

48. Saikal, "Islamism, the Iranian Revolution."

49. Farhi, "Cultural Policies," p. 5.

50. Yodfat, *Soviet Union and Revolutionary Iran*, p. 101.

51. Hiro, *Longest War*, p. 83.

52. Hunter, *Iran's Foreign Policy*, p. 104.

53. Bingbing, "Strategy and Politics," p. 14.

54. Gill, "Chinese Arms Exports to Iran," p. 359.

55. Ibid.

56. Bingbing, "Strategy and Politics," p. 16.

57. Morris, "From Silk to Sanctions," p. 2.

58. Ganai and Pandey, "Case of India and Iran," p. 147.

59. Sisakht, "Foreign Policy of Iran," p. 148.

60. Ibid.

61. "Trying to Remember Khomeini."

Chapter 4. The Islamic Order under Khamenei

1. For a discussion of Khamenei and his views, see Ganji, "Who Is Ali Khamenei?"

2. For a detailed discussion, see Hovsepian-Bearce, *Political Ideology of Ayatollah Khamenei.*

3. Khamenei, quoted in Ibrahim, "Confrontation in the Gulf."

4. For a comprehensive list, see al-Din, "Mardan e Ayatollah Khamenei"; and Khamenei, "Nama haa and Payam haa-e Muqam Moa'zam-e Rahbar-e Hazrat-e Ayatollah Khamenei 1368."

5. Khalaji, "House of the Leader."

6. The presidency, Majles, and Assembly of Experts are the three universally elected bodies for which elections have always taken place constitutionally and on time irrespective of any internal and external difficulties.

7. Tarock, "Iran–Western Europe Relations," pp. 59–60.

8. Cited in Arjomand, *After Khomeini*, p. 66.
9. Cited in Bayat, *Making Islam Democratic*, p. 114.
10. Ansari, "Iran under Ahmadinejad," p. 16.
11. Taghavi, "Iranian Economy," p. 175.
12. Maloney, *Iran's Political Economy*, p. 243.
13. Ibid., pp. 205, 239.
14. Khatami, quoted in Esposito and Voll, "Islam and Democracy."
15. Saikal, *Zone of Crisis*, p. 116.
16. Khatami, *Islam, Dialogue and Civil Society*, pp. 17–18.
17. The arrest and killings of dozens of liberal intellectuals and politicians in 1998 was known as the Chain Murders and led to a confrontation between Khatami and the conservative establishment that controlled the Ministry of Intelligence. See Hovsepian-Bearce, *Political Ideology of Ayatollah Khamenei.*
18. Huntington, "Clash of Civilizations?"
19. Khatami, "Presentation," p. 25.
20. Jehl, "On Trip to Mend Ties."
21. See Saikal, *Iran at the Crossroads*, pp. 59–63.
22. The most detailed and balanced analysis of Iran's nuclear program is Patrikarakos, *Nuclear Iran.*
23. *Iran: Nuclear Intentions and Capabilities*, p. 3.
24. See Gates, *Duty*, pp. 185–86.
25. Kamel, *Political Economy of EU Ties*, p. 128.
26. For a detailed discussion of the policy of dual containment, see Pollock, *Persian Puzzle*, pp. 259–73; and for Israel's role in the Clinton administration's foreign policy toward Iran, see Parsi, *Treacherous Alliance*, chapters 14 and 15.
27. See Brzezinski, Scowcroft, and Murphy, "Differentiated Containment."
28. "President Delivers State of the Union Address."
29. For a detailed discussion, see Saikal, *Modern Afghanistan*, pp. 237–43.
30. Dobbins's account of this episode may be found in Dobbins, "Negotiating with Iran."
31. Gillespie, "September 11, 2001 (9/11)," p. 1514.
32. Naji, "Iranian Students Lose Hope"; see also Recknagel, "Protests Highlight Reformist Students' Frustration."
33. The circumstances of Ahmadinejad's victory are treated more extensively in Ehteshami and Zweiri, *Iran and the Rise of Its Neoconservatives*, chapter 3.
34. Fathi, "Low Turnout in Iran"; see also Abedin, "Iran after the Elections."
35. For more details on the life, character, and politics of Ahmadinejad, see Ansari, "Iran under Ahmadinejad"; Ehteshami and Zweiri, *Iran and the Rise of Its Neoconservatives*; and Naji, *Ahmadinejad.*
36. Pickler, "Did Iran's New Leader Help Take Hostages?"
37. "The Big Squeeze."
38. For an evaluation of Ahmadinejad's first presidency, see Axworthy, *Iran: Empire of the Mind*, chapter 9.

39. Habibi, "Economic Legacy of Mahmoud Ahmadinejad," p. 5.
40. Maloney, *Iran's Political Economy*, p. 330.
41. "Ahmadinejad under Fire on Economy."
42. Warnaar, *Iranian Foreign Policy*, chapters 4 and 5.
43. He infamously claimed that the Holocaust was a myth created by Zionists. See "Ahmadinejad: Holocaust a Myth."
44. For a detailed discussion, see Naji, *Ahmadinejad*, especially chapters 4–6.
45. Rouhani, quoted in Saikal, *Iran at the Crossroads*, p. 68.
46. *Iran News*, October 29, 2013.
47. Saikal, *Zone of Crisis*, p. 119.
48. Saikal, *Iran at the Crossroads*, p. 68.
49. See, for example, Gerecht, "Iran's Revolution: Year 2."
50. Siddique, "Iran Elections."
51. Saikal, *Iran at the Crossroads*, p. 69.
52. Clemons, "Khamenei Is the New Shah."
53. "Khomeini's Disciples in Iran?"
54. Jahanbegloo, "Two Sovereignties," p. 28.
55. Saikal, *Iran at the Crossroads*, p. 70.
56. Ibid.
57. Erdbrink, "Iranian Leader Rebuffs Ahmadinejad."
58. Borger, "Khamenei's Son Takes Control"; Fleishman, "Iran Supreme Leader's Son."
59. Saikal, *Iran at the Crossroads*, p. 71.
60. Ibid., p. 72.
61. Erdbrink, "Iran's Supreme Leader."
62. "Mahmoud Ahmadinejad."
63. For details of Rouhani's views, see Rouhani, *Rawaiti-e Tadbir wa Omid*.
64. Saikal, *Iran at the Crossroads*, p. 88.
65. Ibid., p. 89.
66. Rezalan, "Iran's Supreme Leader."
67. For the full text in English, see Islamic Republic of Iran, "Iran's First Charter of Citizens' Rights," Article 15. For the Persian text, see http://rouhani.ir/files/CitizensRights.pdf.
68. Islamic Republic of Iran, "Iran's First Charter of Citizens' Rights," Article 13.
69. Esfandiari, "Iranian Citizens' Rights Charter."
70. Islamic Republic of Iran, "Iran's First Charter of Citizens' Rights," Article 26.
71. Dehghan, "Hassan Rouhani Takes Oath."
72. For an analysis of "postrevolution" Iran, see "Revolution Is Over."
73. Sheridan, "Baby Boomers of Iran."
74. See Sreberny and Torfeh, *Cultural Revolution in Iran*.
75. Sciolino, "Love Finds a Way in Iran."
76. Samimi, "Online 'Sigheh' in Iran."
77. See Nooshin, "Subversion and Countersubversion."

Chapter 5. Resource Capabilities

1. For a classification of the states on the basis of gross national product, see World Bank, "World Bank Country and Lending Groups."

2. World Bank, "Iran Overview."

3. Crane, Lal, and Martini, *Iran's Political, Demographic, and Economic Vulnerabilities*, p. 83.

4. Bazoobandi, "Iran's Economy and Energy," pp. 29–30.

5. Nasseri and Motevalli, "Iran Inflation at 25-Year Low."

6. Bazoobandi, "Iran's Economy and Energy," p. 27; Khajehpour, "Has Rouhani Achieved His Goals?"

7. Amuzegar, *Islamic Republic of Iran*, p. 7.

8. Population growth was encouraged because of conservative opposition to family planning, which was associated with the Shah's regime. Furthermore, it was seen as necessary for a strong economy and the creation of the "twenty-million-strong Islamic army" that Khomeini envisioned. Ter-Organov, "Islamic Nationalism in Iran," p. 135; also see Roudi, *Iran Is Reversing Its Population Policy*.

9. Amirahmadi, "Economic Costs of the War," p. 261.

10. Maloney, *Iran's Political Economy*, pp. 205, 235.

11. Amuzegar, *Islamic Republic of Iran*, pp. 8–9.

12. A. Komijani, "Macroeconomic Policies and Performance in Iran," p. 184.

13. Amuzegar, *Islamic Republic of Iran*, pp. 9–10.

14. Salehi-Isfahani, "Poverty, Inequality," p. 12.

15. Crane, Lal, and Martini, *Iran's Political, Demographic, and Economic Vulnerabilities*, pp. 89–90.

16. Amuzegar, *Islamic Republic of Iran*, p. 12.

17. DiPaola and Arnsdorf, "Iran Loses $133 Million."

18. Clawson, "Tehran Adds to the Pressure."

19. Maloney, *Iran's Political Economy*, p. 471.

20. Choksy, "Iran's Economic Health."

21. Saikal, "Roots of Iran's Election Crisis," pp. 97–98.

22. Merat, "Ahmadinejad's Economic Legacy."

23. Ibid.

24. IMF, "Islamic Republic of Iran," p. 44.

25. Amirahmadi, "Rouhani's New Budget."

26. The government committed $400 million to see current projects to completion but halted any further projects. Hulpachova, "Iran's Economy."

27. "Iran Widens Cash Handout Cancellations."

28. Smyth, "Deciphering the Iranian Leader's Call."

29. Dehghan, "Iran Earns More from Tax."

30. Bizaer, "Iran's First Non-oil Trade Surplus."

31. "Budget Oil Dependence at Lowest."

32. Bizaer, "Iran's First Non-oil Trade Surplus."

33. Transparency International, "Corruptions Perceptions Index 2016."

34. World Justice Project, "Rule of Law Index 2016," p. 5.

35. http://www.bbc.com/news/world-middle-east-30378662. See "Iran's President Rouhani Warns against Corruption."

36. "Iran Elections: Hardliners Lose Parliament to Rouhani Allies."

37. Ramezani, "Rouhani Shifts Gears on Economy."

38. Ramezani, "Rouhani's Budget Proposal."

39. Salehi-Isfahani, "Oil Wealth," p. 28.

40. Nasseri and Motevalli, "Investing in Iran?"

41. Alizadeh, "Iran's Quandary," pp. 271–72.

42. The ranking was based on criteria such as ease of obtaining credit, paying taxes, resolving insolvency, and enforcing contracts. World Bank, "Doing Business: Economy Rankings."

43. Abidi, *Iran Business Handbook 2016*, p. 5.

44. Wehrey et al., *Rise of the Pasdaran*, p. 12.

45. Ibid., pp. 57–58.

46. Ibid.

47. Mather, "Iran's Political and Economic Crises," p. 506.

48. Wehrey et al., *Rise of the Pasdaran*, pp. 60–61.

49. Hashim, "Iranian Military in Politics," p. 77.

50. Constitution of the Islamic Republic of Iran, Article 147.

51. Borger and Tait, "Financial Power."

52. Khajehpour, "Iran's Budget"; Wilson, "Lifting of Sanctions."

53. Dizaji, Farzanegan, and Naghavi, "Political Institutions."

54. Crane, Lal, and Martini, *Iran's Political, Demographic, and Economic Vulnerabilities*, p. 47.

55. Ibid.

56. IMF, *2015 Article IV Consultation*.

57. A large part of this is due to the fact that *bonyads* and politically linked companies enjoy tax-free status. "Iran Losing $20 Billion."

58. The OECD average was 34.3 percent. For a full list of tax-to-GDP ratios for OECD countries, see OECD, "Revenue Statistics 2017."

59. Saikal, *Iran at the Crossroads*, p. 123.

60. Ibid., p. 124.

61. Salehi-Isfahani, "Oil Wealth," p. 23.

62. Amir-Mokri and Biglari, "Windfall for Iran?," p. 26.

63. Salehi-Isfahani, "Oil Wealth," p. 28.

64. Amir-Mokri and Biglari, "Windfall for Iran?" p. 26.

65. Callen et al., "Economic Diversification."

66. Amir-Mokri and Biglari, "Windfall for Iran?," p. 26.

67. Mraz, Lipkova, and Brockova, "Economic Sanctions," p. 24.

68. Ibid., p. 27.

69. Phippen, "$5 Billion Energy Deal."

70. Glen, "Iran's Economy in 2015."

71. Mohseni, Gallagher, and Ramsay, *Iranian Public Opinion*, p. 8.

72. Ibid.
73. Nasseri, "Rouhani Struggles."
74. "President Rouhani: Iran Needs No One's Permission."
75. Chubin, "Is Iran a Military Threat?," p. 79.
76. Ward, "Continuing Evolution," p. 572.
77. Tira and Guzansky, "Is Iran in Strategic Equilibrium?," p. 8.
78. Chubin, "Is Iran a Military Threat?," p. 72.
79. This does not translate into offensive strength however.
80. US Department of Defense, *Annual Report*, p. 6.
81. Tira and Guzansky, "Is Iran in Strategic Equilibrium?," pp. 8–9.
82. Ward, "Continuing Evolution," p. 567.
83. Forozan, *Military in Post-Revolutionary Iran*, p. 53.
84. IISS, "Chapter Seven," p. 312.
85. Ibid., p. 313.
86. Farzanegan, "Military Spending," p. 248.
87. IISS, "Chapter Seven," pp. 327–31.
88. Tira and Guzansky, "Is Iran in Strategic Equilibrium?," p. 8.
89. Chubin, "Iran and the Arab Spring," p. 43.
90. Forozan, *Military in Post-Revolutionary Iran*, p. 191.
91. Delijani, "Assessment of the Egyptian Military," p. 9.
92. Ibid.
93. Hashim, "Iranian Military in Politics," p. 71.
94. Chubin, "Is Iran a Military Threat?," pp. 66–69.
95. Olson, "Iran's Path," p. 69.
96. Ibid., p. 71.
97. Ibid., p. 63.
98. Hildreth, "Iran's Ballistic Missile," pp. i–ii.
99. Cordesman and Toukan, "Iran and the Gulf Military Balance," p. 181.
100. Czulda, "Defensive Dimension," p. 94.
101. Wehrey et al., *Dangerous but Not Omnipotent*, p. 39.
102. Chubin, "Is Iran a Military Threat?," p. 80.
103. Hanna and Kaye, "Limits of Iranian Power," p. 179.
104. Library of Congress, *Iran's Ministry*, p. 16.
105. Hanna and Kaye, "Limits of Iranian Power," p. 179.
106. Cordesman and Toukan, "Iran and the Gulf Military Balance," p. 60.
107. Hanna and Kaye, "Limits of Iranian Power," p. 178.
108. IISS, "Chapter Seven."
109. US Department of Defense, *Annual Report*, p. 5.
110. Hanna and Kaye, "Limits of Iranian Power," p. 178.
111. Ibid., p. 179.
112. Ibid.
113. Czulda, "Defensive Dimension," p. 100.
114. To this end, Tehran's soft-power policies have received considerable scholarly attention. Former deputy foreign minister of the Islamic Republic Abbas

Maleki, for example, has analyzed Iran's soft-power interactions according to Joseph Nye's three sources of soft power: culture, political values, and foreign policy. Maleki, *Soft Power.*

115. "Foreign Policy Strategy for Upgrading the Islamic Republic of Iran's Economic Position in the New International Conditions," cited in Jenkins, "Explaining Iranian Soft Power Capability," p. 53.

116. See Kagan et al., *Iranian Influence.*

117. Khamenei, "Office of the Leader" [in Persian].

118. Maintaining the policy of neutrality became difficult in the wake of the hostage crisis and the resulting deterioration of relations with the West. Especially in light of the emergence of the US-led unipolar order, the result is that Iranian foreign policy has typically taken, at least rhetorically, an anti-American position.

119. For a detailed discussion, see Chubin, "Iran's Power in Context" and "Iran and the Arab Spring."

120. Golmohammadi, Atanejad, and Shahrebabaki, "Foreign Policy Strategies," pp. 714–15.

121. Wastnidge, "Modalities of Iranian Soft Power," p. 373.

122. Zarif, "What Iran Really Wants," p. 54.

123. Djalili and Kellner, "Iran's Syria Policy," p. 522.

124. See Jenkins, "*Bonyads* as Agents."

125. Thaler et al., *Mullahs, Guards, and* Bonyads, p. 58.

126. Ibid., p. 57.

127. Slavin, *Mullahs, Money, and Militias,* p. 8.

128. Ibid., p. 11.

129. Ibid., p. 8.

130. Ibid.

131. Specifically, the IKRC has 20 offices in Lebanon, 10 in Syria, 130 in Afghanistan, 35 in Azerbaijan, 58 in Tajikistan, 9 in Iraq, and 20 in Comoros. Jenkins, "Explaining Iranian Soft Power Capability," p. 70.

132. Kagan et al., *Iranian Influence,* p. 81.

133. Majidyar and Alfoneh, *Iranian Influence in Afghanistan,* p. 2.

134. Kagan et al., *Iranian Influence,*" p. 81.

135. Jenkins, "Explaining Iranian Soft Power Capability," p. 72.

136. Von Maltzahn, "Iran's Cultural Diplomacy," p. 221.

137. Maloney, "Islamism and Iran's Postrevolutionary Economy," p. 198.

138. Nasr, *Shia Revival,* p. 215.

139. See Wastnidge, "Modalities of Iranian Soft Power," p. 367.

140. Ibid., p. 371.

141. "About Us."

142. Wastnidge, "Modalities of Iranian Soft Power," p. 372.

143. Esfandiary and Tabatabai, "Iran's ISIS Policy," p. 4; see also Badawi, "Iran's Iraqi Market"; Jabbar, "Iraq Looks to Expand Trade."

144. Haynes, "Transnational Religious Actors," p. 461.

145. Slavin, *Mullahs, Money, and Militias,*" pp. 8–11.

146. Shabani, *Iran's Iraq Policy*, p. 4.
147. Salem, *Iraq's Tangled Foreign Interests*, p. 17.
148. See Saikal, "Afghanistan's Geographical Possibilities."
149. Kagan et al., *Iranian Influence*, p. 79.
150. Ibid.
151. Haidar, head of Herat's provincial council, quoted in ibid., p. 80.
152. Wastnidge, "Modalities of Iranian Soft Power," p. 370.
153. Cited in Adelkhah, "Iran Integrates the Concept," p. 8."
154. Price, "Iran and the Soft War," p. 2398.
155. Khamenei, quoted in Mohseni, *Islamic Awakening*, p. 4.
156. Price, "Iran and the Soft War," p. 2400.
157. Specifically, officials viewed it as spreading three forms of propaganda: white, gray (secondhand sources), and black (it is unclear where the information comes from). Ibid., p. 2405.
158. Blout, "Iran's Soft War," p. 34.
159. Price, "Iran and the Soft War," p. 2407.
160. Adelkhah, "Iran Integrates the Concept."
161. "Iran Urged to Loosen Hold on BBC Persia."
162. Sabet and Safshekan, *Soft War*, p. 20.
163. Ibid.
164. Mohseni, *Islamic Awakening*, p. 5.
165. Hanna and Kaye, "Limits of Iranian Power," p. 180.
166. Hunter, "Iran and the Spread of Revolutionary Islam," p. 744.
167. Kagan et al., *Iranian Influence*," p. 85.
168. Haynes, "Transnational Religious Actors," p. 454.

Chapter 6. Regional Relations

1. For a historical overview of Saudi-Iranian relations, see Keynoush, *Saudi Arabia and Iran*.
2. McInnis, "Iran's Strategic Thinking."
3. Quoted in Amiri and Samsu, "Role of Political Elites," p. 112.
4. "Iran Election: Hassan Rouhani in His Own Words."
5. Zarif, "What Iran Really Wants," p. 52.
6. Ibid., p. 56.
7. Author's interview with Foreign Minister Mohammad Javad Zarif, Tehran, January 24, 2017.
8. For an overview of the consolidation of the Syria-Iran alliance from 1979 to 1982 during the early years of the Iran-Iraq War, see Goodarzi, *Syria and Iran*, pp. 11–58.
9. Akbarzadeh and Conduit, "Charting a New Course?," p. 134.
10. Ibid.
11. Morell, "Iran's Grand Strategy."
12. Rieffer-Flanagan, "Islamic Realpolitik," p. 9.

13. Hunter, *Iran's Foreign Policy*, p. 241.
14. "Argentina Seeks Arrest of Iran's Ex-leader."
15. Jedinia, "Return of Iran's Strategic Council."
16. Constitution of the Islamic Republic of Iran, Article 176.
17. Dehghan, "Iran's President."
18. Lob and Mahdavi, "Understanding Iran's Supreme Leader."
19. Kugelman, "Iran Factor in Afghanistan."
20. Christensen, *Strained Alliances*, p. 16.
21. "Official: Iran Ready to Broaden Ties."
22. Tadjbakhsh and Fazeli, "Iran and Its Relationship to Afghanistan," p. 8.
23. For a detailed discussion, see Saikal, "Afghanistan's Geographical Possibilities."
24. Rahman, "India-Iran Relations," p. 33.
25. For an overview of Iran's role during the Afghan civil war, see Milani, "Iran's Policy towards Afghanistan."
26. Boone, "Hamid Karzai."
27. Tadjbakhsh and Fazeli, "Iran and Its Relationship to Afghanistan," p. 7.
28. Oak, "What's between the Taliban and Iran?"
29. Author's interview with Zarif, January 24, 2017.
30. Nasib, "Iran's Dangerous Liaison."
31. "Afghan Officials Accuse Iran of Supporting Taliban."
32. Oak, "What's between the Taliban and Iran?"
33. Torfeh, "Iran's 'Double Game' in Afghanistan."
34. Nader et al., *Iran's Influence*, p. 18.
35. "Ghani: Work on Construction of 21 Water Dams."
36. Aman, "Afghan Water Infrastructure."
37. Strickland, "Why Are Afghan Refugees Leaving Iran?"
38. Koepke, *Iran's Policy on Afghanistan*, p. 4.
39. Strickland, "Why Are Afghan Refugees Leaving Iran?"
40. Remittances from Afghans working in Iran contribute $500 million to Afghanistan's economy. Nader et al., *Iran's Influence*, pp. 20–22.
41. United Nations, *Return of Undocumented Afghans.*
42. United Nations Office on Drugs and Crime, *World Drug Report 2016*, p. 29.
43. "Inside Iran: Millions Continue to Battle Drug Addiction."
44. United Nations Office on Drugs and Crime, *Afghanistan: Opium Survey 2016*, p. 5; "Afghanistan: 43 Percent Rise in Estimated Opium Harvest."
45. United Nations Office on Drugs and Crime, *World Drug Report 2016*, p. xx.
46. See Gulabzoi, "Narco-State of Afghanistan"; also Norland, "Corrupt Combatants."
47. Tran and Dehghan, "Iran Mosque"; "Iran Suicide Bombing."
48. Vatanka, "Iranian-Pakistani Border Incident."
49. For a conceptual discussion of weak states and strong societies, and a discussion of this in relation to Iraq, see Falk, "Framing an Inquiry"; see also Saikal, "Afghanistan and Iraq."

50. Chubin, "Iran and the Arab Spring," p. 43.

51. Filkins, "Shadow Commander."

52. Heydarian, "Iran Gets Close to Iraq."

53. "Iran, Iraq Sign Three Agreements on Economic Cooperation."

54. Esfandiary and Tabatabai, "Iran's ISIS Policy," p. 4; also see Badawi, "Iran's Iraqi Market."

55. Haynes, "Transnational Religious Actors," p. 461.

56. Stephen Schwartz notes that there have been various *fatwahs* declaring Alawites as Muslims since the nineteenth century, the most "definitive" being the *fatwah* given by the Lebanese cleric Musa al-Sadr in 1973. Schwartz, "What Is Really 'Broken' in Syria?"

57. Ibid.

58. Hof and Simon, "Sectarian Violence," pp. 22–26.

59. These volunteer fighters have been referred to as Iran's "foreign legion." Moslih, "Iran 'Foreign Legion'."

60. "Syrian Rebels Say Hostages 'Iranian Soldiers.'"

61. Sullivan, *Hezbollah in Syria*, p. 22.

62. Al-Khalidi, "Exclusive."

63. Wright, "Iran's Generals Are Dying"; "Iranian Revolutionary Guards."

64. Lake, "Iran Spends Billions."

65. Al-Khalidi, "Exclusive."

66. For background on the Houthis and the civil war in Yemen, see Laub, "Yemen in Crisis."

67. Salisbury, *Yemen*, p. 6. In a roundtable discussion in May 2015 in New York, at which the author was present, Zarif confirmed Iran's "good relations with Houthis." He said that he contacted the American Secretary of State John Kerry two weeks earlier with a proposal that if the Saudi-led coalition stopped bombing the Houthis, Tehran would lean on the Houthis to negotiate for a viable resolution of the Yemen conflict, but Riyadh was disinterested and asked Iran to stop interfering in Arab affairs.

68. "Iranian Trade Min. Meets Turkish Economy Minister."

69. Ünal and Ersoy, "Political Economy," p. 147.

70. "Iran and Turkey Aim to Triple Trade to $30 Billion."

71. Workman, "Turkey's Top Trading Partners."

72. Ebrahimi, Yusoff, and "Issues in Iran-Turkey Relations," p. 73.

73. ICG, *Turkey and Iran*," p. 3.

74. Cornell, *Azerbaijan since Independence*, p. 321.

75. Herszenhorn, "Iran Recalls Its Ambassador."

76. "Iran's Azeris Protest over Offensive TV Show."

77. Farris, "Geopolitics Trump Religion."

78. Ramenazi, "Iran Sets Its Sights."

79. Kumar, "Iran and Turkmenistan," p. 129.

80. "Turkmenistan, Iran Seek Closer Ties as Antidote to Isolation."

81. Putz, "Gas Spats."

82. Quoted in Dergham, "Saudi Foreign Minister."

83. Quoted in Goldberg, "Obama Doctrine."

84. Riedel, "Can This Joint Arab Military Force Succeed?"

85. See Rozen, "Inside the Secret US-Iran Diplomacy"; and also Gupta, "Oman."

86. SIPRI, SIPRI Military Expenditure Database.

87. IISS, "Chapter Seven," p. 318.

88. Chughtai, "GCC Military Spending Spree"; see also Perlo-Freeman et al., *World Military Expenditure, 2015*, p. 2.

89. Blanchfield, Wezeman, and Wezeman, "State of Major Arms Transfers."

90. Black, "Saudi Arabia Sees Yemen."

91. McDowall, Stewart, and Rohde, "Yemen's Guerrilla War."

92. "UAE: 'War Is Over' "; see also "UAE Says the 'War Is Over.' "

93. Ghobari, "UN Says 10,000 Killed."

94. Precise data on civilian casualties is unavailable due to the covert nature of the operation and its location in a remote part of Yemen. Carroll, "What Donald Trump Left Out."

95. Indeed, the US State Department criticized Saudi Arabia and its allies for imposing a land, air, and sea blockade on Qatar in a move that observers noted contradicted Trump's earlier support for the kingdom. Heather Nauert, a State Department spokeswoman, questioned the legitimacy of the move, asking, "Were the actions [the blockade of Qatar] really about their concerns regarding Qatar's alleged support for terrorism? Or were they about the long-simmering grievances between and among the GCC countries?" She added that "the more that time goes by, the more doubt is raised about the actions taken by Saudi Arabia and the UAE." Borger, "US Rebukes Saudi Arabia"; see also Rogin, "Inside the Trump-Tillerson Divide."

96. Dergham, "Saudi Foreign Minister."

97. Ismail, *Saudi Clerics*, pp. 55–95.

98. "Saudi Top Cleric Says Iran's Leaders Are 'Not Muslims.' "

99. Graham, "Sheikh Nimr al-Nimr."

100. "Hajj Rift: Top Saudi Cleric Says Iranians 'Aren't Muslims.' "

101. "Fifteen Saudi Shia Sentenced to Death for 'Spying for Iran'."

102. See Henderson, "Nuclear Handshake."

103. Author's discussion with Prince Turki al-Faisal, Australian National University, Canberra, June 4, 2009.

104. "Pakistan, Saudi Arabia Pledge to Further Expand Ties."

105. Sial, *Emerging Dynamics*, p. 3.

106. Siddiqui, "Saudi Arabia Woos Pakistan."

107. Zahra-Malik, "Saudi Arabia Loans Pakistan $1.5 Billion."

108. "Saudi Arabia 'Seeking Pakistan Arms' "; also see Shams, "Is Pakistan Aiding the Syrian Rebels?"

109. Kaminski, "Prince Alwaleed bin Talal."

110. Ahmed, "Pakistan's Tactical Nuclear Weapons."

111. Hussain, "Chief of a Phantom Army."

112. "Iran Not OK with Gen Raheel Heading Islamic Military Alliance: Envoy."

113. For a discussion, see Rashid, "Should Pakistan Ex-army Chief Lead?"

114. Torbey, "Lebanon."

115. Byman, "Hezbollah's Growing Threat."

116. For a discussion on the state of opposition forces in Syria, see Lister, "Al Qaeda."

117. On the warming relationship between the US and Saudi Arabia under President Trump after restraint under his predecessor, see Davis, "Trump Meets Saudi Prince."

118. Djalili and Kellner, "Iran's Syria Policy," p. 397.

119. Afshari, "Khamenei Preaches."

120. Faghihi, "Rouhani to Sunnis."

121. Esfandiary and Tabatabai, "Iran's ISIS Policy," p. 7.

122. Kagan et al., *Iranian Influence*, p. 85.

123. Pollock and Ali, "Iran Gets Negative Reviews."

124. Teti and Abbott, "Relative Importance of Religion," p. 22.

Chapter 7. Relations with Major Powers

1. Wilson, "Navy Missile Downs Iranian Jetliner."

2. Ibrahim, "Downing of Flight 655."

3. Holland and Spetalnick, "Trump Adopts Aggressive Posture."

4. Eisenstadt, "Russian Arms."

5. Ostovar, "Sectarian Dilemmas."

6. Hussain, "US-Iran Relations," pp. 36–40.

7. Wright, "Iran on Guard."

8. Price, "Iran and the Soft War," p. 2402.

9. Hafezi, "Iran's Khamenei Calls for Vigilance."

10. See Nader, *Rouhani's Election*.

11. Cordesman, Gold, and Coughlin-Schulte, "US and Iran," p. vii.

12. IMF, *Regional Economic Outlook*, p. 81.

13. Zakaria, "Iran's Growing State of Desperation."

14. Saikal, *Iran at the Crossroads*, pp. 91–92.

15. See Saikal, *Zone of Crisis*.

16. Saikal, *Iran at the Crossroads*, pp. 96–101.

17. Muzalevsky, "From Frozen Ties," p. 27.

18. Ibid., p. 4.

19. A RAND publication notes that the US and Iran actually had a number of shared interests in Afghanistan. See Nader et al., *Iran's Influence*," p. 9.

20. Saikal, "Middle East and North Africa," p. 2.

21. Although oil and gas still account for more than half of total export revenue. IMF, *2016 Article IV Consultation*, pp. 31–32.

22. "Best Countries for Business: Saudi Arabia."

23. George, "Iran Emerges as 'Market of the Future.' "

24. Muzalevsky, "From Frozen Ties," p. 18.
25. Bazoobandi, "Iran's Economy and Energy," p. 41.
26. Ibid., p. 102.
27. United Nations Security Council, "Resolution 2231."
28. Samore, *Iran Nuclear Deal*, pp. 7–8.
29. Ntousas, *Iran Nuclear Agreement*, p. 29.
30. IAEA, "Additional Protocol."
31. Ntousas, *Iran Nuclear Agreement*.
32. Kissinger and Shultz, "Iran Deal."
33. Krauthammer, "Iran Deal."
34. Rubio, "Iran Nuclear Deal."
35. Pleitgen and Walker, "IAEA Inspects."
36. Bipartisan Policy Center, "JCPOA at One," p. 2.
37. Krauthammer, "Iran Deal."
38. See Moarefy, "Partially Unwinding Sanctions."
39. Bloomfield, "Follow Iran's Money."
40. Jackson, "Obama's Iran Nuclear Deal."
41. McCain, "Senator John McCain."
42. Rogin, "Republics Warn Iran."
43. Borger, "Iran's Supreme Leader." For more information on the conservative opposition to the nuclear deal within Iran, see Saikal, "Iran and the Changing Regional Strategic Environment," pp. 27–28.
44. Hashem, "Khamenei's Strategy."
45. Alsmadi, "Analysis."
46. "Iran Will Not Co-operate with the US, Khamenei Says."
47. Karami, "Khamenei Calls Negotiations."
48. "Iran 'Fills Arak Nuclear Reactor Core with Concrete.' "
49. ICG, *Implementing the Iran Nuclear Deal*, p. 6.
50. European Union External Action, "Iran Nuclear Deal."
51. ICG, *Implementing the Iran Nuclear Deal*, p. 6.
52. "Conversation with Javad Zarif." A senior US official explained that preparing the licenses—given the technology's complexity and legal requirements of ensuring they do not violate lingering UN restrictions on Iran—took a long time, as did Iran's negotiations with Boeing and Airbus.
53. Snider and Dorell, "Boeing's $16B Aircraft Deal."
54. Zengerle, "Extension of Iran Sanctions Act."
55. "Iran Will Halt JCPOA Implementation if Sanctions Re-imposed: Zarif."
56. Author's interview with Javad Zarif, Tehran, January 23, 2017.
57. ICG, *Implementing the Iran Nuclear Deal*, p. 5.
58. "US Slaps New Sanctions on Iran over Missile Test."
59. Farhad Rezaei argues that the criticism along with Trump's unpredictable nature and his increased willingness to use force has reduced the number of missile tests taking place. Rezaei, "Iran's Ballistic Missiles Program."

60. "Iran Has 'Other Options' if Nuclear Deal Falls Through."
61. Erdbrink, "Iran Treads Cautiously."
62. "Iran: Missile Tests Not in Violation of Nuclear Deal."
63. Hafezi, "Iran to Impose Legal Restrictions."
64. "US Accuses Iran of 'Alarming Provocations' amid Nuclear Tensions."
65. Pecquet, "Nuclear Deal Critics."
66. Solomon, "Trump Faces Battle."
67. Parker, "Russia-Iran," p. 8.
68. Kozhanov, "Russian-Iranian Dialogue," p. 2.
69. Kam, "Will Russia?," p. 42.
70. Lynch et al., *Return of Foreign Fighters*," p. 5.
71. Kalinina, "Militarization."
72. Theohary, *Conventional Arms*, p. 36.
73. "Russia, Iran Plan $10bn Arms Supply to Tehran."
74. Majidyar, "Rouhani Visits Moscow"; see also N. Smagin, "How Russia Managed to Double its Exports to Iran in 2016."
75. Kashfi, "Iran Yields to Russia."
76. Ibid.
77. Aliriza, Alterman, and Kuchins, *Turkey, Russia, Iran Nexus*, p. vii.
78. "Russia's Rosneft, Iran's NIOC Eye $30 Bln in Oil and Gas Projects."
79. Ibid.
80. Gvosdev, "Russia and the Precedent Problem."
81. The Tartus base is currently only a limited supply port, but Russia has announced plans to transform it into a permanent, full naval base. Osborn, "Russia to Build."
82. Stubbs and Devitt, "Russia Stance on Assad."
83. Kuchins, "Russia's Contrasting Relations," p. 19.
84. "Iran Successfully Tests Russia-Supplied S-300 Anti-Aircraft System—Media."
85. Vaez, "Waiting for Bushehr."
86. Barnard and Kramer, "Iran Revokes Russia's Use."
87. Ramani, "Why Russia and Israel Are Cooperating."
88. Ahren and Surkes, "Rivlin in Moscow."
89. Borshchevskaya, "Maturing of Israeli-Russian Relations."
90. This has largely been unsuccessful. Katz, "Saudi Arabia and Russia," p. 351.
91. The deal would not be possible without Saudi and Russian cooperation as heads of OPEC and non-OPEC blocks respectively. Martin, "Global Oil Stocks."
92. "Russia: Trade Statistics."
93. Soldatkin, "Russia's Putin, Saudi Prince."
94. Carroll, "Russia and Saudi Arabia."
95. "Non-Oil Trade between UAE, Russia."
96. Yousef and Jasper, "UAE to Build Russian Warplane."
97. IEA, "Emergency Response Systems," p. 531.

98. Thirarath, "Asian Oil Customers."

99. IEA, *Oil & Gas Security*, p. 6.

100. IEA, "Emergency Response Systems," p. 533.

101. Workman, "Crude Oil Imports by Country."

102. https://www.tasnimnews.com/en/news/2017/02/04/1317982/iran-china-bilateral-trade-down-by-7-7. "Iran-China Bilateral Trade Down by 7.7%."

103. Bingbing, "Strategy and Politics," p. 14.

104. Kasting and Fite, *US and Iranian Strategic Competition*, p. 6.

105. Harold and Nader, *China and Iran*, p. 7.

106. Bozorgmehr and Dyer, "China Overtakes EU."

107. Garver, "China and Iran."

108. Scobell and Nader, *China in the Middle East*, p. 60.

109. Harold and Nader, *China and Iran*, pp. 12–13.

110. "Chinese Bank to Finance Petchem Project in Iran."

111. "NIORDC Centered on Upgrading Ageing Refineries."

112. Scott, "Defying Expectations."

113. "Iran, China's CNPC Terminate Contract in South Pars."

114. Esfandiary, "Iran's Unfolding China Drama."

115. "Our Bulldozers, Our Rules."

116. Kaplan, *Revenge of Geography*.

117. Ghoshal, "China's Nuclear Opportunities in Iran."

118. Dean, "Neo–Russia-China-Iran Strategic Triangle."

119. "Top Commander: Iran Offers to Share Anti-Terrorism Expertise with China."

120. Hsu, "China's Relations with Iran."

121. Scott, "Nuclear Deal."

122. Ibid.

123. See van der Kley, "Chinese Security Services."

124. Garver, "China and Iran."

125. Garver, "US Factor," p. 213.

126. Noi, "Iran's Nuclear Programme," pp. 84–85.

127. Geranmayeh, "Engaging with Iran," p. 6.

128. The case was known as the Mykonos Assassinations because of the restaurant where the victims were killed. Rubin, "Europe's Critical Dialogue."

129. Dupont, "EU-Iran Dialogue," p. 98.

130. Moshaver, "Revolution, Theocratic Leadership," p. 297.

131. Ruairi Patterson argues that this position altered during the 2000s because of changes in the leadership and foreign policy directions of France and Germany, as well as the eurozone crisis, which weakened many southern European states who were opposed to sanctions, and finally because the diplomatic, political, and economic costs of adopting sanctions had fallen considerably. Patterson, "EU Sanctions on Iran."

132. European Union, "Statement by Germany."

133. See IMF, *Refugee Surge in Europe*.

134. "President Rouhani: Iran Ready to Increase Anti-Terrorism Cooperation with EU."

135. Mogherini, "Iran Agreement."

136. Parsi, *EU Strategy*, p. 12.

137. European Union European Commission, "European Union."

138. Eurostat, cited in Ehteshami, "Energy Cooperation," p. 47.

Chapter 8. Conclusion

1. The most notable of these is, of course, the 1979 Iranian Revolution itself, where the Shah's failure to manage growing internal dissent ultimately led to his overthrow.

2. See Bozorgmehr, "Iran's Hardliners Push Back."

3. Corruption and growing dissatisfaction with stagnating wages, living standards, and persistently high inflation and unemployment have been widely documented. See, for example, Maloney, *Iran's Political Economy*.

4. Indeed, Salehi-Isfahani notes that the increase in urban poverty under Mahmoud Ahmadinejad was particularly "striking," and that overall inequality has remained at a steady level since the Revolution. Salehi-Isfahani, "Iran: Poverty and Inequality."

5. Hossein Mousavian, "Understanding Iranian Threat Perceptions."

6. See, for example, Bozorgmehr, "Iran Cracks Down."

7. For analysis regarding Rouhani's efforts to contain the powers of the IRGC, see Erdbrink, "Iran Saps Strength."

8. Erdbrink, "Mehdi Karroubi."

9. Sharafedin, "Iran's President."

10. Dehghan, "Hossein Fereidoun."

11. Ibid.

12. Abrahamian, "Reading Hume in Tehran."

13. For an analysis, see Nader, Thaler, and Bohandy, *Next Supreme Leader*.

14. Ross, "Trump Is on a Collision Course."

15. See for an interesting analysis, French, "America's War against ISIS."

16. Cafiero, "Iran's Role."

17. Secretary of Defense James Mattis stated his position in a hearing before Congress on October 3, 2017. See Youssef, "Iran Deal."

18. Davidson, "Iran Business Ties."

19. For details, see ibid.

20. "Rouhani Hits Back at Trump after Nuclear Deal Speech."

21. "Europe Backs Iran Deal, Saudis Hail Trump's Move."

22. Austin Ramzy, "Trump Threatens Iran over Twitter, Warning Rouhani of 'Dire Consequences'," *New York Times*, July 22, 2018.

23. Tabatabai, "Trump Administration."

24. Salim, DeYoung, and El-Ghobashy, "Kurdish Independence Referendum."

25. Cafiero and Karasik, "Kuwait, Oman."

26. Gorka, "US, Iran on Brink."

BIBLIOGRAPHY

Abedin, M. "Iran after the Elections." *Middle East Intelligence Bulletin* 6, no. 2–3 (2004).

Abidi, S. *Iran Business Handbook 2016*. Ahmedabad: Ahmedabad Management Association, 2014.

About Us. Al-Alam News. http://en.alalam.ir/aboutus (accessed February 12, 2017).

Abrahamian, E. "The Causes of the Constitutional Revolution in Iran." *International Journal of Middle Eastern Studies* 10 (1979), 381–414.

———. *A History of Modern Iran*. Cambridge: Cambridge University Press, 2008.

———. *Iran between Two Revolutions*. Princeton, NJ: Princeton University Press, 1982.

———. "The 1953 Coup in Iran." *Science & Society* 65, no. 2 (2001), 182–215.

———. "Reading Hume in Tehran: The Iranian Revolution and the Enlightenment." *Foreign Affairs* 95, no. 3 (2016), 158–64.

Adelkhah, N. "Iran Integrates the Concept of the 'Soft War' into Its Strategic Planning." *Terrorism Monitor* 8, no. 23 (2010), 7–9.

Adib-Moghaddam, A. "Introduction: Ayatollah Ruhollah Khomeini: A Clerical Revolutionary." In *A Critical Introduction to Khomeini*, ed. A. Adib-Moghaddam, 1–18. New York: Cambridge University Press, 2014.

"Afghanistan: 43 Percent Rise in Estimated Opium Harvest." Al Jazeera, October 23, 2016. http://www.aljazeera.com/news/2016/10/afghanistan-43-percent-rise-estimated-opium-harvest-161023074029664.html (accessed November 22, 2017).

"Afghan Officials Accuse Iran of Supporting Taliban." *Middle East Monitor*, November 20, 2016. https://www.middleeastmonitor.com/20161120-afghan-officials-accuse-iran-of-supporting-taliban/ (accessed November 22, 2017).

Afshari, A. "Khamenei Preaches Shiite–Sunni Unity against Islamic State, US." Al-Monitor, October 22, 2014.

"Ahmadinejad: Holocaust a Myth." Al Jazeera, December 14, 2005. http://www.aljazeera.com/archive/2005/12/200849154418141136.html (accessed November 9, 2017).

"Ahmadinejad under Fire on Economy." BBC, April 23, 2008. http://news.bbc.co.uk/2/hi/middle_east/7363293.stm (accessed November 9, 2017).

Ahmed, M. "Pakistan's Tactical Nuclear Weapons and Their Impact on Stability." Carnegie Endowment for International Peace, June 30, 2016. http://carnegieendowment.org/2016/06/30/pakistan-s-tactical-nuclear-weapons-and-their-impact-on-stability-pub-63911 (accessed October 12, 2017).

Ahren, R., and S. Surkes. "Rivlin in Moscow, Set to Warn Putin of Iranian Gains in Syria." *Times of Israel*, March 15, 2016.

Akbarzadeh, S., and D. Conduit. "Charting a New Course? Testing Rouhani's Foreign Policy Agency in the Iran–Syria Relationship." In *Iran in the World: President Rouhani's Foreign Policy*, ed. S. Akbarzadeh and D. Conduit, 133–54. New York: Palgrave Macmillan, 2016.

Akhavi, S. "Islam, Politics and Society in the Thought of Ayatullah Khomeini, Ayatullah Taliqani and Ali Shariati." *Middle Eastern Studies* 24, no. 4 (1988), 404–31.

al-Din, B. S. "Mardan e Ayatollah Khamenei" [The men of Ayatollah Khomeini]. BBC (Persian), September 17, 2011. http://www.bbc.com/persian/iran/2011/09/110916_l13_khamenei_men.shtml (accessed October 12, 2017).

Aliriza, B., J. B. Alterman, and A. C. Kuchins. *The Turkey, Russia, Iran Nexus: Driving Forces and Strategies*. Washington, DC: Center for Strategic & International Studies, 2013.

Alizadeh, P. "Iran's Quandary: Economic Reforms and the 'Structural Trap.'" *Brown Journal of World Affairs* 9, no. 2 (2003), 267–81.

Al-khalidi, S. "Exclusive: Iran's Support for Syria Tested by Oil Price Drop." Reuters, December 21, 2014. http://www.reuters.com/article/us-mideast-crisis-syria-iran-idUSKBN0JX21420141220 (accessed November 22, 2017).

Alpher, J. "Israel and the Iran-Iraq War." In *The Iran–Iraq War: Impact and Implications*, ed. E. Karsh, 154–68. London: Palgrave Macmillan, 1989.

al-Rasheed, M. *A History of Saudi Arabia*. 2nd ed. Cambridge: Cambridge University Press, 2010.

Alsmadi, F. A. "Analysis: Iran's Conservatives Wary of Nuclear Deal." Al Jazeera, July 14, 2015. http://www.aljazeera.com/news/2015/07/analysis-iran-conservatives-wary-nuclear-deal-150713063303207.html (accessed November 28, 2017).

Aman, F. "Afghan Water Infrastructure Threatens Iran, Regional Stability." Al-Monitor, January 7, 2013. http://www.al-monitor.com/pulse/originals/2013/01/afghanwatershortageiranpakistan.html (accessed November 22, 2017).

Amirahmadi, H. "The Economic Costs of the War and the Reconstruction in Iran." In *Modern Capitalism and Islamic Ideology in Iran*, ed. C. Bina and H. Zangeneh, 257–81. London: Macmillan, 1992.

———. "Iran's Development: Evaluation and Challenges." *Third World Quarterly* 17, no. 1 (1996), 123–47.

———. *Revolution and Economic Transition: The Iranian Experience*. Albany: State University of New York Press, 1990.

———. "Rouhani's New Budget Offers Pain without Hope." *National Interest*, February 14, 2015. http://nationalinterest.org/feature/rouhanis-new-budget-offers-pain-without-hope-12249 (accessed October 12, 2017).

Amiri, R. E., and K.H.K. Samsu. "Role of Political Elites in Iran-Saudi Economic Cooperation." *International Journal of Humanities and Social Science* 1, no. 12 (2011), 107–16.

Amir-Mokri, C., and H. Biglari. "A Windfall for Iran? The End of Sanctions and the Iranian Economy." *Foreign Affairs* 94, no. 6 (2015), 25–32.

Amnesty International. "Amnesty International Annual Report 1982." London: Amnesty International, October 1, 1982.

Amuzegar, J. *The Islamic Republic of Iran: Reflections on an Emerging Economy*. Abingdon: Routledge, 2014.

"ANJOMAN (Organization)." *Encyclopaedia Iranica*. http://www.iranicaonline.org/articles/anjoman-gathering-association-society-general-designation-of-many-private-and-public-associations (accessed May 11, 2017).

Ansari, A. M. "Iran under Ahmadinejad: The Politics of Confrontation." Adelphi Paper 393. London: International Institute for Strategic Studies, 2007.

"Argentina Seeks Arrest of Iran's Ex-leader." *New York Times*, November 10, 2016.

Arjomand, S. A. *After Khomeini: Iran under His Successors*. Oxford: Oxford University Press, 2009.

Arreguín-Toft, I. *How the Weak Win Wars: A Theory of Asymmetric Conflict*. Cambridge: Cambridge University Press, 2005.

Asadzade, P. "New Data Shed Light on the Dramatic Protests in Iran." *Washington Post*, January 12, 2018.

Axworthy, M. *Iran: Empire of the Mind: A History from Zoroaster to the Present Day*. London: Penguin, 2008.

Ayubi, N. *Political Islam: Religion and Politics in the Arab World*. London: Routledge, 1991.

Badawi, T. "Iran's Iraqi Market." Carnegie Endowment for International Peace, July 27, 2016. http://carnegieendowment.org/sada/64187 (accessed October 12, 2017).

Baig, J. "Steve Bannon's War with Islam: Trump May Not Even Understand His Adviser's Apocalyptic Vision." *Salon*, February 6, 2016. https://www.alternet.org/visions/steve-bannons-war-islam-trump-may-not-even-understand-his-advisers-apocalyptic-vision (accessed April 18, 2018).

Baktiari, B. *Parliamentary Politics in Revolutionary Iran: The Institutionalization of Factional Politics*. Gainesville: University Press of Florida, 1996.

Baldwin, D. A. *Power and International Relations: A Conceptual Approach*. Princeton, NJ: Princeton University Press, 2016.

Barnard, A., and A. E. Kramer. "Iran Revokes Russia's Use of Air Base, Saying Moscow 'Betrayed Trust.'" *New York Times*, August 22, 2016.

Bashiriyeh, H. *The State and Revolution in Iran: 1962–1982*. Abingdon: Routledge, 2011.

Bayat, A. *Making Islam Democratic: Social Movements and the Post-Islamist Turn*, Stanford, CA: Stanford University Press, 2007.

Bayat, M. "The Iranian Revolution of 1978–79: Fundamentalist or Modern?" *Middle East Journal* 37, no. 1 (1983), 30–42.

Bazoobandi, S. "Iran's Economy and Energy: Back in Business?" In *Iran after the Deal: The Road Ahead*, ed. P. Magri and A. Perteghella, 25–48. Milan: Institute for International Political Studies, 2015.

Beeman, W. O. *The "Great Satan" vs. the "Mad Mullahs": How the United States and Iran Demonize Each Other.* Chicago: University of Chicago Press, 2008.

Bélanger, L., and G. Mace. "Building Role and Region: Middle States and Regionalism in the Americas." In *The Americas in Transition: The Contours of Regionalism,* ed. G. Mace and L. Bélanger, 153–74. Boulder, CO: Lynne Rienner, 1999.

"Best Countries for Business: Saudi Arabia." *Forbes*, December 2016. http://www.forbes.com/places/saudi-arabia/ (accessed November 28, 2017).

"The Big Squeeze." *Economist*, July 19, 2007. http://www.economist.com/node/9466874 (accessed November 9, 2017).

Bingbing, W. "Strategy and Politics in the Gulf as Seen from China." In *China and the Persian Gulf: Implications for the United States*, ed. B. Wakefield and S. L. Levenstein, 10–26. Washington, DC: Woodrow Wilson International Center for Scholars, 2011.

Bipartisan Policy Center. *JCPOA at One*. Washington, DC: Bipartisan Policy Center, July 2016.

Bizaer, M. "What Iran's First Non-oil Trade Surplus Means for Its Economy." Al-Monitor, May 1, 2016. http://www.al-monitor.com/pulse/originals/2016/04/iran-nonoil-trade-balance-turns-positive-first-time-1979.html (accessed November 22, 2017).

Bjorvatn, K., and K. Selvik. "Destructive Competition: Factionalism and Rent-Seeking in Iran." *World Development* 36, no. 11 (2008), 2314–24.

Black, I. "Saudi Arabia Sees Yemen Intervention as Defence of 'Backyard.'" *Guardian*, January 28, 2016.

Blanchfield, K., P. D. Wezeman, and S. T. Wezeman. "The State of Major Arms Transfers in 8 Graphics." SIPRI, February 22, 2017. https://www.sipri.org/commentary/blog/2017/state-major-arms-transfers-8-graphics (accessed October 12, 2017).

Bloomfield, L. P., Jr. "Follow Iran's Money." *Forbes*, February 3, 2016. http://www.forbes.com/sites/realspin/2016/02/03/iran-deal-frozen-financial-assets/#eba60ea5c5d0 (accessed November 28, 2017).

Blout, E. "Iran's Soft War with the West: History, Myth, and Nationalism in the New Communications Age." *SAIS Review of International Affairs* 35, no. 2 (2015), 33–44.

Boone, J. "Hamid Karzai Admits Office Gets 'Bags of Money' from Iran." *Guardian*, October 26, 2010.

Borger, J. "Iran's Supreme Leader Gives Tentative Approval to Nuclear Deal." *Guardian*, October 22, 2015.

———. "Khamenei's Son Takes Control of Iran's Anti-Protest Militia." *Guardian*, July 9, 2009.

———. "US Rebukes Saudi Arabia over Qatar Embargo in Reversal after Trump Comments." *Guardian*, June 21, 2017.

Borger, J., and R. Tait. "The Financial Power of the Revolutionary Guards." *Guardian*, February 16, 2010.

Borshchevskaya, A. "The Maturing of Israeli-Russian Relations." *inFocus Quarterly*, Washington Institute, Spring 2016. http://www.washingtoninstitute.org/policy-analysis/view/the-maturing-of-israeli-russian-relations (accessed October 12, 2017).

Bozorgmehr, N. "Iran Cracks Down on Revolutionary Guards Business Network." *Financial Times*, September 14, 2017.

———. "Iran's Hardliners Push Back against Rouhani's Reform Agenda." *Financial Times*, June 26, 2017.

Bozorgmehr, N., and G. Dyer. "China Overtakes EU as Iran's Top Trade Partner." *Financial Times*, February 9, 2010.

Brzezinski, Z., B. Scowcroft, and R. Murphy. "Differentiated Containment." *Foreign Affairs* 76, no. 3 (1997), 20–30.

"Budget Oil Dependence at Lowest." Shana, June 15, 2015, http://www.shana.ir/en/newsagency/242845/Budget-Oil-Dependence-at-Lowest (accessed November 22, 2017).

Bunyan, J., and H. H. Fisher. *The Bolshevik Revolution, 1917–1918: Documents and Materials*. Stanford, CA: Stanford University Press, 1961.

Byman, D. L. "Hezbollah's Growing Threat against US National Security Interests in the Middle East." Brookings Institution, March 22, 2016. https://www.brookings.edu/testimonies/hezbollahs-growing-threat-against-u-s-national-security-interests-in-the-middle-east/ (accessed April 18, 2018).

Cafiero, G. "Iran's Role in Qatar's New Foreign Policy." Al-Monitor, August 30, 2017. https://www.al-monitor.com/pulse/originals/2017/08/iran-role-qatar-new-foreign-policy-gcc-dispute-saudi-arabia.html (accessed December 6, 2017).

Cafiero, G., and T. Karasik. "Kuwait, Oman, and the Qatar Crisis." Middle East Institute, June 22, 2017. http://www.mei.edu/content/article/kuwait-oman-and-qatar-crisis (accessed April 18, 2018).

Callen, T., R. Cherif, F. Hasanov, A. Hegazy, and P. Khandelwal. "Economic Diversification in the GCC: Past, Present, and Future." Washington, DC: International Monetary Fund, 2014.

Carroll, C. "Russia and Saudi Arabia 'Sign $3bn Arms Deal' as King Salman Visit Shows How Much Relations Have Changed." *Independent*, October 5, 2017.

Carroll, L. "What Donald Trump Left Out about the Yemen Raid That Killed Navy SEAL Ryan Owens." *Politifact*, March 1, 2017. http://www.politifact

.com/truth-o-meter/article/2017/mar/01/what-donald-trump-left-out-about-successful-yemen-/ (accessed November 27, 2017).

Carter, J. "Tehran, Iran Toasts of the President and the Shah at a State Dinner." December 31, 1977. The American Presidency Project. http://www.presidency.ucsb.edu/ws/?pid=7080 (accessed December 4, 2017).

———. "Toasts of the President and the Shah at a Dinner Honoring the Shah." November 15, 1977. The American Presidency Project. http://www.presidency.ucsb.edu/ws/index.php?pid=6938 (accessed December 4, 2017).

Celmer, M. A. *Terrorism, US Strategy, and Reagan Policies*. Westport, CT: Greenwood Press, 1987.

Chapnick, A. "The Middle Power." *Canadian Foreign Policy Journal* 7, no. 2 (1999), 73–82.

Chen, Y.-F. *Making Revolution: The Communist Movement in Eastern and Central China, 1937–1945*. Berkeley: University of California Press, 1986.

"Chinese Bank to Finance Petchem Project in Iran." *Financial Tribune*, December 7, 2016.

Choksy, J. "When It Came to Iran's Economic Health, Mahmoud Ahmadinejad Apparently Cooked the Books." *Forbes: Capital Flows*, September 6, 2013. http://www.forbes.com/sites/realspin/2013/09/06/when-it-came-to-irans-economic-health-mahmoud-ahmadinejad-apparently-cooked-the-books/#75ec0d262758 (accessed November 22, 2017).

Christensen, J. B. *Strained Alliances: Iran's Troubled Relations to Afghanistan and Pakistan*. DIIS Report 2011:03. Copenhagen: Danish Institute for International Studies, 2011.

Chubin, S. "Iran and the Arab Spring: Ascendancy Frustrated." GRC Gulf Papers, Geneva: Gulf Research Center, September 2012.

———. "Iran's Power in Context." *Survival* 51, no. 1 (2009), 165–90.

———. "Is Iran a Military Threat?" *Survival* 56, no. 2 (2014), 65–88.

Chughtai, A. "GCC Military Spending Spree." Al Jazeera, June 4, 2016. http://www.aljazeera.com/indepth/interactive/2015/08/gcc-military-spending-spree-150808120255563.html (accessed November 27, 2017).

Churchill, W. S. *The Second World War: The Grand Alliance*. Boston, MA: Houghton Mifflin Company, 1950.

———. *The Second World War: Triumph and Tragedy*. Harmondsworth: Penguin, 1954.

"CIA Documents Acknowledge Its Role in Iran's 1953 Coup." BBC, August 20, 2013. http://www.bbc.com/news/world-middle-east-23762970 (accessed April 13, 2017).

"Clashes Reported at Funeral of Iranian Dissident Cleric." BBC, December 21, 2009. http://news.bbc.co.uk/2/hi/middle_east/8423794.stm (accessed November 9, 2017).

Clawson, P. "Tehran Adds to the Pressure on Iran's Economy." *Policy Watch* 1983, Washington Institute, September 17, 2012, http://www.washingtoninstitute

.org/policy-analysis/view/tehran-adds-to-the-pressure-on-irans-economy (accessed October 12, 2017).

Clemons, S. "Khamenei Is the New Shah: There Will Be (More) Blood." *Huffington Post,* May 25, 2011. https://www.huffingtonpost.com/steve-clemons/khamenei-is-the-new-shah_b_404505.html (accessed April 18, 2018).

Constitution of the Islamic Republic of Iran. http://www.servat.unibe.ch/icl/ir00000_.html (accessed April 21, 2018).

"A Conversation with Javad Zarif." Interview by Fareed Zakaria. Council on Foreign Relations, New York, September 23, 2016. Video, 59:43, and transcript. https://www.cfr.org/event/conversation-javad-zarif (accessed March 8, 2018).

Cooper, A. F., ed. *Niche Diplomacy: Middle Powers after the Cold War.* Houndmills: Macmillan, 1997.

Cooper, A. S. *The Fall of Heaven: The Pahlavis and the Final Days of Imperial Iran.* New York: Henry Holt and Company, 2016.

Cordesman, A. H., B. Gold, and C. Coughlin-Schulte. "The US and Iran: Sanctions, Energy, Arms Control, and Regime Change." A Report of the CSIS Burke Chair in Strategy. Washington, DC: Center for Strategic & International Studies, 2014.

Cordesman, A. H., and A. Toukan. "Iran and the Gulf Military Balance." Working Draft, October 3, 2016. Washington, DC: Center for Strategic & International Studies.

Cornell, S. E. *Azerbaijan since Independence.* London: Routledge, 2015.

Cottam, R. "Goodbye to America's Shah." *Foreign Policy* 34 (1979), 3–14.

Crane, K., R. Lal, and J. Martini. *Iran's Political, Demographic, and Economic Vulnerabilities.* Santa Monica, CA: RAND, 2008.

Crossette, B. "Iran Drops Rushdie Death Threat, and Britain Renews Teheran Ties." *New York Times,* September 25, 1998.

Czulda, R. "The Defensive Dimension of Iran's Military Doctrine: How Would They Fight?" *Middle East Policy* 23, no. 1 (2016), 92–109.

Dahl, R. A. *A Preface to Democratic Theory.* Chicago: University of Chicago Press, 1956.

Davidson, A. "The Iran Business Ties Trump Didn't Disclose." *New Yorker,* October 20, 2017.

Davis, J. H. "Trump Meets Saudi Prince as US and Kingdom Seek Warmer Relations." *New York Times,* March 14, 2017.

Davis, R. *Typing Politics: The Role of Blogs in American Politics.* Oxford: Oxford University Press, 2009.

Dean, J. W. "Neo–Russia-China-Iran Strategic Triangle." *Veterans Today: Journal for Clandestine Community,* November 30, 2016. http://www.veteranstoday.com/2016/11/30/neo-russia-china-iran-strategic-triangle/ (accessed October 12, 2017).

Dehghan, S. K. "Hassan Rouhani Takes Oath for Second Term with Swipe at Trump." *Guardian,* August 7, 2017.

———. "Hossein Fereidoun, Brother of Iran's President, Is Arrested." *Guardian*, July 17, 2017.

———. "Iran Earns More from Tax Than Oil for First Time in Almost 50 Years." *Guardian*, September 28, 2015.

———. "Iran's President and Supreme Leader in Rift over Minister's Reinstatement." *Guardian*, April 28, 2011.

Dehghan, S. K., and O. Bowcott. "Thatcher Files Show How Iran's Shah Was Denied UK Asylum." *Guardian*, July 22, 2016.

Delijani, P. "An Assessment of the Egyptian Military and the Iranian Revolutionary Guards in Connection to the Emergence Theory." Honors thesis, University of Maine, 2010.

Dergham, R. "Saudi Foreign Minister: Iran Is Biggest Sponsor of Terrorism." Al-Monitor, October 5, 2015. http://www.al-monitor.com/pulse/fr/sites/al monitor/contents/articles/politics/2015/10/saudi-arabia-yemen-syria-crisis -relations-disputes-agreement.html (accessed November 27, 2017).

Diba, F. *Mossadegh: A Political Biography*. London: Croom Helm, 1986.

DiPaola, A., and I. Arnsdorf. "Iran Loses $133 Million a Day on Embargo, Buoying Obama." Bloomberg, August 3, 2012.

Dizaji, S. F., M. R. Farzanegan, and A. Naghavi. "Political Institutions and Government Spending Behavior: Theory and Evidence from Iran." *International Tax and Public Finance* 23, no. 3 (2016), 522–49.

Djalili, M.-R., and T. Kellner. "Iran's Syria Policy in the Wake of the 'Arab Springs.'" *Turkish Review* 4, no. 4 (2014), 396–405.

Dobbins, J. "Negotiating with Iran: Reflections from Personal Experience." *Washington Quarterly* 33, no. 1 (2010), 149–62.

Dupont, P.-E. "The EU-Iran Dialogue in the Context of the Ongoing Nuclear Crisis." *Central European Journal of International and Security Studies* 3, no. 1 (2010), 97–112.

Ebrahimi, M., and K. Yusoff. "The Aftermath of *Coup d'État* against Mohammad Mosaddeq of Iran in 1953: Reflections from British Documents." *TAWARIKH: International Journal for Historical Studies* 2, no. 2 (2011), 203–20.

Ebrahimi, M., K. Yusoff, and M. M. S. Jalili. "Economic, Political, and Strategic Issues in Iran-Turkey Relations, 2002–2015." *Contemporary Review of the Middle East* 4, no. 1 (2017), 67–83.

Ehteshami, A. "Energy Cooperation between the EU and Iran." In *EU–Iran Relations after the Nuclear Deal*, ed. S. Blockmans, A. Ehteshami, and G. Bahgat, 47–51. Brussels: Centre for European Policy Studies, 2016.

———. "Iran as a Middle Power." *Public Diplomacy Magazine* 2 (Summer 2009), 54–56.

Ehteshami, A., and M. Zweiri. *Iran and the Rise of Its Neoconservatives: The Politics of Tehran's Silent Revolution*. London: I. B. Tauris, 2007.

Eisenstadt, M. "Russian Arms and Technology Transfers to Iran: Policy Challenges for the United States." Arms Control Association, March 1, 2001.

https://www.armscontrol.org/act/2001_03/eisenstadt (accessed October 12, 2017).

Elm, M. *Oil, Power, and Principle: Iran's Oil Nationalization and Its Aftermath*, Syracuse, NY: Syracuse University Press, 1992.

Emadi, H. "Exporting Iran's Revolution: The Radicalization of the Shiite Movement in Afghanistan." *Middle Eastern Studies* 31, no. 1 (1995), 1–12.

Enayat, H. "Iran: Khumayni's Concept of the 'Guardianship of the Jurisconsult.'" In *Islam in the Political Process*, ed. J. P. Piscatori, 160–80. Cambridge: Cambridge University Press in association with the Royal Institute of International Affairs, 1983.

"Enteshar-e fayl-e Ayatollah Montazari dar moured-e 'addamhai-e sali hazaro sisadi shastu haft" [The broadcast of tapes of Ayatollah Montazeri about the executions of 1367]. BBC Persian Service. https://soundcloud.com/bbcpersian/1367a (accessed December 4, 2017).

Erdbrink, T. "Enigmatic Leader of Iran Backs Overture, for Now." *New York Times*, September 23, 2013.

———. "Iranian Leader Rebuffs Ahmadinejad over Official's Dismissal." *Washington Post*, April 20, 2011.

———. "Iran Saps Strength of Revolutionary Guards with Arrests and Cutbacks." *New York Times*, October 21, 2017.

———. "Iran's Supreme Leader Advises Ahamadinejad Not to Run for President." *New York Times*, September 26, 2016.

———. "Iran Treads Cautiously with Trump. So Far." *New York Times*, February 3, 2017.

———. "Mehdi Karroubi, Iranian Opposition Leader, Ends Hunger Strike." *New York Times*, August 17, 2017.

Esfandiari, G. "Rohani Officially Launches Iranian Citizens' Rights Charter." Radio Free Europe, December 19, 2016. http://www.rferl.org/a/iran-rohani-launches-citizens-rights-charter/28184867.html (accessed October 12, 2017).

Esfandiary, D. "Iran's Unfolding China Drama." *National Interest*, April 13, 2015. http://nationalinterest.org/blog/the-buzz/irans-unfolding-china-dilemma-12620 (accessed October 12, 2017).

Esfandiary, D., and A. Tabatabai. "Iran's ISIS Policy." *International Affairs* 91, no. 1 (2015), 1–15.

Esposito, J. L., ed. *The Iranian Revolution: Its Global Impact*. Miami: Florida International University Press, 1990.

———. *Islam and Politics*, 4th ed. Syracuse, NY: Syracuse University Press, 1998.

———, ed. *The Oxford Encyclopedia of the Modern Islamic World*. Oxford: Oxford University Press, 1995.

Esposito, J. L., and J. O. Voll. "Islam and Democracy." *Humanities* 2, no. 6 (2001). https://www.neh.gov/humanities/2001/novemberdecember/feature/islam-and-democracy (accessed November 23, 2017).

European Union. "Statement by Germany, United Kingdom, France and the EU High Representative on the Iranian Nuclear Issue." Press release S008/06. Berlin, January 12, 2006.

European Union European Commission. "European Union, Trade in Goods with Iran." Brussels: Directorate-General for Trade, 2017. http://trade.ec.europa.eu/doclib/docs/2006/september/tradoc_113392.pdf (accessed October 12, 2017).

European Union External Action. "Iran Nuclear Deal Already Bringing Positive Results, Mogherini Says." September 23, 2016. https://eeas.europa.eu/headquarters/headquarters-homepage_en/10323/Iran%20nuclear%20deal%20already%20bringing%20positive%20results,%20Mogherini%20says (accessed October 12, 2017).

"Europe Backs Iran Deal, Saudis Hail Trump's Move." BBC, October 13, 2017. http://www.bbc.com/news/world-us-canada-41604513 (accessed December 4, 2017).

Faghihi, R. "Rouhani to Sunnis: Iran Not Seeking 'Shiite Crescent.'" Al-Monitor, December 15, 2016. http://www.al-monitor.com/pulse/originals/2016/12/iran-islamic-unity-conference-rouhani-shiite-crescent.html (accessed November 27, 2017).

Fakhreddin, A. "Unseating Mosaddeq: *The Configuration and Role of Domestic Forces*." In *Mohammad Mosaddeq and the 1953 Coup in Iran*, ed. M. J. Gasiorowski and M. Byrne, 27–101. Syracuse, NY: Syracuse University Press, 2004.

Falk, R. "Framing an Inquiry." In *Weak States, Strong Societies: Power and Authority in the New World Order*, ed. A. Saikal, 9–21. London: I. B. Tauris, 2016.

Farhi, F. "Cultural Policies in the Islamic Republic of Iran." Paper presented at "Iran after 25 Years of Revolution: A Retrospective and a Look Ahead." Woodrow Wilson Center for Scholars, Washington, DC, November 16, 2004.

Farris, C. "Geopolitics Trump Religion in Iran–Azerbaijan Relations." *Diplomat*, August 7, 2013. http://thediplomat.com/2013/08/geopolitics-trump-religion-in-iran-azerbaijan-relations/ (accessed November 27, 2017).

Farzanegan, M. R. "Military Spending and Economic Growth: The Case of Iran." *Defence and Peace Economics* 25, no. 3 (2014), 247–69.

Fathi, N. "Low Turnout in Iran May Aid the Hard-Liners." *New York Times*, February 20, 2004.

Fattahi, K. "Two Weeks in January: America's Secret Engagement with Khomeini." BBC, June 3, 2016. http://www.bbc.com/news/world-us-canada-36431160 (accessed November 9, 2017).

"Fifteen Saudi Shia Sentenced to Death for 'Spying for Iran.'" BBC, December 6, 2016. http://www.bbc.com/news/world-middle-east-38220550 (accessed November 27, 2017).

Filkins, D. "The Shadow Commander." *New Yorker*, September 30, 2013.

———. "The Warrior Monk." *New Yorker*, May 29, 2017.

Fleishman, J. "Iran Supreme Leader's Son Seen as Power Broker with Big Ambitions." *Los Angeles Times*, June 25, 2009.

Forozan, H. *The Military in Post-Revolutionary Iran: The Evolution and Roles of the Revolutionary Guards*. Abingdon: Routledge, 2016.

French, D. "America's War against ISIS Is Evolving into an Invasion of Syria." *National Review*, June 19, 2017.

Fu, Z. *Autocratic Tradition and Chinese Politics*. Cambridge: Cambridge University Press, 1993.

Gambrell, J. "Released Tape Rekindles Memory of 1988 Iran Mass Execution." AP, August 29, 2016. http://bigstory.ap.org/article/cbb4cef79970438fa1edcc1300253d5a/released-tape-rekindles-memory-1988-iran-mass-execution (accessed November 9, 2017).

Ganai, M. A., and A. P. Pandey. "A Case of India and Iran, Political Relationship since Gulf War to 2001." *International Journal of Political Science and Development* 4, no. 5 (2016), 146–9.

Ganji, A. "Who Is Ali Khamenei? The Worldview of Iran's Supreme Leader." *Foreign Affairs*. 92, no. 5 (2013), 24–42, 44–8.

Garver, J. "China and Iran: An Emerging Partnership Post-Sanctions." Middle East Institute, February 8, 2016. http://www.mei.edu/content/china-and-iran-emerging-partnership-post-sanctions#_edn3 (accessed October 12, 2017).

———. "The US Factor in Sino-Iranian Energy Relations." In *Sino-US Energy Triangles: Resource Diplomacy under Hegemony*, ed. D. Zweig and Y. Hao, 207–26. London: Routledge, 2016.

Gates, R. *Duty: Memoirs of a Secretary at War*. New York: Alfred A. Knopf, 2014.

George, M. "Iran Emerges as 'Market of the Future' as Sanctions Removed, Business Executives Flock to Tehran." ABC, January 22, 2016. http://www.abc.net.au/news/2016-01-22/iran-emerges-as-market-of-future-as-sanctions-removed/7107520 (accessed November 28, 2017).

Geranmayeh, E. "Engaging with Iran: A European Agenda." European Council on Foreign Relations, July 14, 2015. http://www.ecfr.eu/publications/summary/engaging_with_iran_a_european_agenda (accessed October 12, 2017).

Gerecht, R. M. "Iran's Revolution: Year 2." *New York Times*, June 14, 2010.

Ghamari-Tabrizi, B. "Contentious Public Religion: Two Conceptions of Islam in Revolutionary Iran: Ali Shari'ati and Abdolkarim Soroush." *International Sociology*, 19, no. 4 (2004), 504–23.

Ghani, C. *Iran and the Rise of Reza Shah: From Qajar Collapse to Pahlavi Power*. London: I. B. Tauris, 1998.

"Ghani: Work on Construction of 21 Water Dams to Start in Near Future." Khaama Press, February 20, 2016. http://www.khaama.com/ghani-work-on-construction-of-21-water-dams-to-start-in-near-future-0120 (accessed November 27, 2017).

Ghobari, M. "UN Says 10,000 Killed in Yemen War, Far More Than Other Estimates." Reuters, August 30, 2016. http://www.reuters.com/article/us-yemen-security-toll-idUSKCN11516W (accessed November 27, 2017).

Ghods, M. R. *Iran in the Twentieth Century: A Political History*. Boulder, CO: Lynne Rienner, 1989.

Gholizadeh, S., and D. W. Hook. "The Discursive Construction of the 1978–1979 Iranian Revolution in the Speeches of Ayatollah Khomeini." *Journal of Community and Applied Social Psychology* 22, no. 2 (2012), 174–86.

Ghoshal, D. "China's Nuclear Opportunities in Iran." *Globalist*, May 30, 2016. https://www.theglobalist.com/china-nuclear-opportunities-in-iran/ (accessed November 28, 2017).

Gill, B. "Chinese Arms Exports to Iran." *China Report* 34, no. 3–4 (1998), 355–79.

Gillespie, A. K. "September 11, 2001 (9/11)." In *Encyclopedia of Global Studies*, vol. 4, ed. H. K. Anheier and M. Juergensmeyer, 1513–15. Los Angeles: Sage, 2012.

Glen, C. "Iran's Economy in 2015." The Iran Primer. United States Institute of Peace. December 17, 2015. http://iranprimer.usip.org/blog/2015/dec/17/irans-economy-2015 (accessed October 12, 2017).

Golan, G. *Soviet Policies in the Middle East: From World War Two to Gorbachev*. Cambridge: Cambridge University Press, 1990.

Goldberg, J. "The Obama Doctrine." *Atlantic*, April 2016.

Golmohammadi, V., H. Atanejad, and E. N. Shahrebabaki. "Foreign Policy Strategies towards Economic Development: Comparative Study of the Republic of Turkey and the Islamic Republic of Iran (2004–2013)." *Mediterranean Journal of Social Sciences* 6, no. 3 (2015), 711–19.

Goodarzi, J. M. *Syria and Iran: Diplomatic Alliance and Power Politics in the Middle East*. London: I. B. Tauris, 2009.

Gorka, A. "US, Iran on Brink of Armed Conflict: War Scenario and Consequences." Strategic Culture Foundation, February 8, 2017.

Gradstein, L. "Israel Develops New Ties with Saudi Arabia and other Gulf States." PRI, April 19, 2017. https://www.pri.org/stories/2017-04-19/israel-develops-new-ties-saudi-arabia-and-other-gulf-states (accessed November 7, 2017).

Graham, D. A. "Sheikh Nimr al-Nimr and the Forgotten Shiites of Saudi Arabia." *Atlantic*, January 5, 2016.

Guerrero, J. G. *The Carter Administration and the Fall of Iran's Pahlavi Dynasty: US–Iran Relations on the Brink of the 1979 Revolution*. Basingstoke: Palgrave Macmillan, 2016.

Gulabzoi, N. "The Narco-State of Afghanistan." *Diplomat*, February 12, 2015. http://thediplomat.com/2015/02/the-narco-state-of-afghanistan/ (accessed November 27, 2017).

Gupta, S. "Oman: The Unsung Hero of the Iranian Nuclear Deal." *International Policy Digest*, July 18, 2015. https://intpolicydigest.org/2015/07/18/oman-the-unsung-hero-of-the-iranian-nuclear-deal/ (accessed November 27, 2017).

Gvosdev, N. K. "Russia and the Precedent Problem." *National Interest*, September 25, 2014. http://nationalinterest.org/feature/russia-the-precedent-problem-11349 (accessed November 9, 2017).

Habibi, N. *The Economic Legacy of Mahmoud Ahmadinejad. Middle East Brief* No. 74. Waltham, MA: Crown Center for Middle East Studies, Brandeis University, June 2013.

Hafezi, P. "Iran's Khamenei Calls for Vigilance against West's 'Soft War': State TV." Reuters, May 26, 2016. http://www.reuters.com/article/us-iran-west-vigilance-idUSKCN0YH10P (accessed November 28, 2017).

———. "Iran to Impose Legal Restrictions on Some US Entities, Individuals: TV." Reuters, February 4, 2017. http://www.reuters.com/article/us-usa-trump-iran-idUSKBN15I2R2?il=0 (accessed November 28, 2017).

"Hajj Rift: Top Saudi Cleric Says Iranians 'Aren't Muslims' after Iran Calls Saudis 'Murderers.'" Russia Today, September 6, 2016. https://www.rt.com/news/358378-iran-saudi-rift-hajj/ (accessed November 27, 2017).

Hanna, M. W., and D. D. Kaye. "The Limits of Iranian Power." *Survival* 57, no. 5 (2015), 173–98.

Harding, N. *Lenin's Political Thought: Theory and Practice in the Democratic and Socialist Revolutions*, Chicago, IL: Haymarket Books, 1977.

Harold, S., and A. Nader. *China and Iran: Economic, Political, and Military Relations*. Santa Monica, CA: RAND, 2012.

Hashem, A. "Khamenei's Strategy Puts US 'Trojan Horse' Out to Pasture." Al-Monitor, December 14, 2015. http://www.al-monitor.com/pulse/en/originals/2015/12/iran-nuclear-deal-divisions-jcpoa-zarif-soleimani.html (accessed November 28, 2017).

Hashim, A. S. "The Iranian Military in Politics, Revolution and War, Part Two." *Middle East Policy* 19, no. 3 (2012), 65–83.

Haynes, J. "Iran and Shia Transnational Religious Actors: Limits of Political Influence." *Civitas-Revista de Ciências Sociais* 14, no. 3 (2014), 450–66.

Henderson, S. "The Nuclear Handshake." Policy Analysis. Washington Institute, November 8, 2013. http://www.washingtoninstitute.org/policy-analysis/view/the-nuclear-handshake (accessed October 12, 2017).

Hen-Tov, E., and N. Gonzalez. "The Militarization of Post-Khomeini Iran: Praetorianism 2.0." *Washington Quarterly* 34, no. 1 (2011), 45–59.

Herszenhorn, D. M. "Iran Recalls Its Ambassador from Azerbaijan." *New York Times*, May 22, 2012.

Hess, G. R. "The Iranian Crisis of 1945–46 and the Cold War." *Political Science Quarterly* 89, no. 1 (1974), 117–46.

Heydarian, J. "Iran Gets Close to Iraq." *Diplomat*, January 24, 2012. http://thediplomat.com/2012/01/iran-gets-close-to-iraq/ (accessed November 27, 2017).

Hildreth, S. *Iran's Ballistic Missile and Space Launch Programs*. Washington, DC: Congressional Research Service, Library of Congress, December 6, 2012.

Hiro, D. *Iran under the Ayatollahs*. Abingdon: Routledge, 2011.
———. *The Longest War: The Iran–Iraq Military Conflict*. New York: Routledge, 1991.
Hof, F. C., and A. Simon. "Sectarian Violence in Syria's Civil War: Causes, Consequences, and Recommendations for Mitigation." Paper commissioned by the Center for the Genocide Prevention, United States Holocaust Memorial Museum, Washington, DC, March 25, 2013.
Holland, S., and M. Spetalnick. "Trump Adopts Aggressive Posture toward Iran after Missile Launch." Reuters, February 2, 2017. https://www.reuters.com/article/us-usa-trump-iran/trump-adopts-aggressive-posture-toward-iran-after-missile-launch-idUSKBN15G5ED (accessed December 4, 2017).
Holliday, S. J. *Defining Iran: Politics of Resistance*. Farnham: Ashgate, 2011.
Hossein Mousavian, S. "Understanding Iranian Threat Perceptions." Al-Monitor, July 14, 2017. https://www.al-monitor.com/pulse/originals/2017/07/iran-threat-perceptions-regime-change-regional-dialogue.html (accessed December 6, 2017).
Houghton, D. P. *US Foreign Policy and the Iran Hostage Crisis*. Cambridge: Cambridge University Press, 2001.
Hovsepian-Bearce, Y. *The Political Ideology of Ayatollah Khamenei: Out of the Mouth of the Supreme Leader of Iran*. London: Routledge, 2015.
Hsu, S. "China's Relations with Iran: A Threat to the West?" *Diplomat*, January 26, 2016. http://thediplomat.com/2016/01/chinas-relations-with-iran-a-threat-to-the-west/ (accessed November 28, 2017).
Hulpachova, M. "Iran's Economy Struggles to Support Ahmadinejad's Ill-Conceived Housing Vision." *Guardian*, January 30, 2014.
Hunter, S. T. "Iran and the Spread of Revolutionary Islam." *Third World Quarterly* 10, no. 2 (1988), 730–49.
———. *Iran's Foreign Policy in the Post-Soviet Era: Resisting the New International Order*. Santa Barbara, CA: Praeger, 2010.
Huntington, S. P. "The Clash of Civilizations?" *Foreign Affairs* 72, no. 3 (1993), 22–49.
Hussain, N. "US-Iran Relations: Issues, Challenges and Prospects." *Policy Perspectives* 12, no. 2 (2015), 29–47.
Hussain, Z. "Chief of a Phantom Army." *Dawn*, March 29, 2017.
IAEA (International Atomic Energy Agency). "Additional Protocol." https://www.iaea.org/topics/additional-protocol (accessed November 28, 2017).
Ibrahim, Y. M. "Confrontation in the Gulf; Resist US in Gulf, Top Iranian Cleric Urges All Muslims." *New York Times*, September 13, 1990.
———. "The Downing of Flight 655; As Iran Mourns, Khomeini Calls for 'War' on US." *New York Times*, July 5, 1988.
ICG (International Crisis Group). *Implementing the Iran Nuclear Deal: A Status Report*. Middle East Report No. 173. Belgium: International Crisis Group. January 16, 2017.

———. *Turkey and Iran: Bitter Friends, Bosom Rivals*. Middle East Briefing No. 51. Brussels: International Crisis Group, December 13, 2016.

IEA (International Energy Agency). "Emergency Response Systems of Individual IEA Partner Countries: The People's Republic of China." In *Energy Supply Security 2014: Emergency Response of IEA Countries*, 501–55. Paris: International Energy Agency, 2014.

———. *Oil & Gas Security: Emergency Response of IEA Countries: People's Republic of China*. Paris: International Energy Agency, 2012. https://www.iea.org/publications/freepublications/publication/China_2012.pdf (accessed February 5, 2017).

IISS (International Institute for Strategic Studies). "Chapter Seven: Middle East and North Africa." *Military Balance* 116, no. 1 (2016), 307–64.

"Imam Khomeini Advised Gorbachev to Study Islam." Institute for Compilation and Publication of Imam Khomeini's Works. December 31, 2014. http://en.imam-khomeini.ir/en/n10495/News/Imam_Khomeini_Advised_Gorbachev_to_Study_Islam (accessed November 9, 2017).

"Imam Khomeini Denounced US Operation in Tabas." Institute for the Compilation and Publication of Imam Khomeini Works. April 27, 2015. http://en.imam-khomeini.ir/en/n11641/News/Imam_Khomeini_Denouced_US_Operation_in_Tabas (accessed November 9, 2017).

IMF (International Monetary Fund). *Islamic Republic of Iran: 2015 Article IV Consultation: Press Release; Staff Report; and Statement by the Executive Director for the Islamic Republic of Iran*. IMF Country Report No. 15/349. Washington, DC: International Monetary Fund, December 2015.

———. *Islamic Republic of Iran: 2016 Article IV Consultation*. IMF Country Report No. 17/62. Washington, DC: International Monetary Fund, February 2017.

———. *The Refugee Surge in Europe: Economic Challenges*. IMF Staff Discussion Note/16/02. January 2016. https://www.imf.org/external/pubs/ft/sdn/2016/sdn1602.pdf (accessed October 12, 2017).

———. *Regional Economic Outlook: Middle East and Central Asia*. World Economic and Financial Surveys. Washington, DC: International Monetary Fund, October 2015. http://www.imf.org/external/pubs/ft/reo/2015/mcd/eng/pdf/mreo1015.pdf (accessed October 12, 2017).

"Inside Iran: Millions Continue to Battle Drug Addiction." *Al Arabiya*, May 21, 2015. https://english.alarabiya.net/en/perspective/features/2015/05/21/Inside-Iran-Millions-continue-battle-drug-addiction.html (accessed November 27, 2017).

"Iran 1953: State Department Finally Releases Updated Official History of Mosaddeq Coup." National Security Archive. June 15, 2017. http://nsarchive.gwu.edu/NSAEBB/NSAEBB598-State-Department-releases-documents-on-US-backed-1953-coup-in-Iran/ (accessed August 2, 2017).

"Iran and Turkey Aim to Triple Trade to $30 Billion." *Express Tribune*, March 5, 2016.

"Iran-China Bilateral Trade Down by 7.7%." Tasnim News Agency, February 4, 2017. https://www.tasnimnews.com/en/news/2017/02/04/1317982/iran-china-bilateral-trade-down-by-7-7 (accessed November 28, 2017).

"Iran, China's CNPC Terminate Contract in South Pars." Mehr News Agency, April 23, 2013. http://en.mehrnews.com/news/54942/Iran-China-s-CNPC-terminate-contract-in-South-Pars (accessed November 28, 2017).

"Iran Deal 'Does Not Belong to One Country': EU's Top Diplomat." Reuters, July 12, 2017. https://www.reuters.com/article/us-iran-nuclear-eu/iran-deal-does-not-belong-to-one-country-eus-top-diplomat-idUSKBN19W2AY (accessed December 5, 2017).

"Iran Election: Hassan Rouhani in His Own Words." BBC, June 15, 2013. http://www.bbc.com/news/world-middle-east-22921680 (accessed November 27, 2017).

"Iran Elections: Hardliners Lose Parliament to Rouhani Allies." BBC, April 30, 2016. http://www.bbc.com/news/world-middle-east-36178276 (accessed November 22, 2017).

"Iran 'Fills Arak Nuclear Reactor Core with Concrete.'" BBC, January 11, 2016. http://www.bbc.com/news/world-middle-east-35285095 (accessed November 28, 2017).

"Iran Has 'Other Options' if Nuclear Deal Falls through under Donald Trump, Foreign Minister Says." ABC, November 11, 2016. http://www.abc.net.au/news/2016-11-11/iran-says-has-options-if-nuclear-deal-fails/8015774 (accessed November 28, 2017).

"Iranian Revolutionary Guards General, Six Basij Volunteers Killed in Syria: Media." Reuters, February 5, 2016. https://www.reuters.com/article/us-mideast-crisis-syria-iran/iranian-revolutionary-guards-general-six-basij-volunteers-killed-in-syria-media-idUSKCN0VE19Z (accessed November 27, 2017).

"Iranian Trade Min. Meets Turkish Economy Minister." Mehr News Agency, January 4, 2017. http://en.mehrnews.com/news/122485/Iranian-trade-min-meets-Turkish-economy-minister (accessed November 27, 2017).

"Iran, Iraq Sign Three Agreements on Economic Cooperation." PressTV, September 6, 2015. http://www.presstv.com/Detail/2015/09/06/428004/iran-iraq-Minister-of-Economic-Affairs-and-Finance-Ali-Tayyebnia-Hoshyar-Zebari-agreement-economic-cooperation (accessed November 27, 2017).

"Iran–Iraq War (1980–1988)." Global Security.org. Last modified July 11, 2011. http://www.globalsecurity.org/military/world/war/iran-iraq.htm (accessed November 9, 2017).

"Iran Losing $20 Billion a Year to Tax Evasion." PressTV, February 19, 2015. http://www.presstv.com/Detail/2015/02/19/398290/Iran-is-losing-between-1220-billion-a-year-through-tax-avoidance-and-evasion-head-of-the-State-Tax-Organization-Ali-Askari-says- (accessed November 22, 2017).

"Iran: Missile Tests Not in Violation of Nuclear Deal." Al Jazeera, February 1, 2017. http://www.aljazeera.com/news/2017/01/iran-missile-tests-violation-nuclear-deal-170131103418904.html (accessed November 28, 2017).

"Iran Not OK with Gen Raheel Heading Islamic Military Alliance: Envoy." *Economic Times*, April 3, 2017.

Iran: Nuclear Intentions and Capabilities. National Intelligence Estimate. National Intelligence Council. November 2017.

"Iran's Azeris Protest over Offensive TV Show." BBC, November 9, 2015. http://www.bbc.com/news/world-middle-east-34770537 (accessed November 27, 2017).

"Iran's 'Hanging Judge' Dies at 76." BBC, November 27, 2003. http://news.bbc.co.uk/2/hi/middle_east/3243912.stm (accessed November 9, 2017)

"Iran's President Rouhani Warns against Corruption." BBC, December 8, 2014. http://www.bbc.com/news/world-middle-east-30378662 (accessed November 22, 2017).

"Iran Successfully Tests Russia-Supplied S-300 Anti-Aircraft System—Media." Russia Today, March 4, 2017. https://www.rt.com/news/379427-iran-tests-russian-s300/ (accessed November 28, 2017).

"Iran Suicide Bombing: Chabahar Mosque Hit by Attack." BBC, December 15, 2010. http://www.bbc.com/news/world-middle-east-11997679 (accessed November 27, 2017).

"Iran Urged to Loosen Hold on BBC Persia." PressTV, April 19, 2009. http://www.payvand.com/news/09/apr/1210.html (accessed November 22, 2017).

"Iran Widens Cash Handout Cancellations." PressTV, August 3, 2015. http://www.presstv.com/Detail/2015/08/03/423069/iran-subsidy-cash-handout-rabiei (accessed November 22, 2017).

"Iran Will Halt JCPOA Implementation if Sanctions Re-imposed: Zarif." PressTV, December 3, 2016. http://www.presstv.ir/Detail/2016/12/03/496313/Iran-India-US-New-Delhi-Mohammad-Javad-Zarif-sanctions-JCPOA (accessed November 28, 2017).

"Iran Will Not Co-Operate with the US, Khamenei Says." BBC, June 3, 2016. http://www.bbc.com/news/world-middle-east-36443315 (accessed November 28, 2017).

Irish, J., and A. Shalal. "Saudi Arabia, Israel Present De Facto United Front against Iran." Reuters, February 19, 2017. https://www.reuters.com/article/us-mideast-crisis-iran/saudi-arabia-israel-present-de-facto-united-front-against-iran-idUSKBN15Y09R (accessed December 4, 2017).

Islamic Republic of Iran. "Iran's First Charter of Citizens' Rights Released." KhabarOnline, December 19, 2016. English version: http://english.khabaronline.ir/print/188133/Islamic-Republic-of-Iran—Hassan-Rouhani-/Politics/Politics (accessed October 12, 2017). Persian version: http://rouhani.ir/files/CitizensRights.pdf (accessed October 12, 2017).

Ismail, R. *Saudi Clerics and Shi'a Islam*. New York: Oxford University Press, 2016.

Jabbar, A. "Iraq Looks to Expand Trade with Iran." Al-Monitor, December 22, 2013. http://www.al-monitor.com/pulse/originals/2013/12/iran-iraq-trade-ties-strengthen.html (accessed November 2017).

Jackson, D. "Netanyahu Blasts Obama's Iran Nuclear Deal." *USA Today*, April 6, 2015.

Jahanbegloo, R. "The Two Sovereignties and the Legitimacy Crisis in Iran." *Constellations: An International Journal of Critical and Democratic Theory* 17, no. 1 (2010), 22–30.

Jedinia, M. "Return of Iran's Strategic Council Might Constrain Rouhani." Al-Monitor, June 27, 2014. http://www.al-monitor.com/pulse/originals/2014/06/return-iran-strategic-council-constrain-rouhani.html (accessed November 27, 2017).

Jehl, D. "On Trip to Mend Ties, Iran's President Meets Saudi Prince." *New York Times*, May 17, 1999.

Jenkins, W. B. "*Bonyads* as Agents and Vehicles of the Islamic Republic's Soft Power." In *Iran in the World: President Rouhani's Foreign Policy*, ed. S. Akbarzadeh and D. Conduit, 155–76. Basingstoke: Palgrave Macmillan, 2016.

———. "Explaining Iranian Soft Power Capability: A Political Economy of the Islamic Republic's Parastatal Foundations." Honors thesis, Australian National University, Canberra, 2014.

Josef, K. "Iranian Revolutionary Guard Corps and Their Influence on the Iranian Government, Military and Economy." *International Annual Scientific Sessions Strategies* 21, no. 1 (2014), 171–5.

Kagan, F. W., A. K. Majidyar, D. Pletka, and M. C. Sullivan. *Iranian Influence in the Levant, Egypt, Iraq, and Afghanistan*. Report. Washington, DC: American Enterprise Institute and Institute for the Study of War, 2012.

Kalinina, N. "Militarization of the Middle East: Russia's Role." *Security Index: A Russian Journal on International Security* 40, no. 2 (2014), 31–45.

Kam, E. "Will Russia and Iran Walk Hand in Hand?" *Strategic Assessment* 19, no. 2 (2016), 41–51.

Kamel, A. M. *The Political Economy of EU Ties with Iraq and Iran: An Assessment of the Trade–Peace Relationship*. New York: Palgrave Macmillan, 2015.

Kaminski, M. "Prince Alwaleed bin Talal: An Ally Frets about American Retreat." *Wall Street Journal*, November 22, 2013.

Kamrava, M. *Revolution in Iran: The Roots of Turmoil*. Abingdon: Routledge, 1990.

Kaplan, R. D. *The Revenge of Geography: What the Map Tells Us about the Coming Conflicts and the Battle against Fate*. New York: Random House, 2012.

Karami, A. "Khamenei Calls Negotiations with US 'Lethal Poison.'" Al-Monitor, August 1, 2016. http://www.al-monitor.com/pulse/originals/2016/08/iran-khamenei-nuclear-deal-sanctions-relief-barjam.html (accessed November 28, 2017).

Kashfi, M. "Iran Yields to Russia in Talks over Caspian Resources." *Oil & Gas Journal*, February 2, 2015.

Kasting, N., and B. Fite. *US and Iranian Strategic Competition: The Impact of China and Russia*. Washington, DC: Center for Strategic & International Studies, November 28, 2012.

Katouzian, H. *Mussadiq and the Struggle for Power in Iran*, London: I. B. Tauris, 1999.

Katz, M. N. "Saudi Arabia and Russia." In *Saudi Arabian Foreign Policy: Conflict and Cooperation*, ed. N. Partrick, 345–57. London: I. B. Tauris, 2016.

Keddie, N. R., with Y. Richard. *Modern Iran: Roots and Results of Revolution*. New Haven, CT: Yale University Press, 2003.

Keynoush, B. *Saudi Arabia and Iran: Friends or Foes?* New York: Palgrave Macmillan, 2016.

Khajehpour, B. "Has Rouhani Achieved His Goals for Iranian Economy?" Al-Monitor, March 14, 2017. http://www.al-monitor.com/pulse/originals/2017/03/iran-rouhani-first-term-economic-management-goals.html (accessed November 22, 2017).

———. "Iran's Budget Tackles Falling Oil Prices." Al-Monitor, December 10, 2014. http://www.al-monitor.com/pulse/originals/2014/12/1394-budget-iran-economy.html (accessed November 22, 2017).

Khalaji, M. "House of the Leader: The Real Power in Iran." Policywatch 1524. Washington Institute, June 1, 2009.

Khamenei, A. "Nama haa and Payam haa-e Muqam Moa'zam-e Rahbar-e Hazrat-e Ayatollah Khamenei 1368" [Letters and messages of his excellency the leader Ayatollah Khamenei 1368, or 1989].

Khamenei, A. "Office of the Leader." [In Persian.] March 20, 2008. http://www.leader.ir/langs/fa/index.php?p=bayanat&id=3744 (accessed February 12, 2017).

Khan, T. "Saudi Prince Mohammed bin Salman's Warning to Iran." *National*, May 3, 2017.

Khatami, S. M. *Islam, Dialogue and Civil Society*. Canberra: Centre for Arab and Islamic Studies (The Middle East and Central Asia), Australia National University, 1999.

———. "Presentation." In *Dialogue among Civilizations: The Round Table on the Eve of the United Nations Millennium Summit*, 21–30. Paris: United Nations Educational Scientific and Cultural Organization, 2000.

Khomeini, R. "Announcement of International Quds Day." For the Islamic Republic of Iran. August 7, 1979. https://lightiran.wordpress.com/the-sufferings-of-palestine/announcement-of-international-quds-day/ (accessed November 9, 2017).

———. "The Granting of Capitulatory Rights to the US: October 27, 1964." In *Islam and Revolution I: Writings and Declarations of Imam Khomeini (1941–1980)*. Translated by H. Algar, 181–88. Berkeley, CA: Mizan Press, 1981.

———. *Islam and Revolution I: Writings and Declarations of Imam Khomeini (1941–1980)*. Translated by H. Algar. Berkeley, CA: Mizan Press, 1981.

———. "Thirty Million Have Stood Up." In *Islam and Revolution I: Writings and Declarations of Imam Khomeini (1941–1980)*. Translated by H. Algar, 321–28, Berkeley, CA: Mizan Press, 1981.

"Khomeini's Disciples in Iran: An Irreconcilable Rift?" *Time Magazine*, February 10, 2010.

Khomeini, S.R.M. *A Clarification of Questions: An Unabridged Translation* of *Resaleh Towzih al-Masael*. Translated by J. Borujerdi. Boulder, CO: Westview Press, 1984.

Kian, A. "Gendered Khomeini." In *A Critical Introduction to Khomeini*, ed. A. Adib-Moghaddam, 170–92. New York: Cambridge University Press, 2014.

Kiani, D. "Iran and Central Asia: A Cultural Perspective." *Iranian Review of Foreign Affairs* 4, no. 4 (2014), 113–38.

Kinzer, S. *All the Shah's Men: An American Coup and the Roots of Middle East Terror*. Hoboken, NJ: John Wiley & Sons, 2003.

Kissinger, H., and G. P. Shultz. "The Iran Deal and Its Consequences." *Wall Street Journal*, April 7, 2015.

Koepke, B. *Iran's Policy on Afghanistan: The Evolution of Strategic Pragmatism*. Stockholm: Stockholm International Peace Research Institute, 2013.

Komijani, A. "Macroeconomic Policies and Performance in Iran." *Asian Economic Papers* 5, no. 1 (2006), 177–86.

Kozhanov, N. "Russian-Iranian Dialogue after 2012: Turning a New Page?" *Russian Analytical Digest* 192 (November 19, 2016), 2–4.

Krasner, S. D. *Defending the National Interest: Raw Materials Investments and US Foreign Policy*. Princeton, NJ: Princeton University Press, 1978.

Krauthammer, C. "The Iran Deal: Anatomy of a Disaster." *Washington Post*, April 10, 2015.

Kuchins, A. C. "Russia's Contrasting Relations with Turkey and Iran." In *The Turkey Russia, Iran Nexus: Driving Forces and Strategies*, ed. B. Aliriza, J. B. Alterman, and A. C. Kuchins, 13–20. Washington, DC: Center for Strategic and International Studies, 2013.

Kugelman, M. "The Iran Factor in Afghanistan." *Foreign Policy*, July 10, 2014. http://foreignpolicy.com/2014/07/10/the-iran-factor-in-afghanistan/ (accessed April 18, 2018).

Kumar, A. "Iran and Turkmenistan: An Overview." *Ars Artium* 3 (January 2015), 128–31.

Lake, E. "Iran Spends Billions to Prop Up Assad." Bloomberg, June 9, 2015. https://www.bloomberg.com/view/articles/2015-06-09/iran-spends-billions-to-prop-up-assad (accessed November 27, 2017).

Laub, Z. "Yemen in Crisis." Backgrounder. Council on Foreign Relations. April 19, 2016. https://www.cfr.org/backgrounder/yemen-crisis (accessed October 12, 2017).

Library of Congress. *Iran's Ministry of Intelligence and Security: A Profile*. Washington, DC: Library of Congress, December 2012.

Lister, C. "Al Qaeda Is Starting to Swallow the Syrian Opposition." *Foreign Policy*, March 15, 2017. http://foreignpolicy.com/2017/03/15/al-qaeda-is-swallowing-the-syrian-opposition/ (accessed April 18, 2018).

Lob, E., and A. H. Mahdavi. "Understanding Iran's Supreme Leader on the Nuclear Deal." *Washington Post*, April 14, 2015.

Lynch, T. F., III, M. Bouffard, K. King, and G. Vickowski. *The Return of Foreign Fighters to Central Asia: Implications for US Counterterrorism Policy*. Strategic Perspectives No. 21. Washington, DC: Institute for National Strategic Studies, National Defense University, 2016.

"Mahmoud Ahmadinejad: Iran Can Be Better Managed." Al Jazeera, April 29, 2017. http://www.aljazeera.com/programmes/talktojazeera/2017/04/mahmoud-ahmadinejad-iran-managed-170422093336025.html (accessed November 9, 2017).

Majidyar, A. "Rouhani Visits Moscow to Bolster Iran-Russia Ties amid Fears of US–Russia Partnership." Middle East Institute, March 23, 2017. http://www.mei.edu/content/article/io/rouhani-goes-moscow-bolster-iran-russia-ties-amid-fears-us-russia-partnership (accessed October 12, 2017).

Majidyar, A., and A. Alfoneh. *Iranian Influence in Afghanistan: Imam Khomeini Relief Committee*." Middle Eastern Outlook No. 4. Washington, DC: American Enterprise Institute for Public Policy Research, July 2010.

Malek, M. H. "Elite Factionalism in the Post-Revolutionary Iran." *Journal of Contemporary Asia* 19, no. 4 (1989), 435–60.

Maleki, A. *Soft Power and Its Implications on Iran*. Tehran: University of Tehran, 2007.

Maloney, S. *Iran's Political Economy since the Revolution*. New York: Cambridge University Press, 2015.

———. "Islamism and Iran's Postrevolutionary Economy: The Case of the *Bonyads*." In *Gods, Guns, and Globalization: Religious Radicalism and International Political Economy*, ed. M. A. Tétreault and R. A. Denemark, 191–218. Boulder, CO: Lynne Rienner, 2004.

Marschall, C. *Iran's Persian Gulf Policy: From Khomeini to Khatami*. London: RoutledgeCurzon, 2003.

Martin, W. "Global Oil Stocks Are Surging after Russia and Saudi Arabia's Historic Deal." Business Insider Australia, December 12, 2016. https://www.businessinsider.nl/oil-stocks-surge-after-russia-saudi-arabia-deal-2016-12/ (accessed April 18, 2018).

Mather, Y. "Iran's Political and Economic Crises." *Critique* 38, no. 3 (2010), 503–18.

McCain, J. "Senator John McCain Opposing the Iran Nuclear Agreement." Floor Statement, September 9, 2015. http://www.mccain.senate.gov/public/index.cfm/floor-statements?ID=677006e7-0969-4031-8617-4751657aea17 (accessed October 12, 2017).

McClory, J., and O. Harvey. "The Soft Power 30: Getting to Grips with the Measurement Challenge." *Global Affairs* 2, no. 3 (2016), 309–19.

McDowall, A., P. Stewart, and D. Rohde. "Yemen's Guerrilla War Tests Military Ambitions of Big-Spending Saudis." Reuters, April 19, 2016. http://www.reuters.com/investigates/special-report/saudi-military/ (accessed November 27, 2017).

McInnis, J. M. "Iran's Strategic Thinking: Origins and Evolution." American Enterprise Institute, May 12, 2015. http://www.aei.org/publication/irans-strategic-thinking-origins-and-evolution/ (accessed October 12, 2017).

Merat, A. R. "Rouhani Deals with Ahmadinejad's Economic Legacy." Al-Monitor, September 11, 2013. http://www.al-monitor.com/pulse/originals/2013/09/ahmadinejad-leaves-rouhani-economic-problems.html (accessed November 22, 2017).

Miglietta, J. P. *American Alliance Policy in the Middle East, 1945–1992: Iran, Israel, and Saudi Arabia*. Lanham, MD: Lexington Books, 2002.

Milani, A. *Eminent Persians: The Men and Women Who Made Modern Iran, 1941–1979*. Vol. 1. Syracuse, NY: Syracuse University Press, 2008.

Milani, M. M. "Iran's Policy towards Afghanistan." *Middle East Journal* 60, no. 2 (2006), 235–56.

Moarefy, S. "Partially Unwinding Sanctions: The Problematic Construct of Sanctions Relief in the JCPOA." *Harvard Law School National Security Journal* (July 15, 2016). http://harvardnsj.org/2016/07/partially-unwinding-sanctions-the-problematic-construct-of-sanctions-relief-in-the-jcpoa/ (accessed October 12, 2017).

Moghadam, V. "Socialism or Anti-imperialism? The Left and Revolution in Iran." *New Left Review* 166 (1987), 5–28.

Mogherini, F. "The Iran Agreement Is a Disaster for ISIS." *Guardian*, July 28, 2015.

Mohseni, E., N. Gallagher, and C. Ramsay. *Iranian Public Opinion, One Year after the Nuclear Deal: A Public Opinion Study*. College Park, MD: Center for International & Security Studies at Maryland, 2016.

Mohseni. P., *The Islamic Awakening: Iran's Grand Narrative of the Arab Uprisings*. Middle East Brief No. 71. Waltham, MA: Crown Center for Middle East Studies, Brandeis University, April 2013.

Moin, B. *Khomeini: Life of the Ayatollah*. London: I. B. Tauris, 1999.

Monshipouri, M., and M. Dorraj. "Iran's Foreign Policy: A Shifting Strategic Landscape." *Middle East Policy* 20, no. 4 (2013), 133–47.

Morell, M. "Iran's Grand Strategy Is to Become a Regional Powerhouse." *Washington Post*, April 3, 2015.

Morello, C. "Iran Accuses U.S. of Bullying Tactics at Security Council Meeting Called to Discuss Unrest in Iran." *Washington Post*, January 5, 2018.

Morgenthau, H. J. *Politics among Nations: The Struggle for Power and Peace*. New York: Alfred A. Knopf, 1948.

Morris, A. "From Silk to Sanctions and Back Again: Contemporary Sino-Iranian Economic Relations." *Al Nakhlah* (Winter 2012), 1–8. http://fletcher.tufts

.edu/~/media/Fletcher/Microsites/al%20Nakhlah/archives/Winter2012/Morris_Final.pdf (accessed March 15, 2018).

Moshaver, Z. "Revolution, Theocratic Leadership and Iran's Foreign Policy: Implications for Iran-EU Relations." *Review of International Affairs* 3, no. 2 (2003), 283–305.

Moslih, H. "Iran 'Foreign Legion' Leans on Afghan Shia in Syria War." Al Jazeera, January 23, 2016. http://www.aljazeera.com/news/2016/01/iran-foreign-legion-leans-afghan-shia-syria-war-160122130355206.html (accessed November 27, 2017).

Mraz, S., L. Lipkova, and K. Brockova. "Economic Sanctions against Iran and Their Effectiveness." *Actual Problems in Economics* 8, no. 182 (2016), 22–28.

Murray, D. *US Foreign Policy and Iran: American-Iranian Relations since the Islamic Revolution*. London: Routledge, 2009.

Muzalevsky, R. *From Frozen Ties to Strategic Engagement: US-Iranian Relationship in 2030*. Carlisle, PA: Strategic Studies Institute and US Army War College Press, May 2015.

Nader, A. *Rouhani's Election: Regime Retrenchment in the Face of Pressure*. Santa Monica, CA: RAND, 2013.

Nader, A., A. G. Scotten, A. I. Rahmani, R. Stewart, and L. Mahnad. *Iran's Influence in Afghanistan: Implications for the US Drawdown*. Santa Monica, CA: RAND, 2014.

Nader, A., D. E. Thaler, and S. R. Bohandy. *The Next Supreme Leader: Succession in the Islamic Republic of Iran*. Santa Monica, CA: RAND, 2011.

Naji, K. *Ahmadinejad: The Secret History of Iran's Radical Leader*. Berkeley, CA: University of California Press, 2008.

———. "Iranian Students Lose Hope in President's Reforms." CNN, July 21, 2003. http://edition.cnn.com/2003/WORLD/meast/07/18/otsc.naji/index.html (accessed November 9, 2017).

Nasib, A. "Iran's Dangerous Liaison with the Taliban." Gandhara, June 26, 2015. http://gandhara.rferl.org/a/afghanistan-iran-taliban/27094526.html (accessed November 27, 2017).

Nasr, V. *The Shia Revival: How Conflicts Within Islam Will Shape the Future*. New York: W. W. Norton, 2006.

Nasseri, L. "Rouhani Struggles to Lift Iranians' Prosperity at His Own Risk." Bloomberg, August 10, 2016. https://www.bloomberg.com/news/articles/2016-08-09/rouhani-support-sinking-across-iran (accessed November 22, 2017).

Nasseri, L., and G. Motevalli. "Investing in Iran? You'd Better Like Tea, Cake and Bureaucracy." Bloomberg, October 6, 2015. http://www.bloomberg.com/news/articles/2015-10-05/investing-in-iran-you-d-better-like-tea-cake-and-bureaucracy (accessed November 22, 2017).

———. "Iran Inflation at 25-Year Low May Spur Rate Cut to Boost Growth." Bloomberg, June 21, 2016. http://www.bloomberg.com/news/articles

/2016-06-21/iran-inflation-at-25-year-low-in-post-sanctions-win-for-rouhani (accessed November 22, 2017).

Newman, A. J. *Safavid Iran: Rebirth of a Persian Empire*. London: I. B. Tauris, 2006.

Nikukah, F. "Iran and Red and Black Colonialism." *Ettela'at*, January 7, 1978.

"NIORDC Centered on Upgrading Ageing Refineries." *Financial Tribune*, March 5, 2017.

Nobari, A.-R., ed. *Iran Erupts*. Stanford, CA: Iran-American Documentation Group, Stanford University, December 1978.

Noi, A. Ü. "Iran's Nuclear Programme: The EU Approach to Iran in Comparison to the US' Approach." *Perceptions* (Spring 2005), 79–102.

"Non-Oil Trade between UAE, Russia Stood at $1.6 Billion in the First Nine Months of 2016." UAEinteract, March 9, 2017. http://www.uaeinteract.com/docs/Non-oil-trade-between-UAE-Russia-stood-at-USUSD16-billion-in-first-nine-months-of-2016/78853.htm (accessed November 28, 2017).

Nooshin, L. "Subversion and Countersubversion: Power, Control and Meaning in the New Iranian Pop Music." In *Music, Power and Politics*, ed. A. J. Randall, 231–72. New York: Routledge, 2005.

Norland, R. "Corrupt Combatants Fight for Control of Lucrative Afghan Drug Trade." *New York Times*, April 6, 2016.

Ntousas, V. *Iran Nuclear Agreement: The Politics of Attainability and the Implications for Iran and the World*. FEPS Policy Brief. Brussels: Foundation for European Progressive Studies, 2015.

Nye, J. S. "Soft Power." *Foreign Policy* 80 (1990), 153–71.

Oak, N. C. "What's between the Taliban and Iran?" *Diplomat*, June 8, 2016. http://thediplomat.com/2016/06/whats-between-the-taliban-and-iran/ (accessed November 27, 2017).

OECD (Organisation for Economic Co-operation and Development). "Revenue Statistics 2017—The United States." OECD Revenue Statistics 2017. https://www.oecd.org/tax/revenue-statistics-united-states.pdf (accessed October 12, 2017).

"Official: Iran Ready to Broaden Ties with Afghanistan's Farah Province." Fars News Agency, June 27, 2014. http://en.farsnews.com/newstext.aspx?nn=13930406000599 (accessed November 27, 2017).

Olson, E. A. "Iran's Path Dependent Military Doctrine." *Strategic Studies Quarterly*, 10, no. 2 (2016), 63–93.

Osborn, A. "Russia to Build Permanent Syrian Naval Base, Eyes Other Outposts." Reuters, October 10, 2016. http://www.reuters.com/article/us-mideast-crisis-syria-russia-tartus-idUSKCN12A0W6 (accessed November 28, 2017).

Ostovar, A. *Sectarian Dilemmas in Iranian Foreign Policy: When Strategy and Identity Politics Collide*. Brief. Washington, DC: Carnegie Endowment for International Peace, 2016.

"Our Bulldozers, Our Rules." *Economist*, July 2, 2016. http://www.economist.com/news/china/21701505-chinas-foreign-policy-could-reshape-good

-part-world-economy-our-bulldozers-our-rules (accessed November 28, 2017).

"Pakistan, Saudi Arabia Pledge to Further Expand Ties." *Dawn*, February 18, 2014.

Pallaver, M. "Power and Its Forms: Hard, Soft, Smart." PhD diss., London School of Economics, 2011.

Parker, J. W. "Russia-Iran: Strategic Partners or Competitors?" Working Paper. Houston, TX: Rice University's Baker Institute for Public Policy, 2016.

Parsa, M. *Democracy in Iran: Why It Failed and How It Might Succeed*. Cambridge, MA: Harvard University Press, 2016.

———. *Social Origins of the Iranian Revolution*. New Brunswick, NJ: Rutgers University Press, 1989.

Parsi, R. *An EU Strategy for Relations with Iran after the Nuclear Deal*. Brussels: Policy Department, EU Directorate-General for External Policies, 2016.

Parsi, T. *Treacherous Alliance: The Secret Dealings of Israel, Iran, and the United States*. New Haven, CT: Yale University Press, 2007.

Patrikarakos, D. *Nuclear Iran: The Birth of an Atomic State*. London: I. B. Tauris, 2012.

Patterson, R. "EU Sanctions on Iran: The European Political Context." *Middle East Policy* 20, no. 1 (2013), 135–46.

Pear, R. "Khomeini Accepts 'Poison' of Ending the War with Iraq; UN Sending Mission." *New York Times*, July 21, 1988.

Pecquet, J. "Nuclear Deal Critics Silence as Trump Says Iran Complying." Al-Monitor, April 19, 2017. http://www.al-monitor.com/pulse/originals/2017/04/jcpoa-cheating-iran-tillerson-congress-sanctions—iaea.html (accessed November 28, 2017).

Pei, M. *From Reform to Revolution: The Demise of Communism in China and the Soviet Union*. Cambridge, MA: Harvard University Press, 1994.

Perlo-Freeman, S., A. Fleurant, P. D. Wezeman, and S. T. Wezeman. *Trends in World Military Expenditure, 2015*. SIPRI Fact Sheet. April 2016.

Perry, M. "James Mattis' 33-Year Grudge Against Iran." *Politico Magazine*, December 4, 2016.

Phippen, J. W. "Iran Signs a $5 Billion Energy Deal with France's Total." *Atlantic*, July 3, 2017.

Pickler, P. "Did Iran's New Leader Help Take Hostages?" *Deseret News*, July 1, 2005.

Ping, J. H. "Middle Power Statecraft: Indonesia and Malaysia." PhD diss., University of Adelaide, 2003.

Pipes, D. *The Rushdie Affair: The Novel, the Ayatollah, and the West*. New Brunswick, NJ: Transaction Publishers, 1990.

Pipes, R. *The Russian Revolution*. New York: Knopf, 1990.

Piscatori, J. "The Rushdie Affair and the Politics of Ambiguity." *International Affairs* 66, no. 4 (1990), 767–89.

Pleitgen, F., and B. Walker. "IAEA Inspects Iran's Parchin Military Site for First Time." CNN, September 21, 2015. http://edition.cnn.com/2015/09/21/middleeast/iran-nuclear-inspection/index.html (accessed November 28, 2017).

Pollock, D., and A. Ali. "Iran Gets Negative Reviews in Iraq, Even from Shiites." Policywatch 1653. Washington Institute, May 4, 2010. http://www.washingtoninstitute.org/policy-analysis/view/iran-gets-negative-reviews-in-iraq-even-from-shiites (accessed October 12, 2017).

Pollock, K. M. *The Persian Puzzle: The Conflict between Iran and America*. New York: Random House, 2004.

Porter, G., "The Untold Story of John Bolton's Campaign for War with Iran." American Conservative, March 22, 2018. http://www.theamericanconservative.com/articles/why-a-john-bolton-appointment-is-scarier-than-you-think-mcmaster-trump/ (accessed April 15, 2018).

"President Delivers State of the Union Address." Washington, DC, January 29, 2002.

"President Rouhani: Iran Needs No One's Permission to Defend Itself." Fars News Agency, August 24, 2014. http://ifpnews.com/news/politics/security/2014/08/president-rouhani-iran-needs-ones-permission-defend/ (accessed November 22, 2017).

"President Rouhani: Iran Ready to Increase Anti-Terrorism Cooperation with EU." Fars News Agency, February 5, 2017. http://en.farsnews.com/newstext.aspx?nn=13951117001261 (accessed November 28, 2017).

Price, M. "Iran and the Soft War." *International Journal of Communication* 6 (2012), 2397–415.

Prys, M. "The Variability of Regional Powers." Paper presented at the SGIR 7th Pan-European Conference on IR. Stockholm, September 9–11, 2010.

Putz, C. "Gas Spats: Turkmenistan Tangles with Iran." *Diplomat*, January 10, 2017. http://thediplomat.com/2017/01/gas-spats-turkmenistan-tangles-with-iran/ (accessed November 27, 2017).

Rahman, K. "India-Iran Relations and Current Regional Dynamics." *Policy Perspectives* 7, no. 2 (2010), 27–49.

Rakel, E. "Conglomerates in Iran: The Political Economy of Islamic Foundations." In *Big Business and Economic Development: Conglomerates and Economic Groups in Developing Countries and Transition Economies under Globalisation*, ed. A. E. Fernández Jilberto and B. Hogenboom, 109–32. Abingdon: Routledge, 2007.

Ramani, S. "Why Russia and Israel Are Cooperating in Syria." World Post, *Huffington Post*, June 23, 2016. http://www.huffingtonpost.com/entry/why-russia-and-israel-are-cooperating-in-syria_us_576bdb68e4b083e0c0235e15 (accessed November 28, 2017).

Ramezani, A. "Iran Sets Its Sights on Armenia." Al-Monitor, November 9, 2015. https://www.al-monitor.com/pulse/originals/2015/11/iran-armenia-cooperation.html (accessed November 27, 2017).

———. "Rouhani's Budget Proposal Reverses Declining Reliance on Oil." Al-Monitor, December 12, 2016. http://www.al-monitor.com/pulse/originals/2016/12/iran-rouhani-cabinet-budget-proposal-2017–1396-oil.html (accessed November 22, 2017).

———. "Rouhani Shifts Gears on Economy." Al-Monitor, October 28, 2015. http://www.al-monitor.com/pulse/originals/2015/10/iran-economic-stimulus-package.html (accessed November 22, 2017).

Rashid, A. "Should Pakistan Ex-army Chief Lead Islamic Military Alliance?" BBC, April 9, 2017. http://www.bbc.com/news/world-asia-39525449 (accessed November 27, 2017).

Recknagel, C. "Iran: Protests Highlight Reformist Students' Frustration with Khatami." Radio Free Europe, June 17, 2003. http://www.rferl.org/a/1103553.html (accessed October 12, 2017).

"The Revolution Is Over." *Economist*, Special Report: Iran, November 1, 2014. http://www.economist.com/sites/default/files/20141101_iran.pdf (accessed November 9, 2017).

Rezaei, F. "Iran's Ballistic Missiles Program: Changing Course in the Trump Era?" *Iran Matters*, May 8, 2017. https://www.belfercenter.org/publication/irans-ballistic-missiles-program-changing-course-trump-era (accessed November 28, 2017).

Rezalan, J. "Iran's Supreme Leader, Ayatollah Ali Khamenei, Endorses Diplomacy over Militarism." *Washington Post*, September 17, 2013.

Riedel, B. "Can This Joint Arab Military Force Succeed Where Others Have Failed?" Brookings Institution, March 30, 2015. https://www.brookings.edu/blog/markaz/2015/03/30/can-this-joint-arab-military-force-succeed-where-others-have-failed/ (accessed October 12, 2017).

Rieffer-Flanagan, B. A. "Islamic Realpolitik: Two-Level Iranian Foreign Policy." *International Journal on World Peace* 26, no. 4 (2009), 7–35.

Rizvi, S. "Ayatollah Denounces US Embassy; Hostages Taken." United Press International, November 5, 1979. http://www.upi.com/Archives/1979/11/05/Ayatollah-denounces-US-embassy-hostages-taken/2330085124217/ (accessed November 9, 2017).

Rogin, J. "Inside the Trump-Tillerson Divide over Qatar." *Washington Post*, June 14, 2017.

———. "Republics Warn Iran—and Obama—That Deal Won't Last." Bloomberg, March 9, 2015. https://www.bloomberg.com/view/articles/2015-03-09/republicans-warn-iran-and-obama-that-deal-won-t-last (accessed November 28, 2017).

Ross, D. "Trump Is on a Collision Course with Iran." *Politico Magazine*, June 20, 2017.

Roudi, F. *Iran Is Reversing Its Population Policy*. Viewpoints No. 7. Washington, DC: Woodrow Wilson Center for Scholars, August 2012, 1–6.

Rouhani, H. *Rawaiti-e Tadbir wa Omid* [Narration of foresight and hope]. Tehran: Center for Strategic Research, 2013.

"Rouhani Hits Back at Trump after Nuclear Deal Speech." Al Jazeera, October 14, 2017. http://www.aljazeera.com/news/2017/10/rouhani-hits-trump-nuclear-deal-speech-171013190257102.html (accessed December 6, 2017).

Roy, O. *Islam and Resistance in Afghanistan*. Cambridge: Cambridge University Press, 1990.

Rozen, L. "Inside the Secret US-Iran Diplomacy That Sealed Nuke Deal." Al-Monitor, August 11, 2015.

Rubin, M. "Europe's Critical Dialogue with Iran: An Assessment." Policywatch 443. Washington Institute, January 10, 2010. http://www.washingtoninstitute.org/policy-analysis/view/europes-critical-dialogue-with-iran-an-assessment (accessed October 12, 2017).

Rubio, M. "Iran Nuclear Deal an Unfolding Disaster." CNN, October 18, 2016. http://edition.cnn.com/2016/10/17/opinions/iran-nuclear-deal-disaster-rubio/index.html (accessed November 28, 2017).

"Rumors Confirmed about Death of MKO Leader, Massoud Rajavi." Fars News Agency, July 10, 2016. http://en.farsnews.com/newstext.aspx?nn=13950420000258 (accessed November 9, 2017).

"Russia, Iran Plan $10bn Arms Supply to Tehran." Russia Today, November 14, 2016. https://www.rt.com/news/366871-russia-iran-weapons-delivery/ (accessed November 28, 2017).

"Russia's Rosneft, Iran's NIOC Eye $30 Bln in Oil and Gas Projects." Reuters, November 1, 2017. https://www.reuters.com/article/russia-iran-oil-idAFR4N1DP01N (accessed November 28, 2017).

"Russia: Trade Statistics." globalEdge, 2016. https://globaledge.msu.edu/countries/russia/tradestats (accessed November 28, 2017).

Sabet, A.G.E. "*Wilayat al-Faqih* and the Meaning of Islamic Government." In *A Critical Introduction to Khomeini*, ed. A. Adib-Moghaddam, 69–87. New York: Cambridge University Press, 2014.

Sabet, F., and R. Safshekan. *Soft War: A New Episode in the Old Conflicts between Iran and the United States*. University of Pennsylvania Scholarly Commons. Philadelphia, PA: Iran Media Program, 2011.

Sadeghi-Boroujerdi, E. "The Origins of Communist Unity: Anti-Colonialism and Revolution in Iran's Tri-Continental Moment." *British Journal of Middle Eastern Studies*, August 1, 2017. https://www.tandfonline.com/doi/abs/10.1080/13530194.2017.1354967?journalCode=cbjm20

Saikal, A. "Afghanistan and Iraq: State-Building in Countries with Strong Societies." In *Weak States, Strong Societies: Power and Authority in the New World Order*, ed. A. Saikal, 107–22. London: I. B. Tauris, 2016.

———. "Afghanistan's Geographical Possibilities." *Survival* 56, no. 3 (2014), 141–56.

———. "Iran and the Changing Regional Strategic Environment." In *Iran in the World: President Rouhani's Foreign Policy*, ed. S. Akbarzadeh and D. Conduit, 17–32. New York: Palgrave Macmillan, 2016.

———. *Iran at the Crossroads*. Cambridge: Polity Press, 2015.

———. "Islamism, the Iranian Revolution, and the Soviet Invasion of Afghanistan." In *The Cambridge History of the Cold War: Volume 3: Endings*, ed. M. P. Leffler and O. A. Westad, 112–34. Cambridge: Cambridge University Press, 2010.

———. "The Middle East and North Africa: An Area of Change and Transition?" In *The Arab World and Iran: A Turbulent Region in Transition*, ed. A. Saikal, 1–6. New York: Palgrave Macmillian, 2016.

———. *Modern Afghanistan: A History of Struggle and Survival*. New rev. ed. London: I. B. Tauris, 2012.

———. *The Rise and Fall of the Shah: Iran from Autocracy to Religious Rule*. Princeton, NJ: Princeton University Press, 2009.

———. "The Roots of Iran's Election Crisis." *Survival* 51, no. 5 (2009), 91–104.

———. *Zone of Crisis: Afghanistan, Pakistan, Iran and Iraq*. London: I. B. Tauris, 2014.

Salehi-Isfahani, D. "Iran: Poverty and Inequality since the Revolution." Brookings-Institution, January 29, 2009. https://www.brookings.edu/opinions/iran-poverty-and-inequality-since-the-revolution/ (accessed April 18, 2018).

———. "Oil Wealth and Economic Growth in Iran." In *Contemporary Iran: Economy, Society, Politics*, ed. A. Gheissari, 3–37. Oxford: Oxford University Press, 2009.

———. "Poverty, Inequality, and Populist Politics in Iran." *Journal of Economic Inequality* 7, no. 1 (2009), 5–28.

Salem, P. *Iraq's Tangled Foreign Interests and Relations*. Washington, DC: Carnegie Middle East Center, December 2013.

Salim, M., K. DeYoung, and T. El-Ghobashy. "Tillerson Says Kurdish Independence Referendum is Illegitimate." *Washington Post*, September 29, 2017.

Salisbury, P. *Yemen and the Saudi-Iranian 'Cold War*. London: Chatham House, 2015.

Samii, A. W. "The Iranian Nuclear Issue and Informal Networks." *Naval War College Review* 59, no. 1 (2006), 63–90.

Samimi, M. "Online 'Sigheh' in Iran: Revolutionary or Restricting?" *Huffington Post*, January 18, 2015. https://www.huffingtonpost.com/mehrnaz-samimi/online-sighehin-iran-revo_b_6182110.html (accessed April 18, 2018).

Samore, G., ed. *The Iran Nuclear Deal: A Definitive Guide*. Cambridge, MA: Belfer Center for Science and International Affairs, Harvard Kennedy School, 2015.

"Saudi Arabia 'Seeking Pakistan Arms for Syrian Rebels.'" *Gulf News*, February 23, 2014.

"Saudi Top Cleric Says Iran's Leaders Are 'Not Muslims.'" BBC, September 6, 2016. http://www.bbc.com/news/world-middle-east-37287434 (accessed November 27, 2017).

Schirazi, A. *The Constitution of Iran: Politics and the State in the Islamic Republic*. London: I. B. Tauris, 1998.

Schwartz, S. S. "What Is Really 'Broken' in Syria?" Gatestone Institute, March 29, 2013. https://www.gatestoneinstitute.org/3651/syria-alawite-shia (accessed October 12, 2017).

Sciolino, E. "Love Finds a Way in Iran; 'Temporary Marriage.'" *New York Times*, October 4, 2000.

Scobell, A., and A. Nader. *China in the Middle East: The Wary Dragon*. Santa Monica, CA: RAND, 2016.

Scott, E. "Defying Expectations: China's Iran Trade and Investments." Middle East Institute, April 6, 2016. http://www.mei.edu/content/map/defying-expectations-china%E2%80%99s-iran-trade-investments (accessed October 12, 2017).

———. "A Nuclear Deal with Chinese Characteristics: China's Role in the P5+1 Talks with Iran." *China Brief* 15, no. 14 (2015). https://jamestown.org/program/a-nuclear-deal-with-chinese-characteristics-chinas-role-in-the-p51-talks-with-iran/ (accessed October 12, 2017).

Secor, L. *Children of Paradise: The Struggle for the Soul of Iran*. New York: Riverhead Books, 2014.

Sedigh, J. *Miliyat wa Enghelab dar Iran* [Nationality and revolution in Iran]. New York: Entisharate Fanus, 1352/1973.

Seifzadeh, H. S. "The Landscape of Factional Politics and Its Future in Iran." *Middle East Journal* 57, no. 1 (2003), 57–75.

Shabani, M. A. *Making Sense of Iran's Iraq Policy: Broader Parameters of Iranian Interests*. Brief. Bonn: Center for Applied Research in Partnership with the Orient, January 30, 2015.

Shams, S. "Is Pakistan Aiding the Syrian Rebels?" Deutsche Welle, March 28, 2014. http://www.dw.com/en/is-pakistan-aiding-syrian-rebels/a-17528187 (accessed November 27, 2017).

Sharafedin, B. "Iran's President Praises Ex-leader Khatami, Defying Media Ban." Reuters, March 7, 2017. https://www.reuters.com/article/us-iran-rouhani-khatami/irans-president-praises-ex-leader-khatami-defying-media-ban-idUSKCN0W91ZT (accessed December 4, 2017).

Sheridan, S. "The Baby Boomers of Iran." *Fordham Political Review* (online), June 6, 2013. http://fordhampoliticalreview.org/the-baby-boomers-of-iran/ (accessed October 12, 2017).

Sial, S. *Emerging Dynamics in Pakistani-Saudi Relations*. Norwegian Peacebuilding Resource Centre Report. Oslo: NOREF, 2015.

Siddique, H. "Iran Elections: Khamenei Warns Protesters to Stay off Streets." *Guardian*, June 20, 2009.

Siddiqui, T. "Saudi Arabia Woos Pakistan with $1.5 Billion Grant. Why Now?" Security Watch. *Christian Science Monitor*, March 28, 2014. https://www.csmonitor.com/World/Security-Watch/Under-the-Radar/2014/0328/Saudi-Arabia-woos-Pakistan-with-1.5-billion-grant.-Why-now (accessed November 27, 2017).

SIPRI (Stockholm International Peace Research Institute). SIPRI Military Expenditure Database. Stockholm International Peace Research Institute, 2017. https://www.sipri.org/databases/milex (accessed October 12, 2017).

Sisakht, A. Y. "Foreign Policy of Iran with India since 1990." PhD diss., University of Mysore, 2012.

Skocpol, T. *State and Social Revolutions: A Comparative Analysis of France, Russia, and China*. Cambridge: Cambridge University Press, 1979.

Slavin, B. *Mullahs, Money, and Militias: How Iran Exerts Its Influence in the Middle East*. USIP Special Report. Washington, DC: United States Institute of Peace, June 1, 2008.

Smagin, N. "How Russia Managed to Double Its Exports to Iran in 2016." Russia Beyond the Headlines, February 17, 2017. https://www.rbth.com/business/2017/02/17/russia-exports-iran-704108 (accessed October 12, 2017).

Smith, W. B. *Moscow Mission, 1946–49*. London: Heinemann, 1950.

Smyth, G. "Deciphering the Iranian Leader's Call for a 'Resistance Economy.'" *Guardian*, April 19, 2016.

Snider, M., and O. Dorell. "Boeing's $16B Aircraft Deal with Iran Air Faces Challenges." *USA Today*, December 11, 2016.

Sohrab, N. "Historicizing Revolutions: Constitutional Revolutions in the Ottoman Empire, Iran, and Russia, 1905–1908." *American Journal of Sociology* 100, no. 6 (1995), 1383–447.

Soldatkin, V. "Russia's Putin, Saudi Prince Praise Dialogue on Oil, Syria." Reuters, May 30, 2017. https://uk.reuters.com/article/uk-russia-saudi-meeting/russias-putin-saudi-prince-praise-dialogue-on-oil-syria-idUKKBN18Q0S1 (accessed December 4, 2017).

Solomon, J. "Trump Faces Battle to Undo Iran Nuclear Deal." *Wall Street Journal*, November 11, 2016.

Sreberny, A., and M. Torfeh, eds. *Cultural Revolution in Iran: Contemporary Popular Culture in the Islamic Republic*. London: I. B. Tauris, 2013.

Strickland, P. "Why Are Afghan Refugees Leaving Iran?" Al Jazeera, May 17, 2016. http://www.aljazeera.com/indepth/features/2016/05/afghan-refugees-leaving-iran-160511103759873.html (accessed November 27, 2017).

Stubbs, J., and P. Devitt. "Russia Stance on Assad Suggests Divergence with Iran." Reuters, November 3, 2015. http://www.reuters.com/article/us-mideast-crisis-syria-russia-idUSKCN0SS0TY20151103 (accessed November 28, 2017).

Sullivan, M. *Hezbollah in Syria*. Middle East Security Report 19. Washington, DC: Institute for the Study of War, 2014.

Summitt, A. R. "For a White Revolution: John F. Kennedy and the Shah of Iran." *Middle East Journal* 58, no. 4 (2004), 560–75.

"Syrian Rebels Say Hostages 'Iranian Soldiers.'" Al Jazeera, August 6, 2012. http://www.aljazeera.com/news/middleeast/2012/08/201284124145698648.html (accessed November 27, 2017).

Tabatabai, A. "How the Trump Administration Is Boosting Iran's Hardliners." *Atlantic*, October 10, 2017.

Tadjbakhsh, S., and M. Fazeli. "Iran and Its Relationship to Afghanistan after the Nuclear Deal: A New Era for Constructive Interaction?" PRIO Paper. Peace Research Institute Oslo, July 2016.

Taghavi, M. "Iranian Economy Entering the Third Millennium." *Discourse: An Iranian Quarterly* 2, no. 3 (2001), 167–78.

Tarock, A. "Iran–Western Europe Relations on the Mend." *British Journal of Middle Eastern Studies* 26, no. 1 (1999), 41–61.

Tazmini, G. *Revolution and Reform in Russia and Iran: Modernisation and Politics in Revolutionary States*. London: I. B. Tauris, 2012.

Ter-Organov, N. "Islamic Nationalism in Iran and Its Ideological, Military and Foreign-Policy Aspects." In *Community, Identity and the State: Comparing Africa, Eurasia, Latin America and the Middle East*, ed. M. Gammer, 132–41. London: Routledge, 2004.

Teti, A., and P. Abbott. "The Relative Importance of Religion and Region in Explaining Differences in Political Economic and Social Attitudes in Iraq in 2014: Findings from the Arab Transformations Public Opinion Survey." Arab Transformations Working Paper 1. University of Aberdeen, 2016.

Thaler, D. E., A. Nader, S. Chubin, J. D. Green, C. Lynch, and F. Wehrey. *Mullahs, Guards, and* Bonyads: *An Exploration of Iranian Leadership Dynamics*. Santa Monica, CA: RAND, 2010.

Theohary, C. A. *Conventional Arms Transfers to Developing Nations, 2008–2015*. Washington, DC: Congressional Research Service, December 19, 2016.

Thirarath, I. "Iran's Big Asian Oil Customers Return." Middle East Institute, August 23, 2016. http://www.mei.edu/content/map/irans-big-asian-oil-customers-return (accessed October 12, 2017).

Tira, R., and Y. Guzansky. "Is Iran in Strategic Equilibrium?" *Strategic Assessment* 18, no. 4 (2016), 7–18.

"Top Commander: Iran Offers to Share Anti-Terrorism Expertise with China." Fars News Agency, November 14, 2016. http://en.farsnews.com/newstext.aspx?nn=13950824001193 (accessed November 28, 2017).

Torbey, C. "Lebanon: Will New President End Political Crisis?" BBC, October 31, 2016. http://www.bbc.com/news/world-middle-east-37821698 (accessed November 27, 2017).

Torfeh, M. "Iran's 'Double Game' in Afghanistan." *Guardian*, March 11, 2010.

Tran, M., and S. K. Dehghan. "Iran Mosque Bombing Kills Dozens." *Guardian*, December 15, 2010.

Transparency International. "Corruptions Perceptions Index 2016." https://www.transparency.org/news/feature/corruption_perceptions_index_2016 (accessed November 22, 2017).

Treverton, G. F., and S. G. Jones. *Measuring National Power*. Santa Monica, CA: RAND, 2005.

"Trump Administration Pledges 'Great Strictness' on Iran Nuclear Deal." Reuters, March 8, 2017. https://in.reuters.com/article/iran-nuclear/trump-administration-pledges-great-strictness-on-iran-nuclear-deal-idINKBN16E2IF (accessed December 6, 2017).

Trump, D. "President Trump's Speech to the Arab Islamic American Summit." May 21, 2017. https://www.whitehouse.gov/the-press-office/2017/05/21/pre

sident-trumps-speech-arab-islamic-american-summit (accessed October 12, 2017).

"Trying to Remember Khomeini—36 Years after the Revolution in Iran." *Guardian*, February 9, 2015.

"Turkey Major Trade Partners." Bridgat, June 2017. http://countries.bridgat.com/Turkey_Trade_Partners.htm (accessed April 21, 2018).

"Turkmenistan, Iran Seek Closer Ties as Antidote to Isolation." Eurasianet.org, July 5, 2016. http://www.eurasianet.org/node/79536 (accessed November 27, 2017).

"UAE Says the 'War Is Over' for Its Troops in Yemen." Deutsche Welle, June 16, 2016. http://www.dw.com/en/uae-says-the-war-is-over-for-its-troops-in-yemen/a-19336750 (accessed November 27, 2017).

"UAE: 'War Is Over' for Emirati Troops in Yemen." Al Jazeera, June 17, 2016. http://www.aljazeera.com/news/2016/06/uae-war-emirati-troops-yemen-160616044956779.html (accessed November 27, 2017).

Ünal, S., and E. Ersoy. "Political Economy of Turkish-Iranian Relations: Three Asymmetries." *Ortadoğu Etütleri* 5, no. 2 (2014), 141–64.

United Nations. *Return of Undocumented Afghans from Pakistan and Iran: 2016 Overview*. International Organization for Migration, 2016. https://afghanistan.iom.int/sites/default/files/Reports/iom_afghanistan_-_return_of_undocumented_afghans_from_pakistan_and_iran_-_2016_overview.pdf (accessed October 12, 2017).

United Nations Office on Drugs and Crime. *Afghanistan: Opium Survey 2016: Executive Summary*. Vienna: United Nations Office on Drugs and Crime; Kabul, Ministry of Counter Narcotics, 2016.

———. *World Drug Report 2016*. Vienna: United Nations Office on Drugs and Crime, 2016.

United Nations Security Council. Resolution 2231. Joint Comprehensive Plan of Action (JCPOA) on the Islamic Republic of Iran's Nuclear Programme." S/RES/2231 (2015), July 20, 2015.

"US Accuses Iran of "Alarming Provocations' amid Nuclear Tensions." BBC, April 20, 2017. http://www.bbc.com/news/world-us-canada-39649683 (accessed December 4, 2017).

US Department of Defense. *Annual Report on Military Power of Iran*. Washington, DC: US Department of Defense, April 2012.

"US Slaps New Sanctions on Iran over Missile Test." Al Jazeera, February 4, 2017. http://www.aljazeera.com/news/2017/02/slaps-sanctions-iran-missile-test-170203154253182.html (accessed November 28, 2017).

Vaez, A. "Waiting for Bushehr." *Foreign Policy*, September 12, 2011. http://foreign-policy.com/2011/09/12/waiting-for-bushehr/ (accessed October 12, 2017).

Van der Kley, D. "Why Might Chinese Security Services Be in Afghanistan?" East Asia Forum, March 7, 2017. http://www.eastasiaforum.org/2017/03/07/why-might-chinese-security-services-be-in-afghanistan/?utm_source

=newsletter&utm_medium=email&utm_campaign=newsletter2017-03-12 (accessed October 12, 2017).

Vatanka, A. "Iranian-Pakistani Border Incident Reveals Deeper Problems." Al-Monitor, October 24, 2014. http://www.al-monitor.com/pulse/originals/2014/10/iran-pakistan-border-gas-pipeline.html (accessed November 27, 2017).

Verrier, A. "Francis Younghusband and the Great Game." *Asian Affairs* 23, no. 1 (1992), pp. 34–43.

Von Maltzahn, N. "Iran's Cultural Diplomacy." In *Iran and the Challenges of the Twenty-First Century: Essays in Honour of Mohammad-Reza Djalili*, ed. H. E. Chehabi, C. Therme, and F. Khosrokhavar, 205–21. Costa Mesa: Mazda, 2013.

Waltz, K. N. *Theory of International Politics*. Reading, MA: Addison-Wesley, 1979.

Ward, S. R. "The Continuing Evolution of Iran's Military Doctrine." *Middle East Journal* 59, no. 4 (2005): 559–76.

Warnaar, M. *Iranian Foreign Policy during Ahmadinejad: Ideology and Actions*. New York: Palgrave Macmillan, 2013.

Wastnidge, E. "The Modalities of Iranian Soft Power: From Cultural Diplomacy to Soft War." *Politics* 35, no. 3–4 (2015), 364–77.

Wehrey, F., J. D. Green, B. Nichiporuk, A. Nader, L. Hansell, R. Nafisi, and S. R. Bohandy. *The Rise of the Pasdaran: Assessing the Domestic Roles of Iran's Islamic Revolutionary Guards Corps*. Santa Monica, CA: RAND, 2009.

Wehrey, F., D. E. Thaler, N. Bensahel, K. Cragin, J. D. Green, D. D. Kaye, N. Oweidat, and J. Li. *Dangerous but Not Omnipotent: Exploring the Reach and Limitations of Iranian Power in the Middle East*. Santa Monica, CA: RAND, 2009.

Wight, M. *Power Politics*. Edited by H. Bull and C. Holbraad. Leicester: Leicester University Press, 1978.

Wilson, G. C. "Navy Missile Downs Iranian Jetliner." *Washington Post*, July 4, 1988.

Wilson, W. T. "Lifting of Sanctions on Iran Complicates Policy Options." Issue Brief No. 4548. Heritage Foundation, May 11, 2016. http://www.heritage.org/report/lifting-sanctions-iran-complicates-policy-options (accessed October 12, 2017).

Workman, D. "Crude Oil Imports by Country." World's Top Exports, May 29, 2017. http://www.worldstopexports.com/crude-oil-imports-by-country/ (accessed October 12, 2017).

———. "Turkey's Top Trading Partners." World's Top Exports, February 16, 2018. http://www.worldstopexports.com/turkeys-top-import-partners/ (accessed April 21, 2018).

World Bank. "Doing Business: Economy Rankings." 2017. http://www.doingbusiness.org/rankings (accessed April 21, 2018).

———. "Iran Overview." February 2017. http://www.worldbank.org/en/country/iran/overview (accessed November 22, 2017).

———. "World Bank Country and Lending Groups." https://datahelpdesk.worldbank.org/knowledgebase/articles/906519-world-bank-country-and-lending-groups (accessed November 22, 2017).

World Justice Project. "World Justice Project (WJP) Rule of Law Index 2016." https://worldjusticeproject.org/our-work/wjp-rule-law-index/wjp-rule-law-index-2016 (accessed October 31, 2017).

Wright, R. "Iran on Guard over US Funds." *Washington Post*, April 28, 2007.

———. "Iran's Generals Are Dying in Syria." *New Yorker*, October 26, 2015.

Ya'alon, M. "Why Iran Is More Dangerous Than Islamic State." *Los Angeles Times*, September 29, 2016.

Yapp, M. "The Legend of the Great Game." *Proceedings of the British Academy: 2000 Lectures and Memoirs* 111 (2001), 179–98.

Yazdi, M. "Patterns of Clerical Political Behavior in Postwar Iran, 1941–53." *Middle Eastern Studies* 26, no. 3 (1990), 281–307.

Yodfat, A. Y. *The Soviet Union and Revolutionary Iran*. Abingdon: Routledge, 2011.

Yousef, D. K., and C. Jasper. "UAE to Build Russian Warplane as Mideast Tensions Rise." Bloomberg, February 21, 2017. https://www.bloomberg.com/news/articles/2017-02-20/u-a-e-to-build-russian-warplane-as-iran-stokes-mideast-tensions (accessed November 28, 2017).

Youssef, N. A. "Iran Deal Is in Interests of US, Mattis Says." *Wall Street Journal*, October 3, 2017.

Zahra-Malik, M. "Saudi Arabia Loans Pakistan $1.5 Billion to Shore Up Economy." Reuters, March 14, 2014. https://www.reuters.com/article/us-pakistan-saudi/saudi-arabia-loans-pakistan-1-5-billion-to-shore-up-economy-idUSBREA2C13G20140313 (accessed December 4, 2017).

Zakaria, F. "Iran's Growing State of Desperation." *Washington Post*, January 4, 2012. https://www.washingtonpost.com/opinions/irans-growing-state-of-desperation/2012/01/04/gIQA6usPbP_story.html?noredirect=on&utm_term=.bbc47cda08b6 (accessed May 8, 2018).

Zarif, M. J. "What Iran Really Wants: Iranian Foreign Policy in the Rouhani Era." *Foreign Affairs* 93. no. 3 (2014), 49–59.

Zengerle, P. "Extension of Iran Sanctions Act Passes US Congress." Reuters, December 2, 2016. https://www.reuters.com/article/us-iran-nuclear-usa-sanctions/extension-of-iran-sanctions-act-passes-u-s-congress-idUSKBN13Q5JW (accessed November 28, 2017).

Zonis, M. *The Political Elite of Iran*. Princeton, NJ: Princeton University Press, 1971.

INDEX